PENGUIN BOOKS

WINDBLOWN WORLD:
THE JOURNALS OF JACK KEROUAC 1947–1954

Jack Kerouac was born in Lowell, Massachusetts in 1922, the youngest of three children in a Franco-American family. He attended local Catholic and public schools and won a scholarship to Columbia University in New York City, where he met Allen Ginsberg and William S. Burroughs. His first novel, *The Town and the City*, appeared in 1950, but it was *On the Road*, first published in 1957, that made Kerouac famous. Publication of his many other books followed, among them *The Subterraneans*, *Big Sur*, and *The Dharma Bums*. Kerouac died in St. Petersburg, Florida, in 1969, at the age of forty-seven.

Douglas Brinkley is the Director of the Theodore Roosevelt Center for American Civilization at Tulane University. He is the award-winning author of fifteen books, including *The Unfinished Presidency: Jimmy Carter's Journey Beyond the White House*; *Wheels for the World: Henry Ford, His Company, and a Century of Progress*; *Rosa Parks*; *Tour of Duty: John Kerry and the Vietnam War*; and *The Boys of Pointe du Hoc: Ronald Reagan, D-Day, and the U.S. Army 2nd Ranger Battalion*. He lives in New Orleans.

WINDBLOWN WORLD

The Journals of Jack Kerouac

1947–1954

Edited and with an introduction by

DOUGLAS BRINKLEY

PENGUIN BOOKS

PENGUIN BOOKS
Published by the Penguin Group
Penguin Group (USA) Inc., 375 Hudson Street, New York, New York 10014, U.S.A.
Penguin Group (Canada), 90 Eglinton Avenue East, Suite 700, Toronto,
Ontario, Canada M4P 2Y3 (a division of Pearson Penguin Canada Inc.)
Penguin Books Ltd, 80 Strand, London WC2R 0RL, England
Penguin Ireland, 25 St Stephen's Green, Dublin 2, Ireland (a division of Penguin Books Ltd)
Penguin Group (Australia), 250 Camberwell Road, Camberwell,
Victoria 3124, Australia (a division of Pearson Australia Group Pty Ltd)
Penguin Books India Pvt Ltd, 11 Community Centre, Panchsheel Park, New Delhi – 110 017, India
Penguin Group (NZ), cnr Airborne and Rosedale Roads, Albany,
Auckland 1310, New Zealand (a division of Pearson New Zealand Ltd)
Penguin Books (South Africa) (Pty) Ltd, 24 Sturdee Avenue,
Rosebank, Johannesburg 2196, South Africa

Penguin Books Ltd, Registered Offices:
80 Strand, London WC2R 0RL, England

First published in the United States of America by Viking Penguin,
a member of Penguin Group (USA) Inc. 2004
Published in Penguin Books 2006

1   3   5   7   9   10   8   6   4   2

Copyright © The Estate of Stella Kerouac, John Sampas, Literary Representative, 2004
Introduction and notes copyright © Douglas Brinkley, 2004
All rights reserved

Grateful acknowledgment is made to the Henry W. and Albert A. Berg Collection of English
and American Literature, The New York Public Library, Astor, Lenox and Tilden Foundations
for permission to reproduce selected pages from Jack Kerouac's journals.

THE LIBRARY OF CONGRESS HAS CATALOGED THE HARDCOVER EDITION AS FOLLOWS:
Kerouac, Jack, 1922–1969.
Windblown world : the journals of Jack Kerouac, 1947–1954 / edited and
with an introduction by Douglas Brinkley.
p.   cm.
ISBN 0-670-03341-3 (hc.)
ISBN 0 14 30.3606 8 (pbk.)
1. Kerouac, Jack, 1922–1969—Diaries.   2. Authors, American—20th century—Diaries.
3. Beat generation—Diaries.   I. Brinkley, Douglas.   II. Title.
PS3521.E735Z478 2004
818'.5403—dc22
[B]   2004054882

Printed in the United States of America
Designed by Carla Bolte • Set in Scala

To John Sampas, David Amram, and Jim Irsay
for inspiring a new generation to discover
the works of an American master

Powerful winds that crack the boughs of November! — and the bright calm sun, untouched by the furies of the earth, abandoning the earth to darkness, and wild forlornness, and night, as men shiver in their coats and hurry home. And then the lights of home glowing in those desolate deeps. There are the stars, though! high and sparkling in a spiritual firmament. We will walk in the windsweeps, gloating in the envelopment of ourselves, seeking the sudden grinning intelligence of humanity below these abysmal beauties. Now the roaring midnight fury and the creaking of our hinges and windows, now the winter, now the understanding of the earth and our being on it: this drama of enigmas and double-depths and sorrows and grave joys, these human things in the elemental vastness of the windblown world.

— Jack Kerouac, November 12, 1947

CONTENTS

Introduction   xi

Cast of Characters   xxix

Acknowledgments   xli

SECTION I

The Town and the City

The Town and the City Worklogs   3

Well, this is the Forest of Arden   131

Psalms   153

SECTION II

On the Road

1949 Journals   181

Rain and Rivers   281

Journal during First Stages of "On the Road"   373

Index   423

INTRODUCTION

Wherever novelist Jack Kerouac wandered in his peripatetic life, he usually kept a spiral notebook or railroad brakeman's ledger with him just in case he wanted to scribble down a spontaneous thought or compose a haiku. This was not an unusual trait for a serious writer. Old-time reporters, in fact, never left home without their cigarettes and notebook, and Kerouac was no different. So Allen Ginsberg knew exactly what he was doing when, in 1953, he snapped the elegiac photograph that adorns this book's cover. There is the handsome Kerouac on an East Village fire escape, gazing out over a sea of New York buildings, brooding like Montgomery Clift under the tenement-filled sky at dusk. With a "Railroad Brakeman Rules Handbook" protruding out of his jacket pocket, this photograph represents the iconic Kerouac; it's as if he offered Ginsberg his best Jack London–like pose for posterity to ponder.

Unlike that photograph, there is nothing posed about these journal entries, published here for the first time. The printed text of this volume of journals draws on material entered by Kerouac in ten notebooks from June 1947 to February 1954. Though these journals are presented here as a single entity, the editing has involved minor interweaving between one notebook and the next. Kerouac's doodles, dead-end rants, and marginalia have not been included. But I've tried to stay as close to the original journals as possible, correcting Kerouac's punctuation and spelling only when it was necessary for clarity's sake. I've also inserted occasional footnotes, as unobtrusively as possible, in order to provide context when necessary.

Read as a whole, *Windblown World* offers riveting proof of Kerouac's deep desire to become a great and enduring American novelist. Brimming with youthful innocence and the coming-of-age struggle to make sense out of a sinful world, these pages reveal an earnest artist trying to discover his authentic voice. Call it "The Education of Jack Kerouac" if you like. Kerouac, in fact, used to say that he "always considered writing my duty on earth." *Windblown World* is a testament to that heartfelt conviction.

Over the past thirty-five years since Kerouac died in Saint Petersburg, Florida, at age forty-seven, over a dozen books have been published detailing his heroic literary career. Certainly the two volumes of his selected letters — edited by Ann Charters — have provided readers with the most enlightened new understanding of what motivated this incurable Massachusetts drifter to dedicate his entire life to his chosen craft. *Windblown World* takes us even deeper into the real world of Jack Kerouac, the spontaneous word slinger, who set out to become the quintessential literary myth-maker of postwar America, creating his "Legend of Duluoz" by spinning romantic tales about his earthly adventures. "I promise I shall never give up, and that I'll die yelling and laughing," Kerouac wrote in a 1949 entry included in this volume. "And that until then I'll rush around this world I insist is holy and pull at everyone's lapel and make them confess to me and to all."

The journal entries included in this volume constitute his confessional outpouring during the period of his life (1947–1954) when he composed his first two published novels: *The Town and the City* and *On the Road*. In his autobiographical novel *Vanity of Duluoz: An Adventurous Education* (1968) Kerouac called the period covered in this book the time of his "misty nebulous New England Idealistic style." Born on March 12, 1922, the youngest of three children in a Franco-American family that had established itself in Lowell, Massachusetts, Jack Kerouac was by the age of ten already aiming to become a writer. His father ran a print shop and published a local newsletter called *The Spotlight*. Young Jack learned about layout at an early age in an atmosphere made intoxicating by the smell of printer's ink. Before long, he began writing and producing his own hand-printed sports sheet, which he showed to friends and acquaintances in Lowell. He attended both Catholic and public schools, and won a scholarship to Columbia University — which, in addition, paid for a year of academic prep work at the Horace Mann School (in New York City). In New York, he fell in with fellow literary-icons-to-be Allen Ginsberg and William S. Burroughs. A broken leg hobbled his college football career, and Kerouac quit Columbia in his sophomore year, eventually joining the merchant marine and then the navy (from which he was honorably discharged). Thus began the restless wandering that would characterize both his legacy and his life.

With ferocious intensity, Kerouac began keeping journals in 1936, as a fourteen-year-old boy in Lowell. His obsessive habit continued for the rest of his life. Long, detailed passages, usually produced daily, are ornamented with poems, drawings, doodles, riddles, psalms, and prayers. "I resort to these diary-logs in order to keep track of lags, and digressions, and moods," Kerouac noted as he began writing *On the Road*. Kerouac's modus operandi in these handwritten journals is one of voluntary simplicity and freedom, of achieving sainthood by being lonesome and poor, with empathy for every sentient creature. Early on, Kerouac wanted no part of the postwar scramble for monetary success: "It is beneath my dignity to participate in life." To Kerouac, the "most ringing sound of all human time" was Jesus' refrain "My kingdom is not of this world."

Kerouac's lifelong devotion to mystical Catholicism comes through very strongly in these pages. His spiral notebooks are adorned with crucifixes, and scarcely a passage appears without invoking glory to God. "Strike me," Kerouac begs God in one passage, "and I will ring like a bell." Always Kerouac is the religious quester, fueled by what scholar John Lardas in *The Bop Apocalypse* (2001) calls his "penchant for immanental mysticism." If *Some of the Dharma* (1997, originally composed from 1953 to 1956) documents Kerouac's evolving acceptance of Buddhism, *Windblown World* bears witness to his lifelong acceptance of Jesus as philosopher-prince: "Christ's teachings were a turning-to, a facing up, a confrontation and confoundment of the terrible enigma of human life. What a miraculous thing! What thoughts Jesus must have had before he 'opened his mouth' on the Mount and spoke his sermon, what long dark silent thoughts."

At a time when Norman Mailer was playing sociologist by studying "White Negro" hipsters, Kerouac sought to depict his fascinatingly inchoate friend Neal Cassady as the modern-day equivalent of the Wild West legends Jim Bridger, Pecos Bill, and Jesse James. Like the Lowell boy he never quite ceased to be, Kerouac saw athletes and range-worn cowboys as the paragons of the true America; these journals teem with references to "folk heroes" and praise for Zane Grey's honest drifters, Herman Melville's confidence men, and Babe Ruth's feats on the diamond and in the barroom. Kerouac, in fact, brought confidence-man Neal Cassady into the American mythical pantheon as "that mad Ahab at the wheel," compelling others to join his roaring drive across Walt Whitman's patchwork Promised Land.

What is also quite evident when reading Kerouac's journals is his tremendous love of "the essential and everlasting America." Like the poet William Carlos Williams, Kerouac is obsessed with explaining his "Americanism." Whether it's the Brooklyn Dodgers or Denver fireworks or the New Jersey Turnpike or Louisiana bayous, Kerouac's journals are infused with poetic imagery about post–World War II American life. No serious writer has ever celebrated American city names with the childlike exuberance of Kerouac. Like Chuck Berry, he tried to rattle off as many American transient name places as possible. A classic Kerouacian line from his journals is "He is in hot K.C., he wants to zoom down to Tulsa and Fort Worth, or out to Denver, Pueblo, Albuquerque — anyplace but here, in the hot Missouri night." He tried to find the midnight essence of all American community both big and small. "Eau Claire belongs to a type of American town I always like: it is on a river and it is dark and the stars shine stark-bright, and there is something *steep* about the night," he writes in 1949 while traveling through Wisconsin. "Such towns are Lowell, Oregon City, Holyoke

Mass., Asheville N.C., Gardiner Maine, St. Cloud, Steubenville O., Lexington Mo., Klamath Falls Ore., and so on — even Frisco of course."

Windblown World is divided into two distinct sections. The first centers around his struggle to get his first novel, *The Town and the City*, written and published. This journal section —"worklogs," as he unpretentiously called them — were composed in Ozone Park, a nondescript working-class neighborhood in New York City's downscale borough of Queens. It's a place that makes no pretense of being a literary Mecca along the lines of Greenwich Village or Harlem or Brooklyn Heights. But it was here from 1947 to 1949 that Jack Kerouac, the father of the Beat Generation, wrote his first published novel, *The Town and the City*, launching a career that would push the limits of American prose.

Kerouac was driven to write *The Town and the City* by the grief he experienced at the death of his father, Leo, from stomach cancer in early 1946. For months, he had lain awake in the second-floor apartment above the drugstore at Thirty-third Avenue and Cross Bay Boulevard listening to his father coughing in dire pain. Every two weeks, a doctor came, and the son watched as fluid from his father's stomach was pumped out into a bucket. Jack and Leo were alone in the apartment when the end finally came, a scene achingly re-created in *The Town and the City*: "'You poor old man, you poor old man,' he cried, kneeling in front of his father. 'My father!' he cried in a loud voice that rang with lonely madness in the empty house.... Peter went outside to a candy store and telephoned his mother at the shoe factory ... and then came back in the house and sat looking at his father for the last time." Leo had always wanted his son to "get a job," and that's what the twenty-four-year-old Jack Kerouac did: he stayed home and started writing *The Town and the City*, which was published by Harcourt, Brace in 1950 under the name "John Kerouac."

In his later masterwork, *On the Road*, Kerouac glossed over the years right after his father's death in a single sentence: "I stayed home all that time, finished my book and began going to school on the GI Bill of Rights." His friend Allen Ginsberg was so impressed by Kerouac's unflappable quest to write the Great American Novel at his mother's kitchen table in Queens that he nicknamed him "The Wizard of Ozone Park." Under the lyrical spell of Thomas Wolfe, whose sweeping novels *Of Time and the River* and *Look Homeward, Angel* romanticized the desolation of the vast rawness that was America, Kerouac had become determined to make himself into just as great a native storyteller. Kerouac admired many facets of Wolfe's writing: his robust prose; his embrace of the autobiographical impulse to create fiction out of one's own myth; his ability to conjure the sadness in nostalgic moments, to find the spiritual in the forlorn, and to celebrate the holiness inherent in the American earth; and the romantic, optimistic tone he retained far into adulthood. According to Kerouac, Wolfe's novels engulfed him in "a torrent of American heaven and hell ... [that] opened my eyes to America as a subject."

In the end, as Regina Weinreich states in *The Spontaneous Poetics of Jack Kerouac,* Wolfe's acolyte did not just imitate his idol in *The Town and the City;* to some extent he one-upped him. In fact, the lead promotional blurb that Harcourt, Brace used to sell Kerouac's first novel came from the distinguished Columbia University literature professor Mark Van Doren, who deemed it "wiser than Wolfe." That seemingly grand accolade also, however, pointed to what would prove to be *The Town and the City*'s Achilles' heel: virtually every reviewer would remark that Kerouac's talent was unoriginal and that he owed Wolfe a tremendous literary debt. The sheer heft of *The Town and the City* — twelve hundred manuscript pages and nearly 300,000 words — caused Kerouac, in an entry in this volume, to deem the book "a veritable Niagara of a novel." In particular, it drew critical comparisons with Wolfe's *Look Homeward, Angel,* which takes place in a fictionalized Asheville, North Carolina, boardinghouse operated by protagonist Eugene Grant's mother. Critics did not miss that the early chapters of Kerouac's novel are set in a similar house in Lowell, Massachusetts, large enough to hold nine ever-growing children. The model for Kerouac's fictionalized Lowell home was the Sampas family and its ten children, including his closest friend, Sebastian Sampas.

In *The Town and the City*, Kerouac documented the disintegration of a large middle-class family — the Martins of Galloway — as its members scattered into New York City and faced different problems. Eventually, the Martin children reunite after World War II when they return to attend their father's funeral in his New Hampshire hometown. The saga offers one of the most moving filial narratives ever written — that of young Peter Martin and his father and their efforts to find themselves and each other. Kerouac fashioned other memorable characters as well: the clan's fastidious mother; Joe Martin, its intrepid wanderer; Francis Martin, the self-styled intellectual who feigns insanity to get out of the navy; Alex Panos, a romantic poet; Kenny Wood, a lost soul; Liz Martin, the embittered wife; Leon Levinsky, a Greenwich Village "hipster," and many others. Five of the Martin boys actually represent aspects of Kerouac himself, a point mirrored in the journals by Kerouac's constant worries over his "schizophrenic personality."

The entire period when Kerouac was writing *The Town and the City* is spanned in these detailed journals, which tell of his tortured efforts to improve the novel's plot and characters. Kerouac is seemingly more interested in his daily word counts than in the tightness of his prose. "Just made one of those great grim decisions of one's life — not to present my manuscript of 'T & C' to any publisher until I've completed it, all 300,000-odd words of it," Kerouac recorded on June 16, 1947. "This means seven months of ascetic gloom and labor — although doubt is no longer my devil, just sadness now."

Over these months, Kerouac, haunted by Christian images, used his journals as a confessional booth where he could catalogue his innermost feelings, indulge his philosophical musing, and pray to God for help through an interior dialogue with himself. The notebooks were, he explained, his "mood log." This log makes clear that Kerouac wanted to give *The Town and the City* a religious cast. To his journal he admitted that he hoped to find inspiration in Leo Tolstoy's moral essays, but instead found the Russian count too self-consciously spiritual, too self-satisfied in his lofty evocations of "good and evil." Thus Kerouac turned to another Russian muse, Fyodor Dostoevsky, whose

Brothers Karamazov has been called a perfect work of fiction. "I concluded that Dostoevsky's wisdom is the highest wisdom in the world, because it's not only Christ's wisdom, but a Karamazov Christ of lusts and glees," Kerouac concluded. "Unlike poor Tolstoy, Dostoevsky never had to retire to morality."

Given that view, it's not surprising to see how often Jesus was on Kerouac's mind as he was writing *The Town and the City*. In fact, he kept the New Testament at his side and prayed to Christ before each work session, and while there is little humor in these *Town and the City* journals/worklogs, there is an abundance of mystical Christian theologizing. "[I]f Jesus were sitting here at my desk tonight, looking out the window at all these people laughing and happy because the great summer vacation is beginning, perhaps he would smile, and thank his Father. I don't know," Kerouac wrote on June 26, 1948. "People must 'live,' and yet I know Jesus has the only answer. If I ever reconcile true Christianity with American life, I will do so by remembering my father Leo, a man who knew both these things."

Whether he achieved that goal or not, *The Town and the City* was published on March 2, 1950, to generally admiring views. Charles Poore in the *New York Times* heralded Kerouac as "a brilliantly promising young novelist" with a "magnificent grasp of the disorderly splendor and squalor of existence." *Newsweek* went so far as to declare Kerouac "the best and most promising of the young novelists whose first works have recently appeared." As scholar Matt Theado notes in *Understanding Jack Kerouac* (2000), Kerouac's wordplay in the novel — for example, "A star-wealthy sky, August cool and calm"— presage his future spontaneous prose experiments most marvelously found in *Visions of Cody* (1972).

But there were quibbles amid the hurrahs. The *Saturday Review* criticized *The Town and the City* as being "radically deficient in structure and style," while the *New Yorker* dismissed the narrative as "ponderous, shambling ... tiresome."

Home-grown validation came, however, when Lowell *Sun* columnist and news editor Charles Sampas — Sebastian's brother — dubbed *The Town and the City* "The Great Lowell Novel" and the newspaper ran along with its story photographs illustrating the people and places evoked in the novel. *The Town and the City* was also received well in Great Britain, although more as a promising effort than as an enduring work of mature literature. When it was published in June 1951 by the now-defunct Eyre and Spottiswoode, British critics generally applauded Kerouac's vigor but decried his disdain for self-editing. Many of the English reviews intimated that if the overly ambitious Kerouac could stop chasing the chimera of "the Great American Novel" and instead find his own voice, he just might have a shot at becoming the F. Scott Fitzgerald of his generation. What they admired in the young Kerouac was his visionary sweep, his exuberance, his genuinely sentimental notion of middle-class American family life expressed in a Wolfe-like rhetorical style that the *Times Literary Supplement* called "informed with genuine power." The *Sunday Mercury* chimed in approvingly that *The Town and the City*'s overall thesis was that "family is stronger than the evils of modern civilization."

Kerouac was quite pleased with the handsome English edition of *The Town and the City,* even more so that it received upbeat reviews in the Liverpool, Newcastle, Nottingham, Belfast, Dublin, and Cardiff papers as well as the London dailies. "I haven't expressed my gladness and gratitude that my book was finally published in England," Kerouac wrote his London editor, a Mr. Frank Morley, on July 27, 1951. "Though remote, the honor is like horns over the sea or something." In the same letter, Kerouac also told Morley that his editor at Harcourt, Brace had rejected his new novel, *On the Road,* that he had hired a new agent and that from now on he was going to be his "own editor." Kerouac then rhapsodized about crossing the Atlantic, soon, just to experience "an English summer night," and about starting a third novel, this one about jazz and bop with his English friend Seymour Wyse as the model for the main character, a "19th Century be-slouched hatted wanderer among the Impressionists through France." In essence, what Kerouac was telling Morley is that by the time *The Town and the City* was published in Britain, its author had moved toward developing that original voice the London critics had urged him to seek, in a work-in-progress called *On the Road*. Thomas Wolfe would no longer be Kerouac's polestar; instead he would look to harmonize with the wailing horns of America's midnight jazz cats, with the fast talk of highway con men, the rants of existential poets, and the prayers of the lonesome priests searching for a new faith from Lowell to Laredo. In fact, even the last third of *The Town and the City* can be seen as the beginning of the Kerouac "road" genre that would win him legions of devoted admirers around the globe. But for all the ardor with which he embraced his critics' exhortations to be more creative, he patently rejected their advice to drop a few adjectives and rein in the rhapsodies — the very traits that would come to distinguish Kerouac's thirty books of prose and poetry.

As these journals make clear, this was Kerouac's first and only attempt at writing a traditional novel. John Kerouac would, of course, soon become the revered Jack Kerouac whose 1957 novel *On the Road* inspired an entire "Beat Generation" to look for holiness in the mundane, God in oneself, and beauty in every shard of broken glass off a bottle in the street. Today fans now make regular pilgrimages to the still-blue-collar Ozone Park, just to read the small oval plaque bolted to the brick apartment house whence Kerouac set off on his many journeys across America half a century ago.

Which leads us to part 2 of *Windblown World*: the journals/travel logs for *On the Road*. Although Kerouac wrote *On the Road* from Ozone Park — and later from Richmond Hill, Queens, and 454 West Twentieth Street in Manhattan — his material came from his various cross-country treks, a rucksack on his back and a trusty notebook in hand. Now, in this volume, we can read what Kerouac himself wrote while crossing over the Mississippi River in Louisiana, climbing up the Continental Divide in Montana on a bus, and getting stuck in a North Dakota Badlands blizzard. We feel the humidity of Biloxi, the bareness of East Texas, and the lostness of Los Angeles. Instead of fictional pseudonyms for his friends, we encounter the real Allen Ginsberg, Neal Cassady, William Burroughs, and Lucien Carr in all their

Beat Generation glory. This is Jack Kerouac unplugged, discovering America for the first time "through the keyhole of my eye."

It is Kerouac's conscious attempts at myth-making that perhaps most astonishes the reader of these journals. While gathering material for *On the Road* in 1949, for example, crisscrossing America in search of kicks, joy, and God, he stopped off in the eastern Montana town of Miles City, and wandered around in the February snow, temperature registering at twenty degrees below. Soon Kerouac had one of his many epiphanies. "In a drugstore window I saw a book on sale — so beautiful!" he wrote in his journal. "*Yellowstone Red*, a story of a man in the early days of the valley, and his tribulations and triumphs. Is this not better reading in Miles City than the Iliad? Their own epic?" Kerouac was intent on creating his own Yellowstone Red story, only in the modern context, where existential jazz musicians and wandering highway speedsters would be celebrated as the new vagabond saints.

On the Road protagonists Dean Moriarty and Sal Paradise were intended as the automobile-age equivalents of Butch Cassidy and the Sundance Kid. "Beyond the glittery street was darkness and beyond the darkness the West," Kerouac wrote in 1951. "I had to go." In the bohemian circus that was the Beat culture, populated by whores, swindlers, hipsters, horn players, hoboes, and charlatans, Kerouac saw himself as the F. Scott Fitzgerald of the post–Jazz Age, whose frantic stories would bring their unorthodox exploits before the Eisenhower era's public at large. But spinning yarns about deviant characters was dangerous business in the days of Joe McCarthy's philistine witch hunts: in 1954, for example, John Steinbeck's own hometown of Salinas, California, launched an effort to keep H. G. Wells's *Outline of History* and Bertrand Russell's *Human Knowledge* out of the public libraries. In San Antonio, where Davy Crockett and scores of other patriots had given their lives for liberty at the Alamo, an effort was underway to tack SUBVERSIVE labels to more than five hundred books by 118 writers, including the likes of Thomas Mann and Geoffrey Chaucer, while the state of Texas passed a law requiring textbook writers not only to state whether or not they were Communists but also to declare the same of every author they cited.

In this bizarre Red Scare atmosphere, Kerouac was either extremely naïve or wildly courageous to claim that *On the Road*'s car thief and con artist Dean Moriarty was "a new kind of American Saint," a petty criminal with a "wild-eyed overburst of American joy." In an era when Zen Buddhist teachings were considered Communist propaganda, Kerouac's quest to make heroes out of hoodwinkers and hoodlums was bound to raise critics' eyebrows and concerns at the FBI.

But as these journals illustrate, it was Kerouac's peculiar genius to find a common ground between the heroes of America's popular culture and Catholic saints, Zen Buddhist masters and Levantine holy men. Neal Cassady was a mix between TV cowboy Hopalong Cassidy and Saint Francis; melding Johnny Appleseed with Buddha turned out Gary Snyder (fictionalized as Japhy Ryder in *The Dharma Bums*). Filtered through Kerouac's fertile imagination and populist view of American cultural history, even Burroughs became an old-time "Kansas Minister with exotic phenomenal fire and mysteries." His characters were a parade of divine outlaws, desolate angels, holy goofs, and subterranean prophets, every one of them unmistakably American. It is through such characters that Kerouac approached in *On the Road* one of the central questions of postwar Western literature: "Whither goest thou, America, in thy shiny car in the night?"

The biblical lingo was no accident. Although Kerouac only hints at his fixation on the death of Christ in his fiction, these journals are another matter entirely. The original pages were garnished with religious imagery and teem with pleas to God to forgive his wayward carnal sins. From childhood until death, Kerouac wrote letters to God, prayers to Jesus, poems to Saint Paul, and psalms to his own salvation. In fact, he found his own meaning for the term "Beat" one rainy afternoon while praying to a statue of the Virgin Mary at Lowell's Saint Jeanne d'Arc Church, which triggered a teary vision. As Kerouac described it, "I heard the holy silence in the church (I was the only one there, it was five P.M., dogs were barking outside, children yelling, the fall leaves, the candles were flickering alone just for me), the vision of the word Beat as being to mean 'beautific.'"

The most enduring myth about Kerouac is one that these journals partially dispel: that he wrote *On the Road* in April 1951 in a three-week frenzy fueled by coffee. According to the legend, one day Kerouac, inspired by his raucous travels with Cassady over the previous three years, stuck a roll of Japanese tracing paper into the typewriter at his Chelsea apartment on West Twentieth Street — so as not to distract his concentration when changing paper — turned on an all-night Harlem jazz radio station, and produced a modern masterpiece. Kerouac's archives, now housed at the New York Public Library, tell a different story from the legend that between April 2 and April 22 he wrote all of *On the Road*, averaging six thousand words a day, logging twelve thousand the first day, and fifteen thousand the last. The thirty-five-year-old author said he "blew out" his holy words like Lester Young on his midnight saxophone those nights, writing fast because the "road is fast." Revisions were for hung-up squares and the culturally constipated too afraid to dig the natural rhythms of their own minds. Once *On the Road* was finished, Kerouac allegedly Scotch-taped the twelve-foot sheets of paper together and delivered the hundred-foot "scroll" to Harcourt, Brace editor Bob Giroux, who, instead of gushing, bellowed at the author, "How the hell can a printer work from this?" Insulted, Kerouac stormed out of the office, although he would later claim that Giroux compared the work to Dostoevsky's and called Kerouac a literary prophet ahead of his time.

This tale of *On the Road* as the product of a fevered burst of divine inspiration is exaggerated. That the manuscript Kerouac typed in Chelsea in April 1951 was the outcome of a fastidious process of outlining, character sketching, chapter drafting, and meticulous trimming is clearly evident from even a cursory glance at what he called his "scribbled secret notebooks." Not only did he have a coherent and detailed one-page plot line for most chapters, but portions of the dialogue had also been written before April. Journal entries were loosely incorporated into the manuscript in the famous marathon typing session, during which he also used a list he had kept of key phrases to be worked into the text denoting ideas that Kerouac would paraphrase from T. S. Eliot, Mark Twain, Thomas Wolfe, William Saroyan, John Donne, Thomas De Quincey, and many other writers.

The most consistent factor throughout the novel's various drafts was the depiction of Cassady as a kind of "Wild West" protagonist of the saga. The real Cassady was a marvelous legendary character — a point continually reconfirmed whether he cropped up as the secret hero of "Howl" or as the sledgehammer-flipping, speed-rapping, manic driver of the Day-Glo bus labeled "Further" with which novelist Ken Kesey "unsettled" America in 1964 — and Kerouac sketched him truthfully, if with the occasional Hollywood touch of Beat-like actors such as Humphrey Bogart and Montgomery Clift.

The journals also show how Kerouac loved Western towns like Butte, Truckee, Medora, Fargo, Spokane, Denver, and Salt Lake City, which he felt had not been given their due in American literature. He writes with romantic verve about the Texas sagebrush, Arizona mosquitoes, and North Dakota snow. Enamored with the pulp fiction of Zane Grey, Kerouac celebrates the Continental Divide as the spiritual vortex where "rain and rivers are decided." It's as if all of Kerouac's wanderings in the West are scored by a Gene Autry looptape, a Great Plains wind always howling at his back.

What these working notes for *On the Road* make clear is that Kerouac, far from clinging solely to the romantic notion of the spontaneous eruption of prose, had already drafted portions of *On the Road* between 1948 and 1950 and typed it onto the Japanese tracing paper. Kerouac denied the care he took largely because it went against the legend he was creating around himself as a "bop-prosody" genius. Kerouac exaggerated his act of literary creation, which was admittedly intense for those high-octane weeks, to prove that he was as spontaneous with words as the blind pianist George Shearing, trumpet player Chet Baker, and guitarist Slim Gaillard were with jazz. Just six weeks after finishing *On the Road*, Kerouac wrote to Cassady that his next novel would be *Hold Your Horn High*, the ultimate romanticized story of a "hot jazz cat."

Kerouac's prolific output, as *Windblown World* proves, was the result of constant "sketching" and creative self-discipline, as well as a belief in the notion of spontaneous prose. This is further manifested in the meticulousness with which Kerouac maintained his journals and worklogs. "Hemingway has nothing over me when it comes to persnickitiness about 'craft,'" he wrote an editor. "Nor any poet." His copious journal volumes are filled not only with regular observations but with chapter drafts, false starts, atmospheric ramblings, and random character profiles as well. "Really, you oughta see it, I'm a genius of organization," Kerouac once wrote his novelist friend John Clellon Holmes. "I should have been a charcoal suit."

Of course, these revelations about Kerouac's disciplined work methods are not entirely new. Throughout the 1950s and 1960s, Viking Press's Malcolm Cowley, who served as editor for *On the Road,* went on record claiming that Kerouac had written versions of his masterpiece before April 1951 and done major rewrites before its eventual publication in 1957. Some of the confusion stemmed from the peculiarity that over the years Kerouac had shown editors two different manuscripts titled *On the Road.* The second was an experimental "spontaneous prose" portrait of Cassady that Kerouac wrote in 1951–52 and retitled "Visions of Neal"; it was published in 1972 as *Visions of Cody.* Still, "*On the Road* was good prose," Cowley recalled. "I wasn't worried about the prose. I was worried about the structure of the book. It seemed to me that in the original draft the story keeps swinging back and forth across the continental United States like a pendulum." Cowley urged Kerouac to consolidate episodes, shorten chapters, rewrite passages, and throw out dead-end tangents. "Well, Jack did something that he would never admit to later," Cowley maintained. "He did a good bit of revision, and it was very good revision. Oh, he would never, never admit to that, because it was his feeling that the stuff ought to come out like toothpaste from a tube and not be changed, and that every word that passed from his typewriter was holy. On the contrary, he revised, and revised well."

And so did Cowley. Worried that Kerouac would reinsert excised passages back into *On the Road,* the editor never sent him galleys, only a box of finished books. Furthermore, Cowley had tweaked sections of the intricate novel without even informing the author, who complained bitterly to Allen Ginsberg, Peter Orlovsky, and Alan Ansen on July 21, 1957. "He yanked much out of *On the Road* ... without my permission or even sight of galley proofs! Oh Shame! Shame on American Business." It left an even bigger bruise on Kerouac's ego when Cowley read some of his other manuscripts — *Doctor Sax, Tristessa,* and *Desolation Angels* — and rejected them all, fretting that Kerouac had "completely ruined" himself as a "publishable writer" by embracing "automatic or self-abuse writing." Cowley believed that Kerouac's first book, *The Town and the City,* was better than anything in his new spate of jazz- and Buddhist-influenced stuff.

Just a few weeks after Gilbert Millstein reviewed *On the Road* glowingly in the *New York Times* on September 5, 1957, Kerouac's audacious work made the best-seller list for several weeks, alongside Ayn Rand's *Atlas Shrugged* and Grace Metalious's *Peyton Place.* Virtually overnight, Kerouac became the "avatar" of the Beat Generation. He appeared on John Wingate's TV show *Nightbeat* to tell millions of viewers he was "waiting for God to show his face." Bright women bored with *Ozzie and Harriet* domesticity swooned over this new James Dean with brains, while literary lions like Nelson Algren, Norman Mailer, and Charles Olson dubbed Kerouac a Great American Writer. PEN — the International Association of Poets, Playwrights, Editors, Essayists and Novelists — invited him to join, but he declined. The Village Vanguard nightclub had him read jazz poetry, and Steve Allen provided piano accompaniment as Kerouac read passages from *Visions of Cody* on Allen's popular TV program.

"Jack was on top of the world," his musician friend David Amram recalled. "Everybody wanted to meet him, to hang with him." Russian artist Marc Chagall wanted to paint the first Beat's portrait with angels fluttering around his head. Photographer Robert Frank asked him to write the introduction to his book of elegiac photographs, *The Americans.* Jackie Kennedy, wife of the future president, said she had read *On the Road* and loved it. Instead of the "little magazines," Kerouac was now commissioned to write articles for *Playboy, Esquire, Escapade, Holiday,* and the *New York World* and *Sun* explaining the Beat Generation. In a letter to Cassady, a bewildered Kerouac reported that "everything exploded."

And there stood the handsome Jack Kerouac with his penetrating blue eyes and football player's build, the victim of his own myth-making, and unsure how to act under the intense glare of the spotlight. Never before had an American literary icon seemed so utterly confused and ill equipped for fame, and certainly nobody could have guessed from reading *On the Road* that the shy Beat author was afraid of cars. "[I] don't know how to drive," he admitted, "just typewrite."

And, it now must be added, write furiously in his notebooks. His prolixity in this regard was truly Herculean. The reader should understand that *Windblown World* constitutes only *some* of the prolific Kerouac's journal entries and worklogs from the 1947 to 1954 period. An entire notebook titled "Road Workbook 'Libreta America,'" for example, is not included here. This journal contains character sketches, detailed outlines, and passages of fiction — a selection of which is included here, at the end of the "Rain and Rivers" journal. It has three short unpublished chapters from an early failed draft of *On the Road* (including a number of tangential passages that include Kerouac's thoughts on his writing, sketches, and other ideas for projects and poems); a long section of spontaneous prose in which he tries to flesh out his *On the Road* characters; and two chapters of an unpublished novel titled *Gone on the Road.* I've also excised most of another journal, which Kerouac labeled "Private Philologies, Riddles and a Ten-Day Writing Log (much of which is just nonsense and words)." I've inserted some fragments from it chronologically into the "1949 Journals."

Because Kerouac has become a cottage industry, it's not hard to envision that someday all of his journals might be published in a perfectly annotated multivolume set. That was not, however, the objective of *Windblown World.* Instead, this volume offers the strongest and most important passages; some of his really sloppy thinking and poor writing was left out. As editor, I've taken the liberty of making internal edits. But I've maintained the intensity of Kerouac's original text to the best of my ability. And while technically *Windblown World* deals with Kerouac's writing of two novels, it also sets the stage for such other works as *Visions of Cody, Doctor Sax,* and *Book of Dreams.*

Unpublished pages aside, what both sections of *Windblown World* have in common is a brooding melancholy that penetrates every page. At times Kerouac is almost suicidal, unable to accept the cruel realities of existence. He seeks spiritual guidance from God, begs for grace and forgiveness while praying for divine intervention. He is always seeing sadness around him, concerned about all the lonely people with dark eyes looking for salvation. "I shall keep in contact with all things that cross my path, and trust all things that do not cross my path, and exert more greatly for further and further visions of the other world, and preach (if I can) in my work, and love, and attempt to hold down my lonely vanities so as to connect more and more with all things (and kinds of people), and believe that my consciousness of life and eternity is not a mistake, or a loneliness, or a foolishness — but a warm dear love of our poor predicament which by the grace of Mysterious God will be solved and made clear to all of us in the end, maybe only," he breathlessly recorded in a run-on journal sentence of August 1949. "Otherwise I cannot live."

Douglas Brinkley
New Orleans
March 20, 2004

CAST OF CHARACTERS

This list provides a quick reference for biographical information on all of the main players in *Windblown World*. However, it is not an all-inclusive catalog of names mentioned in the text. For those that are unknown beyond what Kerouac offers about them, his context will have to do.

Walter Adams   Friend to Kerouac from his Columbia days who lived at the Union Theological Seminary in Manhattan. Adams threw many of the early Beat parties, at which Kerouac forged friendships with others from the bohemian scene.

Ann   A nurse who was a neighbor to Kerouac's sister, Caroline, and her husband in North Carolina. Kerouac had a romantic relationship with her.

George "G. J." Apostolos   Tough and aggressive, Apostolos was among Kerouac's closest boyhood friends in Lowell. Kerouac once described him as "the smuggest sonofoabitch that ever lived." After high school, he enrolled in the Civilian Conservation Corps and helped build Estes Park (today named Rocky Mountain National Park) in Colorado and the Pentagon in Washington, D.C.

A. J. Ayer   British philosopher who occasionally mixed with Kerouac's New York crowd. His *Language, Truth and Logic* (1936) was a widely discussed book of its time.

Jinny Baker   Kerouac's sixteen-year-old girlfriend in the summer of 1948. Kerouac once taped a picture of a model into a journal and wrote "Jinny's exact likeness" above it.

Herb Benjamin   Part of Kerouac's New York crowd who often supplied Kerouac and friends with marijuana.

Caroline "Nin" Kerouac Blake   Kerouac's older sister by three years. Lived in North Carolina with her second husband, **Paul** — like Jack a former collegiate football player — in the period these journals were written. They went to live in Denver with Jack, briefly, in the summer of 1949. A portion of these journals were written while Kerouac was staying at their home in North Carolina, in the summer of 1947 and again shortly after **Paul Jr.**'s birth in June 1948.

Justin Brierly   A Columbia graduate and friend of Neal Cassady and Hal Chase. He worked as a lawyer and teacher in Denver. Fictionalized as Denver D. Doll in *On the Road*.

Beverly Burford   Kerouac met her through Ed White and had a brief romantic relationship with her in Denver in spring/summer 1950. She and her brother, **Bob** — who went on to edit small literary magazines — were lifelong friends to Kerouac thereafter. Fictionalized as Babe Rawlins in *On the Road*.

Joan Vollmer Adams Burroughs   Kerouac met her in 1943 when she shared an apartment near Columbia with his future wife, Edie Parker. She became the common-law wife of William S. Burroughs, by whom she had two children — **Willie** and **Julie**. Burroughs accidentally killed Joan during a game of William Tell in Mexico City, September 1951. Fictionalized as Jane in *On the Road* and as Mary Dennison in *The Town and the City*.

William S. "Bill" Burroughs   Missouri-born, well-traveled, and Harvard-educated, the tall, slender, and reticent Burroughs sought out friends in circles of crime and drugs. He moved to New York in 1944 and became fast friends with Kerouac, Huncke, and Ginsberg. Though he didn't begin writing until age thirty-five, he became a prodigious novelist, authoring Beat classics *Junky* (1953) and *Naked Lunch* (1959). Fictionalized as Will Denison in *The Town and the City* and as Old Bull Lee in *On the Road*.

Bill Cannastra   This rambunctious New York native and Harvard Law graduate threw infamous all-night parties throughout the late 1940s in his loft. Friend to Kerouac until he was decapitated in 1950 when he stuck his head out of a New York City subway.

Mary Carney   The railroad worker's daughter who became Kerouac's high school sweetheart in Lowell. Kerouac later based the title character of *Maggie Cassidy* (1959) on her. Four of their deeply personal love letters are housed in the Berg Collection at the New York Public Library.

Lucien Carr   First met Allen Ginsberg while both were living on the seventh floor of the Union Theological Seminary (used as a Columbia University dorm during World War II). Came from St. Louis — where he was friendly with William Burroughs — to Columbia, met Kerouac in 1943, and introduced him to Allen Ginsberg in 1944. That summer he stabbed David Kammerer to death and spent two years in jail; Kerouac was detained as an accessory after the fact. Worked at United Press International in the period these journals were written and is said to have brought Kerouac teletype paper from his office, on which Kerouac often typed. Fictionalized as Kenny Wood in *The Town and the City* and as Damion in *On the Road*. Often "Lou" in Kerouac's journals.

Carolyn Cassady   Carolyn Robinson, a stunning platinum blonde, met Neal Cassady in Denver in the spring of 1947 and soon became

Carolyn Cassady. While he was still married to LuAnne Henderson, Neal and Carolyn began an affair and were eventually married in April 1948. Fictionalized as Camille in *On the Road*.

LuAnne Cassady Sixteen-year-old, blonde-haired LuAnne Henderson married twenty-year-old Neal Cassady in 1946, and the two of them headed to New York to meet Hal Chase. She returned to Denver after two months, and their marriage quickly withered, but they continued an off-and-on relationship in the following years. Fictionalized as Marylou in *On the Road*.

Neal Cassady A Denver native, Cassady is said to have stolen five hundred cars before his twenty-first birthday and spent a good portion of his adolescence in reform school. In late 1946, at the age of twenty, he left Denver for New York with his new wife, sixteen-year-old LuAnne Henderson. Soon after their arrival in New York, he was introduced to Kerouac and Ginsberg through mutual friend Hal Chase. Cassady and Kerouac — with others — soon began taking their cross-country trips that would become the basis for *On the Road*. Met and married Carolyn Robinson in April 1948. He went on to travel with Ken Kesey in the 1960s. Fictionalized as Dean Moriarty in *On the Road*.

Hal Chase A Denver native, Chase was an anthropology student at Columbia and met Kerouac in 1946. Neal Cassady came to visit Chase in 1946 and he introduced Cassady to Kerouac. In these journals, he is often accompanied by his girlfriend — and later wife — **Ginger.** Fictionalized as Chad King in *On the Road*.

Henri Cru Raised in Paris, Cru was a friend to Kerouac at Horace Mann. Like Kerouac, he had worked as a merchant marine, and he joined Kerouac at Columbia. In 1947, when Cru was living outside of San Francisco, he attempted to sell a film treatment he and Kerouac had prepared. Cru introduced Kerouac to Edie Parker. Fictionalized as Remi Boncoeur in *On the Road*.

David Diamond   Composer and friend to Kerouac in New York, beginning in 1948.

Russell Durgin   Columbia theology student whose Harlem sublet apartment served as lending library and site of many early gatherings for Kerouac's New York friends.

Louis Eno   This childhood friend to Kerouac grew up in the same Centralville neighborhood in Lowell and was also of French-Canadian descent. His father was a judge and often lent his car out for Jack and Louis to go for joyrides.

Rae Everitt   Young literary agent for MCA who ran in the same circles as Kerouac in New York. She would eventually work as agent for Kerouac and John Clellon Holmes.

Jack Fitzgerald   Kerouac's friend and drinking buddy at Horace Mann, Columbia, and afterward. He was a fellow literature and jazz enthusiast. Sometimes referred to as "Fitz." Took a wife, **Jeanne,** and they had a son, **Mike.**

Mike Fournier   This boyhood friend to Kerouac grew up in the same Lowell neighborhood and was a part of the "jock" crowd Kerouac played sports with. Kerouac based *The Town and the City's* Joe Martin largely on Fournier.

Bea Franco   A Mexican migrant worker with whom Kerouac had an affair during his first trip to California in 1947. Their brief romance is fictionalized in Part 1 of *On the Road,* with Bea as Terry.

Allen Ginsberg   Raised in Paterson, New Jersey, Ginsberg went to Columbia as a mentally unstable seventeen-year-old in 1943. There he met Kerouac, who would become a lifelong friend. An active poet at Columbia and in the decades that followed, he went on to pen seminal Beat poems such as "Howl" and "Kaddish"; he won the National Book Award for his collection, *The Fall of America* (1974). Fictionalized as Leon Lavinsky in *The Town and the City* and as Carlo Marx in *On the Road*.

Robert "Bob" Giroux   This 1936 Columbia graduate was a friend to Mark Van Doren. After reading Kerouac's draft of *The Town and the City*, Van Doren recommended it to Giroux, an editor at Harcourt, Brace. Giroux gave Kerouac a contract and worked with him extensively on editing the novel, even visiting Kerouac while he was living in Denver in the summer of 1949. He went on to become a renowned editor and publisher. Kerouac dedicated *The Town and the City* to Giroux.

Beverly Anne Gordon   An eighteen-year-old romantic interest of Kerouac's in the spring of 1948.

Barbara Hale   Girlfriend to Lucien Carr. A wild and adventurous Vassar graduate with long black hair who often wore thick schoolteacher-like spectacles. Worked as a researcher for *Time* in the late forties and early fifties. Her father was the assistant district attorney of New York under Thomas Dewey. An aunt gave her a Model A Ford, which she, Carr, and Kerouac used to get around the city.

Diana Hansen   A New York fashion writer whom Neal Cassady romanced and lived with beginning in the fall of 1949. When she became pregnant with Cassady's child in February 1950, he quickly divorced Carolyn in Mexico and married Hansen in New York that July. Immediately after they married, Cassady left for California and returned to Carolyn. Kerouac calls her "Dianne" or "Diane" in the journals. Fictionalized as Inez in *On the Road*.

Alan Harrington   A regular in Kerouac's New York crowd. Went on to become the author of *The Immortalist* (1969), among other works of both fiction and nonfiction. Fictionalized as Hal Hingham in *On the Road*.

Joan Haverty   Lived with Bill Cannastra until his untimely death in 1950; the tall, dark-haired Haverty married Kerouac that fall. Their brief, rocky marriage ended in June 1951. Joan had become pregnant, and Kerouac believed the father was not he, but one of her restaurant coworkers. She threw him out of their apartment, and they never reconciled. Fictionalized as Laura in *On the Road*.

Al Hinkle   Neal Cassady's friend from Denver who met Kerouac at Columbia. He and his wife, **Helen**, sometimes joined Kerouac on road trips. Al is fictionalized as Ed Dunkel in *On the Road* and Helen as Galatea Dunkel.

John Clellon Holmes   Like Kerouac, Holmes came to New York from Massachusetts. A Columbia student, Holmes met Kerouac in August 1948. After they'd both left Columbia, Holmes took American literature classes with Kerouac at the New School in 1949. He published the novel *Go* in 1952; it fictionalized Kerouac as Gene Pasternak. Holmes wrote the famous essay "This Is the Beat Generation" for the *New York Times Magazine*, November 16, 1952. His wife, during the period of these journals, is **Marian**. Holmes is fictionalized as Tom Saybrook in *On the Road*. Often called "Johnny" in Kerouac's journals.

Herbert "Hunkey" Huncke   Small-time thief, brooding drifter, winsome hustler, and chronic drug addict, Huncke was a friend to William Burroughs as early as 1944 and met Kerouac early on in his time at Columbia. His small stature and scrappy, honest demeanor made him a very well liked member of the New York Beat circle. A sometime writer, Huncke later authored a collection of stories called *The Evening Sun Turned Crimson* (1980) and an autobiography, *Guilty of Everything* (1990). Fictionalized in *The Town and the City* as Junky and in *On the Road* as Elmo Hassel.

Frank Jeffries   Another Denver friend, Jeffries accompanied Kerouac and Neal Cassady on a trip from Denver to Mexico in spring 1950. Kerouac based Part 4 of *On the Road* on that trip, in which Jeffries is fictionalized as Sam Shephard (not to be confused with the actor/playwright).

David Kammerer   A member of the early Beat circle in Greenwich Village, Kammerer introduced William Burroughs to Kerouac in February 1944. Kammerer was infatuated with Lucien Carr and on August 13, 1944, his sexual advances overwhelmed Carr, who stabbed Kammerer to death with a Boy Scout knife and dropped his body in the Hudson River. Carr was convicted of manslaughter and spent two years in jail. Kerouac was detained after the fact as an accessory. The incident is fictionalized in *The Town and the City*, with Kammerer as Waldo Meister.

Alfred Kazin   A well-respected critic and a celebrity instructor at the New School for Social Research in the late forties and fifties. In 1948, Kerouac took a Kazin literature course, for which he composed the essay "Whitman: A Prophet of the Sexual Revolution."

Gabrielle Levesque Kerouac   Jack's mother, whom he lived with in Ozone Park, New York, while writing *The Town and the City*. Jack lived off her income from her job at a shoe factory during this period. Fictionalized as Marge Martin in *The Town and the City* and as Sal Paradise's aunt in *On the Road*. Often "Mémère" in the journals.

Leo Kerouac   Jack's father, Quebec-born of French-Canadian descent. He worked in mills from boyhood and as insurance salesman, printer, and manager of the Pawtucketteville Social Club in Lowell throughout Jack's childhood. He died of stomach cancer in 1946 in Ozone Park, New York, just before these journals begin. Fictionalized as George Martin in *The Town and the City*.

Elbert Lenrow   One of Kerouac's professors at the New School; Kerouac took his "The 20th Century Novel in America" class in the fall of

1948. In January 1994, Lenrow penned a short memoir titled "The Young Jack Kerouac" for *Narrative,* recounting his experience with Kerouac the student.

Tom Livornese   Columbia student, piano player, jazz enthusiast, and friend to Kerouac. Explored the New York music scene with Jack through 1947 and afterward. Often accompanied by his younger sister, **Maria.**

Tony Monacchio   Friend and coworker of Lucien Carr at UPI. A regular in Kerouac's circle in the spring and summer of 1948; often threw the parties at which the early Beats met, drank, and talked.

Adele Morales   A New York artist with whom Kerouac was romantically involved in 1949 and 1950. She would go on to marry Norman Mailer in 1954 and achieved notoriety and infamy in 1960 when he stabbed her at a party in Manhattan. In 1997, she published her memoirs, *The Last Party: Scenes from My Life with Norm.*

Frank Morley   Englishman who worked as an editor at the British publisher Eyre and Spottiswoode. He was responsible for publication of *The Town and the City* in Great Britain.

Connie Murphy   A bright young Irish boy, Murphy was a member of a small group of young intellectual men in Lowell sometimes called The Young Prometheans. The group included Kerouac, Ian and John McDonald, and Sebastian Sampas. Their discussions touched on literature, philosophy, politics, and science. Murphy grew up to be a physicist and medical doctor.

Jim O'Dea   A boyhood pal from Lowell, O'Dea often joined in on the baseball games Kerouac organized and became the local district attorney.

Edie Parker   Kerouac's first wife. They married in August 1944 under strange circumstances: Kerouac had been detained as a material witness after Lucien Carr stabbed David Kammerer to death. Leo Kerouac refused to pay Jack's $500 bond, so Jack promised to marry Edie, his girlfriend, if she posted his bail—which she did. He lived with her in Grosse Pointe, Michigan, until they separated that fall. The marriage was annulled in 1946 by Edie. Fictionalized as Judie Smith in *The Town and the City*.

Duncan Purcell   Acquaintance of Kerouac's through Jack Fitzgerald.

Rhoda   A girl whom Kerouac, Cassady, and Al Hinkle picked up on their legendary New York–to–New Orleans automobile trip in January 1949.

Vicki Russell   A well-known drug dealer in New York who used Allen Ginsberg's apartment as a way station for her marijuana and speed cache. Upon one of her arrests, the *New York Daily News* described her as a "six-foot marijuana-smoking redhead." Herbert Huncke published a story about her exploits entitled "Detroit Redhead 1943–1967."

Roland "Salvey" Salvas   A lanky crack-up, Salvas was a boyhood friend from Lowell.

Sebastian Sampas   Best friend to Kerouac during high school. A poet and member of The Young Prometheans who studied theater arts at Emerson College. He and Kerouac often made trips into Boston together. They kept up a steady correspondence until his death at Anzio in 1944, while serving in the U.S. Army as a medic.

Meyer Shapiro   An art historian who was a professor at Columbia from 1936 to 1973, he also lectured at the New School for Social Research — where Kerouac attended his lectures — from 1936 to 1952.

Louis Simpson   Columbia student and poet who would go on to write more than a dozen books of poetry.

Ed Stringham   Wrote for the *New Yorker* in the 1940s; a friend to Kerouac who introduced him around the intellectual circles in New York.

Allan Temko   Kerouac's classmate at Horace Mann, Temko became an architectural critic and was a friend to Kerouac in New York, Denver, and San Francisco. Fictionalized as Roland Major in *On the Road*.

Ed Uhl   This Colorado rancher befriended a teenage Neal Cassady when he had to work on his ranch in Sterling, Colorado, as a condition of his probation. Kerouac and Cassady stopped at Uhl's ranch briefly while making their way from San Francisco to New York in August 1949. This event is vividly re-created in *On the Road,* in which Uhl is fictionalized as Ed Wall.

Mark Van Doren   Columbia professor and mentor to Kerouac and Allen Ginsberg. Helped move *The Town and the City* toward publication.

Gore Vidal   Returned to New York from Antigua in 1949 to warm critical reception of his novel, *The City and the Pillar* (1948). Vidal ran in the same intellectual social circles of New York (that often gathered at the San Remo and other Greenwich Village bars) as Kerouac. He went on to write dozens of books, both fiction and nonfiction.

Ed White   After his discharge from the navy, White was Hal Chase's roommate at Columbia. White's suggestion to Kerouac that he "sketch" instead of writing traditionally is credited with inspiring Kerouac's move toward spontaneous prose. After graduation, White moved to Denver where he became an architect. Sometimes accompanied by his father, **Frank**. Fictionalized as Tim Grey in *On the Road*.

Don Wolf   While Kerouac's classmate at Horace Mann, Wolf helped him with his music column for the *Horace Mann Record.* Wolf went on to be a popular songwriter who collaborated with Bobby Darin.

Alan Wood-Thomas   Artist and architect, he moved to New York after dropping out of Princeton; on the fringe of Kerouac's circle.

Seymour Wyse   Kerouac's classmate at Horace Mann. A jazz enthusiast of the first order, he would accompany Kerouac to such famous Harlem nightclubs as the Savoy, Minton's, and the Apollo Theatre, and together they developed a "bop ear." Nicknamed "Nutso."

Sarah Yokley   Dated Kerouac in early 1950. Kerouac met her through Lucien Carr, with whom she worked as an editor at UPI. She had dated Carr previously. Sometimes "Sara."

ACKNOWLEDGMENTS

Gratitude must first be accorded to John Sampas for allowing Jack Kerouac's journals to be published. For over a decade, he has overseen the Kerouac estate with great fortitude and leadership. In August 2001, Sampas placed the journals/notebooks/worklogs that constitute *Windblown World* under control of the Berg Collection at the New York Public Library. As of June 2004, the library's Kerouac collection included over 1,050 manuscripts and typescripts, 130 notebooks, and 52 journals dating from 1934 to 1960. There are also 55 additional diaries dating from 1956 to 1969. As for correspondence, the library holds nearly 2,000 Kerouac-related letters.

At Viking Press, my editor, Paul Slovak, was indispensable. Because his firm publishes so many of Kerouac's titles, Slovak has emerged as one of the principal scholars of Beat Generation literature. He knows more about Kerouac and company than anybody else I know. And I'm particularly grateful for his mild-mannered intelligence and editorial savvy. He wisely made sure that *Windblown World* wasn't too long. My Boston attorney George Tobia, who represents the Kerouac Estate, is responsible for putting together the deal that enabled me to edit these diaries/journals. He is a dear friend and an ace lawyer.

A special salute is due to the Kerouac biographers whose works helped my understanding of Kerouac's life when I was editing *Windblown World:* Gerald Nicosia (*Memory Babe: A Critical Biography of Jack Kerouac*), Ann Charters (*Kerouac*), Barry Gifford and Lawrence Lee (*Jack's Book*),

Dennis McNally (*Desolate Angel*) and Regina Weinreich (*Kerouac's Spontaneous Poetics*).

More than any other American writer I've encountered, Kerouac has a truly devoted following. Some of these admirers have helped me better appreciate Kerouac's work. They include David Amram, Ann Douglas, George Condo, Ed Adler, Robert Rauschenberg, Chris Felver, Johnny Depp, James Graverholz, Bob Rosenthal, Carolyn Cassady, Ramblin' Jack Elliott, Anne Waldman, Kevin Willey, Joyce Johnson, Odetta, Mary Montes, Sterling Lord, and Dave Moore. Patrick Fenton kindly shared his wide knowledge of Kerouac's life in Queens. Jeffrey Frank of the *New Yorker* and Cullen Murphy of the *Atlantic Monthly* both deserve special thanks for running excerpts of the journals as I edited them. Portions of my introduction draw from my essay "The American Journey of Jack Kerouac," which first appeared in *The Rolling Stone Book of the Beats,* for which kudos are due to Jann Wenner and editor Holly George-Warren. Special thanks to our friends at Garden District Bookshop: Carolyn Mykulencak, Britton Trice, Ted O'Brien, and Deb Wehmeier.

Finally, at the Eisenhower Center for American Studies, Andrew Travers — who oversees our Kerouac project — helped me prune this volume. Together we waded through notebooks, trying to decipher Kerouac's often illegible scrawl. My debt to him is considerable. Also, Lisa Weisdorffer helped me prepare the manuscript for publication, coming in on a few Sunday afternoons as our deadline approached.

My beautiful wife, Anne, and our daughter, Benton, continue to be the lights of my life.

SECTION I

The Town and the City

The Town and the City Worklogs

June 16 - '47 —

Just made one of those great grim decisions of one's life — not to present my
manuscript of "T+C" to any publisher until
I've completed it, all 380,000-odd words
of it. This means seven months of ascetic
gloom and labor — although doubt is no
longer my devil, just sadness now. I think
I will get this immense work done much
sooner this way, to face up to it and
finish it. Past two years has been work
done in a preliminary mood, a mood of
beginning and not completing. To complete
anything is a horror, an insult to life,
but the work of life needs to get done,
and art is work — what work!! I've
read my manuscript for the first time
and I find it a veritable Niagara of
a novel. This pleases me and moves me,
but it's sorrowful to know that this
is not the age for such art, This is
an excluding age in art — the leaver-
outer Fitzgeralds prevail in the public
imagination over the putter-inner
Wolfes. But so what. All I want
from this book is a living, enough

These meticulous logs of Kerouac's progress on his first novel, *The Town and the City*, filled most of two journals, running from June 1947 to September 1948, when Kerouac completed the manuscript. They begin with Kerouac's summer "mood log." In November 1947, he begins his "winter writing log," which catalogues his progress on *The Town and the City*. Other than a brief portion written in North Carolina, this was all written in New York while Kerouac was living with his mother in the small walk-up apartment above a drugstore at 94-10 Cross Bay Boulevard in the nondescript working-class town of Ozone Park, Queens. Leo Kerouac died in the same apartment in 1946. It had two small bedrooms, a kitchen in which Kerouac wrote each night, and a sitting room with a piano.

The first journal itself measures about 7½ by 8½ inches. The cover has "1947–1948" written at the top, with "NOTES" in bubble lettering below it and "JOURNALS" below that. In the bottom right is:

> John Kerouac
> 1947 N.Y.
> June–December

The second journal these logs were pulled from, like the previous one, measures about 7½ by 8½ inches. On the cover "FURTHER NOTES" is written in block lettering, and below it is written "Well, this is the Forest of Arden." In the bottom-right corner is the following:

> J Kerouac
> 1947–48
> N.Y.C.

JUNE 16 — '47 —

Just made one of those great grim decisions of one's life — not to present my manuscript of "T & C"* to any publisher until I've completed it, all 380,000-odd words of it. This means seven months of ascetic gloom and labor — although doubt is no longer my devil, just sadness now. I think I will get this immense work done much sooner this way, to face up to it and *finish* it. Past two years has been work done in a preliminary mood, a mood of beginning and not completing. To complete anything is a horror, an insult to life, but the *work* of life needs to get done, and art is work — what work!! I've read my manuscript for the first time and I find it a veritable Niagara of a novel. This pleases me and moves me, but it's sorrowful to know that this is not the age for such art. This is an *excluding* age in art — the leaver-outer [F. Scott] Fitzgeralds prevail in the public imagination over the putter-inner [Thomas] Wolfes. But so what. All I want from this book is a living, enough money to make a living, buy a farm and some land, work it, write some more, travel a little, and so on. But enough of this. The next seven(TEEN) months are joyless to view — but there is as much joy in these things, there is more joy, than in flitting around as I've done since early May, when I completed a 100,000-word section (Mood Log). I might as well learn now what it is to see things *as they are* — and the truth is, nobody cares how I fare in these writings. So I must fare in the grimmest, most efficient way there is, alone, unbidden, diligently again, always. The future has a glorious woman for me, and my own children, I'm certain of that — I must come up to them and meet them a man with things accomplished. I don't care to be one of those

*Short for *The Town and the City* (1950), Kerouac's first novel, the writing of which is the subject of much of this journal. He worked on it through most nights into early morning at the kitchen table of the apartment he shared with his mother.

frustrated fathers. Behind me there must be some stupendous deed done — this is the way to marry, the way to prepare for greater deeds and work. So then —

10-DAY MOOD LOG, JUNE 16–26 '47

JUNE 15 (SUNDAY) — I find it almost impossible to get underway again: my mind seems blank and disinterested in these fictions. I give up after **500-words** of a preliminary nature.

MONDAY 16 — Feeling just as hopeless — feeling that I may not, after all, be able to complete anything. But I write **2000-words** pertaining to the chapter, and things begin to break, or crumble & seethe.

TUESDAY 17 — Reluctance! Reluctance always! We hate original work, we human beings. Wrote **1800-words** pertaining. I'm back in these regions of fumbling dark uncertain creation, but it's my one and only world, and I'll do the best I can. What would be the best medium for earnest thoughts if not a novel — earnest thoughts refined, as from crude one, into earnest *motives* — and the *unconscious intuitive drift of great theme* — *thoughts rushing*. I often think a notebook is better — but no, a novel, the very tale of earnestness and life-meaning, is the best thing. ("It will be better for you." — Mohammed)

WEDNESDAY 18 — A great physical lassitude and physical melancholy. I eat a big meal at 1 A.M. and walk two miles* and do some writing — **1800-words**. Something's wrong — I keep saying, "Why do I *have* to write this?" It would be far better if I were asking myself — "Why do I *want* to write this?" That's the greatest writing, the *uncon-*

---

*Famous for taking long, contemplative walks, Kerouac could take the busy street on which he lived — Cross Bay Boulevard — and follow it south across Jamaica Bay and into Rockaway to admire the Atlantic Ocean. Or Kerouac could wander northward toward Jamaica, a bustling neighborhood and hotbed of African-American culture in the forties and fifties. He also often headed ten miles eastward to Lynbrook, where his friend Tom Livornese lived.

scious. Someday I'll learn, someday I'll learn. I've got to do this now, though — how *best* to do it, that's the problem. A monstrous job, but alright if I can only believe in its *sure real* progress. I wish I could write from the point of view of one hero instead of giving everyone in the story his due value — this makes me confused, many times disgusted. After all, I'm human, I have my beliefs. I put nonsense in the mouths of characters I don't like, and this is tedious, discouraging, disgusting. Why doesn't God appear to tell me I'm on the right track? What foolishness!

THURSDAY 19 — Read Tolstoy's moral essays and I writhed and wrestled to the conclusion that morality, moral concept, is a form of melancholy. Not for me, not for me! Moral behaviour, yes, but no concepts whatever. There is a lugubrious senility in morality which is devoid of real life. Let's just say — the substance of things is good, its *form* is good too until the form dries up, and then anyway, being bad, useless, outworn, the substance marches off and leaves the form-husk there. All very general. I concluded that Dostoevsky's wisdom is the highest wisdom in the world, because it is not only Christ's wisdom, but a Karamazov Christ of lusts and glees.* Let's have a morality that does not exclude sheer life — loving! Poor Tolstoy, anguished because he started rich and profligate — yet when a Count retires to the peasants, it's really of some account to the *world* (pun intended.) Tolstoy must have been self-conscious of his moral importance in the eyes of the *world*. But Dostoevsky, Shakespeare — their morality grows in the earth, is hidden there and brooding. Dostoevsky never *had* to retire to morality, he was always it, and everything else also. (Today's busy thoughts.) Wrote **2000-words**, walked at night, saw a terrible auto crackup, but nobody killed.

*Fyodor Dostoevsky's semiautobiographical approach and his concern with Christian morality and philosophy greatly influenced Kerouac and is often pondered in these journals. The "Karamazov Christ" is a reference to a parable in *The Brothers Karamazov* in which Christ returns to sixteenth-century Seville and is imprisoned for having burdened mankind with their freedom. Kerouac sometimes refers to him as "Dusty."

FRIDAY 20 — Things going smoothly again in my soul. Back to the *humility and decency* of writing-life. A Galloway* friend visited me in the afternoon; but wrote again at night. It occurs to me that one of the gutsiest, greatest ideas a writer can have is that he writes about some-one merely "to show what kind of a mad character he is." This idea has to be understood in the American sense. My Galloway friend wants *specific conclusions* from literary art, I agree with him, and I think noth-ing is more specific about a person than the tone and substance of his personality, his being, the fury and feel and look of it. To show "what a mad character" Francis is, I wrote a sketch of someone else in such a way as you may or may not like this someone else, but you see that Francis definitely does *not* like him.† And what is the purpose of these arts and devices? — what is the point of Francis' dislike of someone else? — specifically, that's the kind of character he is, *that's what he does.* This would take too long to explain — at least, this is my mood tonight, a good one, and I got to writing at 1 A.M. and wrote on final draft of this week's 8000-words.

SATURDAY 21 — Day off. Went out in N.Y.

SUNDAY 22 — Another thought that helps a writer as he works along — let him write his novel "the way he'd like to see a novel writ-ten." This helps a great deal freeing you from the fetters of self-doubt and the kind of self-mistrust that leads to over-revision, too much cal-culation, preoccupation with "what others would think." Look at your own work and say, "This is a novel after my own heart!" Because that's what it is anyway, and that's the point — it's *worry* that must be elimi-nated for the sake of individual force. In spite of all this insouciant ad-vice, I myself advanced slowly today, but not poorly, working on the final draft of the chapter. I'm a little rusty. Oh and what a whole lot of

*Galloway, New Hampshire, is the fictionalized Lowell, Massachusetts, in which Kerouac sets *The Town and the City.*
†Francis Martin, the self-styled intellectual from *The Town and the City*, loosely based on Sebastian Sampas.

bunk I could write this morning about my fear that I can't write, I'm ignorant and worst of all, I'm an idiot trying to achieve something I can't possibly do. It's in the will, in the heart! To hell with these rotten doubts. I defy them and spit on them. Merde!

MONDAY 23 — Wrote in the afternoon for several hours, went into N.Y. on business of a minor sort, and came back at night and wrote some more. A day of intense feelings, described elsewhere, a day of great rending thoughts that twist one back to face sudden realities heretofore avoided — and there you are, facing them, like looking into the sun, blinking, admitting the truth. Well, a very dramatic way of growing up, and of describing it. The details of it? — a fraction of those thoughts on paper and I would have enough thematic material to write ten epic American novels (maybe a couple of Siamese novels thrown in.) If the ordinary men, the men who work and keep their silence, by which fact they are not ordinary after all — if, then, the general run of men, were to write down *all* their thoughts or a fraction of them, what a universe of literatures we'd have! And I struggle with these pencil-marks and scribblings.

TUESDAY 24 — Wrote on the final draft. Chapter will be 10,000-wds. long now.

WEDNESDAY 25 — Wrote. Am reading the New Testament, really for the first time.

THURSDAY 26 — Wrote on final draft, working slowly. Went to N.Y. to complete plans for going to sea this summer — I need to make a living.* Can I go about in camel's hair, and leathern gird, and subsist on locust and wild honey? — (I probably could, with practice, but what of my wife, children, and mother? But Jesus would teach *them* to look only to God, too.) Still and all, if Jesus were sitting here at my desk

---

*Kerouac had made plans to sail out of California with Henri Cru as a merchant seaman. He would make the trip to California, but they never sailed.

tonight, looking out the window at all these people laughing and happy because the great summer vacation is beginning, perhaps he would smile, and thank his Father. I don't know. People must "live," and yet I know Jesus has the only answer. If I ever reconcile *true Christianity* with *American life,* I will do so by remembering my father Leo [Kerouac], a man who knew both of these things. This only breaks a little ground on the subject. I must see —

FRIDAY 27 — Completed the work, and placed it in the main manuscript, where it is as a grain of sand on a beach. And what is this beach? Only time will tell — I only know I should do it, I do it. 8,000-words in chapt. + 7,000-words in notebook → 15,000 Now that's all — there is nothing further to say on the subject of my work, which I have created myself, and whose face I do not know. What it is, what will come of it, I repeat, I don't know. It will be there — that's all one can be certain of — it will be there, it will abide and be there, and there's nothing to say. This is darkness and yet this is also light — This is life and work. Don't laugh, this is what it is.

Work of this kind is like a human being: *What* is it, *whence* does it come, where is it going, and why, and when, and *who* will know it? Work like this is something alive, and full of unknowables, and it abides even as you do not know *what* it is.

So I console myself, saying, do not ask me *what* this book is, whence it came, *why* it came and for what purpose, do not point out its imperfections, gaucheries, crudenesses — rather, you might just as well say to me, looking at me in the eyes: — "*What* are you, *whence* came you, *why,* and for what crude imperfect purpose?" —

Remember —
    the flashing exhilirated maddening discoveries and truths of youth, the ones that turn young men into visionary demons and make them unhappy and happier than ever all at once — the truths later dropped with the condescension of "maturity" — these truths come back in true maturity, maturity being nothing less than disciplined earnestness —

these truths will come back to all true men, who make of them no fiery invidious "flag of youth" any more, but make of them what they can — here: — for example — If a boy finds that *idealism* is the highest virtue of man and holds this idea up like a flag in the greedy self-centered world, if a boy once does this, and even *names* and numbers the idealisms, but later discovers that there is also a *practical* world — why, he will still later discover that the idealistic Jesus-soul *is* the only soul!

The life's gone out of it — out of anything which has artificially built itself outward from the substantial essence of itself — let's make this clear — a town is more essential, more substantial, more *living* than a great Rome city, the great Rome city has deviated from the original purpose of a town, a place for people to live in, and become a city, a place for people not to live in, a place for people to hide from life, the earth, the meanings of family and soul and labour — let's make this clear — the life's gone out of it — out of anything which has run astray ("Lead us not into temptation"), anything which has lost itself in cant, artificiality, self-deceit and irrelevent horror, above all, in glittering triviality.

The earth will always be the same — only cities and history will change, even nations will change, governments and governors will go, the things made by men's hands will go, buildings will always crumble — only the earth will remain the same, there will always be men on the earth in the morning, there will always be the things made by God's hand — and all this history of cities and congresses now will go, all modern history is only a glittering Babylon smoking under the sun, delaying the day when men again will have to return to the earth, to the earth of life and God —

— Go ask the Central-American Indian who lives on the green earth that has grown on Mayan rooftops —

James Joyce did say — "History is a nightmare from which I am not yet awake."* But he is awake now, as sure as sunlight.

---

*In Joyce's masterpiece *Ulysses* (1922), Stephen Dedalus tells his class, "History is a nightmare from which I am trying to wake."

We live in the world we see, but we only believe in the world we do not see. Who has believed in the *world* and died with its name on his lips? Who has said, at death, "I believe in the future of this baubel, that triviality, this irrelevence — it will live forever!" Who has died not thinking of the *first* and *last* things, the Alpha and the Omega of life on the earth?

We are come onto this earth and we do not know what we are supposed to do, and in all disorder and confusion, we cry out in our souls — *"There must be truth, for I myself am true! true!" Yet all is false and foolish around us, and we ourselves are falsest and most foolish, and oh what are we supposed to do? What tremendous disorders appear, and where are we in it?* — We don't feel at last that we are true. We feel we are false through and through. But I will soon write a paper entitled — "Strange Reasons for the Abolition of Capital Punishment and Why Men Should No Longer Commit Suicide" — in which I will show that no matter what has been done to the man, he must not be destroyed or destroy himself — because in all the disorder and ghastly ruin of the world and the human imagination, there is still life and the possibility of redemption through the mere seeing of the earth, through wonder, the most abject kind of wonder shuffling down a street, and in this the whole thing is redeemable, and AT LAST, *true!* This is so unspeakable. A murderer must be given a chance to repent — The suicidal man must give himself a chance to wonder again, to *see* again. It's all here — for here is the chiefest thing: If a dead man were allowed to return to the earth, to live again among men on the earth, for *one day* — whatever this soul would *see* and *think*, that is for us now, the living now, that is the only truth, the most central feeling possible to man, the deepest. (And I often wonder: — would this resurrected man waste any time contemplating the good and evil in the world? or would he just feast the eyes of his soul in a hungry viewing of life on earth, of the reality of life on earth, the thing itself: little children, men, women, towns, cities, seasons and seas! A riddle! A riddle!)

Accursed is he who thinks and thinks but is never happy in his thoughts, who can never say — "Here I am, *thinking*." It is no fun, no sport, this eternal thinking of mine which goes on a good twelve hours a day. Why do I do it? It's a form of brooding, I actually look like a *hound-dog* all day. And how my mother is used to it! I think if I were not around the house brooding she would be certain the wheels of the universe had stopped turning. And what do I think about? What thoughts I have! — What thoughts! a whole host, multitude, and world of thoughts, I keep devising new ones and reworking old ones, some of the old ones are concluded and are only thought of as conclusions, whole worlds of new ones come crashing into my feelings, and it never ends. Why do I think? It's my life, right there. That's why I must be alone and thinking six days out of the week, because it's my life. What will these thoughts win me? — They are not of this world. I don't know *what* they are myself!

ON THE TEACHINGS OF JESUS

Christ's teachings were a turning-to, a facing-up, a confrontation and a *confoundment* of the terrible enigma of human life. What a miraculous thing! — what thoughts Jesus must have had before he "opened his mouth" on the Mount and spoke his sermon, what long dark silent thoughts!

First he knew the enigma of life, it was the cause of all sin and trouble; he was a man, he knew what men felt about wanting to live yet doomed to die, about wanting to manage yet cast into great labour and pain and adversity in order to manage, about wanting to eat yet having to kill to eat, about wanting possessions yet having to deprive others for them — he knew how gold was the symbol of men's sweat-and-blood with which an idler could buy men even as they toiled — he knew the fatal meanings of sickness, bereavement, poverty and death on earth — he knew it all — and finally, in a vision, he saw the only *way* to confound all this! "My kingdom is not of this world." Consider that just once more, it is the most ringing sound of all human time —

"My kingdom is not of this world."

Hear its tremendous music, the music of thought, the dark music of dark thought. Of all riddles, this is the only riddle, the Alpha and Omega of riddles — I call it a riddle because it *confounds* the senses —

The riddle of life propounds in the souls of men a moral proposition, to which they respond variously and at all times. All men are aware of the proposition, but most men ignore its meaning, a meaning almost invisible, and live vigorous absentminded lives and 'trouble not themselves.' Other men who know the meaning of the proposition, of fairness and unfairness in the enigmatic situation of life, *seek consciously* to 'trouble not themselves' and would imitate most men, for strength. Finally, some men suffer from knowing all this and almost die, in life, until and if they hold their sorrow well, and seek strength to hold it more.

There are a hundred ways of saying this. 'The Brothers Karamazov' and 'You Can't Go Home Again' say this. I wish I could say it with as much power and clarity. 'Moby Dick' also says this, and [Walt] Whitman says it sometimes. Some others.

———

And the glory of children forever is that they have not begun to perceive that adult human strength depends mostly on forgetfulness.

DOWN SOUTH (1947)*

After ten days in a different part of the world, among different people, in the world itself, and not in the night's-landscape of one's own soul (and an "artist's" soul, at that), after only ten days pursuing different aims and so on, how easily feelings can change, on the surface, and make one realize the mutability of *opinions*. When I said, ten days ago, "My kingdom is not of this world!" — this was only an opinion,

*Kerouac is referring to a two-week trip with his mother to North Carolina to visit his sister, Nin, and her husband, Paul, at the end of June 1947.

perhaps, and not a feeling: because now, again, the world opens up as a place of powerful things for me to feed upon, the excluding moralities vanish in an October rush of excitement, hunger, joy and zeal, the self-disgust of lonely introspection becomes the social gregarious keenness so necessary as a fuel to get one around in things.

I detect a strong dualism — between loneliness, morality, humility, sternness, critical Christianity — and charm, open-mindedness, dask (the attempt at dash), humourousness, Faustian power and lust for experience. These two sets of impulses will never cease to work in me. Which at least makes for good fuel for getting around.

"Getting around" seems to be my most persistent feeling — probably the only basic feeling mentioned in all notebook rhetoric. For what am I? — a "character" (in the American sense.) They call me Kerouac, omitting the first name, as though I were a kind of *figure* in the world, much less a "guy," a "power." This is what they do, smiling when they think of me, even when I spend long winters of loneliness and strive to be stern, silent, majestic. The result is always ... Kerouac. Here I'm giving leeway to what casual acquaintances think of me. The purpose of all this writing is unclear, but it serves unknown needs fortuitously at work and at living.

For what I am is at all times of the least importance, of lesser importance the more I accomplish, of no importance whatever a hundred years from now. The central essence from which we all draw our blood, that's the thing, the place, the Father, the all. I mean this — and when I speak of anything, I hear choruses of unknown past, present, and future voices uttering the words with me. The me and the all, the son and the father. When Christ directs all his motives to God, *over the heads of men*, a man in another history directs all his motives to the All, *over* the heads of men and of his own. The essence of religion, the thing that "will keep you out of a psychiatrist's office" — as though such were the purpose for religion (critical Christianity.) Didn't Jesus warn against the sin of ignoring the madman, to most high exalted point of recognizing no madness anywhere? If little Jude the Obscure refuses to step on worms in the path, he must grow up and assess no living man a worm or a madman: which he fails to follow up.

It is all irreconcilable — the All is irreconcilable. I cannot kill a fish, ere I kill a man, but men eat the little fish, I am a man. To bring morality into the vast *thing* that is organic life, is futile. And futility is the meaning of life, its nobleness — nobleness a thing of principal foremost importance and power, greater than occasional achievement.

Words, words, words — and what are blank pages for?

I keep wondering if "mankind" in Jesus's time was so young and inexperienced in the ways of earthly livelihood that its only recourse was a turning-in to selfless immolation — and if "mankind" now has begun to learn to make a more comfortable life for more men, the American dream, and therefore, changes its life meaning into a "livelihood of man," with religion dead, and "progress" at full sail. Let's mull these things over back in the profound night's-landscape of loneliness in Ozone Park, where work is done, and slightest earthly tremors are felt as great shocks and revelations.

Do I grow stupid away from the blessed "Dostoevsky's Russia" of myself? — the moor of myself, every inch my own creation? — where it becomes clear that too much thinking is worse than none, and that to be specific and grave is like a plow in the hands.

My grave and specific thoughts —

A little mangy dog is tied by a chain to a fence by a Southern poor white family, it whines in the night, it is ill fed, and cruelly treated. Shall I free this dog? — sneak down at night and release him? Will he bark at me, bite me and despise me in the dead of night for meddling in the affairs of this unmoral organic earth. I am not God: What shall I do in this suffering world? Suffer. But is that enough to satisfy the big moral feeling I have. Why should I have a moral feeling on that scale. I am not God. If I were offered the power of miracle, could I yet alleviate the vast organic suffering, without disrupting some inner God's purpose in it all. Why is it that I can bear my own troubles and pain because I believe in fortitude, and have to, of course, but do not grant this fortitude to other and fellow-creatures? If the little mangy dog suffers, and I try to help him, has he not the right to despise me for assuming that he cannot bear his own lot. There's an invisible organic law, to which "Progress" is stone blind — but bless it. *Women love men because they are blind, God loves life because it is blind — and woman and God are love and wrath combined,* the woman will eventually soothe you (as my mother soothed and comforted my dying father) just as surely as God soothes all life in the end, even in death lastly —

We catch a fish, a bass, we call it George, hand it over to a Medieval hook, hang it over the side to live and "keep fresh" with a hook torn through its dumb mouth. We finally go home, lock George up in a dark compartment to suffocate and die, alone, while we drive along in the fresh Carolina air. Oh Jesus! — your fishermen held millions in their nets! Dumb writhing fish, dying and working parched gills in this world. Oh God! — this is all of us, it happens to all of us. What shall we do, where shall we go, and when do we die like this? What is there to say here, that wasn't said — we are doomed to suffering and darkest death. It has been made *hard* for us, *hard!* We are fish wriggling in the net, fighting one another for the watery parts where we can yet breathe. (Therefore the tenant farmer on his gray rickety porch in the noonday sun, poor, humbled, cheated, dying — and therefore the big tobacco man from Wilson with his big 42 foot yatch in the waters, his case of Scotch , his radio, his clean white trousers.) Jesus — your only answer to all things alive! And you have made it *hard, hard,* even as Our Father made it hard. —

So the poor man of poverty and silence, and the big city of talkative cocktail hours. What shall we do about that?

Bless it all — it's God's whole works.

KINSTON, N.C.*
July, 1947

*This small town is in central North Carolina — southeast of Raleigh. Founded in the mid-eighteenth century, it boasts a rich history dating back to the Revolutionary War.

From now on —

    — less notes on the subject of writing —

— and of myself —

    — and more writing.

From now on, no more shouted doubts, no more of the roots of the tree, but the foliage of it. This is a coming of age. *A man must keep his doubts to himself and prove his works instead.*

"THE AMERICAN 'TASTE'"

No human being in the English-speaking world can pronounce the word "taste" in just that way that a certain kind of American pronounces it. It is incredible to hear it. It sounds something like "tayest," it sounds amazing, and it is too rich to be true. It is pronounced by an American who has been "abroad" and who has been to Harvard or Columbia, and who might be rich, but not necessarily. Let us look at him, at this rare, strange creature, let us hear him say, "But my dear Tom, just where is your sense of tayest! Really!" Just where he got the idea that living was a matter of "taste" only God can say. From books written in Europe by continental-phenomenal snobs, from some strange, dark, lonely notion that all the wildness and brutality and vast sweep of American life can be cancelled, in one swoop, by the word "taste" — it's hard to say. But Thomas Wolfe has already covered the satirical aspects of this phenomena, and I leave it to any amateur psychologist to decide the rest. It's unimportant.

"ON A DEEP LIFE"

JULY '47

That kind of lifetime most often observable in obituaries of respectable proportions, and indeed in the obituary sketches of most of this world's lifetimes, the kind of life that can actually be summed up in two or three paragraphs — these lives must surely have been used as cheap coin by the deceased. When you read these obituaries, you often think, "Well at least there's a generation forthcoming from them, who might live a little more intensely." But you know the children of these people will live similar absentminded lives, and die summed up in two paragraphs. A few hollow titles, a few "public services," a medal, some property and means, a diploma for something — that's what they leave for their children to mull over, if indeed their children are capable at all of mulling over anything in the heat of blind acquisitive days. My father's life was so rich and so deep that I still spend my days absorbed in its details, which could fill a book. My father did not die blankly leaving life to be fulfilled, if at all, by his children. He fulfilled it, just as I want to fulfill it in my way, sincerely.

NOVEMBER 1947
(AFTER THE CALIFORNIA TRIP)*

Now I have to get back to "the humility and decency of writing-life." And to the resumption of writing-logs ...

*   *   *

There's something really wrong about being worldly, I'm convinced of that for once and for all, and I'm in a position right now to look into it. How worldly I do sound! But look — I've seen a lot of things. These are just ways of evoking and enunciating the worldly blankness I feel after being away from the controlled madness, the tumultuous sensi-

*This cross-country hitchhiking trip — Kerouac's first — took Kerouac from Ozone Park to see his friend Henri Cru in California, where he ended up working as a security guard at a construction workers' barracks in Marin City. This trip is fictionalized in part 1 of *On the Road*.

WINTER 1947-'48

Hitch-hiking trip July - Oct. 1947

And all the great territories.....

NOVEMBER 1947
(After the California trip)

Now I have to get back to "The
humility and decency of writing-life."
And to the resumption of writing-logs...

*   *   *

There's something really wrong about being
worldly, I'm convinced of that for once
and for all, and I'm in a position right
now to look into it.   How worldly I
do sound!   But look — I've seen a lot
of things.   These are just ways of
evoking and enunciating the worldly
blankness I feel after being away from
the controlled madness, the tumultuous
sensitivity of writing-life for so long.
I don't like the feeling of "Knowing
it all," knowing what I want, how
to get it, all clear, and not "glaring
in" like Carlyle's reality, but just
clear and glistening.   I've got to learn
to walk back to the shadows of truth.

tivity of writing-life for so long. I don't like the feeling of "knowing it all," knowing what I want, how to get it, all clear, and not "glaring in" like Carlyle's reality, but just clear and glistening. I've got to learn to walk back to the shadows of truth.

WINTER WRITING-LOG   1947–1948

NOVEMBER

MON. 3rd — Completed some notes in my notebooks pertaining to the difficulty of getting back to long writing, and then, at 5 o'clock in the evening, as it got dark outside, I resumed on the novel after the long layoff. First, however, with real excitement, I thought about how it would be a great idea to strike out for Northwest Canada with a real good buddy (someone like Hal Chase) and go join the gold rush there. *That too is the shadows of truth!* Anyway, as long as there's a sincere, intense guest — and writing an epic novel is that, too. 12MN — Overpowered by the sadness of not knowing *what* there is in the world, and what I'm doing. Feeling completely indifferent to good and evil, too, to beauty or anything else. I know that *this* is the root of all human troubles, all of them. Indifferent to that knowledge, too. Nothing got written.

TUESDAY 4th — I had to go out and walk in the rain in N.Y. and rage around with my friends. We smashed recordings of Mozart over our heads, I and the daemonic one. We got drunk. I came out of it beautifully, remembering the simple beauty of life, and came home.

WEDNESDAY 5th — Wrote extensive notes. All day it kept occurring to me that there's nothing so manly as the sight of a man writing in great laborious measures and subjecting himself to all the pitfalls of vast mental work. Is that my piddling goal? — manliness?

Doing a lot of thinking, so important to me, really, that I can't write it down. Undergoing an inner revolution.

THURSDAY 6th — Am freeing myself of old shackles, to be described later. I think that I'm about to be free at last. It's really amazing. And it's all so silent, I can't say it. Began writing in a freer style tonight. **1000-words** pertaining, in an hour. Can it last?

FRIDAY 7th — **2500-words** today in a few hours. This may be it — freedom. And mastery! — so long denied me in my long mournful years of work, blind powerful work. Too moved now to explain what all this is. It has to do with everything in my nature and of course, then, in my corresponding work. How I could praise heaven for something like this, towards which I've struggled so long: mastery of my art, instead of slave to it! **1500-more** words at night, just like that. That's five thousand in the past 24 hours. Not that it's easier, it's only *more myself.*

Technically, the great change is from the epic-lyrical feeling for life to the dramatic-moral, without abandoning the lyrical altogether, this goes in the writing. The result has that *invisible* power in it, the power of moral drama, technically the narrative power, with less emphasis on descriptive moods, descriptive obsession (the obsession to sing with the right hand and not let the idle left hand know too much.) This proves that I still can't, and won't, explain this fine change.

SATURDAY 8th — Big American Saturday. Had great conversation with Ed White at night. There is a fine, fair soul of a man, and greatly accomplished, and modest too. His ideas are always simple and true.

SUNDAY NOV. 9th — Read the papers. Lionel Trilling's review of Sherwood Anderson occasioned some interesting thoughts on the subject of Francis Martin. (Now that this new change has come about within me these garrulous logs seem less and less necessary or even worthwhile.) I feel a kind of dumb silence. **2000-words** at night late: and a bare loneliness.

MONDAY NOV. 10 — Worried about money again — but to waste time on little jobs when my writing is reaching climax and mastery is not too sensible. I will spend more time and energy hereafter trying to *sell* my stories, too. The "Christmas in New York"* written in California is highly saleable: when I get it in the mail from the studios I'll make some snap decisions on it, whether magazine-form or book form, or as it is — screen story — and take it around. It wouldn't be bad to make a modest living from writing: no more cotton-picking!

This thought, concerning the change in my writing which now seems so important, came —: that it was not lack of creation that stopped me before, but an excess of it, a thickening of the narrative stream so that it could not flow. Yet tonight I'm really worried about my work. First is it good *now?* — and will the world recognize it as such. The world isn't so dumb after all; I realize that from reading some of my unfinished or unsold novels: they are just no good. I will eventually arrive at a simplicity and a beauty that won't be denied — simplicity, morality, and a beauty, a real lyricism. But the *now,* the *now.* It's getting serious. How do I know if I'm reaching mastery? I have always believed that, in the past when I indulged myself in self-deceiving ecstasies and disgusts. The thinking has got to be real now. Enough, enough. Tonight: **2500-words**, though I wasted time reading my old writings. I can do 4000 a day now. That's a step forward anyway. It's 9500 words in five days, or rather four days, without really getting to it as yet, that is, in amount of time spent. There's something so horribly French-Canadian about my gaucheries here and there in past — and present? — work: — something childish and sincere, yet unintelligent. That word again?

TUESDAY NOV. 11 — Wrote letters in the afternoon. All confused, all confused as Dark Eyes showed up again. We'll see about these lovely interruptions. It's no great tragedy, anyway. And just this moment an-

*Kerouac's screenplay "Christmas in New York" was inspired by O. Henry's short story "The Gift of the Magi."

other period of non-creativeness is striving to come over me. It's like a disease, or rather like a madness. "So what?" rings in the chambers of my head, I challenge everything I see with this hoodlum's thought. *Now, now* I will catch ennui as it tries to catch me, and I will wring its scrawny neck. Ennui is a scrawny gray person, a lounging hoodlum, a lout. No, no, no more smiling joy in life, no charming interest in things and people, just an Apache in a dim street waiting with a knife, and bored, and therefore vicious. Who shall I kill tonight, what shall I destroy? A thrilling wave of physical nausea tries to command my being, just for the sake of variety — a physical sense of sinking and surrendering to base despair and thoughts of knavery, violence, and sarcasm. Lies! Lies! — I only feel like my true self, a dreamy slothful moron dreaming of chaos. More lies! It is at this time that lying is a joy, a life's work. More and more lies. This is the pleasingly sharp-pointed blade I will prick myself with if I let things ride, the marvellous knout to use on myself and others. And what nonsense & crap!

Tonight I'm going to write greatly and love greatly and strangle this folly. I'm catching these damnable changes of purpose in the flesh, red-handed, and throwing them to the winds, just like that. I challenge whatever comes into me at times like this to look me in the eye, I challenge for the possession of my being: — perhaps for variety's sake. Oh yes, I know that I should never have been a writer, it's not in my nature, but we will see this out to the end. **2000-words** tonight.

WEDNESDAY NOV. 12 — Powerful winds that crack the boughs of November! — and the bright calm sun, untouched by the furies of the earth, abandoning the earth to darkness, and wild forlornness, and night, as men shiver in their coats and hurry home. And then the lights of home glowing in those desolate deeps. There are the stars, though! high and sparkling in a spiritual firmament. We will walk in the windsweeps, gloating in the envelopment of ourselves, seeking the sudden grinning intelligence of humanity below these abysmal beauties. Now the roaring midnight fury and the creaking of our hinges and windows, now the winter, now the understanding of the earth and our being on it: this drama of enigmas and double-depths and sorrows and grave joys, these human things in the elemental vastness of the windblown world. **1500-words** tonight. Tomorrow is a day off, otherwise, with a few more words tomorrow, I'd achieve my new schedule goal of 15,000-words per week. By February, the last lines of T & C will be finished and re-finished, and *typed,* and ready for the publisher. Made extensive notes tonight too. Will control these gratuitous energies!

THURSDAY NOV. 13 — Went out on big binge which lasted into —

FRIDAY NOV. 14
    — and

SATURDAY NOV. 15

SUNDAY NOV. 16 — Made extensive notes, Sat. night, about 2000-words. Today read and ate and recuperated. Wrote **4000-words** tonight, wonderfully absorbed too. What more need be said? Talk is cheap. I'm happy.

MONDAY NOV. 17 — I feel very happy today also, and you know, I'm not so worried as before about becoming unhappy, although, of course, I worry a little. And this is not the happiness of a magazine-writer who sends in his gay little philosophy of life to the editor for the one paragraph spread in front of the magazine: This is a serious happiness full of doubts and strengths. I wonder if happiness is possible! It is a state of mind, but I'd hate to be a bore all my life, if only because of those I love around me. Happiness can change into unhappiness just for the sake of change. Like my hand, which I burned with a cigarette the other night: the wound is healing only because the skin is changing. And, similarly, all change is a gateway, a gateway to happiness or unhappiness, in pulses like the heart pulse. Change is a gateway. But these notes aren't nearly as ebullient, and I must say, entertainingly brilliant, as my running thoughts all day & yesterday. **1500-words** tonight, a rather slow night.

TUESDAY NOV. 18 — Sometimes my effort at writing becomes so fluid and smooth that too much is torn out of me at once, and it hurts. This is too much mastery! Accompanied with that feeling is the fear of not being *perfect,* when before, good is good enough, fair is fair enough. Also there's the reluctance to soil white clean paper with imperfections. This is the curse of vanity, I know. **2500-words** tonight. Moving right along — over 20,000 words since 12 days ago, a rate equal to fifty thousand words per month.

WEDNESDAY NOV. 19 — Dark Eyes came to my house tonight and we danced all night long, and into the morning. We sat on the floor, on the beautiful rug my mother made for me, and listened to the royal wedding at six in the morning. My mother was charming when she got up and saw us there. I made Dark Eyes some crepe suzettes. We danced again, & sang.

THURSDAY NOV. 20 — I have Dostoevsky's "Raw Youth" and Stendhal's "Rouge & Noir" in the house now. My impulse is to write a simple sequence in my novel tonight: There's too much of the "pale criminal" with us, and not enough simple beauty. Just look at the people of the world adoring the little Princess and her wedding in London: — is this adoration to be laughed at? The world isn't so complex and daemonic as we writers try to make it, really. A wedding, a young bride — those things are the center of existence, *not* the daemonic relationships of neurotics and fools. I still think Julien Sorel is a nothing. Tonight: — Confused sadness — no writing.

FRIDAY NOV. 21 — A hot-and-cold shower would have roused me to work last night, I bet. **2500-words** today — and after thinking about the book as a whole, I see that the main substance of it is as yet *unwritten.*

Yet there's over 200,000 words done, more than that, close to a quarter-million words and no 'main substance'! But I'm *not* disappointed, indeed I feel refreshed and eager, and I know I can do it without any real trouble. The only problem is time — time presses, I need the money of a career very soon. It's about time, now. What I'm doing with this huge manuscript now is bearing the burdensome mistakes of the past, of novice-writing. But so much there is noble, powerful, and beautiful, that I won't throw it away, so I must carry it with me now.

SATURDAY NOV. 22 — Went out on dull carousals, forced into them, really. Missed the football game, and instead got involved in a silly argument with Burroughs and Ginsberg in the afternoon, about psychoanalysis and about "horror." They are still wrapped up in the same subjects as a year, two years, ago. Everybody likes to stew in the same old juice year after year, myself included.

MONDAY NOV. 24 — Gloomy, rainy, dark day, and tired musing. Maybe it's because Dark Eyes is out of reach for awhile. I'm in a mood now but it doesn't bother me, and I can write in spite of it. A pretty bad day all around. I wrote somewhat at night, but confusedly. That newly-found mastery momentarily lost: but I'm not worried, and besides, 'it's no great tragedy.' That's one of my finest sayings, really. Poof!

TUESDAY NOV. 25 — Took my screen story in to a new agency, Bergh & Winner. *Fiorini,* young editor, may be the man I've been wishing for: serious, intelligent, full of gravity. What will he think of T & C when I show it to him? In this harsh world, a sympathetic editor? — !! Wrote **2000-words** tonight. Hard going right about now, but I mustn't desire it too easy, or grow soft. I feel I have a high destiny, but that it is my fate to work hard at it. It is discouraging to read the great Dostoevsky, but every now and then I get a glimpse of my own unalterable words — or word. I could talk a lot about this right now, but I don't want to. You grow more taciturn after awhile, or go crazy aggravating your heart ... no? yes.

WEDNESDAY NOV. 26 — Went into town again on various businesses. Saw Burroughs and Ginsberg again, this time accidentally. We were all in high spirits. I mention this for some obscure reason. It always amazes me to find myself acting furtively like a Dostoevsky character. I remember saying to myself, "Don't tell them too much about your soul. They're waiting for just that." Which of course they weren't, or they would have to be raving mad, and probably are, as I am. "We were all in high spirits ..." Yet there's a lot of peculiar emotional energy always at work between us and we all know it. Life is a tremendously furtive thing. I finally wheedled something out of my mother. I told her it hurt me to hear her say she was tired of working, even as she adjured me to continue writing and writing for her sake, to spend no time doing anything else. "Yes," she said mournfully, "I know it hurts you, but I say it just the same." And there was nothing malicious whatsoever in this mournful confession. Wrote **2500-words** tonight, probably the best writing I've ever done (argument between George Martin and his son about his leaving college.) But it's always discouraging to spoof out after a few thousand words and to wait for next day's energy. I wish I had the mental energy of ten great novelists! Or could devise some way to get "the most out of myself," as Goethe did, without breaking down (as Goethe did) or without excessive asceticism leading to a blurring of impressions. We'll see. I'm always in a hurry, necessarily too! Really.

THURSDAY NOV. 27 (THANKSGIVING) — Rich duck dinner, a little movie with my mother, and celebrated by reading Dostoevsky at night — "A Raw Youth" — and also the Life of Goethe, he and his "psychic cataclysms" and none the less great for it. My mother and I held long gossipy conversations. I'm learning so much from her nowadays. She speaks of the fat, happy Russian women, the peasant women, and how, if Russia is ruined by Communist Politburos and Sovietism and all that "planned" scientific coldness of the system, Russia might yet be saved when *the women bring the men down to their knees.* (!) — the women, mind you, not the "political" women and the "women"-soldiers of Russia, but the fat, happy peasant women. A really astounding and profound remark. What did Joan Adams Burroughs say about it? "Sounds like a veiled threat of castration." — that particularly in connection with an allied remark my mother had made: "A man is not a man if he doesn't respect women." What about all this! Tonight, wrote **2000-words** (interrupted by visit.)

FRIDAY NOV. 28 — It was today I wrote those 2000 words, not yesterday, but no harm done. Today was one of those days when I can see "mountainous outlines" — the contour and shape itself of my novel, and this is a rare blessing. Consequently I arrived luckily at the key problem of the rest of my novel, and that's that. Only the work remains. (A really amazing solution, too!)

SATURDAY, NOV. 29 — Day off, social "duties" — and a lot of restless, thoughtless barging-around at parties and binges in N.Y.

SUNDAY NOV. 30 — Same thing, same stupid things.

MONDAY DEC. 1 — This is the crucial month. On it, and on its work-project, depends the success of the whole winter — (like a campaign.) No more bingeing-around for weeks now, but *inviolable* work. Tonight: wrote **1000-words**————————— Full of tormented thoughts that come up from a taut and twisted stomach, literally — a hangover, of course, yet a sense of the terrible fatality of life. I know what these thoughts are, and why they hurt so much — close to madness, but I'm not psychotic, nor split off from reality in the slightest, a little bit perhaps, but that [is,] normally at least. And dreams I had during a nap, the mad smile of a man's face, and myself earnest and worried. That mad smile — pleasedness and the insanity of it. If I could only draw that smile I saw in the dream, and the other night. The man who smiles that way knows a lot and despises it all, yet it shouldn't be, it really shouldn't be — and why do I say *that?* — I'm terrified at the sight of madness. It's a horrible sight. Especially in a friend. If you have a friend, and he's insane, undoubtedly insane, and he hates you, but only with a smiling indifferent scorn and not serious hatred, and you yourself don't know how to hate back at him, don't know how he smiles, you even dream of that smile — it's the Devil himself showing through with all the complex diabolism possible, it's the Devil at his evillest. A long drawn-out staring insolent smile breaking out suddenly on a face that has always been gloomy and severe, and sometimes charming — this enough to make me want to cry, as though I were watching my father go mad before my eyes.

TUESDAY DEC. 2 — Feverish night of writing, with my blood pounding, my nerves jangling, yet my whole being incredibly *alive*. It isn't a feeling of comfort but I know it for a visitation of ecstasy, grave thoughtful ecstasy, and I welcome it, even though my very chest is thumping. Wrote *3500-strange-and-exalted words*. It's an ecstasy that's "grave and thoughtful" because I am not possessed by it, I myself possess it and can touch it and examine it. What lonely joys these are! I thank God for them. And with this writing I have completed a large 33,000-word section, and am ready to embark on the last great constructions of the novel. A mountain-peak completed this night, and the last peak in sight, snow-covered and far, but no longer purple from sheer *distance*. (Ah these literary people!) Amen.

WEDNESDAY DEC. 3 — And here is the last great discovery of my "youth" — now I'm no longer a "youth". *I know now what it means to retire from life, and what it means to come to it.* But later, later — Tonight I do feel like living "three lives," in fact, naturally, a thousand lives as well. It's one of those nights when you can't possibly imagine ever being bored again — and I don't think I ever will, either! All the souls to explore! — It's not so necessary to *love*, really, as it is to settle something deep with all of those who really matter. Love and hate are the same thing, differently sifted through personal ... *pride*, or what have you ... personal pride or even just personal-ness. All the souls to explore throughout life, and if you could live a thousand lives, or have the energy of a thousand lives in you! This has always been one of my favorite notions. And all the dark Brooklyns to explore, and ships, and skies, and things — those my old, everpresent ecstasies — and the woods of the earth to explore, to live in. To live is to explore. An adventure of the heart, the mind, the soul. Dostoevsky says it's a sin to be afraid: and of course that's true. I know now tonight that I will endeavor to settle everything that needs to be settled, I'm no longer afraid of settling things anymore, and if I had a thousand lives and energies, and could settle all the varieties that show up in life! There it is — For the first time in my life, I'm really on my knees to life and ready to kiss its hand. What next? And how can I write anything tonight. Tonight I've only just solved the entire novel, that's all, perhaps I'm even quite modest about it all. Solved this novel and signed my life away to fifty other long novels. This is the way it's been tonight, as I just sat around in my chair with my feet up on another chair. In spite of all this, I foresee that I'll *still* have trouble waking up in the mornings from now on.

THURS. DEC. 4 — The happy ending of the "Brothers Karamazov" and also of "A Raw Youth," called "Dickensy" and dull and uninteresting by some critics, is not the laughing mockery of a great genius of understanding, but rather, it seems to me the admission that though human beings do not need "happiness" they might as well be happy. This is like God's gratuitous sunshine after a bad storm, and it is good. I say to these critics: "Don't be ass-holes all your life." Another completely different thought: Americans are socially ignorant, that is, they don't understand the "facts of life" like the French, say — but they have the most beautifully proportioned emotional makeups of any nation, that's why they say Americans are "placid." The sensitivity and violence of Frenchmen and Austrians and what not is only the result of a horrid mixup in their hearts — and too much talk, too. A European in general is carried away by distorted pride. What about that. *Wrote* **2000-words** tonight, beginning on an entirely new kind of section (The War) — and pondering how much it deserves in view of proportions and the necessity of getting my theme towards conclusion. I'll never have to worry about this kind of thing in my other future novels, for reasons unclear to me now, but I just *know*. (More sense later on?)

FRIDAY DEC. 5 — Went into town to get a new topcoat — had dinner at Burroughs — and at night had an astounding conversation with Ginsberg which revealed how deeply similar our visions of life are. It's only that he *had* tried to be clever (i.e. sardonic) about it, but a sorrow has come over him and he speaks without intellectual guile. His vision of life, however, is infinitely more complex than mine, perhaps *riper* too, and in the end, he being a Russian Jew, especially Russian, it is fundamentally different from mine in terms of "space," the feeling he has about space (he's surrounded by it, it is mysteriously incomprehensible to him, and it's the same to him at all times everywhere,) whereas, for me there's a difference I can't really define, except that I'm always keenly conscious of *where* I am and the special atmosphere of where I am. Still, I believe his vision is deeper, though not as grave as mine. And in the end, for him, life at its highest is comedy — people running around in the "Forest of Arden"* and meeting again all the time, and all seeking to love one another, but being so tortured and unhappy about it sometimes that it's funny to watch. My vision emphasizes the urge to brooding self-envelopment while all the love is going on, that is, people have to work and live while they love. It's Russian of him to overlook the meaning of some old man going to bed at night in his red flannels and with a cup of hot toddy and a newspaper — in his vision, that old man must rush out of bed and go and settle something with someone else. These two things do exist, however, self-love and love. His vision is beautiful and more benign than mine, but there's something sweetly true in both visions.

*The setting for William Shakespeare's comedy *As You Like It*. According to biographer Gerald Nicosia, Kerouac seriously discussed the metaphorical meaning of Rosalind's line to Touchstone, "Well, this is the Forest of Arden," with Allen Ginsberg. The two also often repeated it and used it jokingly in conversation by replacing Arden with Manhattan, for instance.

SATURDAY DEC. 6 — As a result of that mad conversation, I dedicated the weekend to a new idea, and tried commencing a new novel. It was splendidly successful (no title yet) and I shall finish it later on after T & C is all done. Went to a movie with my mother, read Stendhal's life.

SUNDAY DEC. 7 — Continued thinking and writing my "new" idea. But a strange thing happened — for the first time in a whole year, more than a year, I fell asleep deliberately on the job, and woke up at dawn sick and nauseous. I took a long walk and almost fainted. Then, it was then, I decided to resume and finish Town & City before anything else. This was my physical system itself, the man itself, revolting against any abandonment of two years of supreme effort, since after all, this "new idea" is not new, and all the magnificent structures of T & C were dedicated laboriously, painfully and patiently to the same end — proof of that is Peter Martin's absorption with "the world itself" in T & C, and other things. However, it is suddenly occurring to me that a great new change is about to take place in mankind and in the world. Don't ask me how I know this. And it's going to be very simple and true, and men will have taken another great step forward. It will be a kind of clear realization of love, and war will eventually seem unreal and even obsolete, and a lot of other things will happen. But madness will rule in high places for a long time yet. All this is going to come up from the people themselves, a great new revolution of the soul. Politics has nothing to do with this. It will be a kind of looking around and noticing of the world, and a simultaneous abandonment of systems of pride and jealousy, in many, many people, and it will spread around swiftly. Enough for now:

MONDAY DEC. 8 — Wrote **3500 words**, swiftly, surely. Am no longer worried about "labor" — just my *mother*.

WEDNESDAY DEC. 10 — Went into town to see Lennie Tristano's opening — great jazz music, "new sounds," ten years ahead of be-bop.

I was alone. Came right back home at 2 A.M. to write, and wrote **2500** splendid words, too. That happy weariness at dawn.

THURSDAY DEC. 11 — At 5 A.M. wrote **1500-words**. Spent most of the night typing and re-working 3,000 words in the manuscript, and thinking of the structures. The world is a structure of souls, nein? And so on —

FRIDAY DEC. 12 — Went into town to see all the kids, the "men and women and things" of the world, and had a great time: Vicki [Russell], Tom [Livornese], Ginger, Ed White, Jack Fitzgerald, Jeanne his wife, Burroughs, Joan [Adams Burroughs], Julie, Bill Garver, Sam Macauley, Hunkey [Herbert Huncke] himself(!) (just out) and all the others wandering in the "sad paradise" of Ginsberg. Spent *days* with Vicki just "goofing off" and then I came out of it walking two miles in Manhattan, alone for sweet musing. Read all the papers —

SATURDAY DEC. 13 — (goofing) —

SUNDAY DEC. 14 — that is, read all the papers tonight.

MONDAY DEC. 15 — Wrote **2000-words**, good ones too.

TUESDAY DEC. 16 — Halfway mark of the month. Re-wrote 2500-words for main ms. And wrote **1000 words** tonight, poor miserable brow-sweated words that they are. Does anything good come out of mere diligence, without the divine intelligence that one should have? If not, I'm hanged if I know how to *work* in this world. Life is easy, but work —

WEDNESDAY DEC. 17 — What a depressed, *beleaguered*, lonely night last night! (Just like the old days.) No work today, went peddling my screen story (in vain, I'm afraid) — but I did get to see that marvellous film "A Tree Grows in Brooklyn." A great story, by a greater director,

Elia Kazan. And I went to see people and none of them were in: it was as though all my friends had suddenly vanished like ghosts in N.Y. This often happens in N.Y., by the way, and it is eerie, and enough to drive one insane when it happens. What is even more eerie is that I ran into two of them on Times Square and they never saw me, and I followed them awhile, and they too eventually vanished (so perhaps it was just an illusion of mine.) This is material for a [Edgar Allan] Poe or "horror" short story. I dreamed up another fantastic story called "Life and Millions," to be described elsewhere. These past few days I've been lost in fantasies and reveries again, the mad & lonely young poet again — which I actually don't welcome, by the way, it's too eerie, unreal, insane, lonesome, joyless and morbid.

THURSDAY DEC. 18 — Got up early, set to work — yet wrote only **1000-words!** — but rewrote 3000 for the main m.s. — and what's funny, spent 2 hours at dawn (my best writing-time) looking for an excerpt among the two million words in the orange crates. Had to find it. Found it. Then I had to go to bed from sheer exhaustion. What a night.

FRIDAY DEC. 19 — Wrote **1500-words**, hard-earned, so hard-earned. I'm going through a difficult period this week: worked like a dog and only produced 5500 words. This is disgusting. No matter how urgent it is for me to finish this book, it takes its own slow damned time, and this is the worst, unhappiest thing I can know. Why is everything so slow? What tiresome experiences.

SATURDAY DEC. 20 — Refrigerator was moved in, etc., and into N.Y. for the night seeing the kids.

SUNDAY DEC. 21 — Had to visit relatives in afternoon. At night, read my "sea diary" of 1942, and what a nice little job it turned out to be, almost Goethean in its sincerity and scope at times. Then I started writing the "Greenland narrative" for my novel, although, since it bears only slightly on the novel's theme, I decided to fuse it swiftly, mood-fully. There's a novel in itself there, with Melvillean possibilities, so I'll generally "save" it for later and extract only the juices I need for now for T & C.* Wrote awhile and went to sleep in an effort to get back on a *day-time* schedule, since my eyes are beginning to ache and water again from too much lamplight.

MONDAY DEC. 22 — But news came of the certainty of a Christmas trip to North Carolina so I closed up the books — for a week.

*   *   *

SUNDAY DEC. 28 — Back again, to the great snow of '47, which I had to go and miss.† No snow at all in eastern N. Carolina. It was a dull trip too, but I got a sort of rest anyway, although I took sick. That makes 12,000-miles of travelling for 1947 for me anyway, which isn't exactly a dull or lazy year — along with the 250,000 words of writing. Tonight, recuperating from an intestinal illness, I gazed at my novel and its imminent conclusion — within 2 months. And what snow outside, what wonderful tons of snow everywhere! I love to see New Yorkers without their infernal cars, for once. They seem to love this respite from the machine.

MONDAY DEC. 29 — I had been thinking of going to some N.Y. or Brooklyn College this year for the sake of the $65-a-month G.I. subsistence, which would pay the rent. But a rested glance at my novel rather (somewhat) convinces me that it will sell to a publisher anyway, and needs all my attention and energy this winter. I can study on my own

---

*Finished in three versions in 1942 and 1943, Kerouac based his novel "The Sea Is My Brother" on his experience as a merchant marine and was heavily influenced by Melville. Other than an excerpt in *Atop an Underwood: Early Stories and Other Writings* (1999), "The Sea Is My Brother" remains unpublished.
†This record-setting snowstorm hit New York City unexpectedly and dumped more than thirty inches of snow on the city on December 26 and 27.

for a whole year after it's out of my hands: reading everything, any-thing I want to read, keeping notebooks, travelling. So I think I'll do nothing but write T & C this winter and the quicker it's off the better all around, rent money or not. Wrote **1000-words** in the afternoon, fit-fully, impatiently — as though I didn't want to write any more. But it may only be the weakness of my illness lingering. I hate to write away from my *theme,* to write build-up material for it, it's far from the goal. Wrote another **2500-words** at night, and that broke it, coralled it, and tied it for good, because I went over a tough hump. Great! Great! — to do things like this, even when I'm sick, that's the happiness of my mad life. Now I see clearly the end of the novel, by six weeks, the middle of February? So many happy things I could say, but that's enough, I'm tired of writing. This makes 25,000-words for this month, December, and 55,000 since I got back from the West. Another 80,000 will finish the novel — eight weeks' good work will do it. Now I'll celebrate New Year's Eve in grand style, happy again. (Make that *twenty* weeks)

WEDNESDAY DEC. 31 — Party at Tom's in Lynbrook, but how sad I was at midnight, without a girl, alone in a room playing "Auld Lang Syne" on the piano with one finger. But afterwards what drinking & yelling, drinking enormously with Jack Fitzgerald, and telling great stories and talking, right into morning —

1948

THURSDAY JAN. 1 — Still drinking with Fitz, at home now, and what a marvellous guy, the best. The most amazing in the world. If he doesn't drink himself to death he'll be a great American writer. Then I had long sweet conversations with my mother.

SATURDAY JAN. 3 — Might as well conclude the holidays. And what kind of night was this I spent? — Just the other day, dreams of guilt,

and tonight, *the deed,* a deed long anticipated — (but all too complicated and treated elsewhere) (Ginger)

SUNDAY JAN. 4 — It's so unusual for me to spend my waking hours
with a sense of my own triumph — and evil — it's not the part — but
again, it's all too much to scribble about. Started writing at night: first,
letters, to Neal [Cassady], etc., then wrote a little in connection with the
City-Episode of the novel, solving plot-obstacles in two big instances.

MONDAY JAN. 5 — My first big workday of 1948 — this is the year of
real success at last. Started writing early in the afternoon and wrote
3000-words. And one thing more: during the night I lay down on my
bed to muse (the dreamy musings that cushion the shock of cerebral
creation): and all of a sudden I sensed the presence of all kinds of gleeful, little things around me, felt it so powerfully that the "gleeful little
things" became almost real, corporeal, moth-shapes, whole swirls and
hosts of them, all around me, I felt like Gulliver, with little things dancing gleefully all over me and around me, and more interesting: it
seemed that these little 'fairy glees' of our life were amazed with me
because I had discovered them, because I had "turned my head and
seen them," and in the simplicity of their little hearts, were pleased
with me, loved me, danced around me, 'their champion and king,'
were happy because I had seen them. And I just lay there grinning and
enjoying their presence & homage. It was one of the loveliest and most
poetic of fancies: and one thing more: I believe in these little things, I
believe they exist, but only at certain wonderful gleeful moments. If I
were an Irish poet, a Celtic bard, I think I'd concentrate exclusively on
these little 'fairy glees' of my heart. And all this only two days after that
deed I mentioned, the seduction of the 'wrong' woman in my life right
now. '*Hurrah for breadth*'?* — I don't really think so after all.

*From Dostoevsky's *A Raw Youth* (1876).

41

TUESDAY JAN. 6 — Wrote all day, as yesterday, and knocked off **2500-words**, and more. Psychological words, mostly, and significantly too, for tomorrow I'm going to see "Crime and Punishment" with John Gielgud, on the stage.* Two days of tremendous work. Must keep it up. Only the *hardest* work will complete T & C.

WEDNESDAY JAN. 7 — Saw "Crime & Punishment" — which I know so well — and it is haunting me again now: but the French movie version with Pierre Blanchar is still the most Dostoyevskyan:† when Raskolnikov goes to give himself up, the Inspector is not in (casually), Raskolnikov wanders out without confessing, but Sonya, Sonya stands there outside *looking* at him, and he goes back in again and converses with a subordinate. When a man presents the world with its own details, and lights them with his celestial visions of unworldly love, that is the highest genius. There is nothing "hammy" about this most honest possible man.

— — — — — — — — —

Wrote **1000-words** at night late. Feel "lost."

SATURDAY JAN. 10 — Spent a lazy afternoon in my bathrobe and slippers, playing the piano, thinking of nothing in particular. 'Tired of writing' for this week — about 10,000 words written this week. At night, went to N.Y.; saw Sarah Vaughan on 52nd St. Feeling another change ...

SUNDAY JAN. 11 — Am reading Thomas Wolfe's "Home Again" and am struck by the simplicity, humbleness, and beauty of his perfectly mature soul in his later years, 35 & 36. This is something only "aging" can produce, as in good Bourbon. American critics are blind to Wolfe's perfect maturity, especially to the simple and magical tone of it. Today,

*One of only two Broadway stagings of *Crime and Punishment,* this National Theatre production starred the prolific British actor and stage director John Gielgud (1904–2000) as Raskolnikoff and ran for a limited forty performances.
†This 1935 film starred French actor Pierre Blanchar (1892–1963) as Raskolnikoff.

read my own novel, or *scanned* it in its entirety. I see that it's almost finished. I have no opinions about it, however, either good or bad, my real feelings are lost *in* it, drowned in it. What is my opinion of this novel? — it is the sum of myself, as far as the written word can go, and my opinion of it is like my opinion of myself: — gleeful and affectionate one day, black with disgust the next day. So no? Wrote **2500-words**, until interrupted by visit from Allen Ginsberg, who came at 4 o'clock in the morning to tell me that he is going mad, but once and if cured he will communicate with other human beings as no one has ever done, *completely*, sweetly, naturally. He described his terror and seemed on the verge of throwing a fit in my house, but didn't. As usual I was oblique with him, but watchful. When he calmed down I read him parts of my novel and he leeringly announced that it was "greater than Melville, in a sense — the great American novel." I did not believe a word he said, but believed everything else he said, which was so interesting. As a matter of fact he castigated me for finding things 'interesting' instead of 'real.' I told him I was just in a good mood, when things seem 'interesting,' but he rushed on to talk about everything else. However, someday I will take off my own mask and tell all about Allen Ginsberg and what he is in the 'real' flesh: he is so close to me, sometimes I can't see him. Right now, I think of him exactly as he thinks of himself, and he even told me his fantasies. It seems to me that he is just like any other human being and I see that this drives him to his wit's ends. How can I help a man who wants to be a monster one minute and a god the next, and never makes up his mind with his earthly will, and goes on wandering to and fro snarling and fawning at people, and never resting, and never wanting to rest, and always accusing me of being stupid because I like to rest once in a while and because I like myself occasionally, and believe in work, and like things and people once in a while. And a man who wants to 'settle' something with me, which I agree to do, whereupon he giggles because it's 'too much.' My main idea about Allen tonight is: — he giggles at everything except his own horror, which precipitates the giggles in the first place. He is locked up inside himself hopelessly to the point where he is actually like a gargoyle-head grinning on the prow of an old ship, and as the old ship proceeds through the waters of the world, the gargoyle-head, undeviating, is grinning and giggling forever as the ship rounds capes, crosses southern seas, passes icebergs and albatrosses, noses into grimy old harbors, stands anchored in flowery lagoons, weathers bright sunshine, gray fog, great storms, blackest night, and finally sinks to the bottom of the ocean, where, amid bubbling muds and weird fishes and sea-light, the gargoyle-head still grins and giggles forever. Yet that's not all.

MONDAY JAN. 12 — Read, and rested from loss of sleep. Decided that "A Raw Youth" is an *evil* book. Later ...

TUESDAY JAN. 13 — Wrote **3000-words**, beginning to approach the feverish conclusions of this big complex story, and I'm in a state of exalted absorption.

WEDNESDAY JAN. 14 — Deliberately rested my mind awhile today, because I want it to reflect while working. At night, wrote **1500-words** — rolling on, on. But what a frenetic story this is! — too much!

THURSDAY JAN. 15 — Wrote over **1000-words** and completed the 'Wartimes' section of my book which I sought vainly (but the best I could) to express by that haunted sadness of that time. I'll have to go over the thing again later and sum it up in some passage: the sadness of uprooted 'war-life.' Today, relaxed and read, while writing slowly, and finally stopping.

FRIDAY JAN. 16 — Went to Manhattoes and drank up a quantity of whiskey with Ken, and Tony Monacchio — who gave me 1500 sheets of good bond paper for my manuscript and will give me 1500 more.* Came home on Saturday,

*Monacchio worked at United Press International with Lucien Carr and both provided typing paper for Kerouac.

SATURDAY JAN. 17 — When I chuckled all night reading Wolfe's experiences with Sinclair Lewis in England,* that is, I didn't *chuckle*, I laughed: one of the happiest nights of my life. Also wrote a sad paragraph.

MONDAY JAN. 19 — Today is the anniversary of this novel. A year ago at this time I had nothing really to show for a year's work (1946) through death and sickness and bereavement and guilt and horror and name your own. On Jan. 19, 1947, I started all over again, secretly, almost sheepishly, and certainly without much real hope. Strange to remember, now, Neal Cassady was around at that time and I kept on writing not to disappoint him. But I soon saw it all again, the whole novel, as I had seen it in March, 1946, when I came home to begin, only to really, yet partially after all, fail —

And now, in a year's time since Jan. 19, '47, I've written 225,000-words from Town & City, which is a lot. Only about 50,000 to go, and still buried under my own avalanche, but it's going to be done now. So this is a great date in my mind, when I began again, and did it. So I begin again, and I shall finish the novel before my 26th birthday, March 12. All this formality of the soul, however, makes it difficult to actually start, especially since I'm beginning today on The City ... How? How? Well, as it should always be, *simply* and *honestly*, from whence arise the most beautiful complexities in literature, and in life. Isn't it honesty *honestly* presented that accounts for all the great original settlements between men and between men and God? There are no official pronouncements, no prepared speeches, no hackneyed manifestoes, no oratorical surveys in the soul — only honesty and speech. There is not even 'style' in the soul? When am I properly going to learn this? So I got down and wrote **1500-words** tonight and got underway beautifully, also pondered the plot, or that is, the complexities.

*Wolfe met *Main Street* (1920) author Sinclair Lewis (1885–1951) for the first time in 1930. The hilarious circumstances of their meeting in London and trip to Surrey — during which Lewis's driver repeatedly got lost and Lewis fell into an alcohol-induced semicoma — is fictionalized in *You Can't Go Home Again*, with Lewis as Lloyd McHarg.

TUESDAY JAN. 20 — I know what to do better than myself ... A passing, true thought, full of mystery. Wrote as best I could, with real pain tonight, just **500-words**, count 'em. There are times when the artisan-architect who writes huge novels suddenly hates himself inscrutably, in such a way that he can't work. I could rope-walk tonight but I will not write. I won't even ask why any more — it passeth understanding by all means.

WEDNESDAY JAN. 21 — Got up early, almost desperate about this week's output, and wrote in slow torture **1000-words**. I simply don't give a damn anyway tonight: too much reverence is worse than none.

THURSDAY JAN. 22 — Tried to write and wrote nothing at all, what I wrote was crossed out. This is one of the worst ones yet, especially after all I've written.

FRIDAY JAN. 23 — Went out finally, last night, but I had already overcome the depression by thinking 'right down' to it — I think. Binge, slight one.

SATURDAY JAN. 24 — Came home: I feel as gay and lighthearted as a little boy, (I think). But all my thoughts are sweet and I can hardly wait to start writing another novel after T & C — a good one, 'really myself' this time. Yet, right now, isn't it true that I don't feel gay and happy, I'm not given a chance to, because I've got too much difficult (not hard, but difficult) — work to do? Aie! Tonight I fought out **1500-words** — tearing my hair.

SUNDAY JAN. 25 — Reading the papers and listening to the radio all day long — and I'm convinced that the so-called 'realities' of 'today's world' are not to be found there among the news items, the editorial comments, the journalese views of the world, and among the book reviews, critical comments, radio programs and what-not of the New York–Hollywood universe. The life of the people themselves, all those who don't know there is such a thing as the 'middleclass,' the life of PEOPLE — And in the same vein, shall I say that the true Russia is not the Russia of "War and Peace" but the Russia of "A Raw Youth" or "Dead Souls" or "The Brothers Karamazov". I believe that war and 'social significance' are totally unreal in the lives of people everywhere: That is why the people themselves seem so incomprehensible when they are unsuccessfully placed among those things: they don't 'react' the way they are expected to by a desperately false and unreal intelligentsia. What I'd like to know is *WHY* these unreal worlds of 'significance' are created by an intelligentsia. More, much more later. However, not to deny anything, all things are of course real. The unreality of the intelligentsia consists of its aims — 'to know everything' — which it never even faintly approaches. Wrote **1500-words** tonight and running into the next day —

MONDAY JAN. 26 — And am now ready at last to embark on the final City Episode. What I have done up till now, such hard work, and only vaguely resembling what I had intended, yet in short, the best I could do. Someday I won't have to say this anymore, I'll have real mastery. And now what about the dramatic furies and moral furies of my City Episode — And to make it *real* I must not plan it too carefully, I'll just let it *grow* like a plant, bit by bit: not logic, but organic. There are a lot of fancy words to describe this, Goethean words, but things are getting too serious to play science. Wrote **2000-words** therefore. Also walked 3 miles, ate 2 big meals, and did 16½ pull-ups tonight. I should have been a financier and all I'd do is sit and count the figures of my wealth, day after day.

TUESDAY JAN. 27 — Had a fist-fight with my novel and drew **2500-**poor-drops-of-blood out of it, and after the smoke of the battle was over, something probably important occurred to me: — to try writing in quick first drafts of just sheer dialogue and sheer description of the action, without pausing to arrange it all in sentence-form, that is, logical and rhythmical and clear. Not that I believe too strongly in clear and

47

logical writing, but I do believe in the kind of writing that gives effortless pleasure to the reader. In the end, I am my own greatest reader. Also, I believe in *sane* writing, as opposed to the psychotic sloppiness of Joyce. Joyce is a man who only gave up trying to communicate to human beings. I myself do that when I'm drunk-weary and full of misery, therefore I know it's not so honest as it's spiteful to blurt out in associations without a true human effort to evoke and give *significant* intelligence to one's sayings. It's a kind of scornful idiocy.

WEDNESDAY JAN. 28 — Out in New York suffering —

THURSDAY JAN. 29 — (really this time!)

FRIDAY JAN 30 — These two days produced vibrations in me, I'm alive and throbbing again. A million new facts were created. I came home thinking, "Now I will tell you what I think of everything." I thought of 'making up my mind' once and for all, but I ended up realizing that I *am* on the right track not ever 'making up my mind.' I still say that my life is a continual effort to achieve perfection of doubt — (and this is more *religious* than it sounds.) My kind of doubt is not wilfully scornful. I also understood that though actually I'm a very dumb guy among many really brilliant and intelligent friends, I myself have a significant intelligence. Whereas they 'know everything' and I don't at all, still, I know the *import* of everything. I'm not 'aware' in their sense, I hardly understand what's going on around me, but I feel everything more than they do, and arrive at their own brilliant effortless conclusions through absorption (like a sponge) and real mental misery. Their brains open up the truth, look in, and withdraw for other uses: my brain receives the truth and sponges it up painfully (my brow contracts like a moron thinking for the first time) and I go away overloaded. They are all jockeying for position in the world, (and I'm meaning psychic position among one another as well as worldly position), while I rush around investigating all the positions and sopping them up one after another. In a sense, I'm mad (and withdrawn from life) while they're sane, human, normal — but in another sense, I speak from the depths of a vision of truth when I say that this continual jockeying for position is the enemy of life in itself. It may be life, 'life is like that,' it may be human and true, but it's also the death-part of life, and our purpose after all is to *live* and be true. We'll see.

Tonight wrote **2500-words**, but with an awful sense of emptiness and musing indifference — that is, I could sit for hours just musing and doing nothing else. I just wrote mechanically, without seizures of feeling or mood of any kind (like [Anthony] Trollope is supposed to have written.) Plainly, I'll have to come around to myself, or something, again. My mother claims that my friends are a bad influence on me, that none of them really wish me well, and all seek to usurp something I have which they don't have. I can't reconcile myself to this, but I know damn well I have always partly agreed with her. In a sense, my mother still wants me to join her in league against the rest of the world, and in another sense she is shrewd and understands clearly the futility of my enthusiasm for an idle life among such friends (who never *work* or care about anything.) But there is madness in everything. I am really confused these days. The realization that I must discover my own will and exert it seems brutal and unfair and unsympathetic and somehow uninteresting. And I know I'm not a *man* yet, I'm not standing erect, with perfect unconscious grace, the way some men do, workingmen, men with families, men who decide and act every day. I'm a 'writer' — and I never should have been a 'writer.' I don't even look like a writer, I look like a lumberjack, or a lumberjack bard like Jack London. I'm a Canuck farmer among the 'eager young students' and I've learned all their airs — I don't even *believe* in them. The only true friend I can imagine at this moment is Mike Fournier of Lowell, from whom I drew the character and personality of Joe Martin in the novel. Also, I'm sick of sadness, and *castration*.

SATURDAY JAN. 31 — Read, went to a movie with Ma ("Cass Timberlane"* — and I like anything from that wonderful man Sinclair Lewis) — and wrote notes. It's so cold I can't stay up at night, I freeze, but in the kitchen I almost manage, I do manage.

FEBRUARY 1948 —

SUNDAY FEB. 1 — Well now, that was 30,500-words for January, slower than I planned, but I'm not in a big hurry any more. I know I can make it now. When March 12† rolls around I ought to be fairly finished, but then I'll want to do some re-writing, and that's allright too. Wrote **3500-words** splendidly, over that by 200, but we'll carry that over for tomorrow. A good start for this month.

MONDAY FEB. 2 — Wrote about 2,000 words but I think I'll cross them out and start another way. The City part of the novel is tricky and a little dangerous for me to do — Hal Chase and Ed White read the City fragment I wrote yesterday (Sunday) and they thought the hero Peter Martin seemed *remote* from the action, which I deliberately must have aimed at, so as not to involve my precious Martins in any madness, at least any Martin but poor Francis. And so on. Work is the main thing, I'll fix things.

TUESDAY FEB. 3 — Went into town and bought Ma a present for her birthday tomorrow, saw Hal and Ed.

WEDNESDAY FEB. 4 — Nice blizzard blowing today. Got back to writing. I had a *true* artistic thought when I woke up: "Town & City is a tremendous story because I'm *making it* tremendous." This is like saying, 'This is going to be a good house because I'm making it good.'

*This 1947 adaptation of Sinclair Lewis's novel of the same name starred Spencer Tracy and Lana Turner.
†March 12 would be Kerouac's twenty-sixth birthday.

It's the super-confidence of a worker with pride, of a craftsman. I think this kind of pride is *not* vain and that it gets one further in work than any modesty of purpose. If a man claims he's doing a modest 'piece of writing' I believe him. There are only two kinds of modesty, false modesty, and — real modesty. Neither of which I'll take. And all this has nothing to do with worldly humility. Wrote 1500-*'sensible'*-words tonight.

THURSDAY FEB. 5 — If there is such a thing as 'fact' or 'facts' in the world, then *everything* is a fact or 'facts.' I have recently heard the 'scholars' speak of 'facts' — and I think they were thinking adversely of my moonstruck creations. Well, after all, if all the world is not a fact, then there is no such thing as 'facts' and so on. All the unfactual fabrications in the world, even in scholarly research at the universities, stem from 'fact.' The pot and the kettle are both black because they serve the same purpose ... and so on. But to create 'facts' is another thing, and tonight I worked myself sick on **2000-words.** I really pushed myself tonight, headache and all, to a most unnatural weariness at 3 A.M. — usually my most vigorous hour. Actually, I'm robust enough to take these things, mental nervousness and all, so I'll just walk it off, I take long walks, and I sleep a lot.

FRIDAY FEB. 6 — Will start checking on my physical and mental condition daily, following from this new plan: to walk 2 miles each night after finishing writing and before going to bed, so as to really *physically* sleep. Tried it last night, along with the pull-ups, and I feel great today, I got up early and *I knew who I was.* You don't realize what a strain it is on the nerves to write or think-of-writing all day long, and to sleep full of nervous dreams, and to wake up not knowing who one is: — this all stems from anxiety about finishing the book, about time 'growing short', etc., and the perpetual strain of invention. Enough of that for now. The condition today: clear-minded, physical feeling the body, but no hunger for food. The position: — happy absorbed thoughts about 'Frisco and things like that. The creation: or *invention:*

several hundred words. Incidentally, I may now forego counting words because I'm going to do a rapid 35,000-word first draft of the City Episode, with corrections later. We'll see. Went through an important and severe self-examination after writing in the afternoon, and it did me good. For instance, supposing all this writing I've been doing for two years, this "Town & City," was just after all one great disorderly manuscript written by a madman in a cracked state, me, and all my dreams of fame and genius and the redemption of my life through high personal success, the delusions of insanity, and the hopes of saving my mother from a life of toil and disappointment, and hopes of my getting a wife's house, land and family, all the fumbling dreams of a madman incapable of even caring for himself — supposing all this were true? and I didn't know it! This was a great fear I must have been unconsciously nurturing, and now it's out. I examined it carefully and saw how it was possibly true in some respects, but untrue according to my knowledge, will, and determined intelligence. This all cleared a mist from my brain somehow. Went out at night to hear Tristano on 52nd street. I was suddenly disgusted with the 'hipsters' who had come there to listen over-enthusiastically to be-bop Howard McGhee jazz.* Also I tried to make women on the subway but gave it up, and will go to dances instead this spring. The question is: how mad am I actually? — and how sane? The answer: — as much as anybody wants to, either way. But at least, it all raises interesting issues. It helped clear a big obstacle of incomprehensibility in my novel's plot. The novel absorbs it all, in the end.

SATURDAY FEB. 7 — Got up early, wrote in the afternoon without much success till 'something broke' and I suddenly began writing with gusto, at which time, though, I had to go into N.Y., where my plans did not materialize, and I came back directly, Saturday night or not, ate, read the papers, talked to Ma, and wrote some more. The *laws*

---

*Howard McGhee (1918–1987), bebop jazz trumpet player.

of writing elude my understanding the closer I examine them, and that's a fact.

SUNDAY FEB. 8 — But I'm thinking of crossing out what I wrote last night, possibly everything I've written in the last two or three weeks. I've hit a dangerous snag. Hal Chase came over today and we talked till late in a fog about how to continue the flow of my novel at this point, technically and spiritually. 15,000 words may have to be revivified before I can continue. The whole thing is absorbing, I don't despair, but time! time! — real calendar time with which I flay myself, because it's been so long now, two years, and i[t] should be due at a publisher's.

MONDAY FEB. 9 — Started all over again at a certain point in the novel, and I won't count words until I've made up the backlog — which is about 10,000 or so. Started all over again *in pencil* which has now proven itself the only way to write sincerely & sensibly. My thoughts can never keep up with a typewriter machine. Wrote till early in the morning.

TUESDAY FEB. 10 — Wrote more; slowly, absorbedly. I decided to start typing out my handwritten manuscript and show it to a publisher, Whittelsey House,* by March 21st. I felt strong at night, hopeful, and also humble, which is the greatest work-feeling possible: strength for work, humility for *knowledge*.

WEDNESDAY FEB. 11 — A big work-day. I typed out 3,500 words of the manuscript, and wrote **2500-words**, new and extra. At this rate I'll never catch up with myself typing out the manuscript. I'm getting deep into the City Episode with its 'atomic disease' nonsense and madness. Oh I pray to God that this will be a true and a good and a splendid book.

*Now defunct, Whittelsey House was a division of the McGraw-Hill Company.

THURSDAY FEB. 12 — If the intellectuals of the '20's thought they were decadent, just wait till you see the '50's — except that in the '50's the great majority of the people will be sounder-souled than they were in the '20's. This is my prediction. Typed 3500 wds., wrote **1000 new** wds.

FRIDAY FEB. 13 — Went into town, talked all night in cafeterias. How I gab away when I come out of my work-loneliness: nobody else can get a word in edgewise, and this is so much like my father.

SATURDAY FEB. 14 — Took Ma to a movie at night.

SUNDAY FEB. 15 — Hung around the house reading, etc. At night typed out 3500 words and scanned the novel.

TUESDAY FEB. 17 — Wrote **2000-words** and typed out 3500-words for manuscript. A day of fine perceptive feelings: — I ran the whole gamut (well, some of it) with joy and knowledge. Walked 2½ miles in Manhattan, from Times Square to 1st Ave. and 14th St., on a beautiful spring-like night. I bought a Lowell newspaper and for the first time in years it seemed that Lowell 'was part of the whole world' after all, a strange fact. I did and thought a thousand things today, a great rich day, lonely but rich. But I won't catalogue it not now.

WEDNESDAY FEB. 18 — Got to work faster now. Only 12,000 words in 18 days this slow meditative month. Today typed 3500 words and wrote a few hundred new words — and I plotted the novel down to its last page. The end clearly in sight for the first time. The whole thing is so long.

THURSDAY FEB. 19 — Got up early, set to work (early for me means one o'clock in the afternoon instead of three o'clock with its waning light) — Wrote: **1500-words**; typed out 3500 wds. in manuscript.

FRIDAY FEB. 20 — Wrote **1500-words** — 1000 of them for the 'sea-chapters' in another section of the novel, rich poetic words that will set that off nicely. Started to go out but came back home to do this writing, in the kitchen. 'Betimes I read books by night as my father slept!' — a thought tonight.

SATURDAY FEB. 21 — Went out drinking beer in Yorkville German-town* with Herr Chase and Herr White. We drank dark beer and talked about women and the world — about women, Stendhal, Sir Thomas Browne, Carlyle, English restraint, linguistics, Wolfe, Shake-speare, the sea, psychology, etc., etc.

SUNDAY FEB. 22 — Ed White and I drank beer till dawn and talked about women, all the women we know, and jazz, the world — and ate prodigiously, and read my Phillip Tourian novel,† and talked with my mother, and played the piano in the saloon down the street.‡ We talked about Denver, Beverly Burford, Bob Burford, Nicky, Ginger, Vicki, Edie [Parker], Bea [Franco], Ruth the nurse, Stasia, Mary [Carney], etc., etc.

MONDAY FEB. 23 — Took Ma to a movie, and at night walked three miles and wrote notes that begin: — "Everything comes from sadness — All the kinsmen, friends, and lovers that one has in the world are like a few drops of water in a paper cup floating in the At-lantican infinity: when the poor cup topples, or is swallowed by a wave, or sinks of its own, or falls apart in the salty surges, the few drops of water vanish forever unreclaimed and irredeemable" — etc.

*Yorkville is a neighborhood on the Upper East Side of Manhattan which at that time was populated almost entirely by people of German and Hungarian descent, and was filled with German restaurants, bakeries, and bars.
†Kerouac collaborated with William Burroughs on a fictionalized account of the Lucien Carr/David Kammerer incident. A working title was "The Phillip Tourian Story," but it eventually became "And the Hippos Were Boiled in Their Tanks." It has never been published.
‡He is referring to a bar at the corner of Cross Bay Boulevard and Doxsey Place, across the street from the Kerouac apartment in Ozone Park. Then it was the Doxey Tavern; as of this writing it is named Glen Patrick's Bar. When Kerouac and his mother had guests, they would often go there, fill up a kettle with beer, and bring it up to the apartment.

TUESDAY FEB. 24 — Back to work-life. Typed out 3500 words, wrote painfully at a few hundred new ones, and read Sinclair Lewis' "Kingsblood Royal" late into the night.* Some work-life. I've been having the worst month of my obscure career — but I think it's due to the strain of typing every workday.

WEDNESDAY FEB. 25 — Typed out 3500 words for the manuscript. Today I feel that the novel is just a poor befuddled heavy-handed novice attempt: — but I do think the moral theme is beautiful and true, so shite on the critics. Wrote **2000-words** pushing myself methodically and painfully and reluctantly back to real driving work. There's no other way, God help me and God damn it.

THURSDAY FEB. 26 — Accounted for **2000-words**, some from earlier writing. This city episode is hell to write. Went to a movie in the evening. Worked late at night ... 'Praying in my room and sighing at the moon from the fullness of my hopes.' (JK)

FRIDAY FEB. 27 — Wrote **1500-words** and typed out 3000-wds. for mss. I'm really working hard now, to redeem this month, to get this whole insane thing over with. It's 21,000-wds. this month now.

SATURDAY FEB. 28 — I'm going to write ceaselessly about the dignity of human beings no matter who and or what they are, and the less dignity a person has the fewer words I'll use. It's the sheer humanness of a man that comes first, whether geek, fag, 'Negro,' or criminal, whether preacher, financier, father, or senator, whether whore, child, or gravedigger. I don't care who or what — and that I should have cared before is an insult to Dostoevsky, Melville, Jesus, and my fathers. Wrote **1000-words** and typed out 2000-words, and on Saturday night too(!)

---

*Lewis's *Kingsblood Royal* (1947) is a novel about an American banker who, in middle age, discovers he is part African.

SUNDAY FEB. 29 — Wrote **1000**-*'bloodletting' words* and that makes 23,000 for the month. Also typed mss. pages today. Tired and absorbed. Read papers.

MONDAY MARCH 1 — Wrote another **1000-words,** and typed out ms. And re-wrote parts I worked on. Now I'm going at it with the rhythm of a blacksmith and I'm afraid to rest by leaving the house. I think this all comes from the fact that in eleven days I'll be hitting my 26th birthday. I want to start living and loving women and travelling all I want at 27, thus the rush. It's great to be working for myself and building something new and huge, and not slaving for someone else and yearning after indefinable future achievements. It's great to be free to work my own way — thanks to my mother and somehow to God too.

TUESDAY MARCH 2 — Typed ms. And went to N.Y. to a movie at night ("Diamond Jim" and "The Spoilers")* and came back and wrote **500-words** at dawn. A beautiful blonde in the subway tried to make me and like a fool I assumed she was a $10-whore and didn't check on it. Yet I'm sick and tired of being a subway-streetcorner romeo, as I seem to always be. Women! women! — and it's always at night somewhere. Betimes the young poet met his fair one at a ball.

WEDNESDAY MARCH 3 — Saw a perfect queenly girl in the library but again I was confused and tongue-locked.† Meanwhile I took out a book on American history and two others on the Oregon and Old Spanish trails. Perhaps I'll see her again, but there's no doubt I'll ex-

---

Diamond Jim (1935) starred Edward Arnold as legendary gambler "Diamond Jim" Brady and depicted his relationship with Lillian Russell. *The Spoilers,* released in 1942, stars Marlene Dietrich, directed by Ray Enright.
†This library at 95-16 Jerome Avenue (now 101st), is where Kerouac researched for his road trips while living in Ozone Park. In *Visions of Cody* (1972), he described it thusly: "A little sort of little kid's library at the corner of Jerome Avenue and Cross Bay Boulevard, where (of course adult books too) old silver-rimmed ladies answered all your questions about (if you were the question-asking type) where to find the Cimarron River."

plore the Uncompahgre River,* in my own way, before 1950. Wrote **2000-words** at night, and then read my splendid books. (11,000-words in past week.)

FRIDAY MARCH 5 — Wrote **500-words**, typed manuscript. Went to N.Y. at night and ran into big crowd of new people. Much drinking, talking, etc. A bunch of decadent youngsters from Kansas whose great-grandfathers cleared Land, fought the terrible Pawnee, built churches. Now their children are, by their own proud admission, 'full of horror and confusion.' And so was I this time, just like them.

SATURDAY MARCH 6 — Binge continued as I caught cold, neglected to eat, bundled with a silly girl in a cold room, etc. Drank 1,000,000 glasses of beer.

SUNDAY MARCH 7 — Came home finally, found good old Hal and dear Ginger waiting for me, playing records, dancing. We talked and drank beer (I got in the bag again), ate, had a big time. I was so glad to see them, more than they knew.

MONDAY MARCH 8 — Then a sort of suffocating cold accompanied with the most terrible nightmares of my life ... Felled as by a sledge-hammer ... Doomish.

TUESDAY MARCH 9 — Still sick, but wrote **500-words**, definitive words, and someday I will leave the sad nightmarish world of my friends which is slowly sickening me. Horror, horror all the time when I see them — and joy when I don't. There ought to be something sane in making a decision. It's only that when I get drunk I want to see everybody and see everything. I want to be a fool and I want to be self-flagellating like them. One thing: I understand this generation well, and all this is part of some shrewd unconscious purpose of mine, as al-

*The Uncompahgre collects its headwaters in the mountains that surround Ouray, Colorado. It flows through southeastern Colorado.

ways. When my work is done with these people, then and then only can I turn to other worlds. And it won't be long now. The novel is now another step nearer completion. And voila, new days are dawning.

WEDNESDAY MARCH 10 — Typed out 3500 wds. of manuscript. Wrote a little in my notebooks. Am reading an American history, and "Overland With Kit Carson"* which contains too little real information but is nevertheless worthwhile. To think of those wolfish Digger Indians! — Melville should have seen *them!* (Eating live lizards, horses, desert rats.) The noble Eutaw justly scorned over Digger friend who is a kind of excremental Gila monster of the desert ... with long dirty hair! Wrote a few hundred words. The Beards' "History of American Civilization"† (or "Rise" is the correct title) is a mighty book, a mighty book — it could have been titled The Great American Saga, it is written so creatively and contains so much. It's another of those great works that humble the reader and at the same time fire him with ambitions.

THURSDAY MARCH 11 — Another wasted day. I've slowed down pretty miserably, but I've been writing steadily since early November. Yet only 35,000-words to go and thus no time to slow down. I read and loafed all day and thought of the plot also.

FRIDAY MAR. 12 — Guess what?! — on my birthday today, wrote **4500-words**(!) — scribbling away till six-thirty in the morning next day. A *real* way to celebrate another coming of age. And *am* I coming of age? (I ask egocentrically) — Hal Chase says I'm just emerging, like "Jim Bridger when he came out of his prairie solitude." My mother and sister and Paul gave me presents (trousers, shirts, ties). I don't scoff at ties, because at the money I make writing I can't positively af-

---

*A pulpy serial of semihistorical fiction, *Overland With Kit Carson* relates the tall tales of the Old West with all of its familiar characters, including Kit Carson (1809–1868).

†The Beards, Charles (1874–1948) and Mary (1876–1958), were historians, social activists, world travelers, and reformers. Together they authored *The Rise of American Civilization* (1927), a much-hailed two-volume revisionist history of America.

ford to make standard salaried jokes about them. But those 4500 words are a new record and it looks like I'll finish the book after all. The only problem left is the *War news* popping up* — I don't want them to blow up the printing presses, not at all.

SATURDAY MARCH 13 — Went to that marvellous movie "Treasure of Sierra Madre"** with Hal and Ginger — Hal was prostrated by the impact of it and could hardly drive home. I read Mark Twain at dawn, and the baseball news, and — the War news too.

SUNDAY MARCH 14 — Home and the papers and the long walk and big dinner. Wrote **3000-words** till 7 o'clock the next morning. A lucky week! — full of easy inspiration and eager energy and hunger.

MONDAY MARCH 15 — Yesterday I wrote 700 words of notes. Now I've got the City Episode defeated I think. Read Mark Twain again tonight and I believe I'm discovering another hero, an American hero in the mainstream with Whitman and Wolfe. Things are opening up anew and broader and CLEARER. Wrote **1500-words** for earlier part of the story, read the St. Louis Sporting News; wrote 1200 more preparatory words till dawn. I'm going like a machine, my "steam's up in the boilers," roaring thunderously —

TUESDAY MARCH 16 — Wrote letter,† went to a movie, then wrote at night, **4000-words,** marvellous words about the river back home for an early chapter in Town and City, which should tie that part and just deliver it prepaid. That's 13,000 words in the past five days, since my birthday, a tremendous speed I've never equalled. Is it my old man

---

*The war news would have concerned Soviet attempts to control Berlin in what would later be deemed "the Berlin crisis."

**John Huston's *The Treasure of the Sierra Madre* (1948) starred Humphrey Bogart in the story of three men on a treasure hunt in Mexico. It won Academy Awards for best director, screenplay, and supporting actor for Walter Huston — the director's father.

†Kerouac wrote a letter to Nin and Paul thanking them for the trousers they sent him for his birthday and inquiring about their new house in Rocky Mount, North Carolina. He also touched on the possibility of war, repeating his "printing presses" quip from his March 12 journal entry.

'hollering at me from the foot of the stairs' as I get older? Well, with another war coming, possibly, there's no need to dwell on my pitiable conflicts, just work. How I talk big *now* — just wait a few days ...

WEDNESDAY MARCH 17 — Wrote about a thousand pertaining words which aren't quite ready for typing. Deliberately resting again, which may be a bad habit. But, on the other hand, I seem to have no interest in writing the City Episode and it's too bad I committed my plot to such things. *There's so much else* I feel like writing. My "City" experiences are hateful.

THURSDAY MARCH 18 — Rested, just reading and sleeping.

FRIDAY MARCH 19 — Movie in evening. Last night I also read my old diaries and their day-by-day records of triumph (with figures and batting averages) and defeat: but the defeat always scornfully passed over. This is the spirit to which I feel myself returning. No more complex masochism for me. Also read a baseball novelette I wrote at seventeen with its erring but indestructible hero ending up a game with an impossible triple play, knocking himself out, winning the pennant single-handed, (driving in the winning runs and beating up the big villain in the course of it all!) I think that was going a little *too* far, unless my sense of values has deteriorated.* But in all seriousness, heroism is still my goal, and I don't care how childish *that* may be, it's it.

SATURDAY MARCH 20 — Went out to N.Y. Came back.

SUNDAY MAR. 21 — Ate and read and thought too much. Wrote **3000-words** till dawn next day. Am a little depressed from drinking-hangover, but depression cannot affect my writing any more, which is a step forward in the discipline of literary work.

*A reference to *Raw Rookie Nerves,* Kerouac's short baseball novel that ends with rookie Freddy Burns turning a triple play that sends his Blue Sox to the World Series. An excerpt of it is published in *Atop an Underwood: Early Stories and Other Writings.*

MONDAY MAR. 22 — Wrote a little — the City Episode has been busted down at last and hogtied for fair. Its climaxes aren't bad at all. Some people will like it better than the rest of the book, even. Today I also decided not to *get drunk* anymore, at least not the way I usually do. It's funny I never thought of this before. I started drinking at eighteen but that's after eight years of occasional boozing, I can't physically take it any more, nor *mentally*. It was at the age of eighteen, too, when melancholy and indecision first came over me — there's a fair connection there. Hangovers knock me off what I could call my *character-stride*. It's the easiest thing in the world for me to fall apart mentally and spiritually when drunk. Thus, no more — it'll take time to stick to it, though, but I shall do so. I seem to have a poor constitution for drinking — and a poorer one for idiocy and incoherence.

TUESDAY MAR. 23 — Completed and wrote **2500-words** today. That's 23,000 for the month. That's some 320,000-words for the entire novel so far, and some 40,000 to go for FINIS. Now if I can only get a dime for each one of those words I'll buy a farm in Colorado and write another book. Or maybe even a *penny* for each word, which is unfortunately more likely. That would mean more years in Ozone Park writing, unless we moved and I got some job to keep up expenses. But a farm is my idea of working for a living, above all things.

WEDNESDAY MAR. 24 — Hal Chase came over to see about the proposed trip to New Hampshire in his car — four of us, including my mother and Ginger. This will take off another week from my schedule, but it would be a nice trip too. Hal and I had a tremendous conversation lasting till dawn. He casually comes up with tremendous ideas sometimes — 'The Orgone theory is a theory of sex-guilt' for instance(!) (That's to say — the *psychology* of the theory itself.)*

---

*Wilhelm Reich's orgone theory purports that all organic material contains a universal life force that can be captured and used to restore psychological well-being to humans.

THURSDAY MAR. 25 — Mom, Hal and I decided to go on a trip to Lowell tomorrow, in Hal's cousin's Buick.

FRIDAY MAR. 26 — And it turned out to be a great thing. One of the real events of my life. Too

MONDAY MAR. 29 — long to explain here. Suffice it to say that 'my premonitions of life were not illusionary,' or something like that. That *clearness* still growing, and part of it all. Tonight I wrote some **3500 words** in a campaign to knock off and finish the novel in April. So many other things are opening up, and as far as writing is concerned so many other kinds of writing. Action is returning to my life, at last, really.

TUESDAY MAR. 30 — Strange joyful meditative day.

WEDNESDAY MARCH 31 — Got out a new passel of books from the library including an agriculture book, but I must write hard and read only when I can. My life's at stake in the novel, or at least, other than that, I'll have to admit that I failed writing it, and I saw that this is not true. It's a matter of work and horse-sense from now on in. I think I see my work for what it is now. My new ambitions, growing clearer, depend on some success in writing — otherwise, they're far off beyond the frustration of literary defeat. All vague, vague, but I'll conclude this notebook just for recording little things, and cover the *change*, or absorb it, elsewhere. Concluding with just a log of writing: Wrote **3500-words** again completing the City Episode dramatically. That's 30,000 wds. for March.

APRIL — SEA ROTTED RAINS OF APRIL -

THURSDAY APRIL 1 — Went out to N.Y. and came back at night, wrote notes. Thought: — you can't be fair in life and strong at the same time: you can't be weak without being useless to others. This is the enigma I'm trying to dramatize in one level of Town & City. Also — when I make judgments I cease to learn, but I never must cease to learn, I never can live if I don't make judgments. Wrote some ... finishing the novel this month, 'putting the cover on it.'

FRIDAY APRIL 2 — Best way to ease eye-strain while working like this is to apply a cold towel to eyes and brow for several minutes. This has cured my watering eyes, — and this is my *surefire* contribution to medical science. (?) Started on Francis N.Y. episode.

SATURDAY APRIL 3 — Went into town, saw Beverly B of Colorado, and some old football teammates.

SUNDAY APRIL 4 — Drove around with Hal and Ginger, sans sleep. Wrote notes on the 'mortification of self; of tortured sensibility, the sense of rudeness' — summed up in the expression: 'Excuse me for living.' *There's* a human enigma!

MONDAY APRIL 5 — Time to put the cover on the novel. Ate big breakfast, studied Herald-Tribune commercial page (planes for Port Said, ships from Bremen, buyers from St. Paul, board-of-directors names, moving-and-the-shining-city of this world's economy — good reading.) Wrote in afternoon. Saw Hal at night, who read parts of novel & discussed it, and likes it.

TUESDAY APRIL 6 — Hal and I conversed all day again, a conversation lasting two days now ... I imagine Dr. Johnson would have done this if he had the time. We veered from the 'abyss' to Goethe to volcanoes to the West to this and that and anything you can name. His conclusion: men come up to the stream of destiny and cannot do otherwise but try to cross it, and since destiny is a Missouri of a stream, like Ahab, Goethe, Wolfe, Old Bill Williams and who-all they all perish — unless they turn back, in which case they die a little later anyhow.

THURSDAY APRIL 8 — Went to Tom Livornese's. This month so far a poor work month.

APRIL 9 — Came back from Tom's — completed **5000 words**. Novel only 20,000 words from completion. My boyhood motto was 'Slow but Sure.' Nearer and nearer. *Just think!*

SATURDAY APRIL 10 — Also walked 5 miles yestiddy. Today: worried about my financial future, thus obliterating the joy of work-almost-completed. I decided to take my novel to Mark Van Doren when it's finished. He remembers my telling him about it 2 years ago (2½ years ago really.) Otherwise a lot of professional people would read it with a jaundiced eye knowing that I am *unpublished,* and it would take years to have it accepted for publication. Moreover Van Doren is my kind of man: humility without pretension, a poet, a 'dreamer,' and a moral guy. The third week of May I should be presenting him with the 380,000-word monstrosity. Tonight: wrote a few hundred words.

SUNDAY APRIL 11 — Slept a lot, walked 3 miles. Wrote up **3000-words** more. Working till *long after dawn* these past weeks, and also sleeping in short fitful bursts.

MONDAY APRIL 12 — But when it comes time to write about the funeral I'll have to rouse all my lyrical and comprehensive muscles.* I think I'll be ready for that last big chapter, in ten days or so. Yesterday I looked through my "1945" notebooks and I never did see a man *suffer* so at 23. What was that all about — or am I falling asleep nowadays? Nah — just extending into something vaster. I want to be a significant writer and I also want to live in a vast and significant way, like Twain almost. That's my present feeling, no Faustian torments that swirl futile and self-destructive around oneself, but a life that reaches out to others like two arms. I wonder if I've discovered seren-

*Kerouac is referring to the earnest telling of George Martin's funeral near the conclusion of *The Town and the City.*

ity at 26? — it sure seems like it. (At 23 I would have said "*It surely seems so.*") There are hints here, and elsewhere, of growth — but growth is never interesting in itself without sympathy somewhere in it. A man's life's got to be just so at every stage that he could not afford to die, and if he did people would miss *more* than just himself. It's vain to say this but self-knowledge *is* vanity. Besides, I'm insane every other day. Let's spread out into the world, etc., etc. All this is to fill the notebook with signs of life whereas actually all the life I've got these days, *all* of it, is pouring into those last chapters every drop. And, big discovery, here and now! — I can no longer write or talk about myself without embarrassment, whereas before it was my meat-pie allright. "Leave me alone," I just said to myself, so let's cut it out and work. Tonight: concluded Francis chapter, which gave me a sense of relief. Plotted Joe chapter, death-chapter, funeral-chapter, and aftermath-chapter — which is *remainder* of the book. Will I *ever* make it? — (at least by first week of May?) —

TUESDAY APRIL 13 — Couldn't sleep till TWO O'CLOCK in the *AFTERNOON* — which shows how upturned I am now, and also how insane, inasmuch as I read till eleven for "relaxation." Slept till 9 o'clock at night. Wrote 1500-words till 4, and retired.

THURS. APRIL 15 — Got up at 6:30 A.M., ate big breakfast — unaccountably popping into a farmer's hours, but it won't last. The picture "Duel in the Sun"* reminds me that I wanted to live unrestrictedly once, that is, live, love, loaf, steal, etc., etc. There's a very *thin* line between all my "concepts." Also, reading about the murderous Murel of 1825 Mississippi fame† I wonder at the *thinner* line among certain other men's 'concepts' — I tremble — and something. God's one

Duel in the Sun (1946), a big David O. Selznick–produced melodrama starring Gregory Peck, Lionel Barrymore, and Jennifer Jones.
†John Murel, legendary murderer and bandit of the Mississippi River. A chapter of Mark Twain's *Life on the Mississippi* is devoted to his story.

time supreme authority over the soul was very necessary once, when men had to struggle to be good. Yet there's neurosis in slothful murderousness; and our present civilization makes it easier to be "good," makes it "pay off" — otherwise? And myself? Myself later at some future cataclysmic time and circumstance? What I want to straighten out is an *organic morality,* or that is, a real manly gentleness, a manly calm among dangers that might bring out the paranoiac cougar in us otherwise. Things like that ... unclear. Tonight I wrote **2000-words,** but the nearer I get to the end the more I fret and worry, I don't know why.

FRIDAY APRIL 16 — Corrupt soul that I have to realize how very corrupt other souls are!!!!! — I've actually lost track for the moment of my word-count, which is a strange lapse of memory for me.

SATURDAY APRIL 17 — Went to N.Y., argued with a girl all night. Also, Ginsberg went mad and begged me to hit him — which spells the end as far as I'm concerned, since it's hard enough to keep sane without visiting the asylum every week. He wanted to know "what else" I had to do in the world that didn't include him, most particularly his concepts (might say) — and when he failed to understand what I half-heartedly tried to explain to him, he asked me to beat him up. I never was so horrified, mortified, and disgusted, not smugly disgusted but just riven by the spectacle of his mad meaningless eyes staring at me in a mockery of human sensibility. He claimed that I was turning away from the truth when I started to leave. I told him I *did* have an unconscious desire to hit him but *he* would be glad later on that I did not. It seems to me I did the most truthful thing there — but at the moment the experience seems so insane, unnecessary, foolish, and pallidly Demonic that I can't think of what to say. I'm through with all that foolishness, and have been for a long time since the days I burned my hands with Celine and fought with Edie and climbed trees with Lucien [Carr], but these Ginsbergs, just coming of daemonic age, assume that no one else has seen their visions of cataclysmic emotion 90% false and 10% childish, and try to foist them on others. I don't want to withdraw from people whom I liked and admired once because of their talent and imagination and charm — and that includes the whole "circle" of the N.Y. "episode" — but if I can't be the way I *want* to be with them, that is friendly, absorbed, occasionally sympathetic and a whole host of other things describing what I *know* to be human fellowship, then there's nothing for me to do but go my own way now into a new phase of life, adult life, or at least, life with good intentions and measures of sincerity and earnest attempts. And I'm tired of satirizing unimportant neurotics anyway, which is all that's left of my relations with them. I go to see them in a happy, fond frame of mind and always come away baffled and disgusted. *This does not happen among my other friends,* therefore I should heed my feelings in these matters and stick to birds of my own feather. "No more hurrahs for breadth." I'm tired of investigating everything and being a 'Faustian' fool seeking out 'all knowledge.' It's plain that it can't be done and should not be done, even by a writer, much less by a writer who must seek to order his own thoughts and work them down to an operational fecundity of sorts. Words, words — and why apologize because I can no longer *agree with everybody* as I tried to do out of insane inhuman pride in my own "universal sympathy." — Such things are for idiots, hypocrites, and mad charlatans of the soul. I will recognize that I'm human and must limit my sympathies, my *active* sympathies, to the life I have and will have, and that any other course is not true. I have been a fool and a liar and a shifty weakling by pretending that I was the friend of these people — Ginsberg, Joan, Carr, Burroughs, [David] Kammerer even, some others — when all the time I must have known that we all naturally disliked each other and were just grimacing incessantly in a comedy of malice. I was the most furtive of the lot, I told myself: "It's allright, you're *learning* a lot." All I learned is that a man must recognize his limits or never be true. Fear of revealing my own intense judgments prevented me from distinguishing between friend and foe. It was as bad, in a lesser way, as the plainsman who tries to convince himself that the drunken Comanche will have as much in common with him as another plainsman. Until the cross-currents of the world become more harmonious, a man is an idiot to 'love all,' he invites his own beautiful but extinguishing doom.

Because I want to live, and work, and raise a family.

SUNDAY APRIL 18 — Rested up for what I hope to be a big week.

MONDAY APRIL 19 — But like the drunken Comanche, I'm glad I know them.

TUESDAY 20 — **1000-words**, slow worrisome going — daytime work now.

WEDNESDAY 21 — Wrote **1500-words**, still crawling painfully —

THURSDAY 22 — Another crawling miserable **1500-words**, **12** hours of it.

FRIDAY 23 — Wrote **2000-words**, concluding things — FEEL GREAT!

SATURDAY 24 — On to final conclusions: (interrupted by friends in N.Y.)

SUNDAY 25 — Talked with H. Huescher for 7 hours straight: came back.

Because I want to live, and work, and raise a family.

SUNDAY APRIL 18 — Rested up for what I hope to be a big week.

MONDAY APRIL 19 — But like the drunken Commanche, I'm glad I know them.

TUESDAY 20 — 1000-words, slow worrisome going — daytime work now.

WEDNESDAY 21 — Wrote 1500-words, still crawling painfully...

THURSDAY 22 — Another crawling miserable 1500-words, 12 hours of it.

FRIDAY 23 — Wrote 2000-words, concluding things — FEEL GREAT!

SATURDAY 24 — On to final conclusions: (interrupted by friends in N.Y.)

SUNDAY 25 — Talked with H. Kuescher for 7 hours straight: came back.

MONDAY 26 — Wrote 1500-good words today, moving along laboriously.

TUESDAY 27 — Good day — 2000-words — lucky creative splurges...

WEDNESDAY 28 — Another big, good day — wrote big letter, and 2000-wds.

THURSDAY 29 — Start 'funeral' — plotting it, — last big chapter. Resting.

FRIDAY 30 — Went out gathering rosebuds, etc. 23,000 for April.

SATURDAY MAY 1 — Physically depressed; also glad that my work
   is just about done on Town & City at last.

SUNDAY MAY 2 — At my mother's prodding, decided to
   show publishers a 150,000-word selection from the
   manuscript. Started preparing it, typing parts,
   writing explanatory interims, revising here and there.

MONDAY MAY 3 — Big day's work preparing 'comprehensive
   selection.' — comprehensive is no understatement, the
   'selection' itself is longer than most novels. Worked
   like a beaver. Time to come out of the warm sweet
   shell of creation, into the dusty market square, and
   prove myself, my work, in the world of men. This
   is changing my whole mood of 2½ years' duration,
   the lonely creative mood. More later.

TUESDAY MAY 4 — Took in the 'selection', the heart and
   guts of 'Town & City', to Scribner's.

   (Diary continued in 'Forest of Arden' notebook.)

   And this is the way a novel gets written,
   in ignorance, fear, sorrow, madness, and
   a kind of psychotic happiness that serves
   as an incubator for the wonders being born.

MONDAY 26 — Wrote **1500-*good words*** today, moving along laboriously.

TUESDAY 27 — Good day — **2000-words** — lucky creative splurges ...

WEDNESDAY 28 — Another big, good day — wrote big letter, and **2000-wds.**

THURSDAY 29 — Start 'funeral' — plotting it, — last big chapter. Resting.

FRIDAY 30 — Went out gathering rosebuds, etc. 23,000 for April.

SATURDAY MAY 1 — Physically depressed: also glad that my work is just about done on Town & City at last.

SUNDAY MAY 2 — At my mother's prodding, decided to show publishers a 150,000-word selection from the manuscript. Started preparing it, typing parts, writing explanatory interims, revising here and there.

MONDAY MAY 3 — Big day's work preparing 'comprehensive selection.' — comprehensive is no understatement, the 'selection' itself is longer than most novels. Worked like a beaver. Time to come out of the warm sweet shell of creation, into the dusty market square, and prove myself, my work, in the world of men. This is changing my whole mood of 2½ years' duration, the lonely creative mood. More later.

TUESDAY MAY 4 — *Took in the 'selection,' the heart and guts of 'Town & City,' to Scribner's.**

---

*Kerouac was attempting to get an excerpt of *The Town and the City* published in *Scribner's Magazine*.

And this is the way a novel gets written, in ignorance, fear, sorrow, madness, and a kind of psychotic happiness that serves as an incubator for the wonders being born.

MAY 1948

WEDNESDAY MAY 5 — Took in 'T & C' and at night got drunk (slightly) with Hal and Fitz — Fitz just became a father and handed out cigars at my prompting. What did we do? — we lined out rows of empty bottles and forgot temporarily our immediate life — plans and struggling endeavors. Hal and Fitz are having 'women-troubles,' or at least, Hal is, and Fitz is a new father. My troubles seem so imaginary and mad, somehow. Later tonight, feeling depressed and very *alone*, I had one of my attacks of fear-of-madness. If the novel is rejected by everybody and judged inferior, muddy, unimportant, a waste of time, the lamentations and incantations of a curiously lonely man — what will that mean to me, what won't it say to me about myself. That I've been silly.

THURSDAY MAY 6 — But today I feel peaceable enough to assume that T & C will be respected by people and readers, and if so, I'll make a further step towards straightening out my life in the world. The past week I've been *blinded* on the subject of cattle raising in Colorado or Arizona. I don't know a thing about it, I'm reading up and asking everywhere. It seems plausible in reality — in myself, wonderful and necessary. With Mike or Paul as partners it could be done, and should be done. I've got to create a home, I need a home, a *homestead,* a base, a place to marry and raise children, a place to work for myself, for a living, for the others. Writing should only be a secondary struggle, otherwise I'll never get along with others lost in those stormy unimaginable seas, alone, peculiarly un-human, necessarily mad and unreachable.

And now, meanwhile, to get back to the work at hand, composing the last 10,000-words of Town & City and typing the manuscript (which, so glad to say, is *carefully* written once and for all and needs no extensive revision, to my judgement.) It's good to feel that I've been a thorough, careful workman and didn't botch up the many scenes I attempted. It's a feeling of natural, organic adequacy, and the hint that I could transfer that to my botched-up life. My life is botched-up because, at 26, I've yet to earn a steady income, I've yet to really *help* anyone in the world, including really taking care of myself, and I've yet to love a woman with any consistency of purpose. Ah I feel strange these days ... As I say, out of the cocoon of lonely creative story-writing, and into the world, the dusty market square, noon, men and women, things — out of that peopled, fabulous moor of myself which is so interesting, *too interesting* for real earthly happiness. When I learn that both are necessary and real to me, when I learn to *feel* that, then I can write again, better than ever, with more knowledge than fury. It occurred to me today too that companionship is the final high value of art — I'm going to work on that. It's the one great thing about Wolfe that makes me love him and hope in him, whereas, as Hal Chase said, 'Dostoevsky leaves me cold and alone and frightened.' Let the litterateurs who live secure comfortable steam-heated city lives on peaceful campuses step forth and announce that Nature, like Dostoevsky, leaves one 'cold and alone and frightened' — I think companionship in the raw catastrophic world is its one 'best, last hope of earth.'* Was Lincoln thinking of the democratic neighborliness of Illinois farmers when he phrased those words? And do the litterateurs, in comfort and ivory-tower security among shelves of books, feel the harshness of that Illinois earth of 1830 when they *read* about it? Do they feel it even today

*From President Abraham Lincoln's annual address to Congress, December 1, 1862: "In giving freedom to the slave, we assure freedom to the free — honorable alike in what we give, and what we preserve. We shall nobly save, or meanly lose, the last best hope of earth."

when they drive across on good roads, in good cars? Let Nature do the freezing and frightening and isolating in this world, let men work and love and fight it off. Let men have a sense of themselves that illuminates their hearts and minds with the beauty of cooperation, neighborliness, companionship. Let the revolutionaries fight with themselves in cities. I don't know, but it seems to me that these ideas, old-fashioned and cliché as they are, are actually, today, this 'modern' day, the fancy damned *zeitgeist* itself.

But, to get back to work. Today I started writing but was a little sick, in the stomach, walked three miles, came back, wrote a paragraph. The sequence of the funeral scene needs outlining, and the humility of writing-life had escaped me in the past nine days of idleness.

FRIDAY MAY 7 — Wrote a sequence of the chapter. This is the last 200-feet to the summit of an unclimbable Everest and I start it gloating, a little afraid, almost helpless. Something about the suspense of the final act, the chagrin of finality and irredeemable loss of expectation. What funny things a man discovers about himself when he writes. Writing is an explosion of interest, it is not something that gets done one by one gravely, and the explosions of interest arrest themselves with a crafty expectant *grin*. All that. Wrote several hundred words slowly, very slowly.

SATURDAY MAY 8 — Wrote with the old vigour, after a shaky musing start, and the count is **2500-words.** Somehow I'm lonesome for the days last December, November, when I was faced with a huge task and writing 'in the middle of it.' Now I'm at the end and feeling more inadequate. It seems that, like a middleaged married man, I have to keep proving my virility to myself, by writing, etc.

SUNDAY MAY 9 — Another **1500-words** tonight, getting the funeral chapter half-finished at least. The last few thousand words are so *formal* I can't get them done, formal because they seem like decorative festoons appended to the statue, like the mummeries of ceremony. But actually they are necessary to the story, completing all the warps and woofs and tying them. Blah blah blah. To get back to the facts, what's what, that is, the facts of my deepest feelings these days: — and yet they are a *something* I can't describe. The words of Jesus impressed me — "Take therefore no thought for the morrow: for the morrow shall take thought for the things of itself. Sufficient unto the day is the evil thereof."* Yes, already worrying about the problems of my next steps ... before their time and forsaking the joys of present fruition, as well as the difficulties thereof.

MONDAY MAY 10 — Today felt like a lucky day, I received my [G.I. Bill] bonus check. I said to myself, "What next?" Wrote **1000-words** more on chapter, good definitive ones. The remainder hangs over my happy conscience. Things are swinging in me ...

TUESDAY MAY 11 — Met Beverly Anne Gordon, accidentally. I saw her, proud, poised, dark, *serious,* lovely — and I made a decision, to follow her to look for the *one* in a million. So I followed her and watched her rollerskating in the rink. Then I came up to her and told her many things. I half-learned to rollerskate, meanwhile. It was a soft exfoliate Spring night, and I had made one of the great decisions of my life, like a veritable Stendhal, in full knowledge and awareness. She has all the amazing qualities of womanhood: a low voice, a statuesque figure, dark midnight eyes, moonlight skin — and youth, the grace of a little girl. And *consciousness.* And *sadness.* And *simplicity.* And finally, the one woman in whose eyes I see humility, not vanity. A proud and secret darkness surrounds her; just right for Colorado; just ripe for six babies. Again, as at sixteen, I am a swain to the witchery of a dark-eyed vivacious brunette. I fell down rollerskating and so help me I was too pleased and absorbed to feel embarrassed. If I had enough money from my Town & City right now, there's no telling what I'd do tomorrow, and where I'd be next week. A strange thing ... on the night of Vic-

*Matthew 6:34.

tory in Europe, V-E day in 1945, she wrote a little poem about God, thanking Him because the war was won — and I ... I wrote a paragraph about the man with the red lining in his cloak. She was fifteen that night, and I was twenty-three. Just think of it! It's as though I'd been saved?

WEDNESDAY MAY 12 — Her birthday today. Took her to a smorgasbord restaurant (Stockholm by name, on 51st St.) — bought her a gardenia — ran out of money — rushed to United Press, borrowed more from Tony Monacchio who was sitting in a corner typing out baseball scores and swearing because the rain wasn't postponing *all* baseball games forever — rushed back to Beverly, whom an affectionate bartender dubbed "little rascal." Such a child with a woman's body! I really don't know what to think, but I'm sure thinking ... No writing.

THURSDAY MAY 13 — Today I heard from another wonderful girl, Peggy Grasse, and I'll see her soon. She's perhaps more beautiful, older (22), graver, more eloquent, and perhaps more *exacting*, I don't know. Meanwhile let's just put it this way: I've got Beverly on the brain, and Peggy too perhaps, and a novel to *finish*. So, until Sunday, I must work, brushing all other consideration and excitements aside. *Now* I see how I got Town & City written, by imprisoning myself in mortal loneliness beautiful and fruitful. Will I always have to do that to write a novel? — and for three-yeared stretches? I should smile I won't! — There's a way of doing everything, whether it's scoring a touchdown, or writing a novel, or living and writing at the same time. Today: — wrote **1000-words**, painful and laborious, painfully *personal* words about the atrocious folly of an idiot, Peter Martin. My next novel will be riper yet. I quit at 4 A.M. exhausted.

FRIDAY MAY 14 — Went to town to pay a debt, and spent some time in the library reading up on Colorado and ranching. But I was feeling strangely sad, as though I were going to lose something soon, myself, or little Beverly. I can't tell how I really feel, or whether I'm in love with love, or what — but she pleases me in so many ways that other girls don't. Is it irresponsible to let things drift until I fall for her irre-deemably? Or perhaps, is it irresponsible to assume that I could make or break our relationship when it should be something working on both sides. In a nutshell, though, I think my sudden love for this girl is a truer expression of myself than anything since my boy's love for Mary Carney in 1939, I think it is *real,* and that my doubts are *recent* and *borrowed* cognitions, or notions, or whatever. If this is a rationali-zation, like a novel, of myself, very well then, it is a rationalization ... but I still feel those tremendous longings for *her* so long dormant in my spirit. All this pitter-patter is due to the fact that someone said she was not 'intelligent' enough to be a companion to my particular con-cerns in the world, and yet when I look up from these wretched con-cerns should I gaze into the cold eyes of an 'intellectual' woman or into the warm eyes of a young love? — a young wife, perhaps? A lot hinges on the reception to my work on Town & City — a lot — in a practical sense. Tonight: — wrote several hundred excellent words.

SATURDAY MAY 15 — Went into town to a party, saw Beverly again — saw Lucien off on a plane in the morning — went to a Yankee-Athletics game with Tony, rained out — came home. This is a sparse summary of the weekend, another one of the strangest in my life. It always seems as though I learn the most on weekends ... and no one has con-sciously realized the tremendous significance of American weekends, from proud sartorial Saturday night with its millions of premonitions of triumph and happiness, to dark Sunday night with its sweet and ter-rified loneliness (in that I see a focus of my 'artistic' vision of life.) To begin in detail about this weekend: each writer has his dream, of course each man has his dream, and my dream, compounded of so many things, of glee and infolding darkness and joy, of sweet compan-ionship under the eaves of home, of sad humility and gravity, of some-thing like little children, home, wonder, sweetness, simplicity, solace in the raw world, of sorrowful contemplation of the chronicle of lives, *human* people, loving, trusting people, a million things, all of them somehow *dark* in that they do not glitter — a dream, too, of a classless society undivided by pomps and worldly vanities and envies — a dream not of perfection in the world but of simple trust, simple desire for happiness and fruition, simple and sincere struggle, and Godliness of intention — something sweet, dark, and how many words do I have to mass to explain it! — well, this, my dream, was shaken this weekend by Beverly. She apparently does not 'trust' me because I 'have no job' — she can't understand who and what I am — and I, believing in a classless society so necessarily, find us divided by class-opinions, or class-cognitions, or whatever it is. There is very little I can talk to her about, there is very little she can tell me that can waken anything in me. We are separated by 'education' and 'class' and these are the very things that are, to me, the enigmatical root of all evil somehow. These are the things, the *divisive* things of the world, that cause so much misunderstanding and cross-currents among a whole world of people who might otherwise get along, as Jesus would have them, sweetly, simply, trustingly. In my dream of eaves and glee and the simple purposeful life I fitted Beverly, because she had all the qualities. Yet, where I might have rejected her on *one count* — the fact that she could not communicate with my more complex concerns (such as these, you see, and they are not so complex) — instead, believing in my dream, I accepted her and wanted her for those earthly qualities that would supplement my *classier* foibles, my writing, my mournful knowledge, my lethargy of contemplation and sympathy — where I might have rejected her, instead *she* rejected me because I apparently was not of her earth. And this is something I refuse to believe, with *moral* terror — this is the divisive unnecessary madness of people again.

It's *her* madness now, not mine, because she fails to notice that I am of her earth as well as of my world — Good God everybody is! Why all those *distinctions*? Why the fear and mistrust? If, on the other hand, she rejected me believing I would not make 'good husband material' due to congenital penury — as exhibited in my dates with her — if she *is* a gold digger, of course then it doesn't matter. But I've no proof she's a gold-digger at all, although I wish I could find out somehow. My dream is shaken — I myself am shaken — I wish everybody on earth would stop looking askance at one another because of some slight infinitesimal difference under the huge universal sky. It's as absurd as the hard-on of a flea, taken all around. Am I as guilty as she in making distinctions and decisions? I picked her out, after all, 'out of millions' — that was my 'idea.' *I* made the first distinction. But now I've lost track of my point if there is any. Suffice it — that I have a dream, an ideal of life more important to me than crass casuality and 'reality,' and that it was shaken because an abyss yawned open in the middle of it. I had a dream of the simple life, I picked a simple girl, and she turns around and wonders if I'm not some kind of drifting tramp because I don't 'have a job,' I *don't work*(!) and so on, because I speak of a farm or ranch. In other words, perhaps, I told her all about myself and she was flabbergasted by the contradictions that to her can never be *put to work*. Ah, I don't know. Here's the crux: — must I in the name of God marry an intellectual girl to be understood and loved? So this is another enigma — to be illuminated further.

After that, seeing Lucien off on his vacation. He was suffering from a catastrophic hangover — there he was, his eyes glued together, shuffling along, in brown-&-white saddle shoes, like some wealthy dissipate in Scott Fitzgerald, mumbling — "Everybody in the world is beautiful and sweet but dumb"* after Tony had given him that description of my particular Beverly. I was amazed by that statement coming from him, in *him* it was a vision, so true. Somehow I got something out of it, I don't remember what, it was a vision of my own I suppose. He went off, as he said, "in the airplane machine," and that was that — and *what* was that. Lucien had 'given up,' it seemed oddly to me, 'he didn't care any more anyway.' My serious dream had to hang together no less. His humble dream of things was truer; my vain and nervous and moralizing dream was more necessary to me, to the 'world', maybe to him. See? — somehow true also. Then I went to the meeting with Beverly, she stood me up, didn't appear, and *that* was

---

*Kerouac was so enamored with Carr's comment that he related it to Allen Ginsberg in a letter and then in his manuscript of *The Town and the City*.

that. But I mustn't quit that dream. Then I went to the ball game with Tony, exhilarated (because I am mad about big league baseball), and God stamped and rained us out. I was defeated and exhausted, all in the mind of course, but in that mind that looks at the world unceasingly and troubles itself unceasingly. Then Tony, who is an epileptic, seemed to have a strange seizure or something — he insisted at least *two hundred actual times* that I go to eat at his sister's house and I had to explain I wanted to go home, *two-hundred-times*. He slumped in the seat, his eyes blazing, poking me and punching me unceasingly, yelling at me. That too was sad and it was 'beautiful and sweet but dumb.' — all of us, all of us. These are Sunday-night thoughts, you can bet your hat on that, and like all true Sunday-night thoughts they are lonely, irrational, confused, beautiful and dark. I only wish that I could find some way of living without dying — but there, again, is my 'education' coming through, my fine poetic perceptions, my Sunday-night sweetmadness. Incidentally, another vision of art: — in the same old world, and words: — art is a HOLIDAY OF DREAMS AND THEMES. Enough, I had a lot to write in this night's pages and I forgot all but the phrases, thought out while working in the Sunday-night-rain. Another phrase — it is a solace in the raw world, a sympathy, that's another *vertu* of art, but I believe I said that the other day, yet, you see, I keep saying it because it *is* a solace to say it and repeat it, so it must be 'awfully true.' Besides, this sadness is soothing, and I am alone, and I lost my love, the brief season is ended. I've got to find that wife, that 'one among millions' — I've just got to. Moreover, having been married once, I suffer from what I'm missing — drowsy sweet-smelling wife in the dumpy sheets at dawn.* And her eyes looking at me. And her hand in mine as I march on bravely into more confusion and sadness and perplexity — that is, as I march on bravely into 'life,' the road that's no bed of thorns or whatever they say (and of course *I*

*Kerouac was briefly married to Edie Parker in 1944. He agreed to marry her in exchange for bail money — he had been detained for questioning in regard to the Lucien Carr–David Kammerer incident.

know what they say.) Goodnight, sweet farewell, goodbye — no loneliness hath man like sweet love softly denied.

MONDAY MAY 17 — Getting underway to finish what I should have finished two weeks ago. No time to lose — by the end of July, I've got to have the whole novel typed so I can go to Colorado and work on a ranch, without leaving any loose ends behind in the East. Tonight: — wrote **2500-words** — mad, good ones, the 'parable of the fish' in the funeral chapter. Somehow, after I wrote the last line of that strange conversation between the three Martin bros. Joe, Francis, and Peter, something *loosened* in me and I became almost radiantly happy. I can't understand it, all kinds of theories could suffice: — say, for instance, that I had reconciled the three warring conflicts in my consciousness, through writing about a kindly rapport among the three brothers who are 'fictional' projections of myself as *seen* by myself. This seems altogether too pat, altho, miraculously, it might be true, which would be amazing. Can't be that it is really, worldly true about the purging, healing effect of 'art' on a serious, comprehensive, even if awkward artist, that he heals himself by working out his inner fights through the labors of his imagination, and so on? I had that moment of joy that was like Dostoevsky's description of the moment before an epileptic fit. Everything was clear and I was *free.* "Now you can have fun," I thought. And I thought, "What the hell did I go and do to myself this time, how did I manage to bind myself up *again*?" More likely, I probably realized that I had really at last finished the novel; all the inner themes are finished for me, the last 4,000 words or so are for the sake of reader's comprehension. It was strange. I took a walk, full of exultance, gratitude, and fear of too-great joy. *Freedom* was the point. However, the previous joy of that has eluded me now (Tuesday), but the change is wrought, has come homing to me for good. At least, I hope so.

TUESDAY MAY 18 — Still waiting for word from Scribner's, it's been two weeks now, and I hope that's a good sign. But I'm still puzzled about last night's amazing, sudden, unaccountable, *unexpected* transformation, from 'silence and sorrow' to the old hungering joy again. Details: — it was no longer *a rigid necessity* any more to 'go away' — to hole up someday on a ranch — to be deliberately *poor* all my life — and I didn't assume any more that Beverly would have been *the* girl for me, I saw that she was, after all, unconversant with me, and would not have been a companion to me in any way — I saw, also, that I would always write, and write greater books, and travel, and 'have fun,' and find a good vivacious intelligent girl someday. These are the details. I guess it's just another case of a perplexed fellow coming to his senses out of some compulsive idea that nature, in its own wisdom, doesn't allow for long, in the interests of sanity. I was shaken up like a raffle-basket and the compulsion loosened, fell apart, and I was 'myself' again. I think! At least, it was interesting — and to be more serious and truthful, I'm very happy it happened. And now — *I'm proud of my life again, and I have faith in it, my life as a writer, telling eagerly, sincerely the million things I know* — my life exactly as I want it, to the devil with what that perplexing ambiguous enigma, 'the others,' think, whatever that is. I have no words to describe the power and the joy of this feeling. There is vast *faith* in it. 'I don't care that I *do* care!' is the odd, colloquial way I think of it. Every good idea and hope and desire I ever had still stands, but from now on, I am unalterably on a course of freedom, confidence, faithful knowledge in myself, and no more kow-towing to the expectations of a compromising world. It'll all be clearer later, I'll explain it. Tonight, wrote: **1500-words**, completing funeral.

WEDNESDAY MAY 19 — That's 10,000-words on the funeral, and now another 5,000-words on *apres-tous,* and the 1,000-page novel is completed — *at last,* after 2½ years. I started writing this story in March of 1946, and now, around May 24, 1948, it'll be all finished. So that's big work well done, and a lot of misery, and I'll just forget it and look ahead. Wrote letters in the afternoon.* At night I had the absolute

*In a letter to Ginsberg dated May 18 Kerouac sums up his short romance with Beverly and tells of Neal Cassady working the Southern Pacific Railroad.

fantods again. The novel is so full of clutter and junk in spots ... in long stretches, like a dump along the river. I got mad as hell thinking of it.

THURSDAY MAY 20 — No word from Scribner's. Their silence and businesslike judicious patience is driving me crazy with tension, worry, expectation, disappointment — everything. And the novel is yet unfinished, really, and the time has come to start typing it and straightening it out. What a job in this weary life of mine, this lazy life. But I'll get down to it. The news that Jesse James is still alive is very thrilling news to me,* and my mother too, but we've noticed that it doesn't seem to impress the New York world at all — which does bear out, in its own way, what I say about New York, that it is a haven for European culture and not American culture. I don't get *personally* mad at these things any more, because that is overdoing things in the name of culture and at the expense of general humanity, but still, I get personally mad at those who scoff at the significance of Jesse James, bandit or not, to the regular American with a sense of his nation's past. Now, if *Gambetta*† were still alive, I suppose that would be big news in New York — or some such European character of the 1880's. The amazing feeling of the American nineteenth century carrying over into the 1940's! — with its evocations of Mark Twain, Bill Hickock, old Abilene, Bill Cody, the James Boys, the Overland, the Pony Express, Melville, Walt Whitman ... and Sitting Bull.

FRIDAY MAY 21 — Scribner's informed me today that "considerations other than literary merit enter into the decision of a publisher." And there I was, for 2½ years, working so patiently to make my book a 'good' and meritorious book. I was plunged down, of course — blacker than ever — full of criminal impulses — and Francis-like in-

*When the real Jesse James died remains a matter of debate; some claim it was as early as 1882 in Saint Joseph, Missouri, but there are accounts of him dying in Guthrie, Oklahoma, in 1948 and in Granbury, Texas, in 1952.
†Leon Gambetta (1838–1882), French republican leader who became a prominent member of the provisional government after the Franco-Prussian War. He was briefly premier before his death.

tellectual bitterness. But I went to New York and thought about it in the streets.

SATURDAY MAY 22 — Then I was swept up in a huge social vortex. Ed White gave me loan of his suit (I had gone to N.Y. in my 'brooding' tramp-clothes, like) so I could fill in for him at a Junior Prom.* (Meanwhile I saw a ballgame, Giants–Cubs, at Polo Grounds with good Tony.) Here's an example: I borrowed a clean shirt from Ed to go to the Prom, leaving with him a dirty shirt, which was not mine, but Tony's, or that is, Lucien's shirt borrowed by Tony. My jackets are at Ed's, other accessories at Tony's, others at Tom's, etc., etc. Here's the picture: — young author, suicidal with sadness and failure, goes brooding in leather jacket. Few hours later: same young author (getting older all the time, though) is strolling in garden by moonlight with a gowned damsel with stars in her eyes, big Buick '48 convertible outside, $20 tab in nightclub, (Tom's money.) And so it goes ... Meanwhile, Connie Murphy's waiting for me [at] home, and I'm also supposed to be at a picnic, which I miss. So I didn't have much opportunity to pout, and now I realize this: — I had to *fight* to write Town and City, so I'll have to *fight* to sell it.

SUNDAY MAY 23 — Weekend concluded in a swirl of hiballs and jazz at Tom's Long Island home. Came home, decided how to start that fight. Think I'll try Mark Van Doren this week — but I must improve the ms. for him a little more, which means typing-work, as of this very moment.

MONDAY MAY 24 — In a furious siege of work today I typed out almost *19,000-words!* 15 hours work.

TUESDAY MAY 25 — Van Doren is gone for the summer, but Allen, who knows a lot about writing, and another guy, read part of my man-

*Kerouac took Maria Livornese (Tom's sixteen-year-old sister) to the Malverne High School Junior Prom; her original date — Ed White — had an impacted wisdom tooth.

uscript and were pretty struck by it, almost amazed. The guy said I should hand in my ms. neatly double-spaced and now I'm inclined to agree with that. Scribner's waded thru a messy lot of paper, mostly; and besides he said Scribner's is the hardest House to 'make.' So I'll type and revise the entire huge thing, starting now, and perhaps get an agent (he suggested a certain good agent;) Agents get to the *editors* themselves, not 'third-rate readers,' and so on — all of which is to convince myself that there is high hope, and that I must 'work on.' But after all this, if no one accepts that 'Town & City,' I'll go crazy in a certain stupid way, and who could blame me! We'll see, we'll see — Allen himself is convinced it will be a success, but he hasn't read the whole vast confusing sprawl of it yet. 'Literary merit' but perhaps no commercial value; yet, too, maybe enough commercial value to suit my needs. As trouble-burdened work, I'll *believe* again.

WEDNESDAY MAY 26 — Came home. Typed 4500 words or so. From now till end of June, typing, typing, revising, and typing. Tonight I had a feeling of good confidence again, *but that's only the fuel, not the destination.* What a mystic remark!?

THURSDAY MAY 27 — Went back to N.Y. to complete the season which ends now with school. Saw everybody, 'millions of people' — Ed, Hal, Ginger, Harold Huescher, Allen, Jack Fitzgerald, Jeanne, his son Mike, his sister (went to a christening there, was a Godfather) went to the Bowery — went to crazy Greenwich Village parties — saw Lucien, Barbara [Hale] — travelled up and down and over around and across Manhattan and Brooklyn in buses, trolleys, subways, cabs — wearing beat-out clothes, then sharp suits, in rain and sunshine, dawn and dusk — talked with a million people (more actual names: Alan Harrington, John Hornsby, Jim Fitzpatrick, Allen Hansen, Mary Pippin Crabtree, [Bill] Cannastra the fabulous mad star, etc.) Went to movies, walked, talked, slept (in Alpha Phi fraternity, where I met a thousand other names, Dean something, Sam White, etc., Whiz somebody, etc.) — I got sore at people, then I was consoled, felt guilty, or felt slighted, had visions, was bored, was riven with awful mortifications, was pleased ... and the whole point is that all that was done, over the space of four days, and drunk throughout, on two dollars which I started out with. Besides, that is, *moreover,* all I owe as I write this is *one dollar.* It never occurs to me what a true beggar and deadbeat I really am, or worse, how painlessly people spend money on me because I'm always thinking and talking about something else — never the point. I ate and drank like a Hollywood producer. In New York, a friendly man who can make his friendliness interesting by being *there,* somehow, can, that is, *could* live without working, and live exceedingly well. People are always having parties in N.Y. Somebody's always got money to pay the check in N.Y. Somebody's always lonely and always willing to do something. It frightens me that I could do this to the ends of my night ... dwindling down always, finally arriving at the Bowery, lasting awhile there, then dying in a doorway too ugly and too old and too mute to be of any use to the lonely generous people with open purses. I guess this is Joe Gould.*

MONDAY MAY 31 — Today, at home, all I know is that I'm afraid of myself ... for living on $2.00 so well for four days, and for all the praise I've been getting for my novel. I can't have a thought without the notion that it must be awfully *good,* because I, the object of their awe, thought the thing up. It's not *me* any more, but some mystical monster that I'm supposed to be. Fame will be like this. The time will come when I'll have to hide in my true dreams and stay there wrapped in humility and glee. Yet all this sounds as though I were saying, "You can't beat sincerity." — but I mean it. The fear of virtue. This, stemming from the masochism of modern vice, modern viciousness really. And I too am modern, naturally, I hate to admit it — I hate to admit that knowledge to me is evil, too. It should be — 'knowing the true

*Joe Gould was a New York City bohemian of the 1940s who achieved minor celebrity after Joseph Mitchell wrote a profile of him for the *New Yorker.* Mitchell eventually wrote an entire book on Gould, *Joe Gould's Secret* (1965). He collected his lifework, "The Oral History of Our Time," in marbled composition books.

purpose of knowledge, peace and joy.' Yet, of course, if I did not become famous, and was pronounced a fool, I would not be unhappier than I am now. Incidentally, there's always the danger of talking and talking meaninglessly, like we do over drinks, forgotten the next day. There's a purpose to knowledge ... salvation. What good are my visions or your visions, beautifully and laboriously worked out in art, if the purpose of it is not to save the something in our souls and make it all beautiful. You've got to feel that you're on your way *there* ... the here and now is tattered and worn. This is exactly what parents have been thinking for their children since Sumeria. It's absurd, surely, but it's also the best thing we ever do. But now I have that fearful feeling that I can *tell all* this very afternoon and that being so there must be a mistake in it, untrue.

Tonight, typed 4000 words, revised, added things, etc. It sounds minute, but it was a long bit of work. I'm getting to be proud of *work* and nothing else ... In other things I have goofy fun, but in work I get a solemn sense of realness. More anon.

JUNE —

TUESDAY JUNE 1 — Went to N.Y. picking up odds & ends. Now Ed Stringham, whom I met just once, who read my chapters (2 or 3), is supposed to be arranging a meeting with Alfred Kazin for me. Kazin is a wheel in the field allright ... we'll see 'wha' hoppeens.' It's very nice of the guy, who seems highly respected by all those people (by Allen Hansen, Auden's 'boy', Alan Harrington, etc.) But the amazing thing is that all this is happening without any of my own finagling. I can't understand it. Ginsberg says I don't understand 'society,' only 'loneliness where everything is hard and grim and hopeless.' That may be so. Alfred Kazin ... I remember when I was 19, getting mad as hell at this critic for attacking Tom Wolfe. Kazin wrote a fine creative introduction to Dostoevsky's 'Raw Youth,' however. Also, Ginsberg wrote a letter to Lionel Trilling for me. And then I have an agent looking for me, and

Lucien's girl (Time Magazine Barbara Hale) says she has a connection at Macmillan, and others. What's happening? It's stupid of me to say that. Meanwhile, goddamit, I've got so much typing to do, and I'm so slow at it. Also I got a letter from Beverly Burford in Colo. And she can get me a job on a ranch in August. Maybe by that time I'll be able to buy one, you might say, one might think, somehow, it seems, or something. THIS is neurosis. A guy the other night said something that disturbed me, that I pretended to be dumb all the time. (Anson.) This is true and why do I do it? Whit — hey!?

This month I should type and revise 600-pages of my manuscript, but there's doubt that I can go that fast, although I'll try. 300-pages 'are ready.' So tonight I began this campaign inauspiciously, typing and revising **12-pages.** I should do at least 25 a day, or 150 a week, to meet this schedule.

WEDNESDAY JUNE 2 — It's Summer and it's hot and I can't work in the burning afternoons. I have a feeling of guilt in that I hate day-time and love night-time and dawn, and the reason is because there's farmer's-blood in me. This is really a strange and important thing. After supper Allen Ginsberg dropped in bringing the remainder of the manuscript which, he said, ended so "big and profound." He thinks I'm going to be a rich man now, really, but worries about what I'll do with money, that is, he can't picture me with money (nor can I). He thinks I'm a true Myshkin, bless his soul, but I'm afraid not* ... The madness has left Allen now and I like him as much as ever, that is, I am involved with him in something as much as ever, but now it's more pleasing than before, therefore it's more friendly. Things are changing in both of us. I am mad, of course about the way he sees the world ... "my father wanted me to become a little school teacher in Patterson

*Prince Myshkin is the morally perfect yet socially outcast protagonist of Dostoevsky's *The Idiot.*

[sic]" ... and "my mother when she was at the mad-town asylum" (forgetting the name of the town where it was) ... And "Bill thinks he's conscious too" ... And a thousand things revealing a sad Ginsbergian world of madness and futile sweetness ... "The embarrassed customs official in Dakar wearing a fez and shorts over his long skinny brown legs came running out in the night after us telling us that we could pass because we'd been so polite to him." This is greatness, he's got to harness it someday.

Tonight, late, and sick from the cold, typed & revised **10 measly pages.**

THURSDAY JUNE 3 — Still sick as a dog but working. Did **24** pages today. I worked out an intricate mathematical thing which determines how assiduously I'm getting my novel typed and revised day after the day. It's too complicated and mad to explain, but suffice it to say that yesterday I was batting .246, and after today's work my "batting average" rose to .306. The point is, I've got to hit like a champion, I've got to catch up and stay with Ted Williams (currently hitting .392 in baseball).* If I can catch him, and *stay* with him, the month of June will be the *final* month of work on Town & City. But the absorbing thing is that I can't possibly bat that high (.392.) without toiling like a fiend (and that's the whole point of my little game.) So it's .306 for now, and depend on it that I'll suffer a batting slump over the weekends, because the *days* themselves figure in the formula (30 days of June), and during the weeks I'll always fatten my figure. To stay over .300 is of course essential in the big leagues ... so I'm doing O.K. as of now, anyway ... (for an outfielder.)

FRIDAY JUNE 4 — Woke up with my .306 average. Worked hard, brought it up to .324.

*Ted Williams would end up hitting .349 in 1948.

SATURDAY JUNE 5 — And today brought it up to the respectable figure of .345 — but news came that my sister is gravely ill in North Carolina from childbirth, so my mother and I took off immediately.

JUNE 6–JUNE 13 — It developed allright, after much worry. She gave birth to a three-pound 7-month infant, by Caesarian. The best of attention at Durham Medical Center saved her life. As well as the baby boy's life.* I came back to do my work, my mother stayed down to care for Nin. Now I really *must* sell my book, make money. While down there Paul and I worked on his garage and around the place, and I got a foretaste of my ambition for a ranch with Paul, Nin, my mother, Mike, his family, myself and my own future family all together. A real homestead and stockade. I suddenly realized that Northern California, around Mendocino Forest, is the place for my big homestead — with San Francisco nearby a hundred miles or so. More on that later. But now I've work and responsibility and human plans ahead of me.

MONDAY JUNE 14 — Arrived home alone, a little sad, but preoccupied with ambitions. I cleared a lot of business today — at the bank, etc., and called up my 'connections.' Then I fell back on the typing. My average is where it was when I unavoidably lost a week — at .345. I must, I *must* be successful. I suddenly realized that the reason for this desire, partly, is because, as a Dostoevskyan writer, I am *expected* to be a failure in the world of success and financial status. But apart from this, without money I cannot bring my human beings all together around me on a homestead, a triple homestead in the California wilds (perhaps near Eel River, or Russian River, near Clear Lake, Longvale, near the Eden Valley Ranch — all around there.)† For a life of family and purpose — while still *inwardly mad* as a writer! Range, range —

*The baby boy was named Paul Blake, Jr.
†Eel River and Russian River snake through Mendocino Forest, cutting deep canyons. Clear Lake, the largest freshwater lake in California, also borders the redwood forest. Eden Valley and Longvale are towns in the area.

experience in all ... And so on, more later. The money not for prestige, but for a homestead of simplicity. So I work now, *alone in the house.*

TUESDAY JUNE 15 — Do you know what this homestead, this ranch is? — what my stature and responsibility in it is?: — it's a footing from which I can be my *childlike self forever.* This means something big ... to me. And apropos of being 'alone in the house' — it is just the saddest, grimmest thing in the world, for a house was made for many, for a family. It is allright to be alone in an upstairs room of a hotel or rooming house or apartment, but not in a *house.* It is allright in an artistic garret ... but spare the poor man alone in his *house.* Last night's sweating, plodding work left me with a .340 average for today to match. This is nowhere near Ted Williams' current .398. I typed and revised — maintained a .327 mark — and went in to town to bring Tony's coat. At about 2 in the morning, just as I stepped out of a White Rose bar, an ecstasy hit me, one of my old fashioned visions, 'full of a million sadnesses and a million wild expectations,' as I thought it. It was tremendous. I won't describe it here, I only mention it as reassurance that I shall always, always be a poet, a 'walking poem' in the flesh. This is reassuring after a dormant feeling in the grave though almost sullen South. What is all this? — It's the fear of losing my 'soul,' the desire to grow poetically in these mysterious sky-nights of the world. But it's a foolish fear, I myself know that it will always be the same. This diary is often superfluous. (The use and juxtaposition of the word 'grave' above is striking ... perhaps I unconsciously associate gravity with a kind of death ... there is much gravity in the South, and no glee whatsoever, even, almost, among the little children, who also seem 'sullen.')

WEDNESDAY JUNE 16 — Work-day, gray and cool and Atlantican. Those foggy Pacific days in 'Frisco are the only things comparable to these gray Atlantic days, those 'work-days' somehow. I used to stay in my room as a child, on days like this, to work. It's one of the levels of my existence: I attach much importance to it. Hot Florida had me depressed in 1947 last year until one gray day I went swimming in the Atlantic (at Daytona Beach) and there, in the grayness of the grave sea, the porpoises rolled and disported like a kind of sea-fleet. When you swim with the dolphins in the gray shaggy Atlantic, you know where your work lies, if you're a poet, and if you were weaned on New England sea-coasts, Autumn, hunger, and gravity.(!). — While writing a scene, I think: "Well, they'll have to understand in their own way, that's all. That's the way *I* understand." — this about the reading public, everybody. Also I think: "It's most intelligent at times, maybe always, to be deliberately unintelligent and short-sighted. What good is 'intelligence' when it does nothing but antagonize the other intelligence of human relationship ..." and so on. While dozing off at dusk a thought came without *invitation* to me ... a very strange phenomena ... it just came, without effort, all worded up. It was such a striking experience that I woke up momentarily before falling asleep. It came like this. "Although your idea of what someone else thinks of you is only paranoiac, unreal, and illusionary, it is part of your relationship with the person, as much a part of it as the actuality of the person's real thoughts. *Paranoia is essential to understanding someone else.*" The words were much better than that, uninvited, but that's the gist of them. Wasn't that weird. While writing, also, I made an interesting slip of the typewriter ... writing 'his nose was bloody,' I typed out, instead, 'hisn was bloody.' Finally I had another one which I forget now, but will remember some day. All this, this fearful rush of thoughts, this terror of visitations, is part of the dangerous business of writing 'full-scale.' I know it well, now. I fear mostly my inability to capture all the things that come, I fear their mysterious source, I fear their fate, I fear *me*, in short. This is true. And, again, I say 'more later' ... you notice the notebook is full of 'so ons' ... that's from the terror of knowing that I can't keep up with all of it. It's like finding a river of flowing gold when you haven't even got a cup to save a cupfull ... you've but a thimble, and that thimble is your pathetic brain and labour and humanness. — Tony came at night, I made crepes, we ate, talked. I typed all day, revised carefully, and maintained a .343 average, climbing 16 points over yesterday.

These figures don't imply the tremendous strain of keeping up and on that way. To reach .390, and to *stay* there, that's almost incredible now as I see how rough it is. There's grave doubt even that I can keep up a pace over .300.

THURSDAY JUNE 17 — Madly, painfully lonesome for a woman these June evenings ... and on I work, work. I see them walking outside and I go crazy ... "no time, no money." — but my desire for a woman is at its highest pitch right now. If my ego were attached to love, as it should be, instead of to work, I'd have me that woman tonight and forever. "No time, no money ..."

Or, yet, why is it that a man trying to do big work by himself, alone, poor, cannot find one little wisp of a woman who will give him her love and time? Why is it that a man with money and success has to drive them away ... or as Hal Chase says, a man with a woman belonging to him, sporting her odor, has to drive them away ... the Lesbians! This experience is going to make me bitter, by God. But an *idea* just came to me. (Meanwhile, of course, you see, I do believe that 'feeling sorry' for oneself is one of the truest things on earth because you can't deny that someone like me, healthy, sexual, even poetic, slashed, pierced, riven with desire and affection for any pretty girl I see, yet unable because of 'time and money' to make love now, *now*, in youth, as they parade indifferently by my window* ... well Goddamit, you just can't deny it! It isn't right! There's too much aloneness in a world yearning, yearning, yearning ... and too many whores, real true whores. To hell with them? No ... the point is, I *want* them. Someday I'll go to France, to Paris, that's what ... where, like Jean Gabin,† you can find a pretty love at the carnival in the night.) (In the night, in the night, in the sky-night and lights, the soft warm knees parting, the breathless clasp, the gasp, the

---

*The kitchen table at which Kerouac wrote was beside a window that overlooked the busy intersection of Cross Bay Boulevard and 133rd Street in Ozone Park, Queens.
†Jean Gabin (1904–1976), French actor, starred in *The Impostor* (1944), Archie Mayo's *Moontide*, and dozens of others in a career that spanned from the 1920s to the 1970s.

tongue, and best of all, the low murmuring voice and what it says.) Well, as I say, I'm going to be bitter about this. This may be sexual inadequacy (no time, no money), but ... just wait, woman, just wait.

Went to bed, after irritating work with a faulty typewriter-hand, with a .350 average.

FRIDAY JUNE 18 — Worked all day, slugged my average up to .353, the highest yet. Tomorrow is an official day off ... I go to meet Ed Stringham and the 'connections,' one of them a composer (David Diamond.) I was irritated today because my manuscript is not as "good" as it should be, but this is an Olympian sense of perfection and not human. It would take me *another year,* maybe longer, to 'perfect' T & C, and that is senseless (It wouldn't be any better anyway, according to human workaday standards.) Allen Ginsberg insists I 'perfect' it, but he's a poet, and a verse-writer is like that. The novelist always has another big story to write, he's got no time to polish his old stories, he's not a decorator, but a builder. Besides I noticed that at least my writing, though unperfected, is original in the original sense of that word ... it is my own thought, nothing gathered from the terminologies of the time, my own words, my own awkward work. During my 'God-sincere' Carlyle period of work and silence, I knew this well (Spring and Summer of 1947.) I was looking at a new novel tonight and I saw how each paragraph was filled with thoughts, terms, words, images, and actions borrowed from the magazine-newspaper language of political and social superficiality — no soul-writing, no 'dark poetry,' no personal vision, no revelation, no work maybe ... just battled-out sentences, a hesitant, empty story, a sparse significance based on something that only exists in newspapers. I don't deny newspapers, I deny lazy thinking, lazy writing, stupid unemotionalism ... (to use their word.) It's *mood,* again, that's first and foremost and even Shakespearian, mood that explains us all, in full, all, all.

If my hand could only 'keep up with my soul' — (but cross out those quotes, I *do* have a soul, and besides, though I am ashamed of my own madness among the regularities of noon's wonderful commerce, I don't care, I shall bury the shame, I'll always find a way to honor among thieving self-lacerations and abasements) — so as I say, if my hand could *capture it*. Here, I think, is one of the secrets that will lead to the miraculous novel of the future; and when I'm finished with T & C in all its aspects, I'm going to discover a way of preserving the big rushing tremendousness in me and in all poets. A certain gadget, the wire-recorder, may help in some respects, although it's a bit awkward to spill your visions into a microphone* ... One big thing is to develop a strenuous accountability (you see it's *moral*, no gadgets invade man's true necessity), and the habit, the daily labor of writing *en passant*, keep a vast and cosmic diary. Imagine such a diary after a year's time ... two million words from which to hew (and *hue*) out a soulful story. Nothing's impossible ... the great novel of the future is going to have all the virtues of Melville, Dostoevsky, Celine, Wolfe, Balzac, Dickens and the poets in it (and Twain.) The novel is undeveloped, it probably needs a new name, and certainly needs more work, more research as it were. A 'soulwork' instead of a 'novel,' although of course such a name is too fancy, and laughable, but it does indicate someone's writing *all-out* for the sake of earnestness and salvation. The idea is that such a work must infold the man like his one undeniable cloak and dream of things ... his 'vision of the world and of the proposition of things,' say.

SATURDAY JUNE 19 — Went into N.Y. and met the composer David Diamond, and others. Diamond is to introduce me to Kazin, I guess, after which my book will start going into the right hands. The typing must be stepped up ... but I go on getting drunk, dammit, as tonight at one of Cannastra's insane parties. Meanwhile, Diamond, speaking casually of Artie Shaw, Lana Turner, Aaron Copland, Alec Wilder, Benny Goodman and other such celebrities (whom, you see, he assumes I may soon meet, or at some time or other) — the point being ... *glamor*,

---

*Kerouac would later do just that in his novel *Visions of Cody*. A large section of the book came directly from conversations between Kerouac and Neal Cassady.

and all that ... well, it just surprises me, that's all, and fascinates me no end. More on this later. I'm getting sick of the tone of this diary and may soon begin a new, bigger one on the typewriter.

SUNDAY JUNE 20 — Went to Dodger game in Brooklyn with Tony, and then to a massive Italian dinner at his sister's house, and then home.

MONDAY JUNE 21 — Received a beautiful batch of letters from everybody ... from Ma, Paul, Neal Cassady, Bill Burroughs in New Orleans, and the address of a beautiful nurse in Durham, N.C., my sister Carolyn's nurse. But Allen G. popped in just as I was reading them and took up my energy, my willing attention, for two days of mad conversation.

TUESDAY JUNE 22 — Including today. 'More later' on everything we talked about in these 2 days.

WEDNESDAY JUNE 23 — And today my attention was similarly taken up by the mad whoopee of the G.O.P. convention in Philly, over the radio.* It is something I really like. Meanwhile I typed a thin sheaf of pages. So much goes on, in myself, and in the world around, that I can't record it as I should in pencil ... so I'll switch to the typewritten diary I mentioned ... and try to recapture all the pathetic 'more anons' of this book. Meanwhile I'll continue here with little things.

THURSDAY JUNE 24 — My typing was held up by all these delays. Now I figure I have at least 450 pages typed and ready, and about 500, or 550, to go — so again, I'll set a pace and a goal, and this time, absolutely keep it. I must do at least 25 pages a day (including revising) which means at July 24 at the latest, thirty days from now, with five or so days off, or a few more. I'll just record the day's pages, and the av-

*The Republican Party nominated New York governor Thomas E. Dewey (1902–1971) for the presidency at the 1948 convention.

erage of day's pages in this final drive (in summer's demented heat.) Typed **30** pages today, using a new kind of self-discipline. That many pages each day, according to last week's batting average discipline, would give me a .600 average. This may be it — ... *has* to be. Kazin, or someone, may want to see the novel soon. And meanwhile I have 3 chapters to really finish up, too. Tonight I also composed a letter to that beautiful nurse in Durham, Ann — and also wrote to Ma and Paul. Saturday night, after that dinner at [Alan] Harrington's, I'll come home and endeavor to write 2 beautiful letters to Cassady and Burroughs, just for the sake of beauty. Anyway I can't spend any more money on Saturdays, I'm down to my last $3.50.

FRIDAY JUNE 25 — Typed **29** pages, going strong. Listened to the Louis knockout of Walcott at night.* Reading "Cattle" and Mark Twain. Enjoying my sense of work and my orderly loneliness.

SATURDAY JUNE 26 — Went to dinner at Alan Harrington's house, met his charming wife and baby Steve. I feel that I have a sincere new friend in Harrington. Although not "my kind of writer" he is my "kind of man." What he's writing now he'll "outgrow," and, vainly, I hope to see him bend his attention to the "world of people, and dark things, and moral furies" later on ... his present work, highly professional, is a satire on the 'American Salesman.' Yet he speaks like Dostoevsky of 'responsibility disappearing till no one is guilty.' And intends a story touching on the Christian condemnation of Judas, who was, somehow, fiercely human and complex, his guilt was not so simple and so condemnable (when you consider Judas the *human*.) Well — we talked for hours at dinner, and Ed Stringham was there, and we all went out later. At six-thirty in the morning I knocked on 'dark-eyes' door ... my '*idea*' of last Thursday the 17th. Suffice it to say that I am loveless. Maybe I'm

*Heavyweight champion Joe Louis knocked out "Jersey Joe" Walcott in the eleventh round at Yankee Stadium, June 25, 1948. It was his last fight before announcing his first retirement.

too 'wild' for protracted love affairs. It's the *world* I need most. I could never say, in a woman's arms, like Wagner's hero: "Let me die!"* I want to *live* ... and see more of the world, & God knows why, and a woman's love is only one of many wild loves. One thing sure: the Goethean passion is not mine. There's too much irritation, restlessness, 'craziness' in me for that languishing condition. I've got to rush off, always. Only two kinds of women suit me: a wild Edie who matches my own impatience and madness and terror, until one of us becomes exhausted, or a simple girl (similar to my mother) who absorbs and understands and accepts all that. Just yesterday a woman in San Francisco smothered her baby to death because she 'didn't want anybody else to touch it.' Yes indeed, 'let me die' in a Wagnerian passion ... I'll buy what Leon Robinson says in "Journey to the End of the Night" — "I'm busy enough trying to stay alive." And add to that ... "and enjoying it weirdly." This begins to point out the peculiar lovelessness of my position in the last 3 years, maybe the last 26 years ... *and I never enjoyed an idea about myself so much, really,* and I guess that means something too: the 'wildness' is the word that pleases me most. By God, it's not every day you find a perfect alibi for yourself, and what's even more amazing is that it's so wildly *true!* Tonight I wrote some laborious and maybe beautiful letters to Neal and Bill, till dawn. I told Neal that the time is coming for me, and my mother, to go to California. Why hang around this crowded, sweaty East, when my book is finished. (These notes include Sunday.)

MONDAY JUNE 28 — Hot disgusting day ... dead and pasty, no wind, nothing, misty, sullen, incredibly stupid. Started late, did **18** pages.

TUESDAY JUNE 29 — Did **27** pages — another disguster of a day. Alan Temko dropped in, en route from San Francisco to Paris, says he wants to 'view America from a distance.' In the Twenties they didn't have to alibi their discontents. But Temko's actions, however dumb,

---

*A reference to "Hark Beloved — Let Me Die!" from *Tristan und Isolde,* an opera by German composer Richard Wagner (1813–1883).

are always lent a beautiful dignity by his person. He is an impressive guy, and occasionally moving. Says he's gone *political* ... If it's true, I guess he turned away from some snobbish claque: — and if 'political,' probably won't write, as he dreamed he would. What a pattern. How many guys I knew who 'were going to write.' They all go political ... a nice gimmick, a nice way to get up in the world too. Creative, too!

Frank Sarubbi then dropped in and we'll run down to No. Carolina this weekend ... I'll get to see my nurse as well as everybody. Read Twain.

WEDNESDAY JUNE 30 — Another disguster, fourth in a row. Give me the cool fogs of Frisco. For the month of June I did approximately — well, with tonight's vast **40** pages, (!) I did, in all, about 320 pages in June ... for a batting average, according to early standards, of .291: — which is enough for the big leagues, but not great. Anyway I'm coming up to the great deadwood of the novel, needing re-writing, and here comes the angry work. Decided not to go to Carolina ... stay home and work, nose to the grindstone.

JULY

THURSDAY JULY 1 — I'm never satisfied with the progress of my work. I won't rest, I won't rest till it's complete complete ... and what a pain in the eye that is. Did **12** pages tonight after Temko came ... We talked. Went to bed at 7 in the morning, revising a chapter.

FRIDAY JULY 2 — And got up on this *beautiful* day at four in the afternoon. What a waste. It's a bright, clear 'California' day. It's the big day for everybody. The beginning of the holiday weekend. At six this evening you'll see them all, dressed up, starting ... a wild excitement in the night ... and I don't think I'll be awake even by then. I wake up at midnight, like a blind bat. At four-thirty now they're all finishing up their work, loading lumber or sorting letters or cleaning up lathes or delivering the last laundry bag or closing the hatches. All of New York tonight, the whole metropolitan skynight of lights, will be a holiday and a humming mysterious vast place. Not I ...

Did 29 pages, working till 8 in the morning. I wonder what the result of all this work will be in the real world, for me. All lost, all awful, all raw, all mistaken and grieved ... Things seem that way sometimes, now. The situation's harsh in a life without beautiful phantasy. But phantasy and glee are truer than malice and skepsis, *that* I know. Who is there in the world who senses and knows *all,* and is at the same time determined to be happy? Find me this manly wonderful man, or woman. Find me the mirage and I will make it all come true, by magical sorcery somehow. "Someone so God-sincere, so deep" and *so sharp.*

SATURDAY JULY 3 — To get to the hymn of images, the facts of living mystery. Big party at Harlem, in Allen's and Russell Durgin's — 'millions of us.' I spent another 3 days without eating or sleeping to speak of, just drinking and wineing and squinting and sweating. There was a vivacious girl right out of the Twenties, redhaired, distraught, sexually frigid (I learned.) With her I walked 3½ miles in a Second Avenue heat wave (on Monday this is) till we got to her 'streamlined Italian apartment' where I lay on the floor looking up out of a dream. Seems like I had sensed it all before. There was misery, and the beautiful ugliness of people, and there was Hunkey — in his evil dawn — telling me he had seen Edie in Detroit and told her that I still loved her. What a surprise that was! — how strange can Hunkey get? Hunkey scares me because he has been the most *miserable* of men, jailed & beaten and cheated and starved and sickened and homeless, and still he knows there's such a thing as love, and my stupidity ... and what else is there in Hunkey's wisdom? What does he know that makes him so human after *all* he *has* known? — it seems to me if I were Hunkey I would be dead now, someone would have killed me long ago. But he's still alive, and strange, and wise, and beat,* and human, and all blood-

*Kerouac's first written use of "beat" as adjective.

and-flesh and *staring* as in a benny depression forever. He is truly more remarkable than Celine's Leon Robinson, really so. He knows more, suffers more ... sort of American in his wider range of terrors. And *do* I love Edie still? — The wife of my youth? Tonight I think so, I think so. And what does *she* know? And *where* are we all? God it's a strange sea-light over all this ... We *are* in the bottom of some ocean; I never realized it before. In my phantasy of glee there is no sea-light and no beatness, just things like the wind blowing through the pines over the kitchen window on an October morning. I'll have to start pulling all these new things together now. And this is why men love dualisms ... they cannot get away from them ... and they feel independent and wise among them.... And they choose about and stumble on to death and the end of phantasy. (or beginning.)

SUNDAY JULY 4 — The party continued on. I stood on the road at dusk and watched the Harlem fireworks here and there, individual little rockets that didn't make blossoms (before the war the fireworks were better.) Everybody was downstairs drinking, talking, sweating, staring, wondering, stumbling, living, dying ... what a funny thing. In the midst of all of Russell Durgin's theology books, too. Lucien plucked on a guitar nervously, Barbara sulked, Irene giggled at me, Fitzpatrick nodded eagerly talking to some girl, another girl from Santa Fe pouted, Ginsberg watched sullenly between knee-jiggles and decided, in his ugly way, that women "don't know their minds." Durgin was drinking, later he stared into the abyss, at dawn, from the fire escape. Alan Harrington puffed on his pipe and should have stayed home, it was no place for the salt of the earth. His friend John [Clellon] Holmes watched with his wild shrewd look. Someone else went up on the roof ... A fire started, died down. It was hot. On the roof I thought of the "Raintree County" type of Fourth of July,* so far from all this, so

*Ross Lockridge, Jr.'s best-selling novel *Raintree County* (1948) is set on July 4, 1872, and told through flashbacks.

much truer, like ... so much more American. Hunkey came at dawn, so strange, so beat, so alert to all.

MONDAY JULY 5 — After I left Irene, I picked up butts from the street and tottered along enjoying myself. I saw a beautiful girl in the subway window, and watched her reflection there as *she* watched me, unknowing. Her young man was so sad and worried by everything ... to lose her meant death. They were the children of love, one flower. I glared at the darkness seriously. Picking up butts in the street involves the highest self-respect in the world, the self-respect of the honest beggar. I came home and collapsed in the sea-light. At midnight my mother came home from No. Carolina, full of thoughts of Nin and Paul. I thought of Edie. Now it's dawn and I'm going to sleep.

TUESDAY JULY 6 — Woke up, ate, felt better, my mother cleaned the house, the sorrow faded back, and I did 25 pages all night. And I composed a letter to Edie, but kept it.

WEDNESDAY JULY 7 — A beautiful cool, clear day. Got letters from Neal, Ed, Allen. Neal doesn't seem to take me seriously about the ranch idea ... I'll have to explain. Ed's communication was gratifying and *true* ... Ed White I underrate too much. Allen's letter was ugly and loveless, he's all poetry and terror. Went to the library, got books. Shook off the weekend's cobwebs ... Did 27 pages all night ... wrote a letter to Neal and then tore it up. All is speculation about this ranch business and I'm sick of speculation (not Tristano's, no.) How quick a mood can change, too. Batting .315 anyway (over that .291.) My eyes drove me nervous and restless today, that's what it was. Too much fast work.

FRIDAY JULY 9 — Did 13 pages only, tired. Discovered 'true thoughts' — which are thoughts that occur in a split-second, all tremendous and full. I can't write a thing in this tonight, however.

SATURDAY JULY 10 — Went to N.Y., walked around a bit, and came right back due to a sore-throat and unusual pounding headache. Drank gallons of cold water to ward off fever and read "Huck Finn" all night. Bought San Francisco papers. Wrote to Neal.* Hot days depress me.

SUNDAY JULY 11 — Hot day. My throat much better after all the ice-water, but headaches persist. What can you do in a muggy disgusting world? Did a little work in the cool night. No thoughts.

MONDAY JULY 12 — Did 27 pages ... batting .328 Working along in casual daze of sorts ... resting.

TUESDAY JULY 13 — Did 19 pages and began totally revising the Francis-Engels chapter ... This great deadwood will ruin my .330 batting average. I now have well over 800 pages done on the ms., with some 200 more to go. And then the novel will be done forever, and the devil can then shove it up. Went to a show with Ma in the evening. Dawn was like a dead blanket of humidity and darkness ... so awful that it was *silly* ... I walked in it amazed.

WEDNESDAY JULY 14 — But today cool winds from the north, from Canada. Woke up analyzing my meaningful dreams of 'gibbering futility.' I understand that you can feel one way and think another way ... for instance, in the dream I felt futile and foolish because I could not even drive a jeep in "the war," so I became impotent. My *thought* on the matter is that war is silly and that there is nothing impotent about me for that. Conclusion ... man is an idiot ... even his *thought* is gibberish, because it is not reconciled with his feeling. It was a good dream, throws light on the chapter I'm working on, because it is the story of all our intellectuals: "They think they're conscious too!" Aside from

*This letter addressed to Neal and his new bride, Carolyn, details Kerouac's hope for the three of them to buy a ranch in Colorado or California (which is why he was reading the San Francisco papers).

that, anyway, cool livable days wake up my thoughts and feelings, I'm an animal allright.

THURSDAY JULY 15 — Painfully groaningly revised **9** pages. Now batting .318. Full of groaning feelings ...

FRIDAY JULY 16 — These must be some of the worst days of my life, I don't know. I feel *old* and finished ... just working with the most *alone* sense I've ever had. 'Nobody left,' it seems, and I feel as though I'll die soon. Now I may be putting a hex on myself as Nigger Jim does about the rattlesnake skin.* Must finish this *soon*. I'm tired. I'd like to live for a change. It's been so long.

Did — that is, revised — **8** more pages groaningly. Also, lately, I feel like a newspaperman: — I've no brains. It's the most empty feeling in the world to feel like a newspaperman racking his head for words, the most superficially-meant words. Batting **.309**

SATURDAY JULY 17 — Saw Tom today, and Allen Temko and wonderful Bob Young — went to Tom's house, then to beach-dance at night, where Tom was playing piano. During the day my left eye went completely Kerplunk — lancing with pain in the nerve. Don't know what this means — but it's pain, and flesh-and-blood. Worked tonight just the same, full of aspirins. I want to finish this work before something really goes wrong with me.

SUNDAY JULY 18 — Rested my eyes in day, worked at night, took walks. Eye will be allright awhile.

MONDAY JULY 19 — Piled up **39** pages. The nearer I get to the final end of this work, the more work there seems to be. My 1946 material is not generally worth the paper it's on. Wearing glasses now, my eyes

*From Mark Twain's *The Adventures of Huckleberry Finn*.

seem perfect. Took a walk with Ma at midnight — she thinks I'm about to work myself sick. But when I'm finished with all this, in 2 weeks or so, by August 4th, W H O O P E E ! — and I mean it! After that, perhaps revisions according to any agreement with an editor, contract, *ADVANCE* — then California and a newspaper job in 'Frisco. Later, later, a ranch, with Neal, Paul, all. A NEW LIFE … (And publication of "The Town and the City" in Fall of 1949.) Hang on, hang on … life's long, energy creates energy, things are allright, hunger piles up, love waits … and when found … grows. Hang on, chile of darkness, nigger Jim on a raft, hang on. Now *shot up* bat. ave. to **.327**.

TUESDAY JULY 20 — Did **22** pages, batting .330 again. Took it easy later at night, otherwise would have done much more. Eyes ached again today. Had a lot of happy, healthy feelings and thoughts for the first time in weeks, it seems. My work is long but it will be done, done, done.

THURSDAY JULY 22 — Did **17** pages, batting **.329** — and I swear to God that I'll *never* be finished with this thing. I've done and completed some 900-pages so far and it looks like another 200 to go, for a mad total of 1,100 pages in the manuscript. I got a packing box today to pack the novel in, five inches deep, but it wasn't deep enough for the pile of paper *so far*.* If the thing weren't closely typed it would be a foot high. But really, honestly, when oh *when* will I be finished! It just gets bigger all the time, more work seems to pile up, it's a monster man …

FRIDAY JULY 23 — Rewrote **10** pages completely, and pretty well (conversation between Francis and Peter in the attic.) Cool weather — feel great.

---

*Kerouac's literary hero, Thomas Wolfe, was known to keep his massive manuscripts piled in huge wooden crates while in progress.

SATURDAY JULY 24 — Went to N.Y., to a party at Allen's, where I met a rose ... a little princess weighted down by the horror of her kingdoms ... a child ... a wise passionate child ... a "nature girl" really, who also sings, dances, paints ... a little Parisienne ... and mostly, a little Goethean love (and just as young.) She went home from the party ... I stayed up late with Vicki, Hunkey, Allen, talking about Dakar and Panama and ships, at dawn ... Then next day, Sunday, little Jinny and I went

SUNDAY JULY 25 — ... to the beach. We played in the waves for hours, lay in the sun. We had dinner at my house, and then the summernight fields and softness and great stars bending close-pack't, and odourous darkness, and flowers and hidden gardens, and the whole universe melting and falling down the skies all crumbled and soft, all blurred and transcendental with milky light, all immortal, all sacrificial and sighing, all too impossible to keep and bear so beautiful and so sad. I wonder why our life must quiver between beauty and guilt, consummation and sadness, desire and regret, immortality and tattered moments unknowable, truth and beautiful meaningful lies, knowledge and the genius of illusion, love and chagrin, "Time" and minutes, what-we-do and what-we-want — or — other poles quivering elsewhere in greater, softer darknesses. Later, at night, wandered in the Bowery enjoying a few beers and thinking love-thoughts, then saw Lucien and Barbara and got out-drunk and staggered home in the morning ... and Allen was crying because he thought nobody wanted to hear his new "silence and transcendence" visions, although, being silent and transcendent, of course, he could not utter them, and we could not utter our understanding, and the Big Error, or (to me) the Big Truth, hovered near touching us almost with its unknown wings. However, there was no reason for me to get so drunk. I think I got drunk for the first time simply because I was happy, no other big reason, and because I was in love, in its living room resting.

MONDAY JULY 26 — Hangoveral day. And got a letter from Ann the little beautiful nurse in the South. I know nothing now, I only relax.

Also, it's not the 'eternal values' that worry me, it's all the tattered moments thousands of them that fall like snowflakes all around our heads, all beautiful, each different, each also 'eternal' ... *but with no name.* And they keep falling and falling until the purity of our understanding of eternal things becomes obscured in a snowstorm of reality, confused 'impurities' pile up on our heads. The feeling of proceeding from purity to impurity of understanding, from morning to ruin, from joyous certainty to something that says 'I know nothing now, I only relax,' this is like Blake's worm flying through the night to reach the rose, and reaching it in slow degrees, like decomposition. But of course, our brains, mostly our kindness of hope, regard the slow ruin of the rose more beautiful and complex and 'true' than mere original purity ... like, say, the rose imbedded in ice doth never change, and we speak of 'change' delightedly (we have to) and somehow, the Iceman cometh. Oh this is fun, and close to it. *'But-with-no-name'* upstairs implies Neal's incessant demand for a 'new psychology,' I mean it's that close to the Big Truth that it settles into the requirements of both Neal's mind and mine. — Couldn't work tonight because of a thousand quivering passions. I love, I love. Someday my wife and I shall go to the rug in the bedroom, every night, and kneel, facing each other, and embrace and kiss, and she shall say, "Because we'll never part," and I will say "Because we'll never part," — and then we'll get up and resume. This is a frenzy, this love. Every night the rug, or all is lost. The most beautiful love there ever was. To say, then, that I can't work because of love, no, no — all my sweating work and suffering was work for love, not only a preparation for love, but part of the love itself, — and all my future work, my future music. It is all love, "The Town & The City", and I mean the love of a girl. It was the labor of attaining a soul which a girl whom I would love could never leave ... God, god, I'm blind, the sentence is mad. Again: — it was the labour of attaining a soul that my love could never hate, and *will* never hate. My "rain" chapter is such beauty that no love of mine can ever and will ever stop loving me. This

Jinny's exact likeness

...l values? that worry
...ed moments thousands
...nowflakes all around
... each different, each
...with no name. And
...tting until the purity
... eternal things becomes
...m of reality, confused
...r heads. The feeling
...to impurity of understand-
...in, from joyous certainty
...I know nothing now, I
...e Blake's worm flying
...ch the rose, and
...ees, like decomposition
...ins, mostly our kindness
...low ruin of the rose
...plex and "true" than
...- like, say, the rose
...never change, and we
...delightedly (we have to)
... iceman cometh. Oh this
is fun, and close to it. 'But-with-no name'
upstairs implies Neal's incessant demand for
a 'new psychology', I mean it's that close
to the Big Truth that it settles into the requirements of both Neal's mind and mine. —
Couldn't work tonight because of a thousand
quivering passions. I love, I love. Someday my
wife and I shall go to the rug in the bedroom,
every night, and kneel, facing each other, and
embrace and kiss, and she shall say; "Because
we'll never part," and I will say, "Because
we'll never part," — and then we'll get up
and resume. This is a frenzy, this love.
Every night the rug, or all is lost. The most
beautiful love there ever was. To say, then,
that I can't work because of love, no, no —
all my sweating work and suffering was work

is how my work is love. She *has* to love me because I am so full of beauty and the work of love. And till I die, too ... Is it not so? "Is this not great gentility?" — Could *I* ever hate Melville or Dostoevsky or Wolfe? Then can she ever hate *me*? Can I hate Shakespeare? Can I but love Twain? Can I do anything but adore Dostoevsky? ... and feel eternal affection for Balzac? — for Celine? Can she but love me? Will I not infold her in my arms as we ride on a bus across Nevada and explain my vision of Nevada to her? Won't I write "I Love You" on the back of the check in a restaurant and show it to her? What will my soul do when she wipes her tears? In slacks or new-look ballerina gown she'll come tripping down the street to me. In the fog we'll walk hand in hand up the steep white streets of San Francisco, with a bottle of Tokay, and "The Encantadas" in my back pocket.* I'll take her with me across the sky-nights and to Paris and to my ranch. She'll kiss the horse on its silky brow, and brood. Because she is mine, mine, and because we'll never part, and we'll kneel on the rug, and have children, and all because work is love, love's words, the vision of love, — and tonight I quiver — ONE FLOWER

TUESDAY JULY 27 — Wearied by ragged literary work in the heat ... did **34** pages, batting **.329**. Can I ever get rid of this lingering past involved in this stupid book. Now I want the bower ...

WEDNESDAY JULY 28 — Yet the bower shuts us off from the rest of the world, not the bower itself, but the greedy jealousy of it. And it is rather exhausting ... No more talk! — no more talk! Just that tonight, after the bower, I saw an old Negro shuffling along in the subway as though he was going over the corn-rows in Carolina, and all my love for the *world* returned. Does this mean that it is impossible for me to love a woman? Really? Or does it mean that I cannot withstand 'grand passions' — yet, after all, grand passions are never meant to last long. My eager gleeful girl is not a grand passion, it's a wife I shall love and

*Herman Melville's "The Encantadas, Or the Enchanted Islands," a series of travel sketches, first appeared in *Putnam's Magazine* in 1894 and later were reprinted in *Piazza Tales* (1856).

live with, a girl who will *allow me my soul* somehow, yet love me. I was jealous of the world for awhile there, and really started to hate everybody because I could not take the attention of my spirit off little Jinny Baker. I was locked up in the madness of blind greedy desire and jealousy ... 'passion,' in short. For me it should be something else, I fear. I fear all limitations. Allow me that fear. It is a fear of the 'artist.' What came over me I don't know. Yesterday it was a cosmic anxiety of love ... all the universe, though more beautiful (the only milky-blurred transcendental one) was slipping out of my grasp as my soul narrowed feverishly upon this girl. For her, yesterday, (though it isn't mentioned above), I would have calmly blown up the universe, or failing to do that I would have run and jumped clear off the edge of the world ... the same world that had taken up 3 years of work in "The Town and The City." I mean this. For her yesterday, and even tonight awhile, I would have gladly been a criminal *of all kinds.* So these are the criminal juices in men, young men, older men, and things are just waiting to bring it all out. My understanding of passion may be warped, but in the throes of it I could have wiped out everything there ever was for me, for anybody else who got in the way, friends, mothers, arts, whole worlds, that's what I could have done yesterday. Can you blame me for being glad that I came out of it partially tonight? — considering the earnestness of my heart heretofore? Or has it been so very earnest? If *one* passion can turn me inside-out ... I know that's earnestness too, but that's not what I mean. I mean *love of life,* of the world, not *just* of one sweet girl. The kind of earnestness that looks up from mere selfhood to all — even though in that one mere selfhood whole universes may be destroyed calmly & happily. Is world-wide earnestness a sublimation, and a false one at that, of love? of passion? Or is passion a murderous madness? ... is passion a kind of lustfulness of soul? — And how did I come out of 'la grande passion' tonight? That's something I don't know, it just came ...

I think, though, I am twisted and neurotic about this. I think there's something 'ugly' in me too, as in Ginsberg, an ugly lie somewhere here. I was worried about wanting to marry her ... and entering her

"Progressive intellectual" world ... and leaving my "glee-world" some-how, my neurotic dream. With her I hate the world. Something's wrong. But now, no marriage, I just simply love her for herself.

That seems to be my new understanding. The plain fact is, Jinny is not ready for a big love, she's but sixteen. Marriage at her age only means imprisonment. I have a guilt about 'affairs', because of what I did to Edie somehow. But — 'affair' is all it can really be, for now. She's young, young ... no world-sorrows yet. And she's as neurotic and self-centered as I am, both of us together are almost a mess.... I think we have different 'values,' though. But the point is she's just a little 'star-tled fawn' and no comprehensions have begun. And something freed me from mad anxiety over her ... as who wouldn't be madly anxious about keeping his 'startled fawn' in the yard forever. And I was. But not so much tonight. Is there such a thing as 'my kind'? There shouldn't be. No class, no kind. I'll sleep on these growing perplexities. My heart is active now ... I don't like it. I'm insane because I don't like love; es-pecially when it's not profoundly reciprocated, of course. That's the point there.

THURSDAY JULY 29 — All my life has been nothing but conflicts. And if there are no conflicts around, why, I'll invent some as quick as that. Did I say yesterday that I was out of love? I'm more heartsick to-day than ever. It all came back ... My old Negro of the corn-rows? — he can go his way, I'll go mine greedy, blind again. She's so young, so beautiful, and so sad that I could cry. That's my feeling. I wouldn't care if she had a dozen lovers as long as I could be *involved* with her. She says she loves Victor Tejeira ... I know Victor, a South American, a poet, gracious and sweet and gentlemanly and fine. No, jealousy of anyone else is not the point. It's my fear that the startled fawn will vanish ... In her world everybody hangs up a Picasso in a conspicuous place. Very well then, for her I will hang up a Picasso in a conspicuous place. How does my knowledge of the decadence of modernism and the sad folly of Progressivism as a mood, as a stupidly obvious rebellion against imaginary grievances, measure against my love for one hundred pounds of girl? What does it matter if I have arrived at great social & spiritual truths in my lonely room and in my massive book and in years of careful meditation and psychological comprehension — what is my art? My knowledge? My poetry? My science? — compared to her little feet? Yes yes yes, I just realized, 'the curl of her little toe.' Old Dmitri, did I say?* I am not Dmitri here, I am greater than Dmitri because I am Dmitri's father, the Father Karamazov himself. It is I wasting fortunes and the love of sons on a girl — and peering anxiously from my miser's window for her arrival. Picasso ... it is Titian and Grant Wood that I really want to hang up. Paris ... it is Montana that I really want to see. The ballet ... it is the all-night movie on Times Square that I really want to see. Mozart ... it is Allen Eager I really want to hear.† But for her ... for her I'll wear a goatee and pretend that I'm a literary genius, and make Proustian remarks, and be obviously *sensitive*. Oh no I won't ... This, America, is the pioneer country of pioneer disciplines strung on a rack and quivering — in quick transition to modern ideas; — and it is all there, even in one love affair between a Canuck farmer and a ballerina, it's all there like a story.

Tonight nevertheless did **23** pages and made some extremely important re-writes and write-ins for the funeral chapter ... which make it much greater. Work is coming to an end, anyway. It's a shame I can't enjoy this prospect! But *who* is Jinny, anyhow, just my little rib, my little love. Why don't I enjoy this instead of moping around like a Goethe about it. *Why?*

FRIDAY JULY 30 — Did **10** pages. At night went to another Allen party, with Harrington — long talks with Harrington, Walter Adams, Diana Hoffman. Louis Simpson was there and I didn't even know it ... he's a good writer. Seymour Lawrence was there, wanted a fragment of

---

*Dmitri, the great sensualist of the Karamazov family in Dostoevsky's *The Brothers Karamazov.*

†Alan Eager (1927–2003), enigmatic jazz clarinetist and saxophonist whose most productive recording period stretched from 1946 to 1948.

my novel for "Wake" magazine in Cambridge.* We'll see ... I don't know. I heard Diamond wants to read my novel now. I think, though, I'll start with Macmillan's first, through Barbara Hale. Had eye-aches again. And the 'sweet' pain of Jinny on my ... on my head, or heart, or whatever. Came home at dawn. I still haven't been able to answer Ann's letter!

SATURDAY JULY 31 — Called Tom Livornese ... and Tommy saw Edie in Detroit. Will see him soon and get the scoop. Wrote to Ann tonight. Did 22 pages, finishing funeral. About 1,000 pages are ready in the ms. A few odds & ends missing here and there, about 100 pages or less. I wonder if I shouldn't show the novel now. I'm certainly tired of working, wish I could rest a few weeks. Today I worked hard on those 22 pages and at night I couldn't see my way through the sea-chapter at all. Batting .331. How grievous is my mind! — mine eyes have seen too much — a lover's complaint, mostly — and general fear and tears and sighing ...

AUGUST — NOT SO AUGUST ... NOT SO CALM ...

SUNDAY AUG. 1 — Tom came over with a jug of wine for my mother, a pint for us, a foot of jazz records — and we started in. Around ten o'clock we got lonesome for women and took off in his Dodge, picked up Jinny, and Vicki, and went swerving around in park-drives, etc., and got tired, and came home. I had a serious talk with Jinny and I see that none of the pain she gave me was her own will. I met her mother, who is not affectionate, and she has no father ... and she is frightened & alone in things. Now I'm *involved* with her at last and it's beautiful. She turns to love affairs with furious compensatory affection and passion, she's lost ... and too young, also, to make an issue of it all. Just, as I said, a little princess, sad. I still don't know what to do with her. We

Wake was a Harvard literary journal, of which Seymour Lawrence was editor and publisher from 1945 to 1953.

hold each other incessantly, it's one endless caress, almost morbid, beautifully endless. We hardly talk. I'm lost, she's lost, we hold each other. She's amazing. That's all there is to it. Finally wrote that letter to Ann, having torn up Saturday's awkward levities ... Everybody's lost, Vicki's lost. Tom says Edie's still afraid of me, that is, to the point of fearing a return of love between us and all its lost overtones, all it would imply. Lost.

MONDAY AUG. 2 — And now, despite all, or perhaps *because* of all, of course, to finish the work of the novel once and for all. Got a letter from Neal, had an urge to answer right away, but would end up losing a day's work on a fresh-beginning Monday, so will wait. Worked, slept, walked, worked grudgingly — then, in the middle of the night, a wonderful interlude for myself: — spaghetti with the blood-red sauce and meatballs, Parmesan, grated cheddar, chicken cuts, with red Italian wine and chocolate ice cream, black demitasse coffee; and a 28 cent Corona cigar; and the life of Goethe (and loves), — all in the kitchen. And I never planned this, I just did it. Then I went back to work at 2:00 A.M. Spent night correcting 50 pages of ancient manuscript and rewriting parts, now a 30-page chapter, to be typed. Went to bed at 7 A.M.

TUESDAY AUG. 3 — Cool rainy day, workday. Started on 'Christmas Eve' chapter, swept on to 'New Year's Eve' and the 'shrouded child sweeter than a bird quivering with phantasy and understanding — amid all and among and alive all, and birds with disillusioned eyes flying high, but not now, O not now' — all new writing, that. A copious day's work, a hundred ancient pages prepared for fifty new ones or so. Then, at four in the morning, carried on with sea-chapter. Drowned happily in work — my Jinny, with her quivering sweet brow, awaits me, anxiously I suppose now that I am 'immersed' in art. Enigmas — mysteries swirling — the mind — the art. On, on —

WEDNESDAY AUG. 4 — Wearying myself with a great overload of revising-work. And I thought I was finished. I'll *never* be finished.

Wrote a letter to Jinny and told her I'd see her Friday. Also told her I was "leaving town soon — just about the time Victor Tejeira visits her, at which time I would fall behind in the game of love, thus, I must create a nostalgia for her, you see. Scheming, working, eating, sleeping, full of the feeling now that I am lost and have no beliefs. And I'm so sick of my novel, and words, words. Once it was the hymn of images and many verbs, now it's muddy poetry and many adjectives and plural nouns — tricks as cheap as my little lie to Jinny about being out of town when her love visits her. He's going to Paris, however, he too ... (Who am I? ...) But is it possible that there's less left to do on the novel? — after these three days 'furious revising'. — I don't frankly believe it. *Ca me navre** — It's not that I'm unhappy, it's only that I want to be in Jinny's arms again, *tonight,* not Friday night ... And I have work, and rivals, and muddy poetry, and sorrows — and I'm *happy.* It's a damnable restless surging after culmination — that's what it is — *When* the novel? *When* fame and money? *When* love? *When?* — what is always wrong with the pitiable *now?* — Blah blah blah, it's the soul, that's all it is. Wrote **2000**-*new-words* at night, 'Lost Father' chapter and completed the preparation of the mad confused sea-chapter. Much work today.

THURSDAY AUG. 5 — Cool, cool day, I'm grateful for these swell workdays, and nice and gray too. Gray workdays are my Thurinigian Forest,† my Weimar, and Jinny is my Italy, you see. I travel back and forth in my coach-and-four over the Alps of conflict ... (That's pretty neat, but a little *too* modern, neat and modern like my sister Carolyn's white walls and Venetian blinds.) Today I start the *big final typing* — let's see how long it takes me. When finished, I take the ms. to MacMillan's, or Van Doren, or Diamond, anywhere. It'll be finished all except *Apres-tous,* which will be a pleasant privilege however, the great last formal chapter ... Also, I've got the fragment "Death of a Father" ready to

*Loosely translated: "That upsets me."
†This expansive German forest's beauty has attracted scores of artists, including Goethe.

mail to Wake Magazine in Cambridge, to mail to the lions who will soften, perhaps to sheepish understanding of death & seriousness.

Isn't it true, also, that a man may eat and sleep and work all week, and be like a lamb in his understanding, and that on the Saturday-end he must ... well, what about his wild need — for a woman, for thighs, for torn-up passion, for drunkenness, and fatiguing sate, and calamitous fury! This is what makes the world go round, *apres tous,* after all, only sometimes it makes the world go round 'till it's dizzy, we complain about that, there are crimes and inconvenient atrocities. But come and ask the man, the lamb, the sleeper — who will be a lion all balls in a moment when he explodes. There's nothing we can do about inconvenience. It's complex, that's all. It's the soul, that's all. That's what it is.

FRIDAY AUG. 6 — Jinny has a temperature, so I took off my gladrags, which I had on, and got back in my work-rags, and went back to work. A beautiful cool night, too ... but I'll see her tomorrow. Tonight I irritably typed out **17-pages**, but for Wake magazine, the fragment, and while in the process came up with some small revisions, for the manuscript copy — 'Death of a Father,' that's what it is. I hope they accept it — if so, I'll appear with some unpublished Whitman. 'A fragment of an unpublished novel' — by 'John Kerouac' — (that's me, you see) — next to 'Unpublished notes by Walt Whitman.' That'll make me famous among the Lions and open the way to money. I forgot to mention I did **27-pages** yesterday, completing 'Charley' ... a big night's work that left me a nervous wreck. Batting **.336** — Tonight I also did revising-work on 'Mickey' chapt.

SATURDAY AUG. 7 — Went to Jinny's for supper — she had also unexpectedly invited Walter Adams: and there was no supper; we went out. I spent my big $4 on flowers and wine, etc. Then back at her house we had Lou & Babara, a get-together. Adams (in love with Jinny) and I talked, as we always do, about various things. He is full of strange hesitant sadness. Then I stormed out on Jinny, the petulant lover, and that's that. I really don't see any reason to describe it or make myself or anyone feel it. Just a girlish prank, she admits it: it would be better if she did not admit it. I expected it, anyway — and 'we're not the same type.' I don't actually care. She threw herself and I caught her, a little surprised, but not over-expectant. Period. It was nice. I shouldn't have torn up her pictures but I did. Lucien & Babara read my 'Death of a Father' and liked it a lot. I mailed it to Wake. Came home.

SUNDAY AUG. 8 — Depression of the lover. But Tom called me up and had me round out a night-clubbing foursome in N.Y. I met *his* love, a wild, charming, mad creature. My date was Esther Jack herself,* I swear. Hal would have loved her. We hit the 3-Devices & much good bebop and Jackie Patis and George Shearing and Oscar Pettiford. I had a long crazy talk with two Negro boys at the bar. Tom drove me back home at his usual speed-clip. The women stayed in New York, Park Avenue or someplace. And I had no feelings.

MONDAY AUG. 9 — Tom popped in as I got up; we talked about his girl, he played piano, and left. Then I got a call from Allen, and Burroughs was in town, so in I went again, and saw Bill, emaciated, sick, beat: and Lou & Babara were there: we talked: I went home. No feelings.

TUESDAY AUG. 10 — Grass will grow and the gods die fast, and everything is true. Something great is about to happen to me: I'm about to love somebody very much, truly, really, this time the 'real thing', but I don't know who. I just feel that. My eyes, incidentally, are hurting worse than ever. This last week of work could be the happiest in 2½ years if it weren't for all these things. I took aspirin and pitched in (after all the interruptions) — and piled up some pages.

THURSDAY AUG. 12 — Still beautifully cool — it's been so for 13 days now. Tonight did **23-pages**, all carefully revised (glee at new

*Esther Jack, the New York socialite from Thomas Wolfe's novels.

Year's.) Batting .345. Eye-aches gone. Haven't heard from *Wake* yet. Feeling very happy these days because I can still 'love the world' as exemplified somehow by the old Negro of the corn-rows and all those associations ... the U.S.A. and all that ... and can at the same time listen to Stravinski with intense appreciation ... which is all somehow due to my affair with Jinny. I'll explain later, it's all a discovery of my own psychology, the deep one that's hard to admit at first because it seems so irrational and stupid.

FRIDAY AUG. 13 — Completed 'glee' — and the 'lost father' — **10-pages.** Wrote a letter to Neal. Numbered my manuscript, it comes to 1,074-pages, with about 25 or less to go with 'Apres-tous.' It was fun numbering the ms. At last. But now, of course, I'm irritable because I think people won't like the book.

Stayed up till 7 A.M. working and just thinking.

SATURDAY AUGUST 14 — Took manuscript (in a packing box) in to Barbara Hale. She started reading it and fell asleep. Lucien read it till dawn. Meanwhile I rushed off to Corinna de Berri's studio and stayed up till 9 A.M. drinking and talking and phoning people, and fooling around. She's an amazing dynamo of a woman, about 38 — used to know Thomas Wolfe. Was Stravinski's love in Paris for awhile. Much married, mad and restless, she retains some of her once-amazing beauty. Tells marvelous absurd stories; also makes impassioned speeches about the 'throb' of America ('Amerrika'). She's 'Niceois,' from Nice, France, or whatnot. A mad new friend for me, although, in a way, she's too many for *me* — with the energy and passion of sixteen women. I am overwhelmed, I need rest after seeing her. Besides, I am perverse about human relationships, I refuse to face them. She called me 'close one,' which is beautiful and too much. Here you see what a real hypocrite I am. However, see however, — enough. That all may not be so.

SUNDAY AUG. 15 — Went to Tom's in Lynbrook and we worked on two tunes, words & music. One of them is possibly saleable — "The very birds are sad, nightingales are weeping ..." More later. Meanwhile we drank Scotch, but my eye-aches didn't come back. Had a great time. He woke up his sister Maria in the middle of the night to make her sing our songs. He loves his little sister.

MONDAY AUG. 16 — Came home. Sea-chapter to work on — and worked on the mournful tangle of it — dozed fitfully at night with my clothes on — wrote some more at dawn. Feeling afraid of work now, 'no courage.' But I've got to do it — the sea-chapter, and then, finally, the last chapter. Tomorrow Barbara and I are supposed to bring the manuscript to Putnam at MacMillan's.

TUESDAY AUG. 17 — Babe Ruth died yesterday, and I ask myself: "'Where is the foundling's father hidden?' — where is Babe Ruth's father?"* Who was it who spawned this Bunyan? — what man, where, what thoughts did he have? Nobody knows. And this is an American mystery, the foundling becomes the king, and the foundling's father is hidden ... and there's greatness in America that this does always happen. — Called Barbara and she's giving the manuscript to MacMillan's, James Putnam, next Tuesday. Meanwhile I'll do the sea-chapter and the last chapter. — And all ye world's minor minds will make symbols of a man's words — ye minds, a pound of knowledge, not an ounce of wit, of sympathy, or human signification. What is the ball of red sun on the horizon? — say ye, the illusion of refraction and facts? ... I say, it is the verse of the soul's signification. Just thoughts — Did **10-pages** of sea-chapter.

WEDNESDAY AUG. 18 — Tom came around, we had supper with my mother in the house and opened a bottle of imported Chianti. Then Tom and I took off for N.Y. and went out with his girl and her aunt Thelma (Esther Jack), to a jazz club again. Had excellent time. That

*The search for Babe Ruth's father notion was later used, to great effect, in *On the Road*, the search for Dean Moriarty's (Neal Cassady's) father.

Thelma is a beautiful little woman, I wish she didn't have to go back to Boston, I wish ... something about her. Although she's 13 years older than I am, she is childlike and wonderful, just like Esther Jack I swear, and a rich sense of life, all that.

WEDNESDAY AUG. 19 — Resumed work. Did **10**-*difficult* pages and have about 10 to go yet. I'm learning now that the 'artist' like every other kind of worker must *work on schedule,* push himself, hurry as much as he can, or, like any other worker, he'll never GET anything and really enough done. It's a lot a bull about the artist's — having all the leisure in the world to 'work.' Work is involved with time; you can't waste time building a house at leisure or you'll never move in. The Utopia for 'artists' fits in with the inherent core of art-work ... laziness and putting-off. So now I know this, after lingering as long as I have on the sea-chapter. I must knock off the final chapter starting tomorrow with the same urgency as the others in the novel, or it will stink, when eventually finished, with the smell of sloth. This is what makes a Hemingway spend ten years between novels* — even a Joyce. Dostoevsky wrote massively — "Crime & Punishment," "The Idiot," "The Possessed," and "The Brothers Karamazov" inside of 12 years, 3 years on an average for each work. And take Shakespeare and Balzac, they had interior deadlines, they wanted to get things done, they wanted to *live,* not loaf. I am going to start another novel soon. Well, that is, *soon* —

FRIDAY AUG. 20 — Did **10-pages** more, a few to go to complete sea-chapter. It's one of the great ones of the book now, whereas originally it was a mess. Work saves all ... Felt wonderful at 9 A.M. without having gone to bed yet (Sat. morn) and methinks soon I'll return to a day-life and go swimming and hiking and whatnot ... now that I'll be through with "Town & City" in a week! This August has been a splendidly cool month.

---

*Hemingway had not published a novel since *For Whom the Bell Tolls* (1940).

SATURDAY AUG. 21 — Finished sea-chapter, one of the great chapters. My 'father-dies' fragment was returned by Seymour Lawrence of Wake Magazine accompanied by a silly letter gently advising me how to write. I cannot describe the disgust I feel, or the anger. Somebody soon — if this keeps up — is about to be brained. I have a thousand exasperated feelings which I won't bother to sum up — they're obvious. For all the flaws in Thomas Wolfe, would I reject the sum of his work, his soul? — but I guess I'd better become an editor myself and make the same criticizing everyone else makes, and learns in college, and be on the safe side. Yes, I deeply regret that I cannot write; yes, boys, forgive me for — for whatever I did that excites your critical faculties. I wish I had faculties like that and just let them loose whenever my eye falls on a written line. It's much easier than work; it's respectable, too. Walter Adams, with a wan smile, says — "Oh yes, James Fenimore Cooper was more English than an Englishman could be, with his fine house, his fine horses, his fine wines, and his fine books — *therefore,* you see ..." — extending the palm of his hand, smiling vaguely. What Mark Twain has to say about Cooper only shows how stupid he must seem in Walter's eyes* ... Well, in that vein, Walter told "that little piss-ass" (as Lucien defines the Wake editor) that I needed an editor to clear my work of "considerable bad writing." Heavens, I certainly couldn't do it myself, I have no talent in that sort of thing, all I ever do is *write* ... which, after all, is the cruder side of the matter. It is the critic and the editor who must straighten things out and give literature its proper meaning. After all, what ungodly things would see the light of print if there weren't editors and critics of all kinds to rearrange things to their own satisfaction. After all, the writer is the child, he must be led by the hand to "craftsmanship." He can know nothing of "craftsmanship" himself, because, naturally, he spends more time writing than studying and pondering the matter. It is the critic who *defines* and "creates attitudes," without which, heaven

---

*In 1895 Twain published "Fenimore Cooper's Literary Offenses," an acerbic essay panning Cooper's novel *Deerslayer* (1841). Twain claimed the novel "scored 114 offenses against literary art out of a possible 115."

knows, our letters would be in an awful dumb state. Yes, it is time to re-examine values. I think I will apply for a job as a Value Re-Examiner someplace, or a Craftsmanship Ponderer, and make a deep study of the matter — go to college till I'm thirty or thirty-five — view America & all life from the perspective of Paris — I think I will do these things now. Yet, that's going a little too far, I think I'd just better struggle along, even without craftsmanship, and deliver my monstrosities into the gentle hands of experts. That will be better for me. *They all agree with me on that score.* Also, it would be awfully nice too if I hurried up and produced another book, and still another, and as many as I can, ere their faculties grow stale from desuetude. The work of life must go on, you know! We're all together in this! After all, you know! We writers must not waste their time! Who knows, someday there might not be editors and critics any more, they might vanish! — and *then* what a fine kettle of fish we'd be in! These blessings cannot always last!

And so on, you know!

SUNDAY AUG. 22 — I married Edie four years ago today. — Took in the sea-chapter to Barbara; saw Lou; and went to a movie with Tony. I might get Tony's United Press sports job in September. I don't know what to do yet.

MONDAY AUG. 23 — Told my mother she ought to go live down South with the family instead of spending all her time slaving in shoe factories in order to earn just enough money to spend on the system of expenses that is our society. In Russia they slave for the State, here they slave for Expenses. There's no difference anywhere ... people just go rushing off to meaningless jobs day after day, you see them coughing in the subways at dawn, and they never rest, they never relax, they never enjoy life, all they do is "Meet Expenses" — beyond food, they squander their souls on things like "rent," "decent clothes," "gas & electricity," "insurance," and a million-and-one "decent" appurtenances. Even the birth of a child involves months and months of "pay-money." Everything "costs money" now. My mother and the whole human race are behaving now like peasants who have just come out of the fields and are just so dreadful tickled because they can buy baubles and doo-dads in stores. The other night she came home with several dollars worth of junk for Nin's baby — even the sweet child is measured in "hourly wages" now. The whole system is incredibly — I don't know *what* incredibly. Insane! And when I told her these things, you might have thought I was blaspheming God Almighty!

Well, those are my sentiments ... As for *me,* the basis of *my* life is going to be a farm somewhere where I'll grow some of my food, and if need be, all of it. Someday I won't do nothing but sit under a tree while my crops are growing (after the proper labor, of course) — and drink home-made wine, and write novels to edify my soul, and play with my kids, and relax, and enjoy life, and goof off, and thumb my nose at the coughing wretches. I tell you they deserve nothing but scorn for this, and the next thing you know, of course, they'll all be marching off to some annihilating war which their vicious leaders will start to keep up appearances (decent honor) and 'meet expenses.' After all, what would happen to the precious system-of-expenses if our exports met with Russian competition. Shit on the Russians, shit on the Americans, shit on them all. I'm going to live life my own "lazy-no-good" way, *that's* what *I'm* going to do. — Tonight I read "Notes From the Underground." The other night I had read "Heart of Darkness," you know. I'm going to do a lot of reading now. Also reading "Tom Sawyer Abroad." I started the final chapter in a relaxed style, just to see how that works. The only trouble with my writing is too many words ... but, you see, "true thoughts" abound in the Town & City, which nullifies the slight harm of wordiness. Now I'll sharpen things. I have another novel in mind — "On the Road"* — which I keep thinking about: about two guys hitch-hiking to California in search of something they don't *really* find, and losing themselves on the road, and coming all the way back hopeful of something *else.* Also, I'm finding a new principle of writing. More later.

*Note that this is Kerouac's first mention of *On the Road* in his journals.

TUESDAY AUG. 24 — Took it easy, took walks, ate. I'm having a real nice rest now, which I didn't anticipate. No trouble with my eyes lately, too. Wrote to Nin & Paul, worked casually on last chapter (like a 'continental novelist'), and enjoyed myself, reading, eating, etc.

WEDNESDAY AUG. 25 — Went into town to see Tony — about job on U.P. I may get it Sept. 17. Tried to find the others; to no avail, and wandered in hot city night, irritated as hell. Slept at Tony's, read in his room, went to a movie next day (that made me wish I could go to sea again if I only *wanted*) — and came home in tremendous 100-degree heat. (101 actually.) The world is like a furnace-breath. Nothing to do or say — this is what the tropics are always like. No wonder white men go bestial in the "colonies."

THURSDAY AUG. 26 — Another day of impossible fiery heat, with a breeze like a prairie fire blowing into the window. The house was 93 degrees hot at 2 in the morning! I just take cold baths and read. I abandon my soul or something in this kind of atmosphere ... thus you see what a precious farce is my soul, after all.

FRIDAY AUG. 27 — Impossible heat continues. I take cold baths and read ... and do nothing else.

SATURDAY AUG. 28 — Impossible heat continues — cold baths, *ice-cold*, and reading ... Dostoevsky's marvellous story "The Gentle Maiden."* — Tom picked me up at night, we went swimming at Point Lookout at midnight.† In his house, later that night, I could not sleep for jungle heat and mosquitoes. But then a tremendous thing happened to me: — I had an ecstatic 7-hour rumination over the "truth of myself," — PRIDE. Yes, there's the subject, at least, in a neurotic like me.

---

*"The Gentle Maiden" (1876), among Dostoevsky's most acclaimed short fiction, depicts the first-person account of a man attempting to find out why his wife has committed suicide. Kerouac was reading a collection of Dostoevsky's short stories at this time, and thoroughly annotated the volume.
†Point Lookout, New York, a small vacation town on Long Island.

I had a picture of the human intensity of men as being represented by some little agitating organism on the forefront of the brain, even on the brow, and that being the everpresent palpitation (the brain's heart) of pride ... pride to humility, back & forth, in the intenser neurotic sense, pride to humility, back and forth. Can you just see that little thing beating away like a heart? — but more mental than a heart, *wilder,* more "intelligent." The source of all our troubles, too, but now I cease, as of this moment, being a philosopher, and turn to the action and mystery and details and human horror and "beauty" of that little thing. Shall I give it a name? — it is just above the eyes, somehow, and incidentally it is *not* the thing that kills us, it is our very life itself, our being, our humanity, our pride. It is all things, in a way. It is our nervous being. But, again, I cease being a "namer" of unnamables ... at least, not so much now as before. My new novel-in-mind ("On the Road") will begin among these new ... precepts? ... thoughts? ... discoveries? Even a calm woman like my mother has that wild pride palpitating on her brow. You see, I've discovered *the* thing. I will be wiser now (and *that's* a prideful statement.) "True thoughts," my new concept mentioned earlier ... the thoughts that come unannounced, unplanned, unforced, vividly *true* in their dazzling light ... led me to this further discovery.* Through all these things, for instance, it was possible for me to realize the following fragmentary things about myself (since "truth" can only be the truth of myself, which I see inside me, and cannot be universalized and vaguely generalized into 'truth for all men' whose *insides* I of course cannot see — trusting, therefore, that the truth in me may be the same in them.) — I realized these true thoughts about myself:

1) *I cannot waste my time loving others when after all, "I am better than they are."* (Do you see the light of that? ... it is an unrepressed thought, and incidentally it is hardly (I think) a geekish exposure of self for the sake of invidious distinction a la "Ginsberg" sort of? Yet it may be. This leads to another one ...

*This concept would later be developed into Kerouac's "first thought, best thought" philosophy, fully elucidated in his brief essay "Essentials for Spontaneous Prose," written in 1953.

2) *I must always justify myself to myself, because the others must not see my faults.* (It's not that I have been so foolish (pride! pride!) in the past as to not know these things, it's only that now, at last, I can weld it all into a statement and an art, as human being and as artist. Before it was necessary to hide these things for fear of 'sterile art.' And that was also a problem of cultural attachment (Kafka is bad for Americans, Wolfe is good, etc., etc.) Also, I yielded to pride without knowing why. Now I may know ...

3) *I am growing older and will die someday* — (This is only Nature, not humanity ... and it doesn't concern me so much anymore.)

4) Greed is pride, vice is pride, morality is pride — all is pride. (But that's only philosophy.)

5) *It is beneath my dignity to participate in life:* — to work at a job like the others, to be a hick farmer like the others, to ride in crowded subways with all the others, to do or be anything like "the others" — too much for *me.*

6) It is possible for me to admit my weaknesses and whimsies and chicaneries without being despised, *even by my mother and sister (and father.)* My soul has been nothing but a day-dream so far, like a Hollywood movie ... a complaint followed by a daydream, a "problem" followed by a "solution."

7) It no longer concerns how bad others can be — what concerns me is how bad *I am.*

8) To be inured to "problems" (as the Delaware were inured to cold winters) is not to have to "solve problems." This is one of the secrets of anti-materialism, so to speak, one of the secrets of social humility (living without waste.) *Mud.*

9) To aim for "truth" is a vicious pridefulness, holier-than-thou in its attitude. I must always turn my face from the others, from a new acquaintance, even, to *impress* him with my aloofness and interest in other things.

10) It is (not) self-laceration to admit the truth about myself. (You see how delicate?)

11) I have struck out at the pride of others and then sat back and expected them to forgive me. I shall tell them to forgive me. I shall tell them how I feel, and ask no forgiveness unless they wish to forgive. And so on — an embarrassment of riches all eluding me at the moment. All this is not at all what I wanted to *confess.* I'm tired now, no sleep. But this is my new work, more anon. The palpitation of pride is the thing: My father saying to Lucien in 1944, "I'm going to buy a rich man's son a drink!" — things like that. The details, the *life* of Solomon's Preacher's words — 'All is Vanity." One of the interesting things about these disclosures of dark self is that it all emerges without Freudian pornography, almost ... it's terribly "clean" and human, in the sense that the little palpitation on the brain is more spiritual, is *all* spirit, and the rest is *merely Nature,* Nature unchangeable, uninteresting, unhuman. You see that? — All this written on Sunday Aug. 29, by the way —

MONDAY AUG. 30 — No sleep, up early in the morning. "It takes much concentration and many steps to make a baby (and a novel?) grow and thrive." The quote is from Ann's letter ... I threw in the novel to see how it would look there among those clear and earnest and *wise* words. How does it look? "Many steps ..." — that's beautiful: It's beautiful and it evokes a picture of lonely integrity such as baby-nurses (and novelists?) must have.

TUESDAY AUG. 31 — Went to N.Y. to buy shoes, etc. Saw a movie, came back home. Got books out of the library — Tolstoy, Twain, Zane Gray, and a volume containing great autobiographical writings from St. Augustine thru Rousseau to Henry Adams, etc. And started work on final chapter for fair, writing several thousand words.

SEPT.

WEDNESDAY SEPT. 1 — Received a card from editorial dept. at MacMillan. Oh I hope they take it — it'll save so much time, I'll start freshly on new things, make immediate plans, start the balls rolling in my sleepy life ... all of them. Actually, I'm ready to grow up if they'll let me, and if they don't let me, how will it be to grow up unremitted for a job of writing like that book? What dolorous pessimisms I'll have! How disappointed & defeated could Ma get too? And the folks — Nin & Paul — how will I ever help them, if the world fails to recognize my work? and *now!!* not when I'm dead. Is it *really* true that diligence gets results — we'll see.

THURSDAY SEPT. 2 — Working on apres-tous still. Went to bed 1:30 A.M. last night, up at 6 A.M. today — Can't really feel this chapter some-how. (And if they don't like my book I can tell you one thing — it's *still* a good-enough book and they can all go to hell. So much for 'pes-simisms.')

Did considerable on last chapter. Read Tolstoy.

FRIDAY SEPT. 3 — Walked among the farmfields in back of the rail-road track this afternoon, in the warm September sun. I think how it would be if the land were mine and the crops my own. In due time, at rosy dawns, I'll be walking my own fields, in California or somewhere. Tolstoy's account of the hay making (scythe-mowing) in "Anna Karen-ina" only confirmed my inner knowledge of those things. Incidentally, at dawn today, I conceived a great story — for now let's call it "The

Partners." Wait till you read it! — I'm going to write it soon, in one long clip without a pause. The story is so psychologically accurate that it almost ends on an impasse, not allowing itself the usual philosophical summation. It concerns the "clear conscience of a transgressor" and the "guilt of a virtuous man," at the same time. It concerns the insufferable conceit of virtue and forgiveness, and the truthfulness of evil, and ends on an impasse — perhaps a killing, for the sake of illuminating the impasse. Tonight: — worked on apres tous, decided it's finished, but must weigh judgment.

SATURDAY SEPT. 4 — Went to N.Y.; dinner at Allan Harrington's, saw Stringham, & Tony & Lou & Barbara at her place afterwards — enjoyable conversations. Got a little looped. Everybody seems to like my book, the things I say, but not *HOW* I say them.

TUESDAY SEPT. 7 — Fourteenth day of lazy work on the last chapter. What a joke. The life of a mind? — not 'rational' thought, but the mere *process* which is undergone when the subconscious mind breaks through to the conscious mind. Hooray! hooray for me!

WEDNESDAY SEPT. 8 — Went to N.Y., picked up a few things, and saw "The Idiot."* (Rogozhin the most wonderful part of the picture. Myshkin was not *confused* enough.) But you'll never guess, this picture set me to thinking about women more than anything else, in a certain way I haven't thought in a long time. Well, the Nastasya of the picture was magnificent, the kind of woman I want (without the madness ... which is of course no longer *her*.) But a woman who *looks* like that. Worked on last chapter again, *and finished it.*

THURSDAY SEPT. 9 — Got form-rejection card from MacMillan's. I'm getting more confident and angrier each time something like this

---

*This French production was the first film adaptation of the novel by Dostoevsky. Released as *L' Idiot* (1946), it received lukewarm reviews and starred Gérard Philipe as Myshkin, Lucien Coedel as Rogozhin, and Edwige Feuillère as Nastasya.

happens, because I *know* "The Town and the City" is a great book in its own awkward way. And I'm going to *sell* it. They won't fool me with their editors who want to skimp everything down to the shallow formulas of this age. How many "forgotten-in-one-month" books must they publish before they realize what they're doing? Just like the movies, and like countless cheap goods that are used up as fast as they're produced, they turn out these cheap 'topical' or 'human-interest-small-village-in-Mexico-representing-the-human-undying-spirit stories' by the week, or books by celebrities, or 'angry' novels full of sex and violence. I'm ready for any battle there is, against anybody, in defense of this excellent book I have written, which comes from the heart and from the brain — it being only incidental, in a significant sense, that it should come from my heart and brain, — and even if I have to go off and starve on the road I won't give up the notion that I should make a living from this book: because I'm convinced that *people themselves will like it* whenever the wall of publishers and critics and editors is torn down. It is they, by Christ, who are my enemies, not "obscurity" or "poverty" or anything like that. It is they, the talking class (*trying to rationalize itself out of a base materialism*) who are the enemy of the people of this country. It is they who build New Yorks and Hollywoods, and flood our radios with inanity, and our papers and magazines with sterilized ideas ... I mean the great "Upper White Collar" class, the Commuters, the Whatnot, the people with snotty 'progressive' daughter six years old and sons who call their fathers 'daddy.' By God, I guess maybe I ought to go back to Canada. But I won't — I'd much rather make the rounds with that baseball bat. Tonight I finished and typed the final chapter. Last sentence of the novel: "There were whoops and greetings and kisses, and then everybody had supper in the kitchen." Do you mean that the folks of this country won't like this last chapter? — or would it be better if I said, "everybody had dinner in the dining room." *But the work is finished.*

Well, this is the Forest of Arden

STATEMENT OF SANITY

I will always worry when I see brutality and loneliness, and I will always be glad when I see people all together and happy. Whenever I deviate from this, I must understand that I am temporarily locked within the doleful psychosis of myself. And when I am thus locked, I should restrain the perverse impulse to tear down the bird's nest, and try to hold in my bitterness with tact and dignity. (If I sound like Aurelius the moralist with my 'musts' and 'shoulds' it should only be apparent to those who make such distinctions out of modern moral barrenness.)

However... The time should come soon when someone like myself may cease defending all 'simple' impulses and statements — (the quotes are a defense) — and merely make them. To defend a simple belief is merely prideful. You want to show that you are conversant with complex doubts. This is as bad as matching long words in an insipid conversational duel with another Freshman. And finally, as far as psychology vs. morality is concerned, I take the position, morally, that psychology is a hesitation-in-analysis and not an action-in-the-world. Knowledge has its place, but the work of life needs to get done. And the smugness of these virtues is not in itself an attack on vice.

What is included here are Kerouac's undated entries in his "Forest of Arden" journal, which was also filled with his *The Town and the City* worklogs from the spring and summer of 1948. The loosely structured essays in this journal concern mostly what Kerouac calls the "artistic-ethical struggles of great writers" and "the despair of 'thinking men.'"

The journal measures about 7½ by 8½ inches. On the cover "FUR-THER NOTES" is written in block lettering; below that is "Well, this is the Forest of Arden," and in the bottom right corner is the following:

J Kerouac

1947–48

N.Y.C.

NOTES CONTINUING THE ARIA

— Mortal men cannot hate each other, they can only be guilty of self-love. However, I do think immortal men, that is, men who would never die, could hate each other if hate is at all possible. Pure hate is impossible, it is only an inversion of self-love, and it probably comes from the fleeting sense that self-love cannot continue forever. But if men lived forever, and could continue self-love indefinitely, I think they would learn how to hate. For hatred implies continuation, and it cannot continue in a mortal world, a world made primarily for love and inverted with the various energies of love. There is a direct similarity in mortality and love, in that they "cannot last," but are necessary; while hatred and immortality are only possibilities. These are strange twistings of thought but they will define themselves later. And I didn't intend them to be anti-Christian, because Christ is the first man to realize that love is the rule of human life. He now looms greater than ever, and I'd be willing to bet that in the next century, Christ (and the few other great men like him) will fill the minds of people as never before.

One thing that overwhelms the sense of good & evil in people is the fact that "they only live once" and the "more the merrier" — the more money, the more fame. It's hard to really understand the tremendous *sense* of *self* that people have because to understand completely, is to leave one's self. And under the sway of terrific selfhood, all of us do say — "I've but one life to live, only one chance to be rich or poor." And this immediately obliterates ideal aspirations. This is why all religions stress immortality, or "another chance in the other world." But no one believes that, and everyone would be "evil" if given half a chance now. The girl who refuses a Hollywood screen test must surely think these very thoughts here, and may change her mind. If she doesn't, she may have something more voluptuous in store, or she may be mildly psychotic, or, what I can't understand at this moment, she may be a perfect loving human —

*　　　*

NEWS ITEM: — "General MacArthur bans kissing in the streets in Tokyo: offenders would get six months in jail."
— Thus, even your perfect loving human is thwarted in his own greatness, the only greatness: Love. Kissing is the ideal result of all the wandering to and fro in the Forest of Arden, kissing is the object of all human life when all is said and done. And a 70-year-old general with delusions of historic(!) greatness (for *what* is history? what?) will not have any of it. It's like I say, humanity will soon achieve greatness, but madness will continue to rule in high places.

Then there's the song by Nellie Lutcher — "I met a guy while walking down the street, I met a guy while walking down the street, he looked at me, I looked at him, he took my hand, and held my hand, he's a real gone guy and I love him 'deed I do — "* Just like that! *This* is the greatness of the Negro, right there, yet I can see how many of our "respectable" White girls would laugh at the words of that song. *Their loving is more prideful.* But still — a great humanity is a coming, I can feel it in my bones, I'm not worried, and I'm glad. More, more to come —

*　　　*　　　*

They're going to drop their systems of pride: this is the main point about future humanity. It's a wonderful thing to contemplate, yet

*Nellie Lutcher (1915–   ), rhythm and blues vocalist.

hardly easy for myself to do even in these moods of love & joy. But I'm doing it by degrees, and it's *easy!* after all: the trick is to get rid of the pride with a conscious loathing of it. The only thing to fear is the inevitable cretin in our souls. Some people are more cretinous than they imagine. It's not evil that's dangerous to the human world, that's the wrong word, it's cretinity that's dangerous. MacArthur's law is the dull musing impulse of a cretin, not the act of a man. A cretin is never afraid of being corrupted. Therefore a cretin wouldn't hesitate at anything: There's the cup of life before him, he doesn't drink, he doesn't fling it away, he just stares at it dullishly and doesn't understand. How do I know this? — this was I at 22, that was the way I was then, I distinctly remember, especially how easy it was to be a cretin, how stupidly pleasant. (Yet I also remember a tremendous dull unhappiness which I don't wish on anyone, either.) No, no, MacArthur, Oh man of destiny, no, no! — They'll put a stop to your law in the backalleys of Tokyo, and in time, maybe tomorrow, in spite of the penalty, in divine human ignorance of the penalty, on the streets themselves. Because this is the Forest of Arden, at heart, and MacArthur's tree is like all the other trees, and the lovers go to and fro beneath the boughs.

*   *   *

The girl with the screentest offer: — she fears an inscrutable kind of corruption, God knows what's in store for her, and I think she's right. But what of her single mortality? What of mine? — What would I do? The screen test is the American form of high Parisian prostitution in Balzac's society, it is the peach-skinned, pure-hearted Norman girl coming to the base Bourgeois sensual Crevels of Paris and losing the virginity of her heart forever. Do I hear someone laughing? No, this is true, and serious, and quite important: ask the old crones around the sewing table, they will speak and tell you. I believe the old crones around that sewing table, I believe they are as old and wise as nature, as the trees of Arden, and *get* you back to your gay hasheesh while I think of this for a moment now.

*   *   *

Do you know what is so utterly sad about the past? — it's because it has no future, the things that came afterwards have all been discredited.

*   *   *

To know that something is necessary, yet not need it for oneself — that's the crime of all "intelligent" and "responsible" men.
"Exterminate the beasts." — KURTZ*

*   *   *

Strip a man of his official capacities for a moment. It is the official capacities of this world that account for it's being so misused and degraded, so uninhabitable. In a half hour, if you strip a man of his official capacities, I might make him an eternal charming friend of mine — but give him back his official capacities next day, and he may very well sentence me to execution. There's the Forest of Arden, my friends, and there's the *World*.

*   *   *

I will tell you: there's a penny on my floor as I write this, which I haven't picked up yet, and I remember dropping a penny on my floor five years ago and someone saying: "Now don't go dropping your gold all over the floor!" I am still prepared to ignore that advice, with fierce pride: — When I can go out in the streets and strew my last dollars everywhere — then! It is understood that a human being may be saved or may not be saved, — (and this is great knowledge to store up

---

*This is a misquote from Joseph Conrad's *Heart of Darkness*, which reads "Exterminate the brutes."

138

for any mad, and necessary, eventuality that may come. What am I saying? — only that the possibility of insane Latter-day-Saintism is not remote from me at all. I don't really worry about it either, or should I say
'though.' — to make it frivolous.)

*   *   *

Art is a retirement from life that is sweet and beautiful and full of wise
genius. While the lovers roam arm-in-arm beneath the boughs of the
Forest, the artist sits under a tree and makes fine pictures and holds
them up to see. He is in love with himself, but he is also in love with
the others, because he shows them his fruits and works and cries —
"See? See?" Then, afterwards, he rests, and goes back to all of them,
back to the arm-in-arm of earthly love, and they love him because he
has done such a beautiful thing, he has celebrated their life and love,
and he has come back to them. They say — "How strange and beautiful is this one! — this soul!" And it is true, as true as it is mysterious
and compelling. "He is of us, he *is* us! — but he is alone beneath his
tree awhile. He will rejoin us with his sweet productions." And they
will say — "He loves God as well as men and women, thus he must be
alone awhile." "And what is God?" "God, Oh God is the sum of it, the
sum of it all." —

Why is "A Raw Youth" an evil book? — because in it, Dostoevsky
mocks, he mocks everything with a real deep and evil unhappiness, he
mocks the simplicities of life (which I grant are more often than not
unreal) — *but:* — he mocks! Now, what is this I'm saying? I'm saying,
let's pay our respects, all we writers of all sorts and talents, to men and
women everywhere, let's respect even their ambiguous dreams, which
we ourselves have more often than non-writing, non-intellecting human beings. When a man *mocks* something, he's mocking his own
abyss, and if Dostoevsky was enraged by the possibility of simple
beauty in life, then it must exist, it must be 'awfully true' that it exists.
Granted, no human situation is 'simple and beautiful' in its entirety,
and granted that words cannot any such situation describe (Mein

Gott!), and granted, furthermore, that it doesn't really matter and so on — but here's what I like: The world is a neutral place in the unspoken state of itself until some 'little thing' of a human being artist comes along and thinks on it, and *speaks,* and turns neutrality into *positiveness,* of any kind, stupid, crass, simple, complex, or otherwise. This itself is greater than the 'degree of awareness' men can have, the mere amiability of human art is a great thing in itself. This is vague, except for one undeniable thing: art should not be used as a cosmic 'gripe' at everything, it should be a sincerity in its deepest sense. This sincerity, to illustrate what I mean, is the thing that makes Dostoevsky go on laboring on "A Raw Youth" for hundreds of pages in spite of his own conclusions: It's his RACE-WIT, his 'old man hollering at him.' —

*   *   *

I have broken bread with thieves and sinners too, and also not for political reasons.

*   *   *

The difference between the 'show-business' crowd in New York and the 'intellectual' crowd is that, instead of being embarrassed by Jimmy Durante malapropisms the intellectuals are embarrassed by Freudian slips of speech. This is almost the only difference, you know? Who know?

*   *   *

Writing, you can do no better than surrender, with humble understanding and perhaps chagrin, and the purging joy of that, the communicative relief of that, to the most personal secrets of yourself with the laborious purposeful hammer of work, into stanzas and stories that draw the universal humanlike irredeemable understanding to them, in the way that grace and beauty always attract in nature — the pool unmuddled by any self-dishonesty either stupid or highly conscious, or by cant, or by comprehension of others made in fear and misunderstanding.

*   *   *

What if I believe in complete knowledge yet decide in favor of limited, honorable action (that is, without abrogating my rights, human and spiritual, to knowledge) — and yet once more, find that honorable action is not always honest action or what's worse, that it's not *fair*. That *fairness* is the key to this thought — (to be developed.) I must at least decide to become a true man now, yet without being unfair. On the other hand I cannot go on being a spiritual 'geek,' because that too is unfair in the sense that I will insult the very purposes of humanity. I will *will* it all now: an honesty and a purpose. And to be more exact, I feel the whole thing in this way! — sympathy is a real feeling but it is quite vast and universal, therefore *indiscriminate,* and leads to a beclouding of personal purpose in the world. And isn't this all too shifty! At least, your 'honorable' man is not always a sympathetic man. The facts only, in things like this. From now on, the facts.

The details are the life of it ...

MARASMUS — "a progressive emaciation or wasting away," which "attracts Bourgeois culture."
EPIGONISM — "degeneracy."

What is the meaning of all this? I just read about those things and I assume that they are Russian inventions, at least 'marasmus.' When I tried to remember 'marasmus' at first, I only hit on something that sounded like 'malamuse' — which, in French meanings ('badly amused') would certainly fit the Russian who invented 'marasmus.' But this is really a serious matter and bodes no good. It is very reminiscent of certain things that are going on in New York right now (1948.) We have our Reichians, our Orgonists, who mostly all smoke marijuana, listen to a frantic 'bop' jazz, believe in homosexuality (epigonism?), and are beginning to recognize the existence of an 'atomic disease' of sorts. And all these people are enemies of 'Bourgeois culture.' There is something definitely afoot, a madness, one not unlike the late Roman cult-madnesses. And, as I say, it hasn't started yet. The despair in France over Existentialism and Dolourism and what-not is nothing compared to what we'll have here. (I think I'll start preparing an article on all this.)

(Concerning the 'bop' music, it is sound, as music, and all that, but further developments have taken it onward to a more musically complex, almost symphonic height tremendous in its implications, yet the 'Reichians' refuse to listen to this new *musical* aspect of it and shriek with a kind of effeminate excitement over the undeveloped 'frantic' aspect of it.)

AMERICA and RUSSIA

The leading idea in America I conclude to be universal livelihood of man, as in Russia the leading idea indisputably is the universal brotherhood of man. Yet there are perversions of both of these ideas, leading to the two kinds of imperialism, American and Russian, in the world today. Yet the bald and exciting fact is that these two ideas may be merged someday.

The American offers world history the first real concrete "way to live." (The popular-propaganda 'way-of-life' idea is actually an abstraction and an illusion, connected with 'American,' which is after all only a matter of local color.) The 'way to live' as offered by American genius in all the practical and technical fields is in the end, however, far from being the mere 'materialism' that the Marxists and malcontented intelligentsia claim it to be. It is most spiritual: it is really the knowledge of how to be happy, healthy and real. Henry Ford and Thomas Edison, millionaires, geniuses and contributors to the great American idea of living, were themselves self-abnegating, almost ascetic, extremely spiritual and humble men in the world ... and everyone knows it. Their aim was not greed and power and wealth, but a 'better way to live' — a thing still to be developed, however, since inferior men always come along to corrupt the uses of great ideas and things. The most exalted Americans were all men of simple tastes and spiritual aims — Thoreau, Twain, William Allen White,* Lincoln, even Washington really. Men like Josephus Daniels† ('the first citizen of North Carolina' — over Thomas Wolfe, Brooklyn-buried?) and F. D. Roosevelt were not great. The American idea is also the exaltation of social humility & decency. With Russia's great Brotherhood idea, all this would grow.

In courses in 'creative writing' at the universities, we are told that a certain amount of restraint, tempered by modern enlightened education, and a close study of the science of writing — plot presentation, character development, and general thematic treatment — are needed in order to successfully probe and analyze and dissect the human foibles and social surfaces which have come to represent life on earth. Of lyric joy, of poetry, of Dostoyevskyan moral fury, of emotional grandeur, of sweep and architectural earnestness, — not a word in the universities. This doesn't begin to express it.

—   —

God as the Should-Be   (THE HUGE GUILT)

The most beautiful idea on the face of the earth is the idea the child has that his father knows everything, knows what should be done at all times and how one should live always.

This is the idea men have of God.

*William Allen White (1868–1944), Pulitzer Prize–winning political journalist.
†Josephus Daniels (1862–1948), owner/editor of the *Raleigh News and Observer* and champion of the Democratic Party, served as ambassador to Mexico under Franklin Roosevelt.

But when the child grows up and learns that his father knows very little more than the child himself, when the child seeks advice and meets with fumbling earnest human words, when the child seeks a way and finds that his father's way is *not enough;* when the child is left cold with the realization that no one knows what to do — no one knows how to live, behave, judge, how to think, see, understand, no one knows, yet everyone tries fumblingly — then the child is in danger of growing cynical about the entire matter, or despairing, or mad.

But that children and fathers should have a notion in their souls that there must be a way, an authority, a great knowledge, a vision, a view of life, a proper manner, a 'seemliness' in all the disorder and sorrow of the world — that is God in men. *That there should be something to turn to for advice* is God — God is the 'should-be' in our souls. No matter if actually there is *nothing* that should be done, no matter if science shows us that we are natural animals and would do better living without 'unnatural qualms,' without inner stress, without scruples or morals or vague trepidations, living like the animals we are, without guilt or horror — that we believe that there *should be* something, that we are *guilty* thereby, is God.

THE PHILOSOPHIC 'WHY'

Let's put it one way: The man who enters the house of doubt-and-wherefore and sneaks out the back way has no right to ask the man who has entered the house of doubt-and-wherefore and explored all the rooms and left the way he came in *why* he should do anything. That's why I was so goddamned mad when a campus philosopher, Martin Spencer Lyons by dubious name, (about 25 years old now, and more cracked than ever) says to me "What are *you* doing?" and I said "Writing a novel," and says to me with the voice of Gabriel, *"WHY?"* Why crap on him, I even know the wall-termites in the house of doubt-and-wherefore by their first names.

Does anyone realize what it means to go in a house one way and sneak out another way?

FOR WHAT DO PEOPLE mean, finally, when they say 'It's a small world after all ...'? Here is the root of human loneliness, to be lost in the too-huge world that is swallowing us all each passing moment. (Described in "Town and City." (Peter's dialogue with Judie Smith.*)   )

Incidentally, all deep novels could very well be entitled, simply, "People" — because that's *all* they're about. But an author chooses a theme, a title, and pretends knowingly, with the knowing understanding of his deep readers, that the theme is *really* a theme apart from people. "Crime and Punishment" is not about crime and punishment so much as it's about Raskolnikov, Sonya, the inspector, his mother and sister, and so on. *The theme is like a holiday that simply brings people together.*

*   *   *

But the secret of life, love, and happiness is *prosaic*. Knowing this truly a person can be happy, really. The minute-tickings of contentment — all that.

*   *   *

Thinking of Billy Eckstine, the handsome Negro singer, who has a marvellous voice, I unconsciously thought — "They don't give him a contract in Hollywood, he's the greatest of them all, they don't give him a nigger's chance ..." There's the true unconscious, the unconscious *truth*, brutal and true. The conscious mind embellishes ...

In California there's a grassy mountainside I know where cattle graze in full view of a Pacific vista. These cattle can see the blue Pacific on a

*Kerouac is referring to the confrontational exchange in Book 4 of *The Town and the City* in which Peter returns from a road trip to find Julie feeling lonely and out of place in New York.

late afternoon when the sun turns dark gold, and the wall of gray fog moving in on the horizon far away over the water, and the Yerba Buena hills of San Francisco jewelled and ivoried and emeralded with city, and the Bay, and the great Bridge, and Mt. Tamalpais gilded vastly in the late light, and the Sausalitos and far Oaklands and El Cerritos across the Bay, and beautiful flowers at their hooves. The air cools, the Pacific sighs, the sun recedes to Japan, 'Frisco and Alcatraz become bright with lights, the grass smells warm and exfoliate in the cool air, darkness produces itself in the whole immense roundabout world, and the cattle stand there awaiting the mournful night of windswept fog, and foghorns in the Bay below, and the occasional precious stars that shine through fog-gaps at midnight. These beasts feed on glory up there. Below, in the morning, the valley rings with heedless sounds, but the cattle are silent.

P.S. After reading this to my mother, I added: "There's all that huge beautiful view and only the cows to enjoy it." It occurred to me that this was my main purpose in writing the paragraph, but I never mentioned it *within the framework of formal, intellectually-communicative writing.* What I've got to learn is my own mind, not the one that was fitted over it like a mortar-board in my booklearning. In America there's a *claw* hanging over our brains, which must be pushed aside else it will clutch and strangle our real selves.

AMERICAN ANGLOPHILES — they represent a wistful desire to get away from the American sprawl of free jobbing and social freedom — they are always interested in the 'nobility,' either actual or spiritual — they resent the inroads that are apparently made on their sense of dignity — they also resent that fierce sense of collective self, or of widespread patriotic self, of American self, which is sneeringly called nationalism. They are Tories, nothing else, even to this day. The Europaphiles are the same, except that their emphasis is made from a sense of 'minority' resentment, and they don't make such a fuss of 'nobility' and 'order.' The 'chaos' of America is nothing but the evaluation made by those who prefer English or European ways of living and working. Actually, there is no such 'chaos' in the heart of the true American culture as found on farms and in smalltowns and certain smaller cities.

*　　*　　*　　*　　*　　*

NOTES ON THE DESPAIR OF 'THINKING MEN'

This is not another tirade of mine against the poor unhappy intelligentsia, not a tirade against that in myself which coincides with their mail-order horror. The 'thinking men', a phrase I actually heard three times in the past 2 days, means another level of men who are more or less independent in their views, with the emphasis on personal real knowledge. I admire these thinking men. I have observed their little notions. Some of them: —

(This is really about Harold Huescher.)

1)   They admire the 'folk,' the people, but their admiration is almost condescending: — They see 'patterns' instead of tableaus among the people; they notice their vigor as a kind of anthropological-economic phenomena — in other words, their admiration is partly an admiration of themselves for being so observant of the people and their 'ways.' Think of all the terms — 'folkways,' 'working-classes,' 'lower economic groups,' and so on, all the braintrust terms which never take blood, music, and grace into account. Their understanding is strictly Olympian, naturalistic, aloof, academical, sparse, 'factually objective,' etc. — and never *participant* or meek-knowing. I think the key is music and poetry: The 'thinking man' goes to the opera but he knows nothing of inner singing, the thing that makes, say, the Puerto Rican what he is in Espan Harlem: and he reads Melville or Shakespeare or Wolfe, but he knows naught of the living grace of people in their own

147

moment-of-self, that is, he cannot penetrate the poetry of a face, a fig-ure, a laugh and sense that *selfhood* there (he only senses his own, and then his studied, borrowed evaluation of theirs.) This is pretty vague due to hurried terminology —

2)   More importantly, the modern thinking man, in his emphasis on despair, seems to have a knack for posing his own fears without chal-lenging them. He seems to think only to the point of defeat, and does not go on from there to any sort of a fight. He seems to enjoy unsolv-able dilemmas which are not challenged, again — a kind of private men-tal masochism, a secret personal drama of *knowing* joylessness. (History may be a drama of attitudes.) The thinking man does not act on his judgements, but lets them ride into space and disappear. He paralyzes his actions. He *loves* defeat. What he really deep-down thinks I can't find out, he won't tell me. He is not *serious* enough with me to ever truly tell me. He loves to be subtle and play little conversational games. He is 'amused' by the 'cream of the jest' of this world, defeat, but that I can't believe. He discourages gravity, seriousness, quick judgment, swift de-cision, impulsiveness, immediate hope. He's been slapped down and 'it won't happen again.' He smiles at his own sympathy and humanity, as if it were a weakness, a fear, a caviling with the facts of 'tough-mindedness.' He does no longer *plan* ... He rides like a chip on the river and prefers not to plod in a line of his own. Incidentally, I think he is very deeply lazy, in a mental sense. He is honest. He is a good man. But he is uprooted from the people, has become a 'thinking man,' and has given up hope. It is not he who has built the bridges. The people did that, the boys from the people who learned to build bridges with-out thinking *why* the river should be crossed, or *what* was beyond.

On this farm or ranch where I'm going, it's not to run away from the generation and what I know so well about it, but to live my own life while I carry on with literary work. The solitude of the garret is neuro-sis through and through, whether it's Dostoevsky, Thoreau, Emily Dickinson, or Wolfe. Literature doesn't necessarily mean neurotic laceration of things. It might also mean knowledge of all men's lives, and knowledge of men's sense of themselves everywhere. It's a lot of things that it hasn't begun to be at all!

Privately, for me, it should be a calm home life to offset the restless mental life. ... Otherwise I'd burn out quick, like Wolfe.

STATEMENT OF SANITY

I will always worry when I see brutality and loneliness, and I will always be glad when I see people all together and happy. Whenever I deviate from this, I must understand that I am temporarily locked within the doleful psychoses of myself. And when I am thus locked, I should restrain the perverse impulse to tear down the bird's nest, and try to hold in my bitterness with tact and dignity. (If I sound like [Marcus] Aurelius the moralist with my 'musts' and 'should' it should only be apparent to those who make such distinctions out of modern moral barrenness.)

However ... The time should come soon when someone like myself may cease defending all 'simple' impulses and statements — (the quotes are a defense) — and merely make them. To *defend* a simple belief is merely prideful. You want to show that you are conversant with complex doubts. This is as bad as matching long words in an insipid conversational duel with another freshman. And finally, as far as psychology vs. morality is concerned, I take the position morally, that psychology is a hesitation-in-analysis and not an action-in-the-world. Knowledge has its place, but the work of *life* needs to get done. And the smugness of these virtues is not in itself an attack on vice.

AND NOW, after accumulation of several days' reading about the artistic-ethical struggles of great writers like Tom Wolfe and Joseph Conrad, and others, at least, those spiritual struggles as imputed to them by critics like [Maxwell] Geismar* and someone called Zabel, — Well,

---

*Maxwell Geismar was a critic at the *New York Review of Books* as well as editor of *The Portable Thomas Wolfe* (1946).

I've come to some conclusions. Does a great writer have to be unhappy? Must he sacrifice his life to his 'art'? If life and 'art' are one and the same thing in a man, how could he possibly sacrifice one half of a solid rock to another unless he sought to split that rock in half? I think that when you say that Conrad and Wolfe sacrificed their lives to their art, you're only saying that they were not writing what they really believed, there was a schism between their hearts and their work, it didn't fit together, it was deranged and unreal on both ends. Why did Wolfe labor so prodigiously to *prove* that he had talent and meanwhile forgetting that he was a man, a human being with a life to live in the world. Everything he did, I admire, including his self-burial, so saintly, in the solitudes of the Brooklyn 'jungle,' but I also see that he was blinded by an unnecessary pride: — he must have said to himself: "So I've no talent, hey? I'll show them! I'll show them I'm no ordinary slob with nothing to do but earn money and raise children and grow old reading Zane Gray" — something like that, something *petulant* all talented people feel at one time or another. If Wolfe was so haunted by time, why didn't he look at it and realize that in time, all things grew and changed and proceeded and he too could grow and change and proceed. It is not Wolfe's writings that are 'immature,' it is the spectacle of a full-grown man still seeking to prove his talent and forgetting all things else about himself — his life, his family, his heart, his happiness, his earthly future. This is also true, to me, of Joseph Conrad, who has never been accused of immaturity, and true of Balzac too.

If all our greatest writers had been men who were constitutionally unhappy and constitutionally defeated in the world, we would have reason to despair of all knowledge and imagination, or if not that, despair of the utter lack of responsibility in imaginative talented men. But there are great writers who were true men in every sense — Mark Twain is one. An uncomplaining man, a man who did not believe that literature is a constant tale of sorrow and nothing else. What does the gloomy sophomore write in his melodramatic tragedy? — certainly not the whole truth. Mark Twain piloted steamboats, dug for silver in Nevada, roamed the West, 'roughed it', told jokes with other men, hunted, worked as foreign correspondent, newspaper editor, lecturer, and was a family man — and yet, he did not have to sacrifice all that to his 'art,' he lived and wrote, he was a full man and a full artist, equally happy and whole as unhappy and unwhole, equally gregarious as he was lonely, equally, healthily, simply all things, and I believe he asked that his work be not compared to 'literature as it is known' because he wasn't doing 'that kind of thing at all.' He *was just writing what he felt like writing, not what he thought 'literature' demanded of him.*

But this is what Wolfe and Conrad, great artists that they were, did continually. They were terribly lonely and unhappy, unnatural men, and *why*, if it wasn't because they felt they had to sacrifice their lives to art. What stupid nonsense that truly is! They split the rock in half, they gazed at themselves in the mirror and thought of themselves as 'artists.' Finally, we had the 'beyond-good-and-evil' nonsense of Nietzsche, Rimbaud, and Gide — NUTS EACH ONE. Let's have another man who lives his life in the world, complete, and also writes great books. I think Zane Gray might have made this with more *work*.

Psalms

PSALM

Thank you, dear Lord, for the work You have
given me, the which, barring angels on
earth, I dedicate to Thee; and slave
on it for Thee, and shape from chaos
and nothingness in Thy Name, and give
my breath to it for Thee; thank you
for the Visions Thou didst give me, for
Thee; and all is for Thee; thank you,
dear Lord, for a world and for Thee.
Infold my heart in Thy warmth forever.

Thank you, Lord God of Hosts, Angel of the
Universe, King of Light and Maker of
Darkness for Thy ways, the which, untrod,
would make of men dumb dancers in
flesh without pain, mind without soul,
thumb without nerve and foot without
dirt; Thank You, O Lord, for small
meeds of truth and warmth Thou
hast poured into this willing vessel, and
Thank you for confusion, mistake, and
horror's sadness, that breed in Thy Name.
Keep my flesh in Thee everlasting.

This journal begins with a series of undated "Psalms," followed by a "Composing Diary" from November 1948 where Kerouac catalogues his work on *Doctor Sax* and *On the Road,* which he was working on concurrently. In the first dated entry, Kerouac writes: "Thus — my new diary begins. And its purpose, simply, to rediscover my *real* voice which is yours too, all our real, one voice, that's so often drowned by criticism and fear." A few pages of entries from the summer and fall of 1950 have been moved from this journal into proper sequence in the "1949 Journals." There is one last psalm on Kerouac's second to last page written in 1950, thanking God for the publication of *The Town and the City.* On his last page, there was an entry dated 1947 that read only "I am a hoodlum and a saint," since cut.

The journal itself is a standard marbled composition notebook. Kerouac has drawn a football, a baseball, a book, musical notes, and a basketball going into a net on the front. "1948" is written in thick marker and on the lines provided on the cover is:

John L. Kerouac

Journal

1939–40

— PSALMODY —

God, I cannot find your face this morning: the night has been split, a morning light has come, and lo! there is the *city*, and there are the city men with their wheels coming to swallow darkness under towers.

Ah! Ah! there's rage here, God, there's a bridge too upon which the wheels collide, beneath which they bring more wheels and tunnels, there's a fire raging here over dull multitudes.

God I have known this city and stayed here trapped and full of rage, I have been a city man, with wheels, and walkings all about inside, I have seen their faces all around me here.

I must see your face this morning, God, Your Face through dusty windowpanes, through steam and furor, I must listen to your voice over these clankings of the city: I am tired, God, I cannot see your face in this *history*.

PSALMS

And when I saw the light of the morning sun streaming in the city, my Saviour, I wept that there was such richness, I wept that Your light was shed upon the sorrowful weary city men, the melancholy women, within their black towers and byways all the light, my Lord: and oh my God now I pray to you — do not remove Your light from us all, and from me — I could not rejoice in more darkness, nor could I pray in the ignorance of the dark: Your light wide over the city and the bridge at morning — and I am saved, my Saviour, saved! By the sun which is a miracle, by the light which is everywhere bright — but Lord: give me power for my psalms, that I may rejoice powerfully, with equal light, give me tears for strength, give me again these mornings of light and purpose and humbleness.

·

And no more psalms exist in me, God? — no more rueful dark-joyed views of You, conceived in lowest loneliness, in darkest silence, in farthest solitude and fear, no more rich ripe singing talents put to use devout — no more?

·

Oh god how I rejoice in sorrows now, as though I had asked You for them, and You had handed them to me, how I rejoice in these sorrows. Like steel I will be, God, growing harder in the forge-fires, grimmer, harder, better: as you direct, Oh lost Lord, as you direct: let me find You now, like new joy on the earth at morning, like a horse in his meadows in the morning seeing the master a-coming across the grass — Like steel, I am now, God, like steel, you have made me strong and hopeful.
  Strike me and I will ring like a bell!

NOTE ON SEASONS
  My darling October, much too brief:
          and winter is lovely too:
  Spring far-echoing, musical and vast,
          only the Summer I hate.
  Yet — Summer is nothing but
          gorgeousness, too————————
  ————————————

MONDAY NOV. 1 — Now with a new novel to be written, I resort to these diary-logs in order to keep track of lags, and digressions, and moods: — although I no longer recognize "moods" as my real enemy but the psychology of accept-or-reject underlying their violence. More on that later. Three times I've started "Doctor Sax," and each start was a false start. My voice has become false somehow since I finished the last 'profundis' passages of 'Town & City' ... you can tell that from the tone of this inauspicious, dishonest opening tone. The New School* is a blight on the beautiful spirit for instance which animated the composition of the foregoing psalms in 1947, poor though they may be in quality. A man cannot create with his words and imaginative constructions anything of human, deepmost value unless he does it by himself without the carping of a 'gadding world.' I'm almost afraid to write now, each word is an insult to the New School & its ilk. And — again! — I've got to rediscover the "humility of writing-life."

I must do this "Doctor Sax" in 2 months; only a short novel, 50,000-wds. or so, in order to present it possibly in a contest by that time, or simply to have another work besides T & C on the market by New Year's. Thus — my new diary begins. And its purpose, simply, to rediscover my *real* voice which is yours too, all our real, one voice, that's so often drowned by criticism and fear.

Started writing at 1:30 A.M. Wrote about **2000-words**, using most of my earlier ragged-starting material. So I haven't really started yet. Went to bed at dawn, thoughtful, a little worried.

TUESDAY NOV. 2 — Continued, after a mile walk, in the afternoon. Begin integrating the "Doctor Sax" mad short-story of 1943 into this present scheme. Finished at 4 A.M., did **2500-words**. Listened to the

---

*Kerouac had begun taking classes at the New School for Social Research in September 1948 on the GI Bill.

amazing election returns, [Harry] Truman winning.* These 4500 words I have are still a hodge-podge of old material and as yet I don't feel *begun*. But you see my feeling — of anxiousness; but, at the same time, how enjoying myself with this little novel! Is it because it is not really "serious"? — That I don't feel torn by the story? Is this what they mean by objectivity? I still have to learn these things once and for myself, not in school, where they flit over the surface of these things in their studies of literature. I feel singularly happy, I feel "Doctor Sax" will be a success for me as well as for the reader. The texture so far is rich, rich. But what do I mean by seriousness — I know I mean mournfulness, real Martin-like people whose every feeling is real enough to touch on the pages. I may get to that when I start on the people and kids in Dr. Sax. If I don't, how truly successful *can* a work of art like this be deemed? No, I don't consider an objective Flaubert-type thing "successful" — tho we know nothing is really objective. Ah, we'll see, we'll see. The point today is this: why am I worried vaguely because it begins to be apparent to me that I can write without 'spiritual torment,' as others have done, and with artistic successfulness. Artistic is one thing, connected with the world; and *spiritual* is another, connected with me and my demented heaven that Harrington jibes at. More on this later. Tonight I also sent out four postcards, took walks; and realized that the greatest source of pathos in Mark Twain, to me, is that he never attempts to place his characters within an infolded, incurled world, a Twain-landscape say, but leaves them naked on the vast plain — whether that plain is the Mississippi Valley states (Missouri, Illinois, Arkansas, Tennessee, Louisiana) — or whether it is Nevada, California, etc. — naked in those vast nights. Simply that he doesn't presume to attempt a closed-in, landscapey, cosmogonical world (as I attempted in T & C) — is pathos, such pathos. Little Huck sometimes never knows *where* he is on the river, Nigger Jim hardly presumes to care ... but you know that Twain is terrified by those things. Dostoevsky

*Harry Truman defeated Republican candidate Thomas Dewey in one of the closest presidential elections in American history.

does this too, but *deliberately* (to show Slavic independence from Nature, as it were.)

WEDNESDAY NOV. 3 — A few short work-hours in the afternoon before school (I go to school to make money for rent and expenses.) Talked to Alfred Kazin after his class. He stumbles about, chatting away, almost getting run over by trucks, eager, stuttering, proud, a little piqued at this world which makes him cast furtive little looks out of the corner of his eye. Calls me "John." Wants to see the whole novel now. From that remote fury of himself he looks at me out of the corner of his eye and says, "It's obvious now that you have *something* there!" I like this guy because he is excited. Then I went to Dave Diamond's, brought cartons, we ate, drank. A writer — Marc Brandel — came in out of the night, very sober, handsome, a little haunted.* I couldn't for instance understand why he was wearing a black sweater under his coat jacket, no tie, raincoat. What did this laborer in stories think of the night, of the streets, of the rain that began to fall. He has written about Central America. He "flew" down there. He is not mysterious, just non-understandable. Then I called Lou, Lou came over to Dave's, Dave played his marvelous "Rounds" and other works. Yes Dave is a spectral artist. But he's always getting mad at me for whatever I do, I, a spectral artist less sober. That's Diamond, sobriety around his mouth, a harsh tongue, crazy frustration (I think.) How the hell should I know? Lucien and I lunged out into the heavy rain (as Peter and Kenneth lunge out of the morgue), full of suicidal intentions. We got blotto; ran into Jas. Putnam in Herdt's on 6th Avenue;† Putnam was blotto; Putnam had been to Barbara's cocktail party a few hours earlier, demanding why I wasn't there; I glowed with joy and retribution, but occasionally tried to restrain J. P. because it was too much for me. The three of us got blotto — more in his apt., on a quart of whiskey. We sat on the floor

*Marc Brandel (1919–1994), a British writer who had two novels already published at the time of this meeting with Kerouac, would go on to become a prolific writer of novels, plays, screenplays, and contributions to popular television shows.
†George Herdt's, a Greenwich Village dive bar.

looking at his poor middle-class guns & fishing reels, his intentions for a lost son. He told us who we were. So much time is spent in this life trying to decide *who* we are ... It's sad when you think all that I really do is only a waste of time and moment's joy. Staggering and reeling in various directions, we parted at dawn ... and that's only a picture of men full of wine, not "modern horror." I'm afraid of "modern" terms. Lou and I picked up a cardboard dresser from the street junk and marched along throwing dry turds and orange peels & old bottles into the drawers. We marched in on poor Barbara like that — Lou wearing an old beat hat picked from the gutter — and started a sideshow with our wares. Barbara joined us sadly. What a sad girl, showing she's this, or that, or something, (sophisticated?), — trying to find who she is. Well, she's a girl who didn't get mad at us for filthying up her rooms at dawn, unexpectedly too. Geekish, I went to school next day, joined Johnny Holmes, we sat in on dull Brom Weber's class. Then we talked all day, strolling, lingering; went to his house, drunk beer. His wife Marian came home mad as hell at him for wasting his time. But he was only basking, and doesn't she wish she could bask too? — a good girl beset by troubles and an inner anger about something. We ate, drank; I called up Harriet Johnson, she came over. (All this, and me without a dollar in my pocket as usual. But John and I learned a lot in our talks that day (another amazing guy, full of the One Prophecy that's rising, rising in the world now — another great friend for me, the taker) — *we* learned, *his* few pennies spent. He said I should take life's gifts as they come. He wants to know why I feel so guilty, why I "lurk") — Goddamit I'll always be guilty of something I'm always, always doing. What a shitty situation I'm in, up here (tap, tap)-) — A mad sex-night with perverse Harriet, a *virgin*. I got mad and stomped around, and she enjoyed even that. Morning, geekish, I arose to linger and talk with Holmes. Again Marian came home, in a better mood this time. Stringham came up bearing a poem, his broken foot, his woozy eyes. We hit a restaurant, then the sad bars, wandered around, laughed, moped, sulked, peered — I myself was at my wit's ends being so dirty and broke. Stringham and I called Diamond and he bawled us out.

"And Alfred won't stand for that either!" — meaning Kazin, meaning wandering around drinking. But that's only men, women, and wine, isn't it? I know less now than ever — absolutely stupid with mournful ignorance. Why is everybody continually building moral laws as though we didn't have enough of them already to burden us with guilt — me anyway. And Stringham too. Let's all just say "the hell with it!" and become *really* creative at last ... free, basking, wandering, idly stopping here and there, tasting, enjoying. Animals at last after the great interruption of ephemeral civilization. And *building* on that, celebrating all that. Went home — talked to Ma briefly in the morning, and took off once more, this time, by arrangement, sixty miles upriver to Poughkeepsie, to see Jack & Jeanne Fitzgerald. There's your Hudson, the haze dusk, the big light ... the afterlight of the world ... the hairy abutments over the water, the mist, the Hudson half moon in the sky — Sing Sing — then night, and Lowell-like squalid Poughkeepsie. Jack's ramshackle house ... books, beer, records, piano, his beautiful angel-baby Mike, — then, for me, a 17-year old peach who wasn't in the house thirty minutes but allowed herself to be pushed upstairs. What pleasures of the flesh! I want to start living again, no holds barred. As with Jinny last summer, a loving, vast, moist, softly undulating little fold — starry, lip-like, mound-like — a kind of eternity to its formless *vastness*. This is what all men want. They look at a girl, they worry about her words of reproach — but they should only consider the eternity of her vaginal folds all wet and desirous for love. Is this not the point of life? The cathedral, the pillar aspire only to this goal — let's admit it for God's sake. Henry Miller makes me cry in "Black Spring" when somebody's widow yields so softly with her fold — so lovingly, so lonely, so desirous — the hero is amazed, "he should have known," he thought she hated everything. Why, of course not. Everybody's deeply sane because of their flesh. Thank God for flesh! Thank God for the sanity of wine and flesh in the midst of all those I.B.M.'s and prisons and diplomats and neurotics and schools and laws and courts and hospitals and suburban homes where children are taught to despise themselves. When shall we again frankly enjoy a bowel movement, like children? All things, all things must tend again to the garden of things. Old Jack — well, there's a guy for you, casting pearls about every time he opens his mouth. What beer we drank! What beautiful and important things I learned. Jack has a great theme, a life-theme, in his vision of his father as "Old Mad Murphy" — who "pisses on everybody and loves and hates everybody," and who "knows there are more than one or two people in the world" (two or three is the way Fitz had it.) His Jeanne is a remarkable girl, radiantly *real* somehow, liberated as it were from the worrying balderdash which burdens most of us today. She cares for the baby with a kind of easy joy. The only chaos in the house is a kind of gentle chaos where Fitz accidentally and gently knocks over bottles and books. There is something radiant about the whole thing. The only sadness is their isolation in a city which would look down on them. But there is no real sadness ... just the square, the horse-trough at the end of their street, deserted, casting a long shadow on a Sunday afternoon. I walked with Fitz. He showed heroic "old mad Murphy's" grocery store, where he died, where he drank, where he lurched down streets. He showed me the places where he played as a kid. We went back to his ramshackle joyous little house and drank beer and made the discovery (while Jeanne was taking a long walk with baby Mike) that on some Monday morning everybody should stay home and do nothing but linger among themselves and bask — no more I.B.M!! no more factories! no more punch-clocks! no more fancy clothes & furniture! no more waste of flesh-and-blood in the maws of civilization! no more of anything but food and drink and love and contemplation of all ourselves! And no more sins and guilt, no more need for sins, no more *guilt for not being guilty!* Nothing but all things, frankly understood at last, rising from sexual energy outward to all human communications and situations. Nothing but the world, its light, and people *in it.* (not *out* of it, as now.)

TUESDAY NOV. 9 — Hitch-hiked back from Poke. A truck-driver, as he rolled his big truck into the Bronx under huge November light, said, finally, after our long agreeing talk, "Life ... is a mystery." I came home and started to write "On the Road," laying "Doctor Sax" aside for awhile — which I have yet to feel (until only lately, working out new ideas.) At night I saw Holmes and Tom Livornese. Big argument about my sex-idea. Can I lose friends by expounding the sexual revolution? We'll see ... I don't think so ... everybody *really* agrees with everybody. I have the feeling these days that I "know everything." And decided to live more and write more, instead of like Diamond living less to write more ... or less? I also feel brash and happy these days. I do anything that comes into my head, and my only guilt is of not being guilty enough ... again.

Wrote **6000-words** of "On the Road," but roughly, swiftly, experimentally — want to see how much a man can do. Will know soon.

WEDNESDAY NOV. 10 — Got letter from Temko in Paris. Wonderful. And great letter from White in Denver. And mad Mayian letter of cavernous terror and St. Francis, from Ginsberg. And Putnam — about my "Wild Trip" story, which we're fixing to sell. Things whirling so much I can't keep up. Two novels, and a third, Town & City, soon to revise — and school, classes, readings, exams, term papers — and all friends — and girls — and booze — and plans to go to Paris in Feb. — to travel U.S.A. in January. Can I do all these things? Can't I? May I?

Ah, the eye of an elephant in its curling head, the looped-up trunk, the craggy hide around it ... Went to Kazin's class at night, after writing **2000-words** in afternoon (1st draft, fast, rough), and had a chat with him, and Harriet. Kazin says, "So you want to be a writer." — with knowing sorrow. But wait till he reads what I have done. As a matter of fact, my writing is a teaching, and it would be impossible for me *to teach if the others already know;* yet I'm always impatient because they don't know what I've done, am doing: but it's better this way. One of the greatest incentives of the writer is the long business of getting his teachings out and accepted — a drive that says, "Ha-ha — wait and see!" Writers deal with one another like Kwakiutls at the potlatch ceremony, saying, "Ya, chief! — you cannot match this!" — and, "Ya, dear,

I'll *outmatch* it!" (Kazin is also a 'writer' now, doing creative book.) Had dull intellectual conversation with Harriet, who is influenced by a Djuna Barnes aesthetic of some sort, and wants a "homogeneous America" like Puritan America. Much 'prettier' — a woman dealing with human beings as interior decoration. Came home at 2 A.M., to write. With Kazin in a 5th Avenue bar, with Harriet in San Remo, Pastor's, and Minetta.* There sat old Joe Gould, no longer eager for conversation: too old now: after an eager half-century of talk: just reading his paper, an old man now like any other. But I love this old guy for what he did, and perhaps his "Oral history" is actually a great book. It may well be. But Joe, like me, must also know that "it is better" to have your teachings go momentarily unrecognized, or one would die all *revealed*. Nein? Carlyle could talk of this ...

In the subway I saw a Negro woman with a bible who might well have been my mother. Did you know that the subway is a great living-room of humanity? How else can men, women, and children sit facing each other, as in a home! The subway is the front parlor of New York, on wheels, rushing through darkness ... darkness ... we all sit there reading, looking at each other, communicating, basking, peering, lurking, seeing ourselves. The subway has never happened before in history — people *face* each other on shelves and it's like 'visiting.' (visitin'.) Wrote another **800-words** at 3 A.M.

THURSDAY NOV. 11 — In the afternoon wrote **1500-words** of "On the Road"; and went to Putnam's in N.Y., fixed the short story, signed at school, saw Lou briefly, & Barbara; saw my New School friends; (and from them I see the interesting fact that the "revolutionary intelligentsia" in this country now do not go to school, they are on all the Times Squares of America smoking hay, talking Reich, reading the papers, listening to bop — the New School intellectuals do not

---

*These are three Greenwich Village bars: San Remo was a Bleecker Street bar and Italian restaurant and legendary writer's hangout; John Clellon Holmes wrote of it in *Go* (1952); and Minetta Tavern was a popular bohemian hangout on MacDougal Street.

count — this is part of the American Sexual Revolution coming, the revolutionaries don't even believe in schools). Then I visited Duncan Purcell and his German wife Edeltrude, and we had a talk of some consequence, though I went away with the distinct feeling they thought I was mad — not only mad, but a criminal of some sort — of course I told them of my unspeakable revolution. That did it! I don't mind they're being Nazis but I wish they were Nazis with a purpose, revolutionaries! — Will I hate myself soon for all this brashness? I don't intend to. I have found a great truth.

FRIDAY NOV. 12 — Wrote **2500-words** in afternoon, after a walk to the library, down the street here in Ozone. Then signed at school in N.Y., went roaming Times Square with the Holmeses, came home. Thinking up mad new ideas for "On the Road."

SATURDAY NOV. 13 — Nothing matters but my writing, after love. (I may be losing my school-money for negligence. I'm always negligent about silly formalities — why don't they just give me my subsistence allowance, I've nothing to learn in school, especially *that* pale school, seat of anemic revolutions.) Today, spent a pretty day at home, football game on television in Linden's bar, papers, eats — and a movie at night with Ma. Windy Autumnal day. My new novel is growing in my mind. At night, resumed, wrote **3000-words.** But I wonder if I can do Doctor Sax too. "On the Road" is a sure bet. It reads "for everybody." It fulfills Mike Fournier's desire, expressed last Spring, that I write "true action" stories. And it is vast, complex, sad, funny. The quality of the writing is poor — or yet it may be better than T & C, I don't really know. Hit sack at 4:30 A.M.

SUNDAY NOV. 14 — Halfway mark of November coming. Wrote **2000-words.** Decided perhaps the best way to do "Doctor Sax" is on a kind of "higher" Al Capp* kick — but right now wrapped in the Road.

*Al Capp (1909–1979), creator of the comic strip *L'il Abner.*

MONDAY NOV. 15 — Signed at school, and then went to Alan Wood-Thomas' art opening at Carlsback studios. Everybody there. Ran into Don Wolf, now a songwriter, after 8 years (since Horace Mann.) Don and his Gershwinesque-looking partner Alan Brandt (a brilliant Broadway-type personality) wrote "Now He Tells Me" for Nat King Cole. Met Alan Wood-Thomas, a swell guy, manly, sincere, smart, dreamy, and a good artist — & his mad, vast wife Annabella (cute trick). Scores of people streamed into John Holmes' after the preview — the owner of the studio, cavorted just like Oscar Nietzscke and Dick Kelly do at parties, dancing and prancing alone. Later, got drunk with John and Herb Benjamin, a madman who says he writes "lush" Djuna Barnes novels, who says the novel is a dance. The important thing about Herb is that he's hip, open, sweet, — I was real drunk and spouted Shakespeare. Holmes and I had another almost-angry discussion concerning political consciousness. I slept there with all my clothes on, rose, talked with John four hours — then went to Tony's, waited, slept — then went home. Wrote two torn-souled letters to Neal and Fitzgerald ... as though it were my last night on earth. I never was so strangely maddened, & God knows why ... The letter to Neal asked for forgiveness, and inscrutably, so did the letter to Fitz. To Neal & Carolyn I said, "I kiss your feet because I don't want to die, lives, you lives" — (how I meant it!) These things are inexpressible and lovely, and *are* love. I reminded Fitz that we both sought to love our fathers' lives. In each letter there was the expression of my new "free" feeling, as evidenced from the fact that I also spoke to their wives in the letters. To me this is a break-up of my fear of women as other than sexual souls — a coming of realization that they are my sisters, that they *are* unequivocally fellow-creatures. This is deep with me, thus the incoherence and naivete. Previous to this I have always usually *categorized* women, that is, I told them different things than men as though they were angels and not humans — what we call "gallantry" and "seductiveness." (Clark Gable.)

WEDNESDAY NOV. 16 — Got up late, did nothing but fill out a new address book. Feeling guilty of my recent "brashness" and "indecency." Ate, and went to Kazin's class. Talked to Bill Welborne after, — a mad new guy. Then I came home & inadequately wrote **700-words** of the Road — that is, things kept happening I didn't intend. Is this the truest kind of writing, though? — compulsive, even fearful, even unspeakable. I am so close to this now that I can't say. Went to bed sadly.

THURSDAY NOV. 17 — Went to school. Saw Dick and Marilyn Neumann, and Welborne, read Sando Burger & his girl Carol, the wife of John Taleyke, an old acquaintance from the days of Burroughs. Long day of varied conversing. Funny that when I left the house in Ozone I was sad because I had no concepts to justify joy, and felt gloomy and beat anyway, but just watching all these people filled me with something great. Came home to write. Also with the conviction that Dr. Sax *must* be done sometime — because Welborne himself thinks of The Shadow as a beyond-evil Gothic figure, without my first mentioning it. A Dr. Sax is waiting, therefore, to be actualized into myth. John Holmes was first to remind me of this (after I myself saw it.) But John's understanding of my "On the Road" fills me with a vision of my own purpose I could not. **1000**-*more-mysterious-words* that get away from me in a trance of writing as I type along. I've always been afraid of trying this — this may be it. This may be the greatest "break" in my writing since last November when I "opened up" from a previous verbal-emotional prison. This may even lead me (Ginsberg thinks so) to that state of writing which Mark Van Doren characterizes as "easy or impossible." I told Allen all about this, and he said such writing "floats lightly over an abyss, like a balloon, like reality." (Specifically, certain passages in my 'Remember? Okay' — chapter in "On the Road," where the boys Ray and Warren conduct irresponsible, incomprehensible conversations in the midst of their hurryings to buses and destinations.) To float lightly over an abyss is like life, when, unpremeditated, we lose our preconceptions in the swirl and danger of real things happening and become full of swift, flitting, nameless fret, sometimes sudden unexpected joy, sometimes fits — all of it criss-crossing and intertwisting and looping around the central, certainly celestial knowledge we *all have* about what we're really up to. But this description is so sad — it's nowhere near. Real intellectual concentration in a work of art is after all only a thing in itself — an analysis, an 'insight' like Proust(?) — it is not life itself, as in Dostoevsky and Shakespeare and sometimes even in Celine. A 'balloon', exactly what we feel as we flit in life like Whitman's kingfishers over the brook.* What engrosses me most now is this irresponsibility we have in the midst of so many specific actions, such as shopping, riding subways, reading, sleeping, even lovemaking. In this irresponsibility I see the bubbles of our life, bubbles which seem actually to be made of the glaze-mist that fills our eyes at moments of eager fun — even at moments of grief. It's *pink!* (I'm not being flamboyant, just serious.) Pink bubbles popping out from our eyes and bursting brilliantly in the great sunlight of our... central life.

FRIDAY NOV. 18 — Wrote **3000-words** in the afternoon, good ones again (tho not so fearfully compulsive; "I knew what I was doing.") We'll know what that means someday ... About the pink bubbles: these considerations, or investigations, or loomings, of mine are for the future. I don't overlook the fact that this is a decade of prosperity and that we have been enabled to turn our attention to love, whereas, in the 30's, economic problems made this virtually impossible. But for the day when atomic energy shall have partially solved economic problems, as I believe they will be (or mankind won't grow, and it always grows), for that day when we'll arrive at the last, greatest problems of life and death in the soul, I proffer these seemingly irrelevent considerations of mine. These things will be foremost then — the 'problems' of basking and love, the sexual pervasive. Whitman has already pointed

*Kingfishers are common in the works of Walt Whitman. From *Specimen Days* (1892): "I write this sitting by a creek watching my two kingfishers at their sundown sport ..."

the way. By the very fact, also, that people have bubbles in their eyes I am convinced that they won't destroy the world. Something else will happen: We have meannesses and inexplicable cruelty, and fits of destruction, but we also have bubbles, balloons, and flowers — the irresponsible joyousness checking the responsible wrath, for what is more "responsible," more "answerable," than judgment? When the judgments of wrath disappear, it will only be because we no longer can stand the weight of "character" (as it is called.) Our codes are life-hatings, nothing less. But our pink mist is life-loving. Can you see this pink mist of joy being allowed at West Point, gray stony seat of honor and codes and responsibility? — where men stand erect only because of a code, not because of a joy.

A huge party took place at night, at Johnny's. First I had dinner at Sando's, with Carol Bernard and Welborne. Sando used to be a junky — knew Huncke and Vicki, was married to Stephanie Stewart. We had a good dinner in their 5th floor Raskolnik apartment in the Bowery, and then met a kid from Detroit at Grand Central, who said he was Tennessee Williams' tea-connection. Then all to Holmes. Here's the roster of this vast party (if I can remember it all) — Us, and the Holmeses, hosts, and a beautiful blonde in black Persian slacks called Grace; and Rae Everitt, (my 'date'), and Harriet Johnson, Herb Benjamin (great, funny guy, a male Ruth Sloane); and Ginsberg; Bill Welborne, and Conrad Hamanaka a Japanese writer; Ed Stringham, Susan, A. J. Ayer a philosopher, with party; Lucien and Barbara; over twenty people, and I know I forgot somebody. Herb had plenty of tea — we consumed four quarts of whiskey — everybody wandered out for walks. I had one with Grace, who is married, a really beautiful doll with whom I refused to start anything due to knowledge of her position and intentions, that is, it would involve nothing but frustration and agony for me, because I could "go" for her, and she doesn't really care(?), and is married, and coquettish anyway. She played everybody. It was a good party. It was so pretty to see Lucien and Marian drunk together (and old Holmes went off someplace with Rae.) Harriet and Herb took a shower together. Welborne left, sore because no liquor.

Hamanaka stayed till dawn. Herb imitated Gypsy Rose Lee. At dawn we dispersed in the rain. Good party.

SATURDAY NOV. 19 — Stayed home, eating, shopping, dozing, talking to Ma. When am I going to hear from Little, Brown? — and Atlantic Monthly? Any day now, what was once my greatest ambition, success as a writer (payment and recognition), will occur. I can't believe it — *and I never think about it.* I'm just recording this. ("A good sign," I tell myself deeply — therefore no difference in my ambition?) Wrote at night: — **1500-words**; the story lags too much?

SUNDAY NOV. 20 — Got up late, walked, watched semi-pro football game, etc. Wrote **2500-words** afternoon and night. Also wrote first draft of essay on "Whitman: A Prophet of the Sexual Revolution", for Kazin's course at New School. And wrote a letter to Alan Harrington demanding to know more about his bronco-busting rootin'-tootin' Indian half-brothers in Arizona. (He pays no attention to them.) In today's writing I got at a good portrait of a young Negro street-haunter (Paul Jefferson.) The novel is opening up now to many characters from "Town & City" — to Liz Martin, Junkey, Buddy Fredericks, Levinsky, later Denison. All my novels will be tied together like Balzac's: This is due to my "sense" of American life as a unity, for me. Due to a feeling ... and it works well.

MONDAY NOV. 21 — Went to New School, signed. (It's like signing for checks, that's all it is to me — the School bores me.) I cut the class and walked a mile ½ to a movie on Times square, 2 old films from the '30's, "Captains Courageous" and "San Francisco."* Those pictures they made then had the power to make one genuinely cry ... no more nowadays with false 'toughness' of heroes. I recall now how "Captains Courageous" made me start writing a novel at 13 — I wonder what

*Captains Courageous (1937) was a Victor Fleming film — based on the Rudyard Kipling book — starring Spencer Tracy, Lionel Barrymore, and other notables; San Francisco (1936) was a Clark Gable romance picture.

happened to that first chapter that I wrote. (Sis emptied my "files" in 1935.) Came home, ate, wrote. — **1000-words**. Shaping up — the characters are more *real* as I reconsider them, & work on.

TUESDAY NOV. 22 — Wrote over **5000-***'miraculous'*-words, wrote all day long and night. (Levinsky in Beckwell's telling of Rembrandt's Christ and Chaplin's angels, and all the others.) I dood it today. Feel good. And I quit not because tired, but for the hell of it.

WEDNESDAY NOV. 23 — Dreamed in the afternoon. At night after supper went to Kazin's class. (In the afternoon I also wrote a letter to Harrington and did some research in Ginsberg's letters for "On the Road.") Ginsberg (and Harriet) were sitting there in Kazin's. A good lecture on Melville's "Redburn." After, Kazin had a few beers with Allen and I. He said things about Diamond that gives me a new vision of Dave — said "He has a hard time, (or a bad time of it) living." I decided to have a serious talk with Dave (who's mad at me lately.) Instead, with Lucien-Archangel, we all (Allen, Barbara, Bob Niles, I) — got sick drunk. At dawn I carried Allen and Lucien over each shoulder, for a block, in my stockinged feet — lost my pencil, too. Slept in Lucien's car. Staggered home at 9 A.M. Too much, too much. Sick, too. Diamond is right. But it's Lucien for whom I always seem to want to die ... and all of us, even poor, sweet, angry Barbara. How she hates me. It was one of those Lucien-daemonic nights ... fights, dances, pukings from balconies, fallings-down-stairs, shouts, and final half-expirings from alcoholic surfeit ... in gutters, gutters, the same old Rimbaud gutters. How sad — what a pain I feel when I think of Lou, who knows all, is killing himself, glows, shines, dies, the sublime Harpo Marx Lucien. He is in his eternity, a bird sitting over the hundred fathoms ... a newspaperman middleclass Hunkey, and a Rimbaud, a Don Birman,* a angel of death.

*Don Birman is the alcoholic main character in director Billy Wilder's film *The Lost Weekend* (1945).

THURSDAY NOV. 24 — Thanksgiving. Walked 2½ miles for ice cream. Duck dinner, talks with Great Ma. (Wrote a letter to Aunt Louise also, yesterday.) Tom came at night. We ate ice cream, rode in his car, played piano — Thanksgiving Tom, who is lost.

FRIDAY NOV. 25 — Went to movies in N.Y. with Ma — Stan Kenton, French picture, etc. She wore her best clothes and how I love my mother, my sweet, dear little mother ... a *person* like all the other treats I happen to know so accidentally. What thoughts I've been having since that binge, from whiskey-sickness which always induces visions. My mother is just "it." I brood over her with such delight. I think Hal Chase is crazy for mistrusting me ... I hope Hal comes back to me. I love people. I know now how geekish we all feel. I am not worth kissing anybody's feet, not even that so poseful. Why don't we all die? Why do we live with such pain of living? Why do I feel pain when I think of Marian, or Lucien, or Burroughs? — a pain that is just "it." Everything is "it." It's got it.* We'll know when ... When I think of them all, and hateful me *in the middle* (reason, see, so hateful.) What a big hole in the world! And in that hole, that amputation, there it is ... why we don't die. "She will not put the notion at rest (that I dislike (or dislove) her) (Marian) until she sees you again." How *avid* we are! How can I hate anyone as much as I hate myself? — therefore, we all love each other don't we?

It's not true that you must love yourself to love others, as Ann Brabham said. You must hate yourself with that pain, then you cross the shadow-bridges to the other side of eternity, where their avid faces twitch, pale, gone, gone ... Above I said "I love people." What an asinine thing to say. *That* was self-love. I have no right to be loved, haven't I? It's all somewhere around here and it's the reason why we don't die. For we know superciliousness does not come from a supercilious

*Throughout Kerouac's published *On the Road*, Dean Moriarty speaks of his search for the enigmatic "it."

source ... and many other things. I've lost all my warm consolations, I sit on the hundred fathoms — everybody please love me.

SATURDAY NOV. 26 — Home in afternoon. Wrote letter to Paul about he & Nin & baby Paul coming to live with us. Saw last moments of great Army-Navy game in the bar.* Ate, talked to Ma (who said she'd never be sick if her kids would come and live with her, especially little baby Paul) — and I went to N.Y. Holmeses and — (this includes his mother, sister, and wife Marian) — I had big talk about society. John says we're "products" of society, I say we only use it from out of our fundamental natures to serve ends which may not always be "fundamental" on top. Argument, really, between a modern Liberal and an anachronistic Catholic (me.) Herb Benjamin came and we went to a Cannastra party, where I hooked up with a Pennsylvania girl called Ann Truxell, an artist; and we went back to John's. In the morning she was gone; much high school stuff occurred. I don't care particularly here because I don't know her anyhow. In the afternoon, more long talks with the whole Holmes family, upstairs. Then we went to Alan Wood-Thomas's house, where I saw his little daughters, his wife Annabella (Lowell-like), and Pauline ... beautiful Pauline, Alan's model. It was a strange, sad, moving day + night. Little LeeAnne, five, told me about the house she'd get when she grew up. Pauline I fell for ... she's a mother, too, and sings with her 2-year-old daughter Marcie ... a prodigious, melancholy child. Pauline's husband appears from hearsay to be cruel, tho this may not actually be true. Pauline is a Neal-type girl, much trouble all her life ... a warm-hearted, Edie-naïve girl, tall, beautiful, Lombardian. Hope to see her again. But I was struck by the fact that "everybody" is married, or are lovers, except me. Why is that? It must be me. Alan Wood-Thomas sketched everybody ... strange how he does that, "his own way" of basking. John was in an intense, ripe mood. It was moving; they said Pauline had a "crush" on me. What do I do now?

*Considered by many the greatest game in the long history of Army-Navy football, this 1948 matchup between 0–8 Navy and 8–0 Army ended in a 21–21 tie.

MONDAY NOV. 29 — The whole Pauline feeling is undefined, I'll let time eat the matter out. I got a beautiful letter from great Jack Fitzgerald. What the hell is Little, Brown doing with my ms., with my time? — I sent them a prodding letter. Full of feelings these days, & curiously for once at ease with these feelings and with other people. Even when little LeeAnne sat on my lap I did not feel like a monster. Maybe I'll get rid of all that now, because it's only bull after all, as Ed White repeatedly used to maintain. It may even be true, by God, that all of us make myths continually and that therefore ... there is no reality. I am not no dashing mad Kerouac, I'm a sad wondering guy (Wood-Thomas' sketch of me is truer, a 55-year-old meditative workman) — and similarly, my pictures of others have been equally untrue and absurd: but since we even have pictures of ourselves, there must be no reality anywhere, or, that is, reality is the sum total of our myths, a canvas out of which everything shows (as in Dostoevsky) with little left out, a cross-section of individual phantasmal creations (in the sense that the daydream is a creation, a whole production.) The energy of this creation, as Casey used to point out at Columbia (Fitz told me this), is the energy of life and art. Yet the watch-repairer has no illusions; I repaired a watch-bracelet Saturday, no illusions about it, *except* that I hooked it up intricately in *my own way* since I couldn't make the instructions work. The reality is there, tho not so simple as Burroughs' Factualism reality. Phooey! — and why pick on Bill at this point. Lucien has always said that he listens to another music than the one we think we're making. Then he says "He-he." — so wise the Archangel of Death. Our fantastic creations *are* our relationships — that is, the mere fact of fantasy is the focal point of communication. And this is all words, words, — another music.

PSALM

Thank you, dear Lord, for the work You have given me, the which, barring angels on earth, I dedicate to Thee; and slave on it for Thee, and shape from chaos and nothingness in Thy name, and give my breath to it for Thee; thank you for the Visions Thou didst give me, for Thee; and all is for Thee; thank you, dear Lord, for a world and for Thee. Infold my heart in Thy warmth forever.

Thank you, Lord God of Hosts, Angel of the universe, King of Light and Maker of Darkness for Thy ways, the which, untrod, would make of men dumb dancers in flesh without pain, mind without soul, thumb without nerve and foot without dirt; thank you, O Lord, for small meeds of truth and warmth Thou hast poured into this willing vessel, and thank you for confusion, mistake, and Horror's sadness, that breed in Thy Name. Keep my flesh in Thee everlasting.

SECTION II

On the Road

1949 Journals

1949

ROAD-LOG

Wed. 27 — Started "On the Road" with a brief
500-wd. stint of 2, 3 hours duration, in
the small hours of the morning. I find
that I am "hotter" than ever — tho on
closer examination afterwards I figure
I may only be over-pleased with words,
and not structurally sound yet (after
a long layoff.) My interest in work
is at a high pitch. My aim is to
have much of "Road" done, if not all,
by the time T&C is published next
winter. I quit school today so I can
do nothing but write. — Now I want to
expand the original 500 words which, in
the heat of work, 'discovered' an important
opening unity.

Thus. 28 — Stayed home playing with baby, eating,
writing letters, walking; movie at night.
Some family trouble - not serious — concerning
debts. Wrote at night. It appears that
I must have been _learning_ in the past
8 months of work on Sax, and poetry.
My prose is different, richer in texture.
What I've got to do is keep the flow,
the old flow, nevertheless intact. I
think one of the best rules for prose-writing
today is to write as far opposite from contemporary prose as possible — it's a
useful rule in itself... actually. — Wrote
500-words — (more, actually, but making up
for yesterday's miscalculated count.)
I figure for the whole novel, right now,
at 225,000 words. Some ways off, eh?

Though Kerouac labeled this his "1949 Journals," this 122-page semi-daily journal actually runs from April 1949 to April 1950. It chronicles Kerouac's daily life, his reaction to the publication of *The Town and the City*, and his progress with *On the Road*, *Doctor Sax*, and other stories as well as some of the trips that would later be fictionalized in the published version of *On the Road*. Some of the entries included here were pulled from Kerouac's "Private Philologies" journal and inserted to fit the chronology.

In the four-plus months between the end of the "Psalms" diary and the start of this one, Kerouac had taken his first road trip with Neal Cassady — which is fictionalized in part 2 of *On the Road* and some of which is covered in the "Rain and Rivers" journal. He returned to Ozone Park in mid-February and resumed classes at the New School. In March, soon after Professor Mark Van Doren had recommended *The Town and the City* to Harcourt, Brace editor Robert Giroux, it was accepted.

A portion of the entries included here detail Kerouac's stay in Westwood, Colorado, in early summer 1949. He traveled there alone by bus in May and convinced his mother and sister (with her family) to settle there permanently. They came but by early July all but Jack had left. His mother returned to New York and moved into the second floor of a small house at 94-21 134th Street in Richmond Hill, Queens — less than three miles from Ozone Park — where Kerouac returned later in the year. Their block was loud with the commotion of motor traffic coming in and out of Manhattan and the clamor of the Long Island Railroad, which also ran nearby.

The journal itself is a spiral notebook that measures about 6 by 9½ inches. "CASH" is printed on the cover, and the pages are ruled vertically for financial bookkeeping. Kerouac has written "1949 Journals" on the cover.

APRIL 1949

ROAD-LOG

WED. 27 — Started "On the Road" with a brief **500-wd.** stint of 2, 3 hours duration, in the small hours of the morning. I find that I am "hotter" than ever — tho on closer examination afterwards I figure I may only be over pleased with *words,* and not structurally sound yet (after a long layoff.) My interest in work is at a high pitch. My aim is to have much of "Road" done, if not all, by the time T & C is published next winter. I quit school today so I can do nothing but write. — Now I want to expand the original 500 words which, in the heat of work, 'discovered' an important opening unity.

THURS. 28 — Stayed home playing with baby, eating, writing letters, walking, movie at night. Some family trouble, not serious — concerning debts. Wrote at night. It appears I must have been *learning* in the past 8 months of work on Sax, and poetry. My prose is different, richer in texture. What I've got to do is keep the flow, the old flow, nevertheless intact. I think one of the best rules for prose-writing today is to write as far opposite from contemporary prose as possible — it's a useful rule in itself ... actually. — Wrote **500-words** — (more, actually, but making up for yesterday's miscalculated count.) I figure for the whole novel, right now, at 225,000 words. Some ways off eh?

FRI. 29
Went into N.Y. to pick up new wine sports-coat & pearl slacks — a $40 outfit. Saw Allen. Something's wrong with my soul that I refuse to feel

and grieve in this monetary notebook — but Allen is grievous. Saw Holmes, Stringham & Tom too. Felt even a little hostile & stern to everybody. Something's wrong with my soul, but this does not mean that I'm not happy these days. Spoke to Lou on phone. Stared at the waters off the Battery and felt that I was saying goodbye to New York in my ... (soul?). Something's definitely changing in me: instead of feeling as much as I used to ("the tension is off," said Allen), I have been mulling with some feeling over the fact that I've stopped "feeling." I no longer feel wild & eager. I think this is bad. But on the other hand, as I say, I'm saying "goodbye to N.Y." like the Red Moultrie of my novel.* Ah well — all's well. Even Allen will be allright. Everything seems against the law today, too — which is a doomish thing. I also was conscious of too much malice in the world, like harsh Nature which man must control, or die. Ruminated later at home.

And at 4 in the morning wrote **500-words** again, with the admonition to "Keep it moving." Thank God for work!

FRI. 29 — Wrote to the boys [Ed White and Hal Chase] in Paris in the afternoon and in the evening went to N.Y. with Nin & Paul to buy a bed — also to see about jeeps. At night we had a late jolly snack. Then I settled down in the kitchen after everybody was in bed and read and wrote. Wrote **1200-words**; fluid words, and maybe the novel begins to be underway at last. Feel good about that. Went to bed at dawn. (Also wrote in my wonderful 'Rain and Rivers' notebook.)

SAT. 30 — Went to Jamaica [Queens] with $40 and bought some Arrow shirts, slacks, ties, and a good pair of shoes. My wardrobe is complete except for cuff-links and socks. It is certainly a sin to sharp up like this — (what would the Lamb think?) — but such is life: a sin in itself, almost. At night dozed at home, and then took a walk in the Saturday night Ozone Park. Abandoning the sloppy pen. Wrote my 250-word biography for Harcourt, Brace; and wrote **1000-words** on the novel. To

*Red Moultrie was the central character in Kerouac's original conception of *On the Road.*

keep building it up is the point. Funny, too, how unsufferingly I can write now. This is perhaps the greatest Grace that has fallen on my head lately. Sometimes I'm mystified by this good fortune. God is good to me — He need not be. I am not the Lamb, not the Lamb.

— MAY —

The May, the soft, airy May ...

SUN. 1 — Went to bed this morning at ten, because I wanted to enjoy Sunday morning. Got up at 5, went for a walk, read a little, wrote a little, and hit sack early. Just a musing day. "Sketched" a little — that is, I write a prose sketch, which can always find its way into my novel later on. Read "Faerie Queene."

MON. 2 — Nin & I took pictures in my room in the afternoon, for use in H-B publicity. All these days are leisurely, playful, casual; followed by the meditative night ... far more easy on the nerves than my old 'T & C' days & nights of darkness and terrified perspiration. It's because I have a family now, and my talent is recognized. — And what about the poor people everywhere? Who is going to give a bed to a household where children sleep on floormats, six in a room? Who is going to buy the high vitamin pills for the undernourished, sickly infant? Who is going to comfort them in the darkness? (for when you're poor, the darkness is less rich: or is that really so?) What does the millionaire Al Capp do with his time & his money & his appetites? — he is not the billionaire Fatback he satirizes? Is there an honest millionaire? — one who could throw his money away, & return to his earlier life, his habits of poverty and hope? Is there Jesus in the land?

Do we need a Jesus? — is the time coming? And will this Lamb reveal? Shall he reveal the secrets of joy in the land, and shrouds? For all this is too much of a scramble for me, and already I foresee, I foresee ...

I foresee Waste in my own house, and Dull Lust, and Laziness, and Snarling Sin. I am thinking. I believe that if I make a lot of money, after a good farmstead & lands, & tools, that there is something I will do ... something like old Tolstoy, and only because I am serious about this whole thing, i.e., my life, and yours, and the feeling for God. And because I fear corruption more than anything else in the world. I will not *learn* riches, I am not Solomon; I am he who watches the Lamb; I am he who has adopted the Sorrows; I am he, John L. Kerouac, the Serious, the Severe, the Stubborn, the Unappeased; he who is pursued by the Hooded Wayfarer; he who wants Eyes; he who Waits; he who is Not Pleasant, and has Silences; he who Walks; he who Watches, and has Hidden Thoughts; he who Grinds the Stone and even the Faces — with Eyes.

He who is not Satisfied.

He who Hates Satisfaction.

He who loves the White Valley of the Lamb.

He who Eschews, and Waits, and Watches, and Sleeps, and Wakes in Anticipation of the Lamb, the Lamb so Meek on the Mountainside.

May 2nd

Patient have I grown, and Waterfalls.... For the White Valley of the Lamb, and the White Angel of the Shrouds, and the Land of Rainbows and Eagles, are not Far. Beware my Eyes are Grindstones! ... but my soul it is not water: it is Milk, it is Milk. For I saw the Shrouded Angel standing in the Hooded Tree, and Golden Firmaments on High, and Gold, and Gold. And the Dusky Rose that glows in Golden Rain, and Rain, and Rain.

Wrote **1000**-*good-words* at night (about where 'ragamuffin dolls and little dusts do lie.') Novel going slow but sure.

TUES. 3rd — Went after my clothes. Saw a ballgame at night in Polo Grounds — a big delightful spectacle, and good game. Slept at Holmes' — talked, drank beer.

WED. 4th — Went to look for Hal Chase but he wasn't in. Came home tired: played ball with Paul after a nap. At night we all went out in the convertible and had ice-cream. All day I've been struck by the Sadness of May ... Saw such a beautiful girl on the ballfield. Oh but the sadness of the May — and even though the May's for all, it's not for me: — as the pictures of me taken Monday attest. They are studies of a madman. Oh but the sadness of the May: what odorous night, what soft eyes stealing into mine, what plaints sighing in the lilac-hedge, what moon! And mad-eyed me. Soon, soon, I must marry the Queen of the May.

At night I wrote about **1000-words.**

THURS. 5 — here's what I think of De Quincey — he is conscious of his reputation as De Quincey, and so absorbed in this that his work is useless, i.e., it reveals nothing; moreover he does not know how to conceal his consciousness of himself-as-a De Quincey, which is a little dumb and vague; and conscious also of *all* his virtues — *all* of them — he is therefore the victim of that one great non-virtue. Today I wrote many letters and straightened out my little affairs, including Adele [Morales]. And I took the sweet child, Little Paul [Blake, Jr.], for a trip to Cathay* ... in the stroller: — by gigantic machines, great hedges, strange dogs, large children, immense plains, rivers, lakes (they were puddles), and where Malayan birds fluttered in amber lagoons. He also saw a Brobdinagian horse, and many strange forests. Either he felt like Marco Polo (it was 2-mile walk) or I myself am the child. *All absorbed in the freshness of the dream* ... this is fatherhood. I was very happy. He held his maple leaf fluttering like a flag, and rode into Cathay standing like a charioteer. I even explained things to him, & stopped before monstrous plants to let him understand. I picked flowers for him. We came back via another continent. At night I read De Quincey, and Blake, Blake ...

*This is an allusion to Marco Polo's famous boyhood trip from Venice to Cathay (China) with his father and uncle.

Nicholas Grimald* is not a bad poet either. "A Venus imp ..." he says. Nor is [Robert] Herrick to be denied, not so at all, no sir, not Herrick.**

Wrote 700-useless words that will all be crossed out. My first impasse in Road.

FRI. 6 — Estimated that the moving bill to Colorado would come to about $300.00. I'm itching to do this. So's everybody but Paul, who is worried about going so far away from his old folks in Carolina. I'd like to get a sportswriting job in Denver to begin with — later wheatfarm.

WED. May 11
After the weekend in Poughkeepsie at Jack Fitzgerald's, I decided, now, to go out to Denver immediately and find a house. Will go alone, hitch-hiking, in the red, red night. Harrisburg, Pittsburg, Columbus, Indianapolis, Hannibal Mo., St. Joe, Last Chance, & Denver.†

SUNDAY MAY 22 — Took a walk up to Morrison Rd. to buy this notebook and had a beer in a big Sunday afternoon roadhouse up there on the ridge. How less sad Sunday afternoon is in the West. I sat near the back door and listened to the mid-American music and looked out on the fields of golden green and the great mountains. Walking around the fields with my notebooks I might have been Rubens and all this my Netherlands. Came home, ate, and made preparatory notes at night. Starting "On the Road" back in Ozone, and here, is difficult. I wrote one full year before starting T & C, (1946) — but this mustn't happen

*Nicholas Grimald (1519–1562), Rennaissance poet, wrote "A True Love."
**Robert Herrick (1591–1674), Episcopal minister and poet; his *Hesperides* (1648) included twelve hundred poems, including the oft-quoted "To the Virgins, to Make Much of Time."
†Kerouac ended up traveling by bus. Portions of that trip are detailed in the "Rain and Rivers" journal. Most of the following entries — in Westwood, Colorado — were pulled from Kerouac's "Private Philologies" journal, which is otherwise not included in this volume.

:— PRIVATE PHILOLOGIES —: (page 15)
:— RIDDLES —: [much of which is just nonsense + words-]
AND A
TEN-DAY WRITING LOG   Westwood, Colo.

LOG SUNDAY MAY 22 — Took a walk up to Morrison Rd. to buy this notebook and had a beer in a big Sunday afternoon roadhouse up there on the ridge. How less sad Sunday afternoon is in the West. I sat near the back door and listened to the mid-American music and looked out on the fields of golden green and the great mountains. Walking around the fields with my notebooks I might have been Rubens and all this my Netherlands. Came home, ate, and made preparatory notes at night. Starting "On the Road" back in Ozone, and here, is difficult. I wrote one full year before starting T+C, (1946) — but this mustn't happen again. Writing is my work now both in the world and the "moor of myself" — so I've got to <u>move</u>. Planned an earlier beginning before the 8,000 words already written in N.Y. first 2 weeks of May. Went to bed after midnight reading a Western dime novel.

MONDAY MAY 23 — Got up refreshed at nine, walked to the grocery store, came back and ate breakfast. It's a sin how happy I can be living alone like a hermit. Mailed some letters I had written yesterday. Drank coffee on the back steps, where the Western wind in bright afternoon airs hums across the grass. (Why do I read Western dime novels? — for the beautiful and authentic descriptions of benchlands, desert heat, horses, night stars, and so forth; the characterizations are of course non-authentic—)—
Worked in the afternoon, and till eleven at night, knocking off <u>1500-words</u> or so. I sometimes wonder if On the Road will be any good, although very likely it will be popular. It's not at all like T+C. I suppose that's allowable —(but sad)— now.

JKerouac—
6100 W. Center
Westwood, Colo.
May-1949
"On the Road"

again. Writing is my work now both in the world and the "moor of my-self" — so I've got to *move*. Planned an earlier beginning before the 8,000 words already written in N.Y. first 2 weeks of May. Went to bed after midnight reading a Western dime novel.

MONDAY MAY 23 — Got up refreshed at nine, walked to the grocery store, came back and ate breakfast. It's a sin how happy I can be liv-ing alone like a hermit. Mailed some letters I had written yesterday. Drank coffee on the back steps, where the Western wind in the bright afternoon airs hums across the grass. (Why do I read Western dime novels? — for the beautiful and authentic descriptions of benchlands, desert heat, horses, night stars, and so forth; the characterizations are of course non-authentic.) — I worked in the afternoon, and till eleven at night, knocking off **1500-words** or so. I sometimes wonder if On the Road will be any good, although very likely it will be popular. It's not at all like T & C. I suppose that's allowable — (but sad) — now.

> JKerouac————
> 6100 W. Center
> Westwood, Colo.
> May — 1949
> "On the Road"

TUESDAY MAY 24 — Woke up at 9:30 with the first "worried mind" in a week, since I've been here. Just a kind of haggard sorrow — and later some worries about money until my next stipend from the pub-lishers. This is a better kind of money-worry than before T & C was bought, for then I had nothing, absolutely nothing. What they call the 'proverbial shoestring' was for me then a mad mysticism. Hal and Ed White must feel today what I used to feel then — a loveless existence in a greedy money-world. I still feel that way even though I know I'll have *some* money all my life from writing, and will never starve or have to hole up in a canyon, eating vegetables like Huescher, or wash dishes in the great-city slops. Someday perhaps I myself will look back on those days (before selling book) with the same kind of wonder that we now look back upon the pioneers living in the wilderness on their wits and grit — someday when some form of social insurance will be in effect for all mortal beings. Because most of the jobs nowadays by which you can earn just enough to live are insupportable to imaginative men ... like Hal, Ed, Allen, Bill B. and numerous others. It is just as difficult for that kind of man to punch a clock and do the same stupid thing all day as it is for an unimaginative man to go hungry — for that too is "going hungry." I am continually amazed nowadays that an actual Progress is underway in spite of everything. This Progress should aim at meaningful work and social security and greater facilities for minimal comfort for all — so that energies may be liberated for the great things that will come in the Atomic Energy Age. In that day then will be opportunity to arrive at the final questions of life ... whatever they really are. I feel that I'm working on the periphery of these final things, as all poets have always done ... and even Einstein in his deepest investigations. "Solving problems," as Dan Burmeister insists, is essential now (and may or may not be a tendency in late-civilization anxiety) — but after that there is the question of the knowable that is now called 'unknowable.' I feel that the most important facts in human life are of a moral nature: — communication between souls (or minds), recognition of what the Lamb means, the putting-aside of vanity as impractical and destructive (psychoanalysis points there), and the consolation of the mortal enigma by means of a recognition of the State of Gratitude which was once called the Fear of God. And many other things as yet unplumbed.

But these are all sunny Colorado reflections and may not apply in the Dark Corridor where something far stranger is burgeoning (I mean Allen.) It may be that Allen is deliberately insane to justify his mother, or that he has really seen the Last Truth of the Giggling Lings. Even if that were so, I, as Ling, could not use it. (All this refers to the fable "Ling's Woe.") Then again, since all of us are really the same man, he may, or I may only be fooling now.

Finally I recognize this at least as an *absorption* of the life-mind ... which may be the only thing we have, like flowers that have nothing but petals that grow. *All is likely.* "This was life," as I wrote yesterday in Road. Ripeness is all.

There is a dynamic philosophy behind the Progress of the 20th Century, but we need to reach the depths of a Static Metaphysical Admission — a Manifesto of Confessions — as well, or the dynamics will just explode out of control like Kafka's penal machine. Perhaps something like this should happen: after the age of five, every human being should become a shmoo and feed the little ones; shmoos with wings like guardian angels.

There should be no great shmoos to kick Good Old Gus across the valley. This is not the Lamb, not peace. Even Good Old Gus, at his depths, is standing alone weeping on the plain looking around for confirmation of his tears; and his vanity is his evil. Dostoevsky knew that even about Father Karamazov.

Worked all day, wrote **2000-words**. Not too satisfied, but enough. Retired at night with papers & the Western dime novel. Anxious for the folks to get here, especially Ma: — what a joy it will be for her! Heh heh heh — (a cackle of satisfaction on my part, you see.)

WEDNESDAY MAY 25 — Went to Denver University and to the home of the Whites. The Denver campus is beautiful and interesting. I walked into the rambling structure of the Students Union just as a jukebox was booming Charley Ventura ... first bop in weeks. My hair stood on end. I floated in. I realized that the music of a generation whether it is swing, jazz, or bop — (at least this law applies to 20th century America) — is a keypoint of mood, an identification, and a seeking-out. Anyway, I looked for Dan, drank milkshakes, sat in the grass, looked at the gals, visited the buildings, etc., and finally hitch-hiked in the hot afternoon countryside to the Whites' house. This is the house they built themselves, that Ed and [Frank] Jeffries and Burt worked on all winter. Frank White was there. I was somewhat amazed by him. He is more like Ed than people think ... the same quick understanding of all statements; in fact, the same fore-knowledge of the trend of what one is about to say. Also he has the same cool, modest ability of much variety. His only drawback is a garrulousness that one can't follow due to his tumbling speech and in-ward-preoccupation with details. Then the rest of the family arrived for supper. Mrs. White made me feel most at home (like Frank.) Of course I was unexpected and shouldn't have crashed in so casually. Jeanne seemed thoughtful about something else. After supper Frank and I drove back to the D.U. campus, where he spoke on cosmic ray research of some kind, to a physics class. They applauded his talk admiringly; I was unable myself to follow the scientific language. Another speaker, on geophysics, was Wally Mureray, friend of Frank's, whom I liked. He was born & raised in Leadville [, Colorado,] and like his father & grandfather has mining in his blood. Also he's a genuine mining type while being a scientist: — a remarkable combination. We met Dan Burmeister at his social science seminar and there ensued an endless argument between the physical scientists and the social scientist, with much reference to relativity, Oppenheim, atomic research, etc. I finally announced (in flood-tides) that it was all a "continuum of ambiguity." Okay? — for rel-ativity is just the idea that one point of reference is as good as another. We got mellow on beer; went home. Frank drove me home.

THURSDAY MAY 26 — Then today (while I continued my hermit do-mesticity in the empty house ... as a matter of fact tried to fix the wellpump just as it seemed to fix itself) the kid on the street here, Jerry, asked me to accompany him to the amusement park, Lakeside, in the evening. His mother, Johnny they call her, drove us to the park. (Her husband has disappeared somewhere.) It was the Sad Fair again. I took a few rides with Jerry (who seems to be looking for a father of some sort.) However a waitress didn't believe I was 21 and wanted proof before she gave me a beer. Jerry (14) drank rootbeer. We rode around a sad little lake in a toy railroad; in the high ferris wheel, etc., and ate hotdogs and ice cream. Still and all, it was a "sinister" night ... sinister-seeming ... and I became depressed — for two days. A park cop threatened to arrest Jerry because he was fooling around with the tame fish at the motorboat dock. Then, when we rode home in an old truck after a Roy Rogers movie, a car almost rammed us in the back. It was strange. In the first place I couldn't understand anything. I doubt if the driver of the old truck knew we were in the back. Between us sat his little son, mysteriously wrapp'd in a blanket. *No one noticed the fact we almost got rammed by the car ...* or that is, they didn't care at all. Then, in the dark sinister country night, as Jerry and I walked home, a car of drunks almost plowed us off the road. Everything was sinister ... like for Joe Christmas.

FRIDAY MAY 27 — Depressed all day. Full of my own private hurt and haunt. Jerry brought over a little kitty for me ... it has sick eyes. It needs meat. It hangs around me mewing for affection. It is somewhat like that lost kid, incomprehensibly lonely. I feed the cat and do my best to achieve a talk with Jerry — and with his incomprehensible mother, who asked me to go riding in a rodeo tomorrow. That is, Sunday. My depression cannot see the light of these things. What did I do all day? — I can't remember any more. Part of my sadness stems from the fact my family's wasting time getting out here. Why? I hated myself all day, too ... hurt and haunted by hurt.

SATURDAY MAY 28 — After a mopey day, I perked up and went to the beerjoints on the ridge. Gad, some beautiful waitresses up there. I really enjoyed the cowboy music ... ate french fries at the bar, etc. There are some good people out this way, just as I had guessed. Came home and slept, to be ready for the Ghostly Rodeo.

SUNDAY MAY 29 — So I rode in a rodeo ... of sorts. Johnny picked me up and we drove to a farm-ranch, and slicked down four horses. A remarkable woman called Doodie runs the place and dominates immense horses, including a 17-hand Palomino, with fiery contemptuous love ... in other words, a real horsewoman. Her son Art is a mild, happy kid growing up among horses. We mounted the four horses and started off for Golden, 15 miles west. I have not ridden extensively since 1934, so I was saddle-sore pretty soon ... but enjoyed it nevertheless. My horse Toppy, a strawberry roan colt, had a tender mouth so I could not rein him up too hard. We joined two other women, one a haughty bitch on an Arabian thoroughbred, and the other a most marvelous woman with flaming red hair and no teeth. She said, "I hate women who don't say *shit* when they've got a mouthful of it." We cantered and walked and trotted to Golden. I had a beer in a bar; then we mounted again and the first thing you know we were joined by a whole posse of riders, and first thing you know, on a dirt road, something happened psychologically, I yelled "Woohee!" and off some of us went lickity-cut down the road in a race. My roan loved to run, and "he run." Up in a glorious mountain meadow we raced around while, by arrangement, a photographer took pictures with a motion picture technicolor camera ... I still don't know under what auspices. We did Indian-circle runs, and Figure-Eights, and galloped *en masse* down a draw, and had a good time. We drank beer in the saddle. Going back to Golden we raced furiously across lots and down into a creek-bed and up out of it flying and hell-for-leather over fields gopher-holes or no gopher-holes. I've never been afraid of a horse falling somehow anyway. After another beer we started back ... and the kid and I really had a race. He was in the road and I in the field parallel, and it was even. Then he beat me on the road ... but he's a lighter rider, and used his reins on both flanks, something I didn't bother to do. — Finally we got back exhausted, a 30-mile day. I went to bed immediately ... With some muscles and one bad blister.

MONDAY MAY 30 — And today I was scheduled to ride in the rodeo at Table-Top (ride a bronc for all I incomprehensibly know) but of course I was too sore. I'm sorry I missed this. Meanwhile some neighbors around here are gossiping about Johnny (Jerry's mother) and me ... an old hen across the street. This sort of thing goes on even here. Best thing to do, is nothing. What does it matter anyway? — No harm in it that's *real* harm (like jail, etc.) Rested all day. Wrote at night. Still and all, consider how horrible it is to have an old woman like that peeking from out her shades all day, trying to figure out what you're doing behind yours, and starting "scandalous" stories about you. Gad! It's *funny* only in a horrible way. (Francis Martin.)

But how I love horses!

Next year: *mountain ranch.*

And tonight re-examined my literary life and I'm worried somewhat about losing touch with it in these natural-life atmospheres. After all, great art only flourishes in a *school* ... even if that school is only friendship with poets like Allen, Lucien, Bill, Hunkey & Neal and Holmes ... and Van Doren & [Elbert] Lenrow too, of course.

: — J U N E — :

IN COLORADO, 1949

TUESDAY JUNE 1 — I'm thinking of making On the Road a vast story of those I know as well as a study of rain and rivers. Allen expresses weariness with my "rain-&-rivers" preoccupation now, but I think it's only because I have not explained manifestly what they mean: as I did in the notebook "Record" on pages covering 'New Orleans to Tucson.' That's clear in my mind.

There is never a real goldstrike, or a real "scientific advance," only a revelation in the heart on one day or the next, subject to horrible change and further revelation. "Revelation is Revolution," as Holmes says, insofar of course, as it is a *change,* miserably from mere day to day.

There is no heaven and no reward, and no judgment either (Allen says his lawyers "will be judged"): — no: — there is only a continuum of living across preordained spaces, followed by the continuum of the Mystery of Death. That death is a Mystery makes Death acceptable therefore; because Mystery never ends but continues.

— Still waiting for the family.

WEDNESDAY JUNE 1 — Fixed the well-pump at nine o'clock this morning. Got dirt out of the valve and tightened a loose cylinder around the pipe, and raised the pressure to 50. For awhile there I was *enraged* because I thought my one-year-lease was on a house with a dry well. It is Okay, I think — 122 feet deep. On top of that it rained today.

Rain is not only poetic in the West, but necessary. So I say "Rain you bastard!" — and it rains. I've been goofing off these two days just listening to the radio, playing with the cat, playing solitary stud-poker, and thinking up On the Road more. *I need my typewriter.* No furniture, no family, nothing. I can't understand all this delay. It took me 60 hours to get out here, and another 48 hours to get a house. It's taken them close to three weeks ... and all I do is wait, wait, wait. I don't think Paul wants to leave the East actually ... he is wasting time in North Carolina. His mother has a husband to support her, and a grandchild, and 2 other children in the East; therefore, there's no tragedy in Paul moving out West, inasmuch as he can visit her occasionally also. So I don't understand all this delay. They arrived in N.C. last Tuesday, and here it is nine days later — and the 1650-mile trip is a 3½ day drive. So they're staying there at least a whole week, and here I am in an empty house paying rent. This I don't like ... A waste of time and money, and a waste of a good thing, and silly. Got a letter from Beverly Burford *Pierceall* today ... now married, living in Colorado Springs, whose Pikes Peak I can see from the kitchen window. Wrote back at night.

THURSDAY JUNE 2 — And tonight the family is finally arriving; got a telegram in the morning. I'm now down to my last actual penny (1 cent), excluding the $20 bill I'm hiding for the lawn (part of the deal on this lease is to plant a lawn.) So now things will start vibrating and we'll get our home going. Only thing is: — where is the furniture truck? Hal Chase ought to be home by now. And soon I'll hear from Giroux and decide about June 15, and a job, and my writing-schedule (months) for Road. — Last night I went to bed reading the New Testament. My own interpretation of Christ I will write soon: essentially the same, that he was the *first*, perhaps the *last*, to recognize the facing-up of a man to life's final enigma as the only important activity on earth. Although times have changed since then, and "Christianity" is actually Christian in method by now (socialism), still, the time has yet to come for a true "accounting," a true Christlike world. The King who comes on an Ass, meek. "True progress shall lie in men's hearts." Do you hear me, Hunkey of the Fires? — Also, I planned to write a "Literary Autobiography of a Young Writer" within a few years, preferably while in Paris. I'm full of ideas, yet not of real work. I keep saying I need my typewriter — I do, and my desk, books, papers too. I wish I had the will and energy of ten writers (as I did in 1947.) The 1948 work on T & C was a Gift from God, for I had long ago gone on my knees like Handel prior to his Messiah-work, and Received that.

But thank God for *everything*. The other night I saw that.

MONDAY JUNE 13 (Colorado)
Trying to get settled in Colorado, jobs and so forth. Will start a new journal soon.

Typing up some 10,000 words of "On the Road" and organizing them — the true beginning now.

Editor [Bob] Giroux is flying out on July 15.

Seeing a lot of Justin Brierly.

Leased small house on outskirts of W. Denver, where plains wash down from mountains. Beautiful summer is mine. Family arrived. Money troubles. And rainy mud; and dry well.

JUNE 28 — You're not really writing a book till you begin to *take liberties* with it. I've begun to do this with On the Road now.

Also, consider that I, in writing about fire, am that close to it that I may be burned. Now that I need "Levinsky and the Angels on Times Square"* I realize that Vicki has it; and she being indicted, the police probably have the manuscript now. But I want it back.

Everybody in America sitting in the movie, avidly watching the crazy-serious gray screen — for what it has to show. It is so much better to explore things like that than silly imaginary questions like "Should teenage girls marry?" — better and more intelligent, the 'social scientists' to the contrary.

*An allusion to *The Town and the City* and Leon Levinsky, the character based on Allen Ginsberg.

Roll your own bones,

go moan alone —

Go, go, roll your own bones,

alone.

Bother me no more.

JULY

COLORADO

JULY 4th

My mother went back to her job in N.Y. today. She will get an apartment in Long Island. Next year I'll buy her a house there. She left at one on the Rock Island. Poor vagabonding widow-woman! In a month, after Giroux, I'm going to Mexico and then N.Y. — perhaps Detroit en route. The big American night keeps closing in, redder and darker all the time. There is no home.

Began writing "The Rose of the Rainy Night" yesterday for amusement.

A heavy melancholy, almost like pleasure, oppresses me now.

"On the Road" proceeding strangely.

Poor Red Moultrie.

All we do is moan alone.

But more and more as I grow older I see the beautiful dream of life expanding till it is much more important than gray life itself — a dark, red dream the color of the cockatoo. Night, like a balm, soothes dumb wounds of prickly day-dark & rainy night!

I am grown more mystic than ever now.

Today was one of the saddest days I've ever seen. Tonight my eyes are pale from it. — In the morning we drove my Ma to the depot, bringing with us the little baby in his diapers. A hot day. Sad, empty holiday streets in downtown Denver and no fireworks. In the depot we wheeled the baby around on marble floors. His little yells were mingled with the "roar of time" up in the dome. I checked my mother's suitcase in anticipation of a little sendoff stroll, to a bar, or something, but we only sat sadly. Poor Paul read a Mechanix Magazine. Then the train came. As I write this at midnight now she's somewhere near Omaha ...

In the afternoon Paul & Nin & the baby and I tried to make a go of it with a picnic at Berkeley Lake. But we only sat sadly and ate tasteless sandwiches, under gray skies and left. The child was still in his little diapers ... somewhat cold now, so we came home. We had a kind of winnie roast in the backyard, & toasted marshmallows till dark. This was Okay.

But at the fireworks at Denver U. Stadium great crowds had been waiting since twilight, sleepy children and all; yet no sooner did the shots begin in the sky than these unhappy people trailed home before the show ended, as though they were too unhappy to see what they had waited for.

A glass of beer makes me happy, though.

Like Jack Fitzgerald I'll start being an Angel Drunk.

—   —

It's so true — the children know more than we do. Now I'm *certain*. Here's why: — Here's why: The Selfish Giant

Scene: When Red returns to Denver after a 10-year absence, the scene in the real estate office where he goes to inquire after his father. The young real estate man whom he fished with giving him the cold shoulder; decoding a difficult legal paper for his own old man; the raw cowhands coming in to pay a commission to effeminate real estate golfers (the tall, flabby, rosy man with the Panama hat.) The white desert of 17th St. & Stout. All this makes Red very sad for his old Denver. Then the graduation exercises for Holmes' kid brother at the auditorium, the stern-voiced valedictorian; then the high school teacher's luncheon and the headmaster. Everything is rosy for the high school kids, but Red knows so many, including Vern, who don't go to school and don't buy something about it ... some rosy conspiracy against suffering; by parents, teachers & children: a conspiracy made in the security of established social power.

What of all the beat kids? the so-called "delinquents" and even the D.P. kids? Well there are D.P. kids right here in America —

      ... dispossessed poor ...

(and all the dispossessed peacemakers in life.)

VOYAGE FROM DENVER TO FRISCO BACK TO N.Y.

AUGUST 1949 — 5,000-miles on the road.
Closed up the house in Denver, went to Frisco in a '49 Ford for $11, stayed three days, came back to Denver with Neal in a '48 Plymouth; stayed in Denver a few days; came on to Chicago in a '47 Cadillac limousine, dug Chicago one night with Neal; bus to Detroit; three days in Detroit trying to understand Edie; on to N.Y. with Neal in a '49 Chrysler at $5 each.

This memorable voyage described elsewhere sometime. (In "Rain & Rivers" book.)

Now living in Richmond Hill. Continue ragged work on "On the Road." Giroux and I preparing "Town & City" for printer, on Sept. 27th. Got another $250.00 advance till Xmas.

Very, very *ennuyee* ... (in the French-Canadian sense, meaning *unhappy & sick*.) But "work saves all?" "The details are the life of it?"

Will go to Paris in early 1950 and finish "Road" and dig French gals and streets of Paris. Also, will begin "Myth of Rainy Night" which will be the 3rd novel.

AUGUST '49

Richmond Hill, N.Y.

CONTINUATION OF THE LAMENTATION

TUES. 29 — Resuming true serious work I find that I have grown lazy in my heart. It's not that I don't want to scribble and scrabble as of yore, but merely that I no longer want to think down to the bottom of things — no more a fisherman of the deep. And why that is — for one thing, indirectly speaking, I cannot for instance as yet understand why my father is dead ... no meaning, all unseemly, and incomplete. It seems he is not dead at all. I haven't cross't the bridge to knowing that he is dead. It hangs on me that I can no longer be serious with myself because ... because ... Everyone and everything are so ambiguous around me now. With Allen even I cannot agree on a serious contract of understanding. He regards himself a "poor, broken spirit in a hospital," and doesn't know how really crazy he is for not caring to admit he knows this is a pose out of pique. So what if he has suffered? — And Edie: not a care, not a straight, long care in the world. She never even looked at me once with anything approaching seriousness. She was tired and wanted to sleep, and drove home and left me to walk 4 miles — not pique so much, just tired. Neal — we have reached great understandings which he really forgets, since in any case he only accomplished his end of them out of sheer technique and long experience of dealing with souls that appear to be like mine? On top of that I have had several *burdens* to carry from silly people who don't know their own minds. I'm tired of these ambiguities and ignorances and indifferences. I want to be serious.

And because I am surrounded by such people it almost seems futile for me to try to fish deep in my work ... they don't care anyway. They don't *know*. I am addressing myself, like the laughing-lady in front of the fun house at whom everyone stares with hanging mouths.

Are there no connoisseurs?

No lovers of love?

Is this the way the world is going to end, — in *indifference*? Where are the serious, consequential, undeniable true fires? Where are the old prophets and scriveners of the Scriptures? Where is the Lamb? Where are the little ones? What has happened to parable? — to the Word? — even to mere tales and seriousness?

What's all this frivolous science?

Why do people wander around in unseriousness and forget even that? Where is the serious child?

The fact is, my father's death was not serious at all. You don't even die any more, you just slip away past the last streetlamp like Celine's people do. It's not even a mockery of anything. An accident.

Who cares about naturalism?

This is why I can't fish deep now. O come to me, love, hurry up for Christ's sake — the Muse is not enough, and there are no laurel wreaths.

I want a soul.

I want a soul.

I want a soul.

I want my little girl.

I insist that life is holy, and that we must be reverent of one another, always. This is the only truth: it has been said so, a thousand million times.

—   —

It's easy to be Olympian. "Dr. Sax" will be easy, I'll laugh from my hilltop at the types of man — the indifferent, the helpless, the complainer. But in "Road" I have to lay my chips down on my number. All bets, please!

Hurry up please it's time!

All bets! — Then the wheel rolls, and what comes up? Win or lose, something's bound to come up, naturally.

Much of my meditation on "Road" therefore has been on problems of the soul, not mere language and mystery as in Sax.

So this, what I'm doing tonight.

WED. 30 — Yesterday, also, I scribbled about a thousand words of preparatory material. The questions I had all decided while writing "T & C" are now being reviewed, with greater stupidity however. Today I dealt with the adolescent question of "why do men go on living." So long ago I had said — "There is no Why." Today I watched the workingmen on the big construction job behind the house, and wondered why. That's enough.

I feel that I'm the only person in the world who doesn't know the feeling of calm irreverence — the only madman in the world therefore — the only broken fish. All the others are perfectly contented with pure life. I am not. I want a pure understanding, and then pure life. What is that woman thinking on the doorstep across the street? She wants a husband. To understand love and the consciousness of love with him? — to enter into a conspiracy concerning eternity with him?

No — to absentmindedly, greedily screw in bed; and absentmindedly raise children; and absentmindedly die; to lie in an absentminded grave — *and let God worry about the rest.*

Not for me.

I'm going to decide the thing myself, even if I have to burn in the attempt.

Meanwhile I'm continually astonished that people really don't love each other. *How can they do it?*

(So now I'm psychotic finally.)

Can it be possible that all these people go on every day merely because it affords them a chance to flatter themselves? — the women with ribbons & flirtations, and the men with boasts, and the children with cock-o'-the walk triumphs, and the old people with vengeful memories?

If this is so, if the world is like this, how long can I survive on such air? Are these just animals?

No matter what one may say about pure life and joy, I don't believe it is enough, I just don't believe any of it ... the insouciance.

So why were these workingmen digging great holes? — so what use are old Faust's canals when no one cares about the furthest lights and the sadness at the end of the canal.

Clearly I'd better hurry up and die. There's no place for me in such a world.

Nobody loves, nobody loves. These are the lees of love.

And I can't stand despair just as I can't breathe when there's no air. Now I must change or die —

How shall I change? I simply don't know how to change ... like a tortoise of the Gallapagos, too, that runs up a thwart a rock and pushes there a year or so. Melville says, "By what evil spirit enchanted?"

Who therefore is enchanting me?

The Church of Rome has an answer twice as absurd as mine ... whatever mine may be. Did you think the Devil would be so intense as to care to enchant his best victims? If only the devil *did* exist! Nothing of the sort can exist in such a dull, sensual, absentminded world, and would be laughed at.

And all we have left is details — pfui! This is why I say I don't care for naturalism, or that is, *why should I write*. There's nothing to write about. The only man who seemed to care, George Martin, is dead and gone. I don't even remember if Leo Kerouac was really completely like that.

It was all in my head.

Don't talk to me about pure life — it's just pure bull.

ENNUI

Life is not enough.

So what do I want?

I want a purpose in eternity, something to decide on from which I'll never deviate now in whatever dark existence or other follows. And what is this decision?

Some kind of fever of understanding, some vision, some love, which will bridge and transcend from this life to the others, some serious, final, and unchangeable sight of the universe. This is what I mean by "I want Eyes." (Dead eyes see. — A. G.)*

Why should I want this? — Because there isn't enough here on earth to want, or that is, not a single thing here exists that I do want.

Why don't I want life on earth? Why is it not enough?

Because it does not flood my soul and place fevers in my brain and make me cry for happiness.

Why do you want to feel?

Because reason and the body of facts, science and truth, do not make me feel, and do not bridge eternity, and in fact choke me like stale, close air.

ennui

You've said all that
of course I've said all that.
What do you want?
I want to be on fire.
Why?
Because I am inflammable. I
am serious.

---

*From Allen Ginsberg's "Stanzas: Written at Night in Radio City" (1949), the full quote reads "As so the saints beyond/cry to men their dead eyes see."

You've said all that —
Of course I've said all that.
You don't know what you want,
And you say life is not enough.
Life is not enough.
Then what is enough?
To feel — or I die.
What will you feel?
Fires.
Then go ahead and burn.
But life is not on fire.
Then die.
Corporeally?

———

Yes.   ← *Flippancy*

My book will be a great success. They'll all say "What's the matter with these writers?" Recall the recent suicide of the Raintree County author.*

So now you care what everybody will say.

Does this mean that I have to admit I'm one with the body of mankind?

Is that what worries you? Who speaks of self-flattery now.

Leave me alone. Woe.

Oh now it deteriorates into a clinical matter merely? I thought for awhile you were a true flame.

So again the tone of unseriousness and dull facts begin. Woe.

Men have lived by that tone for ages.

What the hell do I care? Woe.

I thought you cared.

I care for care, not for uncare.

———

*Ross Lockridge, Jr., author of the best-selling novel *Raintree County*, committed suicide by carbon monoxide in 1948, at age thirty-three.

Go drop dead someplace. Oh.

Try and make me. Woe.

Is that all you want to do — fight? What kind of eternity is that? Oh.

Once I believed in functioning, and created illusions consciously to keep on functioning, which I did. Woe.

And now even illusions elude you?

Naturally. O woe.

You see, it is a real enigma, not just the word "enigma."

Yes.

There. Oh.

Seriousness

To continue: here's a quote from the incredible Balzac: —

"... All electric phenomena (is) erratic and unaccountable in its manifestations.... Men of science will recognize the great part played by electricity in human thinking power."

When I can no longer understand my own laborious understandings of the world, when my mind stops working, when my heart stops dead and my soul is stultified, when I am on the verge of suicide (as today), perhaps it is just something like a power failure because I have lost *contact* with the whole of the Universe? Why do I lose contact? And why, after years of depressions and moods like these, have I not come up with an answer to it?

Life is not enough if you lose contact with the other world, which is simply the perspective we have never seen but which apprises us of the intention of the whole of the universe — which is eventual contact among all things, the electrical togetherness of actual eternity. The other world — mentioned first as the Word of God in the Scriptures, and designated by the great St. Thomas Aquinas as being beyond reason and necessary to man. The perspective of this other world, this other *understanding* which we have not seen, is beyond all present kens of mine but I suspect that it is very strange and yet when we finally see it we'll all say, "Of course, of course, yes, yes!"

When I say I want to burn and I want to feel and I want to bridge from this life to the others, that is what I meant: — to go to the other world, or that is, keep in contact with it till I get there.

Am I really privately serious now? I think so. This *lacrimae rerum;* my happiness, depends on the recognition of the other world while I am in this one, or I cannot stand this one. I must be in contact with as much of this world (through means of variety of sensuality, i.e., experience of loves of all kinds) and I must be in contact with the Holy Final Whirlwinds that collect the ragged forms into one Whole Form.

ennui

This is why life is holy: because it is not a lonely accident. Therefore, again, we must love and be reverent of one another, till the day when we are all angels looking back.

Those who are not reverent now may be the most reverent then (in their other, electrical, spiritual form.)

Will there be a Judgment Day?

No need to judge the living or the dead; only the happy and the unhappy with tears of pity.

(But I am not intelligent enough yet to go much further with these guesses and divinations.)

How shall I live on?

I shall keep in contact with all things that cross my path, and trust all things that do not cross my path, and exert more greatly for further and further visions of the other world, and preach (if I can) in my work, and love, and attempt to hold down my lonely vanities so as to contact more and more with all things (and kinds of people), and believe that my consciousness of life and eternity is not a mistake, or a loneliness, or a foolishness, — but a warm dear love of our poor predicament which by the grace of Mysterious God will be solved and made clear to all of us in the end, maybe only.

Otherwise I cannot live.

And if this is only an illusion, therefore it is excreate, and has come to pass nevertheless, in some odd, dreamlike, likely way.

It is in any case impossible to depend on the "body of facts" at this stage of life when I begin to see the impossibility of crass mortality. I must begin to use my other senses to discover what I need.

Moreover, anyway, lately I have had strange visions of whirlwinds around the commonplace heads of people. There is no mistaking a great clue like that.

Still the puzzle is not clear.

Except that my "power failure" is over and all the lights are shining again. If by any chance it turns out that these are only the electricities of an animal, pure, crass, pushing and shoving and swarming world — of which I am reluctantly one — that none of us are spirit, but just Fellaheen flesh sweating and food for maggots — then still I won't believe it anyway.

Strangely enough, at this juncture, I am confronted by a rich, charming, intelligent man, some English lord or other, or some American actor of great sophistication, saying, "Really now, old man, you do worry too much."

What does this type of man mean? Is this the calm, irreverent woman on the doorstep again? I'll bet it is, really, old man —

"I say, Jack, won't you have some tea? — or read the Times, or *something*. Really, poor fellow, you'll drive yourself balmy. After all, you know — "

"After all *what*?"

"Oh — just after all ..."

"Well? — what about 'after all'? After all this what will happen to our souls? Eh?"

"Really, you odd ball, I'm rather happy with my wife. I shouldn't trouble myself about eternity and all that sort of thing if I were you."

The maid comes in. The charming man has the audacity to select various cakes and crumpets without having decided on the ends of time.

"By God, Roger," I cry, "how can you be so cool about it."

"Really, Jack, after all — it *is* time to eat." (He dares to eat a peach.)*

He sighs. "May I say one thing? Once, as you, I wrestled over these problems to the point of course where I was prime for the loony-bin. I saw the futility of trying to understand what is evidently a bad business and not even a proper good mystery. Oh — I just decided to live ... and let live, if I may. I read Eliot. I find it's quite enough on the subject. Among the novels I prefer Trollope. But beyond that, poor Jack, please, *please!* It's really not the thing to do."

"But what will you be thinking at the moment of your death?" I cry leaping up and overturning tea-things.

He stoops and picks them up himself, with a strange humility that breaks my heart.

"When the time comes, dear fellow, I'll obviously be thinking something or other. But the time has not quite come, I hope. I suppose when it does come I'll be frightened by your whirlwinds and the next thing you know I'll be dead. Quite dead."

"Is that supposed to answer my question?"

"Do be kind, Jack, and make your weekend a pleasant one for all of us. Tomorrow we'll motor to Cannes and stare at the sea, if you wish."

"At night?!!"

"At night. Anything to please you, — old man. You really ought to speak to Gwendolyn. She's a *fiend* on the subject. Dear me, you've spilt most of the tea on the carpet."

— Or if I went to an old railroad brakeman for an answer to my plea, he would say:

"Some's bastards, some's ain't, that's all."

"But what about dying?"

"Well — we all die."

"Naturally."

"Yeah. Naturally."

---

*From "The Love Song of J. Alfred Prufrock," by T. S. Eliot: "Do I dare to eat a peach?"

— Or some Negro tenorman:

"Hey daddy, what will happen when we die? What's life for? Why don't we all love one another? What's the matter? What does it all mean?"

"Man," says he, "don't hang me up with them questions. I want my kicks and when I can't get my kicks no more, then I'm *daid*. Okay poppa?" And he smiles.

Meanwhile I walk in the road at night, in utter darkness, and no one will help me but my own mad self.

And now it's raining outdoors.

(Ah! — I just don't want to be reduced to the kind of writing that makes fatality implicit without ever having to mention it outright.)

I'm serious about this. I want to talk about it. I want to communicate with Dostoevsky in heaven, and ask old Melville if he's still discouraged, and Wolfe why he let himself die at 38.

I don't want to give up.

I promise I shall never give up, and that I'll die yelling and laughing. And that until then I'll rush around this world I insist is holy and pull at everyone's lapel and make them confess to me and to all.

This way I'll really find out something in time.

— Time to write now, I guess.

Yet better than all this poor philosophizing was that night in Denver at the softball game, where, in a fever of sad understanding, I saw beyond mere "Whys" and questionings and ennuis such as these that occupy the last eighteen pages.

Even the details are dear here:

LE COEUR ET L'ARBRE

I had just seen Bob Giroux off on the airplane to N.Y., and walked & hitched back from the airport in a mammoth plains dusk, I, a speck on the surface of the sad red earth. At lilac evening I was arrived among the lights of 27th & Welton, the Denver Negrotown.

With Giroux at rather empty Central City I had seen that my being a published writer was going to be merely a sad affair — not that he intended to show me that. I only saw how sad he was, and therefore how the best & highest that the 'world' had to offer was in fact empty, spiritless; because after all he was, and is, a great New Yorker, a man of affair, a success at 35, a famous young editor. That was why I told him there were 'no laurel wreaths,' i.e., the poet did not find ecstasies in worldly success and fame, nor even in fortune & means, in anything like acclaim or regard, nothing. He quite sensibly told me the laurel wreath is only worn in the moment of writing. Of course.

But that night my dream of glory was turned gray fact, and I walked on Welton Street wishing I was a 'nigger;' because I saw that the best the 'white world' had to offer was not enough ecstasy for me, not enough life, joy, kicks, darkness, music, not enough *night*.

I remember: I stopped at a little shack-place where a man sold hot, red chili in paper containers. I bought some and ate it strolling in the dark mysterious streets. I also wished I was a Denver Mexican, or even a Jap, Toshio Mori! anything but a 'white man' disillusioned by the best of his own 'white world.' (And all my life I had had *white ambitions!*)

As I strolled I passed the dark porch steps of Mexican & Negro homes. Soft voices were there, and occasionally the dusky leg of some mysterious, sensual girl; and dark men who owned them; and little children who were growing up with the same idea — the idea of life-as-you-will. In fact a group of Negro women came by and one of the younger ones detached herself from mother-like elders to come to me and say — "Hello Eddy."

As I said to Allen in a letter, I knew I was really Eddy. But this is untrue. I knew damn well I wasn't so fortunate as to be Eddy — some white kid who dug the colored girls down there. I was merely myself.

So sad I was — in the violet dark, strolling — wishing I could exchange worlds with the happy, true-minded, ecstatic Negroes of America. Moreover all this reminded me of Neal and Louanne who knew this place so well and had been children here and nearby. How I wished I could find them! — I looked up and down the street! — How

I'd been cheated out of actual life! — How I yearned to be suddenly transformed into an Eddy, a Neal, a jazz musician, a nigger, anything hereabouts, a construction worker, a softball pitcher, anything in these wild, dark, mysterious, humming streets of the Denver night — anything but myself so pale & unhappy, so 'white-collar,' so dim.

So finally down at 23rd & Welton the great softball game was going on under floodlights which also partially illuminated the gas tank. What a cruel touch! — now it was the nostalgia of the Gas House Kids. And a great eager crowd roared at every play. The strange young heroes, of all kinds, white, colored, Mexican, Indian, were on the field performing with utter seriousness. Most awful of all: — They were just sandlot kids in uniform, while I, with my 'white ambitions,' had to go and be a professional-type athlete of the highest variety, in my college days.

I hated myself thinking of it. Never in my life had I ever been innocent enough to play ball this way before all the families & girls of the neighborhood, at night under lights, near the gas tank all the kids know — no, I had to go and be a college punk, playing before punks & coeds in stadiums, and join fraternities, and wear sports jackets instead of Levis and sweatshirts.

Some people are just made to wish they were other than what they are, only so they may wish and wish and wish. This is my star.

Oh the sadness of the lights that night! I sat on the bleachers and watched the game. The pitcher looked just like Neal. A blonde in the seats looked just like Louanne. It was the Denver night here in the streets of the real Denver, and all I did was die. What had I gone and done with my life, shutting off all the doors to real, boyish, human joy like this, what had gnawed in me to make me strive to be 'different' from all this.

Now it was too late.

Near me sat an old Negro who apparently watched the games every night. Next to him was an old white man, then a Mexican family, then some girls, some boys — all humanity, the lot. Across the street Negro families sat on their front steps talking and looking up at the starry night through the trees and just sitting in the softness and sometimes watching the game. Many cars passed in the street meanwhile, and stopped at the corner when the light turned red.

There was excitement and the air was filled with the vibration of really joyous life that knows nothing of disappointment and 'white' sorrows, and all.

The old Negro man had a can of beer in his coat pocket, which he proceeded to open; and the old man enviously eyed the can & groped in his pocket to see if he could buy a can too.

How I died!

Down in Denver all I did was die, anyway — never saw anything like it.

I walked away from there to the dumb downtown streets of Denver, for the trolley at Colfax & Broadway; where is the big dumb Capitol building with its lit-up dome and swarded lawns. Later I walked the pitchblack roads up at Alameda and came to the house I'd spent my $1000 on for nothing, where my sister and brother-in-law were sitting worrying about money and work and insurance and security and all that ... in the *white-tiled* kitchen.

It seems that I have an infinite capacity to be unhappy. How I can be so stupid as to waste my life away being unhappy like this! What am I going to do? When will I realize that I have a great life of my own?

Well, there's still time before it's too late ...

(And I don't understand it.)

: —— :

[From Aug. 30 to Sept. 5 I then went on a long session of drinking, music, & people in N.Y.C. Met Lee Nevels, a Negress; stayed at Bob's apt.]

Official Log of "The Hip Generation"

SEPTEMBER '49   Richmond Hill
                                          (On the Road)

TUES. 6 — Tried to get going on the Hip Generation last night, but just really dawdled ritually. This is the new title for On the Road, and also it changes certain ideas concerning it. A Saga of Cities, Streets & the Bebop Night. I haven't really worked since May 1948. Have I forgotten how to work? Time to get going. I have the Fall and Winter, seven months, and if I can average 25,000 a month as I used to, I'd have my 200,000-word novel by April, at which time I want to go to France & Italy and to do the Myth of the Rainy Night, or Doctor Sax.

But I have no real heart for these things any more. I don't suffer ... r ... r ...

Right now as I write this I am very happy and I haven't got a thought in my head. Art is unhappiness (?) Dawdle, dawdle. — Reading La Vita Nuova.*

WED. 7 — Let's see if I can write a novel, as they say I can.

: — S E P T E M B E R   R A I N — :

Today, did **700-words** (new), and wrote a divine page on Beatitude; and revised what I had done yesterday; and meditated; and ate; and walked, and talked, and planned another page on Bliss.

---

*La Vita Nuova (c. 1292), a lesser-known poem by Dante.

THURS. 8 — Work with Giroux in town. Will work at the office also next week. Etc. Let's keep the mundane out of this. Thought a line — Death & nervous breakdowns are always the same, but the materials are never the same. Do seasons suppose I do not know this? Etc. Just sublime!

FRI. 9 — What shall I do tonight? — this raw Autumnal night. Where shall I go? Feel so good these days (& months) that I don't have to do anything. But will go see the gang — bold noble Neal, mad Allen, haunted Lucien, sweet Seymour [Wyse], or dusky darling Lee (she of the bebop night.) And where is Clem of the fires? Old Bull? Will write letters too. Have decided new plot-constructives for "Hip Generation" too. Going along gladly.

Stayed home and wrote **1300**-*goodly* words. That's 3000 in four days, just the pace I want. When I get to the words already written (and numbered in first part of this log last May) the pace will accelerate unnaturally. I want an average of 20,000 a month at least — or about 150,000 by March, the novel practically. In the work itself I find the novel unfold, and really in no other way, and that is a rule about plots. — My writing is good. Also careful about structures, and the Structure. So I'm underway.

Bawk? Hey? What Tom Malone?

J'ai lit la vie nouvelle, j'ai vue la vie nouveau. Notice English sounds of this: —

JAYLEE-LAVEE-NOOVELL
JAYVUE-LAVEE-NUOVO ... a chant.

SAT. 9 — Weekend with Holmes, Seymour, & Neal — music and talk. Feel wonderful knowledges growing in me all the time now. Ho?

MON. 11 — Worked at Harcourt-B office on the ms. With Bob. Wrote 1500-words for Town & City insert, which was good job.

TUES. 12 — Work at office. Another 700-word insert job ... written in "T & C style," & quite without pain. Bob and I eat lavish meals, go to French movies, drink good drinks in places like the Plaza bar. He's great.

WED. 13 — Work at office. I have Alfred Harcourt's office to myself ... Lucien visited me there with Sarah ... — Ate big lobster dinner because I feel so successful, spending all of my dough, this rainy evening.

THURS. 14 — Work at office. Many 300-word inserts all this week. Saw Neal at parking-lot.

FRI. 15 — Work at office — hardly ever home. Sleep at Seymour's occasionally. Have stomach cramps suddenly ... for several days.

SAT. 16 — Work at office. Party at Johnny's at night ... everybody there, including Lee. A sordid, sarcastic party it was. The Beautiful Children suddenly show their sullen eye. Slept at Seymour's.

SUN. 17 — Work at office (almost finished.) Bob gave me Ouspensky book. Came home to Richmond Hill and saw Ma and ate. Wrote inserts at home. So.

MON. 18 — At the office today there was a wire from Lucien: — "Without discipline Kerouac will be tiny. Stand man, don't wilt in these hobo enervating rose bushes."

What's that? — I know well — Lucien is right again. He means about my work, first, being overly influenced by chi-chi poetic ideas, and the lack of discipline in that. Second, about my being ... about my "easing up" in the soul and growing lazy there; my not disciplining my soul for the sake of decency and form, a throwback to his old idea of my "complete disreputability." Sordidness. Etc. How strange that he should think of me, anyhow, even though I am not sure what he really means. Who ever is?

Worked at Bob's house, wrote a Kenny Wood connective, came home at 3 A.M.

TUES. 20 — Oh to be what everyone wants me to be, all at the same time — so there wouldn't be any unneccessary fuss all around. What do I do to atone for my sins? — I feel sorry, that's all.

Went to bright, sunny Jamaica this afternoon and accomplished little errands.

Love, that heals the belly and disease delays.

WED. 21 — After a little work in the office, Bob and I put on our tuxedos and went to the ballet Russe at the Met. It is the most exquisite of the arts — and one can die a strange little death after seeing the ballet for the first time (although I did not die.) It's just understood. Watching from the wings, the girls en masse in blue light are like a vision; they all look Oriental, or Russian, too. Bob and I visited the currently great dancer of them all, Leon Danellian, in his dressingroom, among strange balletomanes, [Alexandra] Danilova sat in a chair. There were telegrams tacked on the wall, and the old Death's Head Impresario of the Ballet looking like an ancient John Kingsland. Gore Vidal was there with his mother. Everybody keeps saying "I like her better than I do Gore." It's the fashion among them. Our group consisted of John Kelly (a millionaire of the arts & Wall Street I guess), and Gore Vidal and Mrs. Vidal, Danellian and his sister, a certain Don Gaynor who is like the sinister intellectual at parties in British films, and later (after dispersals) John LaTouche* and Burgess Meredith (who is funny.) La-Touche is also funny, and extremely lovable ... he stood on his head for us. He knows everybody, even [Greta] Garbo. He just came back from the Congo. He is like a Lowell guy in a Moody street saloon. Also, Dr. Shrappe of Columbia was with us, witty, and lonely.

We spent $55 in the Blue Angel just for drinks and a supper. I

*John La Touche (1917–1956), lyricist for Broadway musicals and movies.

gunned the little French hatcheck girl and made a date with her. Berthy's her name — so great. But this evening I learned that I have to change now — being so much "in demand" socially it just is impossible to accept all invitations to lunch, and equally impossible to try to communicate with everybody, even *agree* with everybody as I've always done out of mere joy. Now I'll have to start *selecting*. Isn't that awful? But it's a fact I have to face.

It appears that I am terrifically naïve. "Yes, yes!" I say to everybody. "Sure, I'll meet you there!" "Oh yes, I'll call you!" "Fine, fine, I'd love to go there." And on top of that, running after every pretty girl I see (in my tuxedo) making dates that obscurely conflict with everything else ... a bloody mess. Finally, I simply go home and sleep all day. It is not done.

Nobody understands me. They think I'm crazy. All I want to do is be agreeable and polite, then go off on my own as always. It is not done.

Neal's vision is something like this. And Tchelitchev's.* Very funny, anyhow. To think of the hundreds of people I already know, and the hundreds more a-coming, and me trying to see them all and agree with theses of their souls — and all of it practically at the same time because there is so little time.

I'd better stay put ... if I can.

Berthy is a sizzling little Parisienne. At least we will meet in Paris; as for now she's married to a New Yorker, and is soon divorcing him, and has cute little dark-eyes scruples that I want to devour out of sight.

Came home with a toothache. Did not go to cocktails with Kelly and Vidal, as arranged, because I've got to start right now withdrawing from an all-too-swirling scene that would only consume my time and maybe in the end my joy. I'm talking about *swirls* — hundreds of swirls leading off from that.

Where is he who walked beneath the stars, looking up, alone?

Right here, God help him.

One thing at a time.

---

*Pavel Tchelitchev (1898–1957), Russian figurative artist and painter.

SEPT. 22–28 — In this space of time, we completed revision on the manuscript and gave it to the printer; and I had my bad tooth pulled, was sick 2 days; met Ed White on the pier; saw Lee, saw Tristano; and followed the hot pennant races. Tonight, 28th, I wrote six letters. Am now ready to resume On the Road.

THURS. 29 — I've got to admit I'm stuck with *On the Road*. For the first time in years I DON'T KNOW WHAT TO DO, I SIMPLY DO NOT HAVE A SINGLE REAL IDEA WHAT TO DO.

OCTOBER   has come again,

1949   come again,

again ...

What will I do? I can't write any more.

MON. 3 — But that's easily settled. A little thought on the matter. I decided I am not one of the hipsters, therefore I am free and objective thinking about them and writing their story. Nor am I Red Moultrie, so I can stand back and scan *him*. I am not even Smitty, I'm none of them.* I am only describing evidential phenomena for the sake of my own personal salvation in works and the salvation and treasuring of human life according to *my own intentions*. What else can there truly be?

Everything else in life, who I will marry, what my health will be like, where I'll live, who I'll love, is unknown and almost unimportant to me, since I belong to God and am working blindly at His Bright Bidding, according to *His Intentions,* as manifestable around mine, which are smaller but no less destined and ordained.

*Ray "Smitty" Smith was Red Moultrie's traveling companion in Kerouac's original conception of *On the Road*. Years later, Kerouac made "Ray Smith" his alter ego in *The Dharma Bums* (1958).

Furthermore, in this life I need nothing and no one insofar as my destined life is concerned, which is the life of mere work in the Ways and eventually in the One Bright Way of the Flaming Soothsayer.

This does not presuppose that I will not die of joy. "The body calls it death, the heart remorse." I will call it joy as far as I can make it, and because the soul is dead, I can only wait.

When Grace descends upon me, I shall recognize it as such, and know Beatitude, but beyond that I cannot grapple with myself to untangle the intertwining ferns in the vale, and vines, which are the result of Divine Intentions intended to mystify and make pure our corrupted wills on earth. I see that God does not wish man to grapple with himself, he only wishes obedient sorrow in the tangled path that leads to His Bright Clearing, where it will be understood that all things are just so, and just so, and just so, in perfection of the Incorruptible Will.

What does God mean? He means it that we will obey His Swirling Commands until He Proclaims Rest for all.

Why so?

Merely, I think, in preparation for an end to this restless nature, which He Has Made as a means of demonstrating the meaning of Absolute Contemplative Light, for we whom He Wishes to enfold in His Bosom forever. An end to *this* — a preparation for *that which never ends.*

The world really does not matter, but God has made it so, and so it matters in God, and he Hath Aims for it, which we cannot know without the understanding of obedience.

There is nothing to do but to give praise.

This is my ethic of "art," and why so.

TUES. 4 — Piled up almost a thousand words, but they're not typed and "sealed." Registered at the New School, G.I. subsistence, for courses on Thursdays and Fridays. Saw Marian & John Holmes, Seymour, Lucien, Sarah Yokley, called Bob, paid up debts, and saw Tristano at night; and came home through the ferns of the vale, no rosebushes.

WED. 5 — Heard great [Don] Newcombe–[Allie] Reynolds pitching duel in 1st game of Series, on radio.* Wrote letters; notes. Feelings of self-sufficiency continue. Remembered that two years ago, at this time, I was walking along railroad tracks in Selma, California, and then too it was Dodgers-Yankees World Series. That since then I completed "Town & City," sold it; traveled to California twice again, began "On the Road"; went to school; began "Doctor Sax"; lived in Denver a summer; decided on my wife Edie; made good; and proceeded beautifully in contradistinction to earlier fumbling years like 1945 and 1946.

Will I be as satisfied in October 1951?

By then I shall have written On the Road, The Imbecile's Xmas, and perhaps all of Doctor Sax; and short stories; and shall have had a Guggenheim Fellowship and travelled all Europe; shall have had bought a house, perhaps a car; shall have perhaps married; shall have certainly loved several beautiful women in ragged measures; shall have had made many new friends, and met the greats of the world; shall have had decided on later, greater books, and poems; shall have died further; shall have come nearer yet to God; shall have weathered illnesses and toil, and binges, and lost hair, and gained wrinkles.

And shall have been stricken with mysteries.

And shall have been lonely.

And shall have been mad.

And shall have been pompous.

And shall have been meek.

And shall have been foolish.

And shall have been cruel, and faithless, and dense-headed; and shall have been on fire, and shall have been like unto rocks, cold, dry, clinkered, cracked; and shall have been funny, and shall have been stupid; and shall have wondered, and shall have raged, raved, scowled, squirted, squeeked, shmeeked, shrieked, shrunken, shriven, shat; and shall have been a bone, and shall have been a bush: shall have slept,

*This famous Brooklyn Dodgers–New York Yankees World Series matchup was scoreless until the bottom of the ninth inning, when Tommy Heinrich won it for the Yankees on a solo home run.

shall have waked, shall have cried, railed, kicked, pondered, crawled, begged, seeked, squirmed, simpered, gabbed, gawked, craned, crowded, shmowded — you know, everything I do and you do and none of it making one either more foolish or more divine, only older and I should say funnier, because of God.

So I think I shall have also become a comedian

O saints! O harlequins! O poets! O monks! O dancers! O fools! O woe, oh-Ho, O moan, Oh, Oh, Oh, Oh me, Oh-yo, Oh, Oh, doe, low, Joe, grow, so, Moe, no, go, whoa, beau, yo-yo, go twiddle your own yo-yo. O mo!

(It takes talent to be a comedian. So I shall attend the School of Comedians now, the Registrar is Comical, and the Courses are Crazy, and the Students Groan.)

THUS. 6 TO SUN. 9 — Went to school and sat out several lectures. Ephraim Fischoff fascinated me and made me think of a school like the new School for Comedians. Think of such a school:

WED. 6:30–8	WM. BURROUGHS, "HOW TO PLAY HORSES."
WED. 4:20–6	H. HUNCKE, "WHAT TO DO WHEN YOU'RE BEAT."
WED. 8:30–10	JOAN ADAMS, "THE ATOMIC DISEASE AND ITS MANIFESTATIONS."
THURS. 4:20–6	N. CASSADY, "HOW TO DIG THE STREETS."
THURS. 6:30–8	A. GINSBERG, "HUNGARIAN POLITICS."
THURS. 8:30–10	L. CARR, "THE FAIR AND FOUL IN OUR WORLD."
FRI. 4:20–6	J. KEROUAC, "RIDDLES AND ROSES."
FRI. 6:30–8	W. BURROUGHS, "SEMANTIC CONFUSION."
FRI. 8:30–10	A. GINSBERG, "THE TYPES AND MEANING OF VISIONS."
MON. 4:20–6	N. CASSADY, "LOVE, SEX, AND THE SOUL."
MON. 6:30–8	H. HUNCKE, "MODERN DRUGS."
MON. 8:30–10	JOAN ADAMS, "THE MEANING OF THE VEIL."
TUES. 4:20–6	L. CARR, "THE APPRECIATION OF THE VALE."

TUES. 6:30–8	A. *GINSBERG*, "SEMINAR: POETRY, PAINTING, DEAD EYES AND THE UNKNOWN."
TUES. 8:30–10	W. *BURROUGHS*, "THE IMMORTAL BARD."
TUES. 8:30–10	N. *CASSADY*, "NEW PSYCHOLOGY, NEW PHILOSOPHY, NEW MORALITY."
WED. 4:20–6	J. *KEROUAC*, "THE MYTH OF THE RAINY NIGHT."

Registration closes any day now. Hurry!!! The Spring term in the New School for Comedians will be even wilder.

H. *HUNCKE*, "MANIFESTATIONS OF ELECTRICAL PHENOMENA IN TEXAS AND THE CARIBBEAN."
W. *BURROUGHS*, "SUPERNATURAL ELEMENTS IN HORSEPLAYING."
A. *GINSBERG*, "THE DOLMEN REALMS."
N. *CASSADY*, "THE GREEN TEA VISIONS."
L. *CARR*, "DOLLS AND POLLYWOGS."
J. *KEROUAC*, "THE HOLY FINAL WHIRLWINDS."
JOAN ADAMS, "HINTS."

And a General Seminar and Chorus, conducted by Aldophus Asher Ghoulens, held each Friday Midnight in the Grotto of the moon, admission by application only to Monsieur H. Hex, 429 Hoax Street, Grampion Hills. Fee: — Gifts, including Puppets, Roaches, Roses, Rainwater, Socks, Maps, Onions, Fingertips, Roast beef, Confessions, and Frogs.

Requirements: Sixty points in elementary realization, largesse, comedown, sorrow, and truest love.

—   —

That's the school, there the faculty, thus the courses. Could one learn there? Don't you think one could really learn there? Learn something you never learn in school?

October 1949

THUS. 6 to SUN. 9 — Went to school and sat
out several lectures. Ephraim Fischoff fascinated
me and made me think of a school like
the New School for Comedians. Think of
such a school:—
    WED. 6:30-8 WM. BURROUGHS, "HOW TO
PLAY HORSES,"
    WED. 4:20-6 H. HUNCKE, "WHAT TO DO
WHEN YOU'RE BEAT."
    WED. 8:30-10 JOAN ADAMS, "THE ATOMIC
DISEASE AND ITS MANIFESTATIONS."
    THURS. 4:20-6 N. CASSADY, "HOW TO DIG
THE STREETS."
    THURS. 6:30-8 A. GINSBERG, "HUNGARIAN
POLITICS."
    THURS. 8:30-10 L. CARR, "THE FAIR AND
FOUL IN OUR WORLD."
    FRI. 4:20-6 J. KEROUAC, "RIDDLES AND
ROSES."
    FRI. 6:30-8 W. BURROUGHS, "SEMANTIC
CONFUSION."
    FRI. 8:30-10 A. GINSBERG, "THE TYPES
AND MEANING OF VISIONS."
    MON. 4:20-6 N. CASSADY, "LOVE, SEX,
AND THE SOUL."
    MON. 6:30-8 H. HUNCKE, "MODERN DRUGS."
    MON. 8:30-10 JOAN ADAMS, "THE MEANING
OF THE VEIL."
    TUES. 4:20-6 L. CARR, "THE APPRECIATION
OF THE VALE"
    TUES. 6:30-8 A. GINSBERG, "SEMINAR:
POETRY, PAINTING, DEAD EYES AND THE
UNKNOWN."
    TUES. 8:30-10 W. BURROUGHS, "THE IMMORTAL
BARD."
    TUES. 8:30-10 N. CASSADY, "NEW PSYCHOLOGY,
NEW PHILOSOPHY, NEW MORALITY."
    WED. 4:20-6 J. KEROUAC, "THE MYTH
OF THE RAINY NIGHT."

O Arkansaw!————————

Anyway, tonight, I feel, is my night for knowing. Tonight — Oct. 9, 1949 — I think that at last I have arrived at a pure knowledge. I don't want to lose it. This is knowledge based on fact.

The thing to know about facts is that there are so many, and so many kinds, and that in dealing with them one must not obtrude one's coy, camping haggledy-diddle upon their unalterable and universal quality ... This quality is the quality of truthsomeness. Facts are true. They are made to be recognized as true. There are natural facts and there are supernatural facts.

In writing, therefore, it is not meet to wrangle against the facts, or grapple with them out of a pouting sense of being "left out" or something. Join the facts! This is like joining humanity.

Of someone as remarkable as Lucien or Burroughs, or Dostoevsky or Cezanne, it is said, always, "Of course there's no other like him," — but this is always said of characters like that; thus now we finally realize that it is inane to go on saying that for its own dumb sake. When at last you say of yourself "There's no other like me, but that's what is always said of a character like me," it is then you join humanity and admit something about yourself ... something not so indispensable after all, something that can only join humanity and join the facts. (This is of course hard to explain, just as it is hard to make appreciable the fact that my pencil's lead just now glittered on the page.)

It is purity.

Cezanne is Cezanne, but so am I, and I am no more than what the others gave me and taught me. I am no more being led around by the hand in this hexed mystery of life than I am leading others by the hand. We all know what we're doing. Stop balking! Stop the machine! Join humanity, which is all of us alike. Everybody has eyes and everybody knows how to peek, including infants. (This is why, although so tragic, the killer Howard Unruh* said he shot "someone in the window" when all the time it was but a 2-year old child in that window, peeking at him; or perhaps just looking out the window; but certainly knowing of what windows look upon, and why windows are, and what life, and eyes, are. "Tragic," I say, because the child is dead and the killer is mad.)

All mad people are only being coy. One of the greatest problems in our life is the problem of coyness, or prurience. Prurience is all our most solemn absurdities, such as propaganda, war, chauvinism, precariousism and the like.

Prurience is the deepest of lies.

Pure knowledge of all the facts, and there are so many, and so many kinds, is now my aim and my seriousness. I must stop lying even to myself, stop that machine. These knowledges are also supported by thousands of years of knowing culminated in present day summations such as anthropology, psychology, theology, sociology of religion, psychoanalysis, semantics, and a general over-all survey of knowledge as we can only "know" it. Therefore I feel that it may yet be possible for men to know more, and better, than they've ever known before; and in my field, the novel, there may yet be written greater works than ever, in all time. Even the New Testament may be exceeded in all ways — artistically, psychologically, spiritually, and folkwisely — because of a definite step forward, or step *down*, due to visions and application of knowledges in our century and centuries to come.

Men have not begun. They are far from declining as a whole or in cultures. There is something we haven't done yet.

There is a certain knowledge of death as yet unplumbed, too, which I shall touch upon in my next lecture. *I don't believe that anybody ever really died, or that the unborn are really not among us.*

There is simply no connection between men and time. Men are only involved in space and place. My father for instance is no further from me now than New Hampshire, first; and the progress of his corrosion, second; and his position among the whirlings, lastly. I admit that his exis-

*September 6, 1949, twenty-eight-year-old World War II veteran Howard Unruh shot twenty-six people in his Camden, New Jersey, neighborhood, killing thirteen.

tence haunts me. He cannot be dead. Nor Sebastian [Sampas]. I believe that I am communicating with them without really knowing it, and also communicating my own selves of pre-birth and possible pre-existence.

This [is] why we, unlike animals, know what we're doing when we *wink the eye*. Animals know how to laugh, perhaps (tho I don't think really) how to *wink*.

When someone winks at me I take this as perhaps being a serious invocation to memory of some fact we both entertained, and still do entertain, in living; and living has no limit. Therefore the wink may be a hint of several centuries old between us, or older, with the intention of communicating to me something I have forgotten due to sheer prurience and inability to understand or be straight.

(Why is my pencil shining so?) (The lead, the lead ... and it only happens occasionally.)

I still recall the simple old shoe of life, the bleak fact of ordinary existence; I'm not trying to be fancy. I don't believe I should have to explain this, however.

All this is truthful, serious and simply.

Pure knowledge is important to me, but I want also to apply it in my work where it really belongs, in a formal sense, therefore I'll work on my book now. I think perhaps there is in the nature of straight naturalism a strange elusive deepdown prurience I never noted before ... "elusive" because the face of naturalism is so *grave*, therefore misleading.

There are a great many things I want to talk about. I hope this night is not merely a 'season' of ripeness, but the true discovery of pure knowledge which may never depart once earned so raggedly. I am tired of my machine, of course.

It is well to remember that facts are true, but this does not prevent them from being *mysterious* also. Do not fear mystery.

My Smitty in "On the Road" has a simple, almost childish method of arriving at pure knowledge of the world. He stands somewhere, at home or on a streetcorner or in a subway, and closes his eyes. He stares at the darkness in his eyes, then opens them wide, looks, and says "Why?" All this is a complicated thing. The effect is to make the world

show its mystery, its skirts, as it were at an odd, embarrassing moment. The *hex* of the mystery shows its presence. There's your streetcorner, your folks wandering like spooks, your lights, darkness,
pavements ... what is all this? Who's this? — or, who's the hoax, what's
the hex. Why is this being done? *Why is reality like this and not like something else?* Childlike Smitty is demanding an explanation; he is wondering at the wall of the world; he wants God to *come down.*
Archetypically he is only "invoking the gods," though his reason may
not be for practical purposes of harvest or success in battle. Only for
reasons of pure knowledge and the essence of knowledge. The
essences in his brainpan are not there for nothing, the swirls in his
wondering soul and about his head are not there for nothing. He is not
demanding *power,* only love, which is pure knowledge of the unknown.

Why do we love? — because the beloved is unknown *to all but us.* Is
this not the feeling of love? What, if nothing else, do we think each
time we see our beloved's lovable and unprecedented face, if it is not
"Why?" This is the deepest Why, the Why that does not whine. The
Why of Whys. Thus it is, too, when we stare at God's face, his "reality"
of a streetcorner or a tree, or anything.

Allen Ginsberg says that what he means by "dead eyes see" is
merely that "face of the universe" with that knowingness of the Why.
"That's when we see at last," he maintains, "with our dead; or buried,
eyes." — 'The crystal lost in stone' is this dead eye; almost like an eye
we're not allowed, to put it on one level. "We see the dolmen realms."
So I told him that one night in 1946 I dreamt I saw, in the sky at night,
great skeletal machines of some kind, like radar equipment, in one
grand mass proceeding slowly through the clouds with a distant humming noise like formations of airplanes very far off. Hardly anyone
might have noticed them with me, in that dream, they were so casually
there, and stealthy. I was terrified, too. Allen says this is the dolmen
realms of eternity, but when I pointed out that machines are but a recent invention, he instructed me that in eternity machines may well
exist anytime, also all things before or after, and both, and all.

I think I see ... as if it has always been promised. One has to learn history and the stupid study of cause and effect, to enter into an understanding of eternity so far as we may know it. Cause-and-effect is also a prurience of mind and soul, because it pettishly demands surface answers to bottomless matters, though it is not for me to deny the right of men to build bridges over voids.

But why walk on such a bridge; an elephant can do that; only a man can stare at the void and know it. Only a man cares, not elephants and asses.

God is waiting for us in bleak eternity.

After all, too, in all this "mysticism" there is certainly no need to play with magic numbers. I am defending myself. Gurdjieff makes much of the numbers 3, 7, 4, and Dante of 9. There are *four* seasons, but they merge and flow into one another. There are *seven* seas, but they are really the same water disconnected partially by continents. There are *three* units to the genitalia, but it is one and the same organ. Or *three* spirits in man — Father, Son, Holy Ghost — all that is merged too. There are *seven* levels of knowledge, says G., but there can be 17 too, and it all overlaps. Dante, who is a greater man, makes of 9 only because of love, after all ... the eras of Beatrice.

I offer no shmathematics. It's all old shoe.

— — — — — — —

To remember for On the Road: If you can't get a girl in the
                                                      Springtime
                                             You can't get a girl
                                                      at all.

— —

Over this long weekend I saw everybody again, but particularly I shall treasure Sat. night when Neal, Lucien, Allen and I wandered together ... first a kind of party in the St. Moritz* where some "creepy" Denver people were (Lou's description), then Lenrow's apt. and drinks, music,

*St. Moritz, a posh hotel on Central Park South.

God is waiting for us in bleak eternity.

After all, too, in all this "mysticism" there is certainly no need to play with magic numbers. I am defending myself. Gurdjieff makes much of the numbers 3, 7, 4, and Dante of 9. There are four seasons, but they merge and flow into one another. There are seven seas, but they are really the same water disconnected partially by continents. There are three units to the genitalia, but it is one and the same organ. Or three spirits in man — Father, Son, Holy Ghost — all that is merged too. There are seven levels of knowledge, says G—, but there can be 17 too, and it all overlaps. Dante, who is a greater man, makes of 9 only because of love, after all... the eras of Beatrice. I offer no shmathematics. It's all old shoe.

————o————o————o————

To remember for on the Road { If you can't get a girl in the Springtime You can't get a girl at all.

Over this long weekend I saw everybody again, but particularly I shall treasure Sat. night when Neal, Lucien, Allen and I wandered together... first a kind of party in the St. Moritz when some "creepy" Denver people were (Lou's description), then Lenrow's apt. and drinks, music, talk; then Sarah's house for roast beef at 4 A.M. I was astonished by these four dearest comrades of mine, all at the same time astonishing me. (I am one of the four when with them.) I thank God I know Lou, Neal, and Allen. I look to them for all the knowledge I need now. I will always love them, each one + enmasse.

talk; then Sarah's house for roast beef at 4 A.M. I was astonished by these four dearest comrades of mine, *all at the same time* astonishing me. (I am one of the four when with them.) I thank God I know Lou, Neal, and Allen. I look to them for all the knowledge I need now. I will always love them, each one & en masse.

I only hope for their admiration and regard. I trust them. They are not evil because they know evil so well. They are my brothers. I would not have lived but to know them. I treasure them, I hoard them forever, I believe them. I am astonished when they turn and notice me and ask me to speak. When I do speak, it strikes me strange that they should seek to understand what I say and pay such attention to my soul. — In due course of time we'll all be old men, and married, and more or less separate in that way, but I know we will always continue, and beyond to the whirlwinds. I say all this only because I never made a formal statement of what I feel for Cassady, Carr, and Ginsberg; and Carr, Ginsberg and Cassady; and Ginsberg, Cassady and Carr.

MON. 10–THUS. 13 — Wrote further in the stubborn work-realms. — O private haunt and hurt, shame and scandal of my star, which is censure from the beasts, sore humility — sorrows of an air importuned by clay. Doleful, doleful day; dread of angels. Romage among the beasts, "we fools of nature," — pigs. O spright! — or sprig! This air doth tremble and cannot of its own meek motion penetrate; dead soul, air, flapped by paws and commotion. Ye so sullen, secret, eyelid-reddened beasts leave off. I have my forlorn reasons. "What is necessary is to discourage others from bothering about you. The rest is just vicious." (Celine.) Specifically, the world is full of beasts and I am not a beast. Remember 'the only broken fish'? Hark.

*"Horatio, I am dead."**

FRI. 14–SUN. 16 — Long weekend in town seeing Giroux, Meyer Shapiro, Holmes, Seymour; Lucien, Neal; Lee; Muriel Jacobs. Jazz on

---

*Hamlet to Horatio in act 5, scene 2, of Shakespeare's *Hamlet,* after the death of Gertrude, Claudius, and Laertes — just before Hamlet's death.

52nd street and in Brooklyn; W. C. Fields movies; classes at New School. Parties here & there. Food, drink. The works. Wearily came home at noon Sunday and slept all afternoon.

Filled with thoughts.

How I admire W. C. Fields! — What a great oldtimer he was. None like him. I'll write something about him soon, my personal ideas. "Ain't you got no Red Eye?" "Ain't you an old Follies girl?" "I snookered that one." "Those Grampion hills." "Mocha-java." "The enterprise I am about to embark upon is fraught with eminent peril, and not fit for a young lady of your tender years." "Don't you want to wear diaphanous gowns? And get enough to eat?" With his straw hat, his short steps, his belly, his wonderful face hid beneath a bulbous puff of beaten flesh, his twisted mouth, his knowledge of American life, of women, of children, of fellow-barflies, and of death ("the fellow in the bright night-gown.") His utter lovelessness in the world. Bumping into everything blindly. Making everybody laugh. The line he himself wrote, addressed to him: "You're as funny as a cry for help." How he blows foam off a beer, an Old Mad Murphy of time; how he is alone among foolish people who don't *see* his soul.

Shakespeare never was sadder.

A hounded old reprobate, a clown, a drunkard of eternity, and "Man."

MON. 17 — Last night wrote several hundred goodly words. Still impossible to say "Road" has really begun. There are 25,000 words sealed in for certain, but this has been the case since May, since which time I've been writing, but *cutting* also. At same time, I really began On the Road in October of 1948, an entire year ago. Not much to show for a year, *but the first year is always slow.* What kind of needless plodding is this? If it turns out as good and as *true* as T & C then it's definitely worth it. I want to finish it by next Spring, so I may be free in Europe to study and make notes for Dr. Sax merely (while perhaps writing the play Imbecile's Xmas.) Who knows? And besides, I don't care so much for Europe. I'm more interested in 3rd Avenue now. — Am reading

Thomas Merton's confession. Also went back to Joyce's thesis on Shakespeare in "Ulysses"* and am reading Hamlet line by line (also deciding how I would act it.) Also Donne's Holy Sonnets, and the magnificent speeches of Ahab in Moby Dick. Full of interests. The novel is about to *move*, too; I feel it. Fullblown are Red & Smitty now, and Pomcry to come.

— Once, when my mother was a little girl, she had two teeth filled and her father decided they ought to be filled with gold. How gladly she looked ahead to a lifetime with her gold teeth; "gold never falls out." But when her little son [Gerard] died in 1926,† all her teeth had to be taken out following an illness, gold and all, and they never gave her back her gold. O death! death! death! (This is what I want to write, not *stylistic* crap!)

WED. 19 — I don't know anything except that parts make a whole. And that though the world is populated by beasts and ignoramuses, there are still a few people worth living for, here and there. Because parts make a whole, I cannot be swayed *one way or the other* by any part, person, event, idea or season any more. This is what they call "peace," but it is only a part of the whole, and all I really know *is what there is not*. What there *is* — ???

Love is what there is, poor love.
Love! Shmove! —
I say, be reasonable. Kind is kind.

THURS. 20–SUN. 23 — Went into town to school and signed at all the classes without attending. On Thurs. night Holmes and Seymour and I made some astounding "prophetic" voice-music recordings that sound like Tristano's "Intuition." I did a few boyishly sad Hamlet soliloquies. Next day I went to dentist, saw Allen, Muriel; and Cannastra,

*A reference to the "Telemachus" chapter of James Joyce's *Ulysses* in which Stephen Dedalus expounds his theories regarding Hamlet's heredity.
†Gerard Kerouac was Jack's older brother; he died at age nine in 1926.

Hornsbein in San Remo. Came home and Allen and I talked till dawn over my notebooks and various papers; but in the morning my mother was anxious over having a "jailbird" in the house. I cannot and will not try to straighten out any nonsense anywhere any more. What's Hecuba to me?

Saturday evening I indulged myself in reading. A dark, deep, profound night — especially when ruminating over the Saxon barbarians of giant-dreams and bloody desolation that led suddenly to sweet and gentle Caedmon, the coming of the Cross.* Lorca's poems about the Civil Guard in Spain also plunged me in dreadful thoughts; and reading about copkillers and their electrocution in Chicago.

I also read Taine on Shakespeare;† a great deal of Merton; and ended up the long reading-night in the Walpurgis of "Ulysses." Mainly, I had further visions of Doctor Sax. The "mundane serpent" is in the Eddas, and escaped destruction in the Flood; will reappear at Snake Hill. The Medieval wizards and vampire-attendants are fools who do not understand true evil, for Doctor Sax goes back further than heretical witchcraft, goes back to the gory abysses of dragons and the great death-orgies of Franks, back to the mighty fury of snow-gods and fire-gods contending for the destruction of all things before Christ. Doctor Sax will be the greatest book I have ever written. I may do it before I'm 30, or spend my life at it; or both, in two versions youngman and oldman. Such are the fruits of reading ... I should read more. An "indulgence" I call it. Sunday I took a long walk thinking of starvation. Imagining myself a hobo just in from Montana, hungry — all that. Sunday night I resumed work-of-the-moment, On the Road. — And what long, long contemplation I have ... My life is like a river of meditations. I sit motionless for an hour straight, wandering through my mind as one picking berries and packing them in proper boxes, all for 'later consumption' of some kind, or

---

*Saint Caedmon lived in the seventh century and wrote biblical poems know as Caedmonian verse.

†Hippolyte-Adolphe Taine (1828–1893), French critic and historian.

pressing in the wine-vats of more formful thought such as accompanies artwork. Poosh!

And all for what? What is knowledge? — What is knowledge?

Van Doren once said, "It's more fun than anything to know something." One knows so seldom.

MON. 24–WED. 26 — A period of "depression" that I sought to ward off by going into town to see friends. Saw Giroux; the Holmeses; had a woman; saw Neal and Dianne. Came home in the rainy night ... I had distinct knowledges of how much time I waste in "brooding" around while life rages on all around. A perusal of a history of the American movies, showing how young and grand were people like Valentino, Barthelmess, Mary Pickford, Chaplin, Gloria Swanson, Garbo, Leslie Howard, Gable, even W. S. Hart, Wallace Reid, Doug Fairbanks Sr. in the early days (naturally); showing me how I'm wasting my own youth; a long talk with Holmes about this sadness; a perusal of Wm. Blake's great carefree proverbs (of Hell) showing how one ought to *live*, especially a poet, a soothsayer, a prophet; a poor, mere photograph of Harry Truman showing how little a President has time to mope, sulk, and dog his days with rumination of sorrows; a talk with Neal, watching how excited he is about life ... All this, and the rainy night, conspired to hurl me into decisions about my introspective paralysis — to come out of that, *and into the sunny world.* To stop wasting time! — To write and write! — Go out with more women! — Meet more people! — Walk the streets at night! — Eat ... see ... dream ... go to excesses ... never mind the sad, dull restraints. — Some people find their days a succession of events of the heart, the body, the soul ... mine have too long been a succession of meditative woes. (Came to some conclusions thereby about Moultrie in On the Road; imagine a hitch-hiking, penniless, mystical Hamlet.) I will *stop, stop, stop* crying very soon! It's gone too far already. Even Neal is worried. I should be delirious with joy; I sold my book, I was saved. It is an insistent morbidity ten times worse than that of Francis Martin in T & C. It is a weariness of the world and of all worlds. It is a downfall of an early exuberance, falling farther because heavier, breaking easier because more fragile, enchained by its own disenchantment all the longer.

Every now and then in these dark days I thank God for sudden visions of joy.

I'm going back to my old ways.

NEXT DAY — Where is the soul located? Somewhere in the frame of the flesh, manifesting itself by use of poor fleshly device ... the look of the eye, the curl of the lips, the balance of the hip and of the head on the shoulder. The soul does all that. It uses what it has, and what it has plus what it intends is the picture of the abyss that I am trying to paint. For though the soul be dead insomuch as it is only a receivership of grace, it is also alive the moment of receiving, & writhes thus. But the Soul of souls is far from dead, and far from these words, words, words.

ALSO: — Two Rules

1)   Never mind the hex and the mystery that fills your days with dolourous wonder.

2)   Never mind the worries pertaining to the interior structures and the interior substantial plans of your work. Delight in things.

I.E., To hell with it; don't worry; simply do.

THUS. 27 — The only thing that is interesting is the action of a man who knows all about inaction and woe. (On this level.)

FRI. 28 — Yesterday and today went to school; sat in on interesting lectures by Wm. Troy, Shapiro, et al; had talks with Holmes, Allen, and with Geo. Bouwman at his home in Brooklyn; a few beers on the antique Brooklyn waterfront, Spanish whores, etc; saw Ruth Sloane; get Muriel and battled around two days with her, a sweet girl; party at Neal's and Dianne's; met Joe Killian there; Neal and I got high, dug our girls; souls; next day I traded in new G.I. books for several delightful used books (Confidence Man, 17th Century Lyrics, On Love by Stendhal, The Possessed, some Proust, Chekhov, Arabian Nights, Turgenieff, Oxford English Prose, and I kept my Hopkins and Yeats.) My library will always be small and distinctive and useful.

These past days were delightful.

Moreover, on Sat. night, I had the biggest dream, vision and trance since last May, at home in Richmond Hill, and wrote it up in a 2,000-word summary "A Structure of Knowledge Concerning Pure Substance Becoming Through the Medium of the Points True Spirit; Wherein Airy Graces shall Commune in Heaven."

Serious and important. More anon in this bk.

SUN. OCT. 30 — To delight in the thing itself, in all the appurtenances of "woeful" life on earth, like the very artist who loves the feel of his paint, or the mathematician who sees Genii in numbers, and so in the case of the spiritual man in the spirit itself ... the very spright and sprig of fleshly intercomprehension ... this is what is to be arrived at. Why should this be my book of Woes? The Black Book of Woes.

Among other things I want, now, to begin an appreciation of how everyone realizes the impossibility of contact and how they airily hint.

— Resting up and eating. Saw a movie. Still don't feel On the Road is begun. However, in the work itself I will find my way. As I go along (and especially during tonight's definitive work) I find that I want a different structure as well as a different style in this work, in contrast to T & C ... Each chapter as a line of verse in the general epic poem, instead of each chapter as a broad-streamed prose statement in the general epic novel. That is why I want to use short chapters, each with verselike heading, and very many such chapters; slowly, deeply, moodily unfolding the moody story and its long outreaching voyage into strange space. And to run up a pace of such short chapters till they are like a string of pearls. Not a river-like novel; but a novel like poetry, or rather, a narrative poem, an epos in mosaic, a kind of Arabesque preoccupation ... free to wander from the laws of the "novel" as laid down by Austens & Fieldings into an area of greater spiritual pith (which cannot be reached without this technical device, for me anyway) where the Wm. Blakes & Melvilles and even spotty, short-chaptered Celine, dwell. I want to say things that only Melville has allowed himself to say in "The Novel." And Joyce.

I'm not interested in The Novel, but in what I want to write about. I want, as in 1947, to bust out from the European narrative into the Mood Chapters of an American poetic "sprawl" — if you can call careful chapters and careful prose a sprawl. If this is not agreeable to the public, what can I say? As an Architect I will nevertheless see that all is solid in this. We'll see.

It is a terrible thing to contemplate the fact that editors like Giroux, in their vast experience of reading, are able to select those aspects of the novel that read best and therefore feel conscience-free to remove whatever which in the author's crucible of torn imaginings seems most pithy, but to reader most delaying in his hot sin of "wanting to see what happens."

Come a day there will when narrative excitement will be referred to its nearest kin and cousin, pornography, and authors of exact imagination will be free, as Joyce felt free, to wind out their moody shrouds about the riddle of the tale being told.

There is no reason in this world why I am not free to do this myself even now.

I am prepared for all ascetic necessaries and a downfall of worldly success if so sadly need be. Hear me Bob? (Pfft!)

"Shroudings
&
Diddlings"

Each chapter an illuminative point, like a dream; and with that strange continuity of purpose that all our dreams and all our days have, in processional life. Each chapter a dewy star newly perceived ... in the heavens which nevertheless in milky blur are Whole. Such a novel ... such a "moodwork" as I once called it, or soulwork — or Shrouded Tale. —
———————— And what a pity it is that all those in whom the youth reposes his hopes, in manhood of success (as now) are gone ... Margaret (with whom I discussed the future under summer's apple tree), Edie, — wife of my youth; my father; and Sebastian. Women have their own way of dying from a man's life. Now, those who know me only in gaunt thoughtful manhood, think me a stranger from the void. My mother is the first and last to know me all. As for Mary, Mary, Quite Contrary, she put the sorcerous gown about my eyes & finisht me off proper ... now a bawdy slut of the Moody St. night, I hear. Beyond this there can only be pale repetition, and a flowering from out the forgotten nutriment, as the petal is but the fruit of abandoned earth.

Yet there is no end to the joy of sweet, sweet life. The honey rain is falling ...

There is a tree in this breast. I feel it spreading all the time. It's early Spring. I will tell you when the leaves start falling. They will never start falling.

There is an evergrowing tree in this breast.

—   —

MON. OCT. 31 — Halloween walk at night; worked.

TUES. NOV. 1 — Worked badly last night. Feelings of nameless-impotence in writing. However, the proofs for T & C are now pouring in at office, and tomorrow we begin final work. The hang-up with composition of On the Road spoils the pleasure of publishing Town & City. Such is my sullen nature. I can do everything well but work, it now seems. Used to be other way around.

But as I read the laborious 10,000 words of October, I see that this is really a better novel than T & C!! — from which I decide that I will just have to get used to the idea of writing slower than before ... twice as slow. On the Road is rich, and moves along richly, with a great deal of depth in every line. Moultrie is a magnificent character who already moves the feelings like a veritable George Martin. Also, the scope of the novel is a world in itself and not only that but an inevitable world. I'm "doing it again," obviously. Must resign myself to the slow pace of the true prose-laborer. Okay.

By April, then, I might have about 100,000 words written and *decided upon* — which is the meat of the job. I might have 150 thous. too, or almost whole thing.

So writing gets harder, but better. Okay.

Rain tonight, cold November rain.

NOV. 2–NOV. 6 — Working at the Harcourt office on the galley proofs. Bob has done a splendid job of revision. It may be that where a story like T & C is concerned, the story is more important than the poetry.

How should I know?

— I GIVE UP —

All I know is that as I grow older, I keep getting more and more forgetful of the things that happen day in, day out. On Tuesday I do forget Monday's gnaw — completely — and by the same token, Sunday's strange angels and airy theory. I give up.

I have now given up.

It's all up to the Angel ...

Facts? details? — parties this weekend, one by Jay Landesman whose "Neurotica" was banned and all the intellectuals were fuming with joy.* Had a fight with Muriel and saw her snarl, whilst she saw my deepest infidelity of the heart. Saw Allen, Neal, Seymour — Diane — visited the Met Museum — saw Zorita in the Times Square snake-horror movie.† Had my picture taken for book-jacket by photographer Elliott Elwitt, a kid of nineteen or so.

Did not know what was going on anywhere.

Did not know who I was.

Did see the works of God. Did hear the cry for eternity in the streets. Heard God coming. Saw the fiery sign in the sky.

And gave up.

My new epitaph is as follows:

— DIGNIFIED BY DEATH —

NOV. 7–13 — A week of hectic galley-proof work and running around N.Y. to school, office, dentist, appointments, drinking, etc. Jack Fitzgerald visited me. The Brooklyn police incident.

I decided further on On the Road — I have my "new idea" germinating ... a form midway between the play and the novel for it. My sister and Baby Paul are with us. Delight.

The truth is, life is too much woe and everybody feels awful. But they can take it.

NOV. 14–17 — Strange thoughts of art these days. To think that I would "start all over" again in my field. Have I not mastered the narrative novel? — (even though my Book of Sorrows (The original ms. of

---

*Jay Landesman (1919–   ), founder of *Neurotica*, a poetry journal "by neurotics, for neurotics."
†*I Married a Savage* (1949), starring burlesque dancer Zorita (1915–2001), featured her signature dance with a boa constrictor.

The Town and the City, 1095 P.) has been edited into a 'good work of fiction' now.) Mastered is the art of evoking masses by masses. Now I want to evoke something else. Action will prove, and logic disproves, that combining the intensification of the play with the scope of the novel is possible. What is my tradition? In form, Melville of Confidence Man & parts of Moby Dick; the later Joyce; monologue poetry & plays of Eliot. In substance: all that the eye needs, from Skeleton to Fie, from Blake to Fum. Substance is always there, it's the Bowl of History that changes, & man must wind his garments about him.

Perhaps I can amass a humble fortune with my 'Town & City' now (signs are favorable), as if God had never wanted me to worry about bread, first by dint of family aid and the later aid of a widow Mother, and now by the Patronage of the Bank Account, to whom I shall dedicate future works as a Spenser to his Lord.

A shroud of silence is descending. Either that or I'm mistaken.

*

Shrouds are necessary.

Epiphany, come one.
"BLOOM: (Bends his blushing face into his armpit and simpers with
           forefinger in mouth.) *'O, I know what you're hinting at now.'* "*
A versification of common speech into simple 'rhymes' of pure language.

What T. E. Hulme says of "saying anything is saying nothing."

Brevity being the soul of wit, epiphany may not only be of character but of plot, of scene, of very swirl.

Okay.

————————

*From the "Circe" chapter of James Joyce's *Ulysses*.

Shrouds are necessary.

Epiphany, come on.

"BLOOM: (Bends his blushing face into his
armpit and simpers with forefinger
in mouth.) 'O, I know what
you're hinting at now.'"

A versification of common speech into
simple 'rhymes,' of pure language.
What T. E. Hulme says of "saying anything
is saying nothing."

Brevity being the soul of wit, epiphany
may not only be of character, but of plot,
of scene, of very swirl.

Okay.

THE BOKE OF Shrouds

Working on "Levinsky and the Geeks" for a
sophisticated magazine — not working, really, it's
but editing of original chapter. Just for "laughs." *

Afflicted by my leg-ailment again (phlebitis.)
Reading the Lamb — Blake. Read "Aspects
of the Novel" — Joyce's stories — really reading
a lot. Spent 2 days on my back.

Squeezed On the Road for elixirs.

Thought of my life — what I will write
and how I will live.

Spent still another 5 days on my back.
Read prodigiously.

* Women who read Vogue will be amused by sweet Levinsky

Working on "Levinsky and the Geeks" for a sophisticated magazine — not working, really, it's but editing of original chapter. Just for "laughs." Women who read Vogue will be amused by sweet Levinsky.

Afflicted by my leg-ailment again (phlebitis.)

Reading The Lamb — Blake. Read "Aspects of the Novel" — Joyce's stories — really reading a lot. Spent 2 days on my back.

Squeezed On the Road for elixirs.

Thought of my life — what I will write and how I will live.

Spent still another 5 days on my back. Read prodigiously.

NOV. 30

I was reading Melville's Confidence Man when suddenly Celine's *Mort a Credit* wiped it clean off my mind. I've only just now remembered that I was in the middle of C-Man a few days ago. I need no further proof to know that in the truest sense Celine towers above Melville. Celine is not the artist, not the poet that Melville is — but he swamps him under from sheer weight of tragic fury. There's no getting around this, not at all. Every beautiful sentence in The Encantadas is but a pale pearl drenching in the tempests of Celine, of Shakespeare, Beethoven, Homer too.

It's not the words that count, but the rush of what is said.

The people do not read Spenser, do not read Melville, do not read Hopkins, do not read E. M. Forster, do not read James Joyce, do not read Stendhal, do not read Ouspensky, T. S. Eliot or Proust — *they read Swift, Tolstoy and Twain; they read Cervantes, Rabelais & Balzac.*

They don't read Donne, they read *Dickens;* they don't read Gide, they read *Celine,* they don't read Turgenev, they read *Pushkin & Dostoevsky;* & *Chekhov* they see; *Shakespeare* they see. They don't see Congreve,* don't see —

---

*William Congreve (1670–1729), English playwright, mostly of Restoration comedies.

What is art? Artness?

No. A poor means of evoking what's to be evoked, of uttering the truth.

In my recent absorptions anent "Road" I'd been wrapped in a shroud of words and arty designs. That's not life — not how one really feels. Not passion!

Here goes again on Road.

Great God, how much must I pirouette to get back to myself! *Psste!*

The experience of life is a regular series of deflections that finally results in a circle of despair.

Such circles also exist in small daily doses.

It is a circle; it is really despair. However, the straight line will take you only to death at once. (Censoring my weak-kneed apologetic optimism.)

DEC. 2nd —

Again laid up with phlebitis. Using penicillin. Things under control.

Since every circle has a center, the "circle of despair," formed by a series of deflections from pale forgotten goals [o], circumferentiates nevertheless one dark haunting *thing* [*].

The thing is ... ???

To me, "this thing" is that Shrouded Stranger I dreamt once. It is ever-present and ever-pursuing. One may swirl nearer and nearer to that shroud, *and it may only be* our haunted sense of the *thing*, which is ever unnameable and is really our chiefest plaint ... as plaint may be a song as well. Ecclesiasticus.

The thing is central to our existence, and alone is our everlasting companion after parents and wives and children and friends may fade away. Wolfe's "brother Loneliness," Melville's "inscrutable thing," Blake's "gate of Wrath," Emily Dickinson's "third event," Shakespeare's "nature"? — God?

One can almost point with the finger. It's also every man's "mystery" and deepest being. — I would also find it most of all in L.-F. Celine's

The experience of life is a regular series
of deflections that finally results in
a circle of despair.

FIG. 1

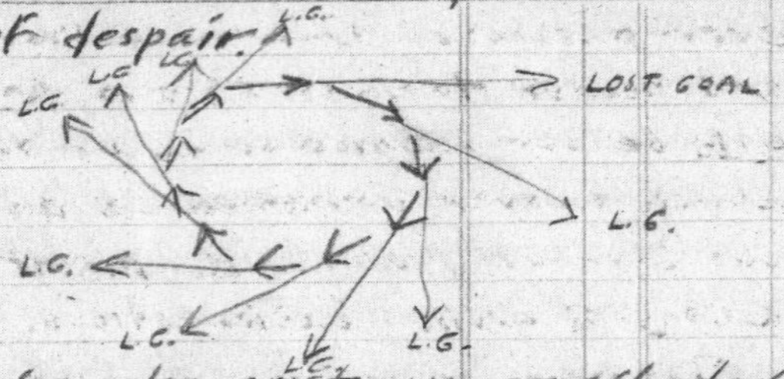

> LOST GOAL

L.G.

Such circles also exist in small daily
doses.

▬▬▬ It is a circle; it is ◄▬ really
despair. However, ▬▬▬▬ The straight line
will take you only to death at once.
[Censoring my weak-kneed apologetic optimism.]

DEC. 2nd ━━

Again laid up with phlebitis. Using
penicillin. Things under control.

FIG. 2

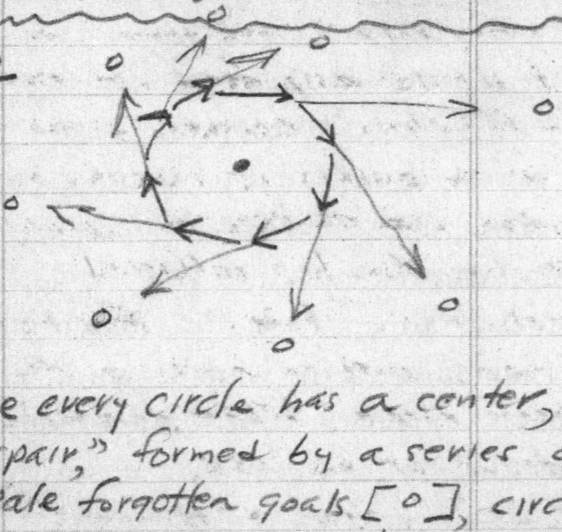

Since every circle has a center, the "circle
of despair," formed by a series of deflections
from pale forgotten goals [o], circumferentiates
nevertheless one dark haunting thing [•].
This thing is ... ???

climactic visions of "death" as he pushes it through for both Leon Robinson and de Pereires ... What's left after everything else has collapsed.

It's really one's "Fate." For Fate is never a man's wish so much as the
center of his life's circle ... That damnable unavoidable focus of his luck.

Also Yeats' "falcon" & "falconer."

"The Shrouded Falconer"

Nonsense and Roses.

Heaven & Earth

— Here in the vale of Airs all is serene, but down in the Valley of
Roars it seems much more exciting. May we go down there? Will we be
allright down there?

— No; there's danger; you'll never come back.

— Even then, this vale is dull — though safe. What's the danger in
the valley below?

— Life and death of earth, my friend.

— I wish we could be safe down there.

— No.

A NOVEL

My name, though it might sound real strange to you because I'm a colored man, has always been Whitey White. This is my name according
to the law, and in my birth papers, & everywhere I go.

The first thing I remember is the winter night in Brooklyn when
there was a lot of noise down on the street — fire wagons, cop cruisers,
a crowd, and my bleeding uncle tied in handcuffs to a policeman —
and the moaning of my Aunt Lucy in the room next to mine, and
everybody jumping on the top floor. "Hush your mouth!" said my Ma
when I started in to yell."

* — This would be a novel in one of the few pure idioms in American speech, City Negro, or Harlemese; with the story-matter that attends it. Very wild!!

"He was up there on the bandstand blowing and blowing till the sweat come out! He says to me, "Hey!" and he goes right on jumping and jumping with that old taped-up horn up there."

Rhythm, too. "Hey now, man!"

*   *   *

*IT'S NOT THE WORDS THAT COUNT BUT THE RUSH OF TRUTH WHICH USES WORDS FOR ITS PURPOSES; as a virtuoso performing on his instrument may use any combination of notes within a beat (the word) but it is the melody of the bar that matters. It's not the design, but the picture; not the curve, but the form. On and on in inane comparison ...

An artist cannot translate the passionate intensity of life without working in passion himself. Scholar's scholar, critic's critic, but the artist burns and beats and blows and jumps and rushes. It is all a matter of virtue, i.e., virtuosity. What the hell! Shit's not pink.

More notes later.

These things have a verisimilitude depending on their resemblance to the beat of life.

ANOTHER NOTE: —

People aren't interested in the facts but in ejaculations.

— That is why straight naturalism fails to express life.

An art like Balzac's is a glorious shower of fantastic ejaculations — a fountain of life, a gushing spring, an incredible spray. Who wants Dos Passos' old camera eye? — or Proust's subtleties? Everybody wants to GO!

So must the author, becoming oblivious to all petty details, in the heat of his huffing & puffing, zealous, fiery soul, GO!

The more fantastic the better, the sadder, the truer about life.

Novelists should write about rational people? — Trilling's "Middle of the Journey"? — write about intellectuals? The only time I knew Trilling he pulled the most absurd irrational mask it has been my honor to observe: after Ginsberg was thrown out of college, and I had been mixed up in this downfall and barred from the Columbia campus, Trilling refused to recognize me on the street in the most farcical way, because so solemn, as if I'd suddenly acquired leprosy and it was his rational duty to himself a Liberal Enlightener of Intellectuals to repair at a safe distance from the area of my septic running sores. From down the street I waved at him eagerly ... He hurried on deep in thought. Finally he came face to face with me at a drugstore counter behind which I implacably was stationed washing dishes. There was nothing he could do; he forced a wan smile — I greeted him. Having paid for his coffee, he hurriedly drank it; and rushed off as soon as he could. But people were milling at the door, he couldn't get out fast enough ... He burst out of the drugstore, breathed with relief; he hurried to his rational chores.

This is what I saw him do. I can take no crap from such men about my own work, especially when I am no longer barred from that imaginary campus-club of theirs.

Is this bug on rationality just another trick to disenfranchise every poor joker in the world who hasn't a chance to bother?

No education, just ejaculation

———————

SUNDAY DEC. 11 — Merde. Now they point out to me that other young writers are "incorruptible;" a former girl of mine wants to hit me over the head with a hammer; a destitute scribbler accuses me of being complacent in my success; they ask that I subscribe to liberal magazines; they gossip that I have allowed myself to be commercialized; they all give me fishy-eyed looks. This is what one gets for addressing one's love to the world.

From now on, nuttin' but shrouds.

I won't even write a diary. My life is in danger. I have become a curmudgeon. My closest friends accuse me of alienating my loyalties. Many people hint of their troubles ...

The only actual friend I have is Bob Giroux (actively). My brother.

Although no simpleton, you might think I was, for all this drivelling.

One night Neal, even Neal, rushed up and grabbed the pencil out of my hand to write a burning thought down, as though The Master's Pencil made no difference to *him* the Potential. How do they expect me to be blind? What the hell do I care about their drivellings?

At least I do my drivelling in private.

Goodbye, ass holes.

The novelist must never give bare facts, but soliloquize them with a reason which is inseparable from the mood of the work in the whole. Otherwise it's journalism.

DEC. 13 — Tonight I had a dream that I wandered across the fields of the U.S. and came to a house which was my own, until, inside, I realized it was *not so any more*. I could tell this by the "project in the backyard," which was not my kind of project: — a huge multi-funnel, black, like an intricate furnace-blower of some kind. And there I was, in what used to be my room, fumbling with some tools I thought were mine. I got scared. At that moment the man of the house came in. It was my father. I hid in the pantry; I retreated to the kitchen-toolroom. The woman came in. The child was out in the yard. Frantically I climbed out through the window, and in the moment of being discovered, ran wildly across the yard, eluding the big woman's attempted tackle, yelling "Off-tackle, hip!" — and ran clear back across a tiny dreamlike America to my "plowing" in a peaceful dale.

DEC. 14 — Saw a great show at Bop City. Lionel Hampton's wild "going" band; and George Shearing at piano. Was with Neal, who has one-arm room in E. 76th St. slums, and is writing his novel on the Harcourt typewriter I got. Told Neal how I had changed in past month.

Was surprised that when you change, others seem to change too(!). We discussed this by the stove in the parking lot shack.

Today also had steak with Harcourt salesmen at noon; a drink with Bob at Waldorf Bar; a chat with Holmes in Bickford's. I write all this because of satisfactoriness & *range* of this day, and will like to recall details of it later.

Meanwhile, On the Road is on the road, that is, moving.

— —

When you say: "I'm going to change," and really mean it, at first it doesn't seem you are changing at all, but in a few months, imperceptibly, it has happened. Life is slow and moody ... and earnest it *proceeds.*

DEC 19 — Nowadays if I kept a writing-log, would say, "Tonight wrote equivalent of 3000-words on a 300-word page."

*   *   *   *   *

Anything in the world can be rationalized. That's not true? Reason is false? — reason is not false? It doesn't matter.

Life is strange, is strange, is strange.

"Criminals or children — which is Man." But there's innocent evil, and there's experienced good.

DEC. 20 dawn — Slow painful work on "Road." Lucidity should be a flow.

*

Night is no romantic time to write, as afternoon-critics say, but when, brooding on the innocent sleep of the world, trances come, visions of the possibilities of the heart, and in the silence, altars to this are meticulously fashioned and chiseled to perfection.

To me it is also the bebop night, and when freight trains roll; and I, completely undisturbed in the dream of my creations which sell at noon(!), unlike the creations of said critics ... (If they want to talk about 'romanticism.')

— * —

Things Everybody Know but Never Talk About

1) Dean says "Look at that belly!" — pointing to the poster of a movie actress. If it were suggested he actually meet this woman, how the youngster would clam up in awe of the awesome world. And say — "Think of all the things between that broad and me! Miles of people, agents, nightclubs, producers, money, right connections! Yet how I would love her, every hidden bit! — as no man ever *dared!*" People never talk of the things, the time and night and bigness, that separate them. "I love her better than anybody. I'll never see her. It's all involved & awful."

: — :

Life is not strange, not strange, not strange.

Or ever that crude I'd be —
That, when life denys of me
I, in ire's worst digressing,
Should of innocence make oppressing.

MAY 19, 1950 — Five months later.

All the time spent in Richmond Hill since last August when I arrived from California via Denver and had that tremendous depression described on page 23 to 46, seems like one amorphous mass of time ... "nothing happened" — the depression is more vivid in my memory this May-morn than publication of "Town & City" — and I wonder why this is so, almost as if there is *no time* in New York life. Yet a great many things happened, in every way, money, and women, and travel (to Boston, Poughkeepsie, New Hope Pa.) and friends, events, shows, meals, dreams, about 75,000 words of miscellaneous writing, and so forth. Maybe my life is not inclosed in diaries any more. Seems strange. In any case this is the morning of my new departure to the West and to Mexico City, till September 1950.

Last night was sad & rainy. My mother ironed my clothes; we had a snack, talked; occasionally looked at each other with a furtive sadness. Perhaps I'm writing all this to warn all travelers — the night before the journey is like the night before death. This was how I felt. Where am I really going, and what for? Why must I always travel from here to there, as if it mattered where one is?

Why am I such a failure in love? For if my love affair with Sara had been successful, "here" or "there" would no longer matter at all, but as it is I can't stay in New York and "lose face" with the associations of her that abound here. I really travel because I'm loveless. I'm going to another life, by dying like this.

But I'm not sad. The truth is that I've yet to meet the true wife of my life, and I will find her somewhere. Travel is a hint of that. What dull nonsense one speaks when one speaks from the chagrined heart. No poesie.

But she was too haughty for my kind.

Nothing is left in this experienced soul of mine except repetition — soon the wise & humble man in me, latent, will become a master of compromise — and then I shall be old and workaday. No harm in that.

Let me say further, in French translated into English —

"I go because I'm crazy. One must work, not play. You don't know how to work any more, you're an idiot. Arrange your life and shut your mouth. You know damn well you won't work in Mexico — in Denver you won't have time. You're spending your money and that's all. Poor dope. One good day you'll no longer be able to do anything, and then it will be too late. If you can't find a way of living today, you won't find it tomorrow. Stop waiting and start."

"Shall I take this trip? — I have to, it's all arranged."

"Yes, go. Go away. Do what you like. Go play, go be the fool. When you return you'll be older, that's all."

"What'll I do when I return?"

"The same thing you could do now."

"What is that?"

"Work and make your life. Find a woman and marry. Have children and shut your mouth. Be a man and not a child."

"Where will I live?"

"Live where you want!! It's all the same, damn fool! Go live in the field, go live on the dump, it's all the same."

"Haven't you a word of advice without condemnation for what I'm about to do?"

Sullen silence ... then — "Advice your ass. You don't need advice. You know what you're doing. Under the circumstances of your trip, if something happens, stop. Stop running like a mouse over the surface of the earth. Life's not long and you're not young."

These are the words of my "French-Canadian older brother" who came to me, almost incarnate, in a tea-vision two weeks ago and has been with me ever since. His words strike home & heavy.

I listen to him with fear & respect. He told me he was "un ambassadeur du Bon Dieu" that morning he appeared in my room, standing scornfully in the corner, with a fishy eye lowered on the silly narcotic in the bed. That first morning he acknowledged several things I asked him — like, for instance, Ginsberg & Meyer Shapiro & Kazin were great men because they were not trying to dejew themselves & therefore I should not try to defrench myself. As simple as that. He told me Carr was a silly ass; that Neal was okay even if 'un excite'; he told me to slap my lady love down and make her *mind;* and such as things as that, all simple, direct and true. He even told me to go to church and shut up. He hinted I should go to Lowell, or Canada, or France, and become a Frenchman again and write in French, and shut up. He keeps telling me to shut up. When I can't sleep because my mind is ringing with gongs of English thought & sentences, he says, "*Pense en Francais,*" knowing I will calm down and go to sleep in simplicity.

I'm taking this brother with me on this trip to Mexico and see what happens.

Many times he says, "Eat!" and I get up and eat.

I think he is my original self returning after all the years since I was a child trying to become "un Anglais" in Lowell from shame of being a Canuck; I never realized before I had undergone the same feelings any Jew, Greek, Negro or Italian feels in America, so cleverly had I concealed them, even from myself, so cleverly and with such talented, sullen aplomb for a kid. Wrote a novel at *eleven,* "Peter"(!) He reminded me my father had started the same sad business in his own life, by mingling with 'les Anglais,' which really means *non-French.* These are the unmistakable truths. Soon I will resolve the thing by Anglicizing my Frenchness, or Frenchifying my English, whichever way it works. There are pitfalls I will have to examine: for instance, getting a "French wife" may only be regressive, like going back to the simple relationship with my sister, as kids. This may all only be interesting material, or madness, or as I hope, an eventual comedown to the roots of my true self.

In any case, seven months in New York, and nothing seems to have happened and here I go again. I'm bringing my "Road" manuscript with me.

There is nothing to say. Someday we'll all have died, and will anything have been settled? — anything done?

I'll see to it that it is, *mon frere.*

PARIS

Joyce ate at Fouquet's, and spent evenings at Madame Lapeyre's bistrot at Rue de Grenelle & Rue de Borgonne.

Celine's Raney ... and Rue St. Denis was his "sick-street."

Kerouac made it every night on San Juan de Letran, and ate at times at La Cucaracha.

: — Sublimities — :

SUBLIMITIES TO LEARN*

[Giovanni] Boccaccio's great poems *IL FILOSTRATO; LA TESEIDE.*
Chaucer's *TROILUS AND CHRYSEYDE*
THE RED BOOK OF HERGEST
THE BOOK OF BALLYMOTE
THE SPECKLED BOOK
Taliesin's SPOILS OF ANNWN
The *MABINOGION*
THE PANEGYRIC OF LLUDD THE GREAT
THE BOOK OF THE DUN COW
The *BOOK OF LEINSTER*
The *BOOK OF LECAIN*
The *YELLOW BOOK OF LECAIN*
Dr. O'Donovan's *ANNALS OF THE FOUR MASTERS*
THE BLACK BOOK OF CHERMARTHEN
The *MYRVIAN ARCHAEOLOGY*
Petrarch's SONNETS
OXIONENSE of Duns Scotus
St. Augustine's *CITY OF GOD; TRINITY*

---

*The following is a list of medieval and Renaissance literature. Kerouac probably became interested in them through Carl Ploetz's *Epitome of Ancient, Mediaeval, and Modern History* (1905), which he was reading at the time.

Poems of Prudentius
Thompson's *LIFE of LOYOLA*

Expressions
The smile in his work ...
What to do with one's eternity?
The fair style in her loving-art.
You don't know what a vale is. — The dusky bee.
The last lay of the world.
What's the hex? Who's the hoax?
I am growing ooder. My shmowd falls.
Impassible death. Look into my fire.
Influences are strong — (a key.)
"Mad about the void." — (ALLEN.)
"The great gelatinous world." — (LUCIEN).
The pathos of enemies. Hugeness of others.
Mismeshment of gears. Coo you too!
Irking nature. — Browse in lullal noons.
Shame and scandal of my star.
A sentence is impressing a thought into one's service.
Hang your hat in a whore-shack.
Ginsberg's — a dark mind. Neal's — a shining mind.
Common skeleton. Nor deeper peer.
Valley of the Roars. Vale of Airs.
Everything slumped a-heap among the gut-bones.
Radioactive holy water ... use it while it's hot.
October dawn: — dew on the dead leaves.
Don't if around with your therefores.
Lullal noon & lily drowse, and buzz & fuzz.
J. Fitzgerald — "This cold lonesome darkness."
The gone abyss.

Farting through silk and shittin' pink.
The rich fart thru silk, the poor shit thru burlap

"On the Road" is my vehicle with which as a lyric poet, as lay prophet, and as the possessor of a responsibility to my own personality (whatever it rages to do) I wish to evoke that indescribable sad music of the night in America — for reasons which are never deeper than *the music*. Bop only begins to express that American music. It is the actual inner sound of a country.

There are saints, and there are scholars; and the difference is always there. Absorbing and-or avoiding.

In Denver last summer all I did was stare at the *plains* for three months, for reasons, reasons.

There's a noise in the void I hear: there's a vision of the void; there's a complaint in the abyss — there's a cry in the bleak air: the realm is haunted. *Man haunts the earth.* Man is on a ledge *noising* his life. The pit of night receiveth. God hovers over in his shrouds. Look out!

More than a rock in my belly, I have a waterfall in my brain; a rose in my eye, a beautiful eye; and what's in my heart but a mountainside, and what's in my skull: a light. And in my throat a bird. And I have in my soul, in my arm, in my mind, in my blood, in my bean a grindstone of plaints which grinds rock into water, and the water is warmed by fires, and sweetened by elixirs, and becomes the pool of contemplation of the dearness of life. In my mind I cry. In my heart I think. In my eye I love. In my breast I see. In my soul I become. In my shroud I will die. In my grave I will change.

But enough poetry. Art is secondary.

Plaintiveness is all.

(In my sleep I referred to myself, in French, not as a "writer" but as *arrangeur* — he who arranges matters; at the same time, I associated this fraction with eating supper (*manger.*) I woke up to remember this.)

FEB. 1 — A night at the opera with Bob & Kelly. A banquet for 300 millionaires. Gene Tunney was there. Afterwards *Birdland* with Neal; champagne in the lounge of the Yale Club. The past month of January has been crazy ... beginning New Year's Eve with that fantastic party that ended for me in Princeton, N.J. and the Lyndons. A thousand swirling things all untold.

FEB. 7 — Tonight I mused & worked simultaneously on four major projects ... "Road," "Sax," "Simpleton" and a juvenile football novel (the latter may be major only in terms of $). (Altho kids in Lowell read it avidly when I wrote it at 17.) Busy day & night. I realize now that if I feel like it, any moment I may start *camping* and decide to be bored & depressed, just for a change. And that's what *that* is, or anything. Tonight I wrote the "serpent of evil" poem ... "all three sighed the sigh of life, and the serpent inched." Needless to say, I also cramm'd my 'Rain & Rivers' travelbook further. That makes *five* projects in all ... in today's fine range. One of those far-seeing days, when you're your own great-statesman of personal history, and see it all like a prophetic protocol ... within the dreamlike bleakness.

FEB. 10 — Mark Twain's "The Mysterious Stranger" is an undiscussed masterpiece, in some ways more profoundly all-inclusive than Melville's last-work (as the Stranger is Twain's) — Billy Budd. "Life is a dream," says Twain's beautiful Satan, but it is said in a context more terrible than anyone's before. "You are but a vagrant thought wandering forlornly in shoreless eternities." — and — *"All the dream-marks are there."*

  Last night — party at Varda's, to which I took Adele [Morales]: later, party at Holmeses, which I left and won't return. Adele and I had wonderful warm hours together. The other night, at Neal's birthday party, I also felt like not returning. Next month I'm off with my new map; don't know where.

FEB. 18 — In twelve days my Town & City will be published and the reviews will appear. Will I be rich or poor? Will I be famous or forgotten? Am ready for this with my "philosophy of simplicity" (something which ties in a philosophy of poverty with inward joy, as I was in 1947 & 1948.)

EARLY 1950

Notebook

Imposing title for the sake of modest future reference. Also, the year, in personal and universal history, is a landmark, for obvious reasons.

SAT. FEB. 18 — "You oughta be out in the forest like a big old grizzly bear." "How come you ain't out there?" "I'm a lady'" "They got lady-bears out there." "Aw baby ..." This is "Double-Crossing Blues," which is playing this moment over Symphony Sid. The girl is only 13 years old. All of a sudden the forest looms around in the night. Great simple art is always suddenly inexplicable and forever understood; it looms, like the forest.

Now I start work on my Chad Gavin* ... Stayed home tonight, Saturday night, always a good night to work, and started by reading 50 pages of the Possessed. Then I drafted opening chapter-plan for Chad Gavin — Walked four miles at 5 A.M. Read 40 pages of Cesar Birotteau [a.k.a. Balzac]. I've been grinding & grinding my mind on the Road idea for years now, yet when Balzac warns "don't confuse the fermentations of an empty head with the germination of an idea," I feel he refers to someone like me. But I'm doing my best. Lost in such thought, produced no wordage tonight. But the 'Road' plot is rich because of the "years" — no other reason.

J. Kerouac
94-21 134th St.
RICHMOND HILL, N.Y.

---

*Chad Gavin was an original character concept for On the Road.

SUN. FEB. 19 — Rose at 4:30, read papers, ate, walked. To "begin at the beginning," therefore — A splendid night of coordinative work; prepared 3,000 words for typing, the mysterious-opening-songful-explanation chapter, which has taken months to evolve. Now I go on to chapter Two, history of Old Wade. I won't count words till they're typed. A hundred ideas rushed in tonight. Laura has a "girlish" whimper when Chad kisses her, although ordinarily she is sly & strange & absentminded. At one point — at climax — she kids him: "I'm not that kind of date." Suddenly answers: — Come to me for the first time! Come to me for the first time!" But all this will appear in the pages of the manuscript ... much later.

At first tonight I was sick in stomach, and harassed. Nevertheless the work came through, & work saved all as of yore. Ah what gladness to be able to do it again. Determination is the key; push through the reluctance. It's one lonely unbeatable will, against silence & darkness which has no defence. The way I, and my material, are organized now, I can have over 50,000 words to show Bob when he gets back from Italy April 1st — publishable words.

Should I postpone western trip & do this first? (Hmm!) We'll see. Must add something every day from now on — that'll do it as nothing else can. Joy is the certainty of wishing — sorrow is the uncertainty of ... something else. As I write this a mournful whistle repeatedly, distressedly blows in the windy night outside. Ah machine! nothing can save thee! And the winds rattle the windowpane in terror. But inside me here, I'm all right. 'Tis but the skill of the soul in its crafty workshop.

MON. FEB. 20 — Went to school in freezing cold to sign; then to Adele's for a chat; & walked to Times Square (1½ miles), then home in the subway with papers. A notice about my book in Lowell Sunday Sun. I gloat more & more in the fact that I may be rich & famous soon, yet continue to walk around in my ragged coat & hunting-cap in the winters — a kind of "young student" in the subways reading The Possessed; scrubbing pennies & meditating whether I should go in the all-night movie or not ... *when all the world is mine*. No greater, truer feeling. The same way when I go traveling around the country in buses (instead of hitch-hiking) and sleep in old hotels like those facing the riverfront in St. Louis ... the *interesting* hotels; and buses where the passengers are *interesting* instead of Time & Life stereotypes. This properly explains why my 'raggedness' is not a pose, but a real means to joy & learning. How can I *learn* and *see* if I make an asinine plane-traveler & convention-hotel guest (Elks "convention") of myself ... and thrust myself forth in the public eye.

T. S. Eliot, Nobel Prize poet, travels as 'Tom Eliot' in old ships; that is why he is old Tiresias ... I shall be young Orestes for the nonce.* Came home at one o'clock, ate bacon & eggs, and settled down to some kind of work. Incidentally everybody in Dostoevsky says "H'm" all the time, interiorly ... that is the key to his vision of man — "H'm." (what mysteries?) (What's he mean by that?) — I wonder if my own "sound" in T & C was not "Hah?" The key to my vision — "Hah?" As though to say, "I know perfectly what's going on, but I'll pretend I don't even hear." To which Dusty replies, "H'm." — What is the sound in Balzac? Later I'll guess it. Maybe it's "Hup! Hup!" — everybody rushing through passions and fortunes, crazily. In Celine it's an oath; in Melville, a hiss. In Twain, it's the word "satisfied." In Celine it's "Wah! Wah!" — or "Hoik! hoik!"

TUES. FEB. 21 — Wrote a hundred words or so, and decided to relax awhile; and went into N.Y. to hear bop. In a cafeteria on 50th and 8th Avenue I made notes about the "hipster generation" which is so much like Dusty's 'nihilist' generation, the possessed, in one way; and so different in another. No secret societies for the hipster, only the secret bebop night. But it is the spectacle of a generation's formal departure from the parent-generation's idea of people ... therefore I see a parallel in old Stepan's annoyance at the "squeal" in his son Pyotr Verhovensky's voice, and my own annoyance at Levinsky's giggle and now Dean

*Tiresias and Orestes are Greek mythological characters: Tiresias the blind soothsayer and Orestes, son of Agamemnon and young avenger of his murder.

Pomeray's "Go!" (especially its connection with the Genet feeling in French hipster-criminal circles, when for instance he looks at a picture of guerillas shooting people in the Philippine jungles and cries: "They really *go* out there!!") did that, in a laundromat on 3rd Avenue. Also, the time in Denver when I half-shamefacedly asked Neal if he could ever "reconcile Christ with the black c —— t" he keeps drooling about, nay shouting, and months later he unexpectedly (in New York, in a recording) mocked me for asking it. N.'s "black c —— t"* it must be understood is mainly a sadistic image; a la Rimbaud, if you wish, but I've had my fill of Phillip Tourian Rimbauds. N.'s "black c —— t" is not Geo. Bouman's love of wild Havana nights, but violence if necessary. How can you reconcile "the king that comes on an ass, meek," with *that kind* (pun intended.) Laugh! Laugh! — I believe in my own stupid seriousness, and I am not unaware of what is charming, after all.

Heard Dizzy Gillespie at Bop City and crossed the street to Birdland to hear Tristano, Miles Davis, Goetz, et al. There too, I had an idea: when Tristano played his abstract, no-beat, Bartok-like "Intuition" a colored guy yelled, "Play some music!" at this — the 'cool' Negro scanning the old-fashioned 'hot' Negro with disdain. But I agree with the hot. *Play some music.* An art which expresses the mind of mind, and not the mind of life (the idea of mortal life on earth), is a dead art. An art which is not manifest to 'everybody,' is a dead art. An art dies when it describes itself instead of life — when it turns from the expression of man's feelings in the void, to a mere description of the void. From drama to abstract lines, an art expires. Shakespeare, Homer, Rembrandt, Tolstoy, Celine, Mark Twain, are manifest to all ... in their best works. The Beethoven of symphonies is greater than the Beethoven of last-quartet 'interpretations of music.' Puccini's best operas in their simple sentiment are worth a thousand abstract modern works of music-study like those of Schoenberg, et al. — At 4 A.M. I ate in Ham n' Eggs Heaven, a huge breakfast. Came home.

*A similar tape-recorded and transcribed Kerouac-Cassady dialogue is included in *Visions of Cody* (1972).

At nine A.M. I received a telegram:

"Dear Jack: Tom died in a crash. (signed) Benedict A. Livornese."
Tom's uncle?

How was I to know this was a gag? — innocently sent out by Tom
himself? The full account of this fantastic incident — how I mourned
all day, how I dropped everything in a bleak grief, how I went out to
Lynbrook in the icy night (falling twice on the ground) and bought a
mass In Memoriam at a Catholic church, how I came to the House of
Sorrows to pay my respects, and how I heard *bebop* from within and
saw Tom running to open the door — all that will be found in a story I
will write for the magazines. It has a Mark Twain sorrowful-funniness
about it. And I never was more happy & ecstatic that Tom was alive.
I've hardly slept since — but more of all this later, in the story. It's too
much now ... really so.

THURS. FEB. 23 — Jack Fitzgerald reports that Edie phoned him
from Detroit and claims she wants to come East but "Kerouac won't let
her." What another fantastic business! Life is full of plots. So much so
I've hardly time to write Road. Woke up at 4 A.M. Friday morning to
work — all turned upside down by everything ... and so glad no one's
died, & glad for everything.

I'll always do what I love.

FRI. FEB. 24 — Worked all morning preparing my big opening-inci-
dent chapter, though I was weary from upset sleep ... mind was very
sharp. I'm proud of result, especially Chad and Laura. This one chapter shows up everybody's soul — and I am learning to write! Learned
a big secret this very selfsame weary morning — i.e., You establish relationships between the souls of all concerned, on all sides, and then
use the naturalistic material for the purpose of placing said relationships in their earthly position. For relationship is "eternal." As Kazin

says, it is the "diamond upon which existence rests." A great learning for me ... the way to do it, the technical secret. For instance: first I establish Laura's relationship with Chad, which is 'calculated silence' and then I use the naturalistic material (in this case the horses) to put into motion and dramatize the eternal fact of her calculated silence, in the way she rides near him without a word. Thus.

Received Allan Temko's marvelous article about me in the Feb. 11 issue of the Rocky Mountain Herald. I'm amazed no end. And where is he now? He hasn't written a word. Strange, angry, radiant, sad man. Article was sent by Justin Brierly, who also says not a word. Plots on all sides! I'm so happy I'll go up in smoke! Bah!

At night, the party at Tom's house where — a sad cavalier — I lost my beautiful Grace to him (he charms like a movie-star ... "piano & cocktails.") I was pretty sad ... and left. But such things have happened to me before ... ownership of a woman is not the burning issue of the day. What is the burning issue of the day? — impregnation of said woman, and some 'I-know-how-to-live' decision for the offspring. Fitz came to the party. Holmeses & Bouwmans also there ... pink wine, steaks, television fights. Fitz came to my house next day. We went to Poughkeepsie. Thirty hours of talk ensued.

SAT. FEB. 25 — The sad fact about the modern American small city like Poughkeepsie is that it has none of the strength of the metropolis and yet all the ugly pettiness. Fitzgerald is a martyr of the guilty Poughkeepsie night wherein petty men slop around wondering what's gone wrong with their souls. Fitz says simply "They're dead." What dismal streets ... what dismal lives ... what futurelessness & hapless woe. Thousands of drunkards in bars. But out of this wreckage rises a Cleo — a veritable Cleophus — the "Negro Neal" I met there this weekend — actually a "Negro Allen" in substance. He says Christ is at each our shoulders, and all is well. He takes a glass of water and teaches me to *taste the goodness of water* for the 'first time' — (of course I have done so as a kid imagining myself in the desert.) The future of

America lies in the spirituality and strength of a Negro like Cleo ... I know it now ... and in all those who understand and receive him. The Larchmont commuters are a thing of the past already. It is simplicity and raw strength, rising out of the American *ground,* that will save us. We will be saved. Only the Larchmont commuters and the Pough-keepsie slobs ("What are you getting out of life? Haven't you got a tele-vision set yet?") are despairing in their Time & Life & Fortune deadend ... poor imitative fools of a shadow that glitters. There are great undiscov-ered peoples in America ... just as in Russia. The nameless kid shot by cops in a Brooklyn street rouses no public sentiment — because he is a 'hoodlum' — but the moment he is resurrected as a scion of a wealthy family, and that family is the future family of earth, there will be furors. (Carl Sandburg: "Exclusive is the ugliest word in English.") Our class-laws will collapse ... otherwise America will collapse ... and America will not collapse. You feel it in the busy streets, especially in the White Rose bars at noon when workingmen are eating ham-on-rye and drinking a beer; the smoke & talk; the swing of things; the sound of things going on, going up ... Allen G. writes: "We are used to think-ing of ourselves in sophisticated Life & Fortune power thoughts, but it may actually be that we are swollen with pitiful pride and History will bypass us (even me and you) in the next half century." The key word is PRIDE. Allen forgets that he, and Cleo, are the discoverers of a humil-ity which will transform the days we're in —

As for the Liberals — the "intellectuals" who write about "crimi-nals" but don't want the Neals in their houses — Fitz says, "They want to accept the touchable untouchables." That is the old story of the Lib-erals ... always Mr. & Mrs. Halfway, always the "respectable" reserva-tions. It is not the oldfashioned fear of 'scandal' but a Liberal fear of 'consequences.' America will collapse just as Allen says if we don't gird up — face the shits — tell them off — fear nothing — go on with the knowledges, the true optimisms of Twain and Whitman (respectively) towards a great big oldfashioned Biblical curse within the land ... a shock-treatment ... a fearful looksee at the abyss ... a prayer like a groan ... a vision of ourselves ... a little more guts and less brainy cleverness.

I swear to God the one great symbol of a disintegrating America is the Dave Garroway television show from Chicago!* — what a sophisticated, serpentine, be-horn-rimmed, suave, half-homo, half-ninny spectacle it presents ... with all the *insinuation* behind it. The key word is insinuation, I don't know why ... I'll know later.

If an H-bomb hit New York and I had a lethal pill in my pocket, and was trapped in a tunnel among screaming mortals, I still think I wouldn't swallow that pill.

Is that the insinuation? Also implied in suave Viennese psychoanalysis.

"Swollen with pitiful pride ..." Come on, let's come down. "America! — America make haste and come down; for unto this day salvation has come unto your house." The words of Jesus ... substituting America for Zachariah. There will come a day when the night will be the sleeping-time because we won't need the night as a guilt-absorber.

MON. FEB. 27 — Came home in snowy cold on N.Y. Central train, sat on canvas bags, train 4 hours late. Slept in afternoon. Wrote at night in cold, cold house ... Soon, tho, it will be Spring, and I will go West — always West. This summer I think I'll get a newspaper job and an apartment or small house in 'Frisco ... Soon, too, I want to get married. I want my own house so that it can stand for what I stand.

Letters today from Kelly, Ed White & Allen.

TUES. FEB. 28 — My new plans for March: — soon as I get my money, I'll join the morning club at the "Y" and workout almost every weekday. Also, black coffee (no cream & sugar); chinning from the door (which has no real grip so I can only do 10 or 11 or 12); and *less sleep.* I'd been getting fat and lazy. Time for action, time for a new life, for my real life. I'll be 28 in two weeks ... a goodly age. Two meals a day instead of three. Much traveling. No stagnation. No more formal sorrows! No more metaphysical awe! Action ... production-speed ... grace

---

*Dave Garroway (1913–1982) hosted the Chicago-based variety show *Dave Garroway at Large* before becoming the first host of NBC's *Today* show in 1952.

... turn the world into an early-Saroyan short story, with mature purposes & absorptions. *Go!* And a writing delirium from true thoughts instead of stale rehashes ... of established intellection. Also, I'm going to *express* more and record less in 'On the Road' — I'm going to point out ways instead of describing paths. — Saw a picture of Bob Giroux in Portugal, in the Daily Mirror, today; with the Catholic pilgrims going to Rome. Zowie! — "Then longer all folk to go on pilgrimages."* Bob's is a pilgrimage in the church of the world, the Jesuit; mine is a pilgrimage in the church of heaven, it-hath-no-name. Likewise we together seek, and are brothers in the spirit. 'May praise be worthy of that Venus-star.' Hello! Hello! — Hulloa! Hulloa! — Zoom! Don't talk to me about the Soviet state ... those gloomballs are dead.

There are no 'villains' in Dostoevsky. That is why he is the "truest of the true." He sees everything at the same time; and he commands his own mind. — You have to believe in life, live life, before you can accomplish anything *in its favor.* That is why dour, Goethe-like, scholarly, regular-houred, rational-souled State Department diplomats have done nothing for mankind. It takes a Ben Franklin for jobs like that. ('Not everybody's a Franklin?' Why live if not for excellence? What kind of an age is this that flatters its own decadent weakness in the name of smart cocktail talk — and mocks excellence.)

What does the old Chinaman think around the block? Just walked by his laundry, at dawn, and he's already up. A man six millenniums old — he neither hates nor loves the world — he works to keep his hands busy — he looks at man with a fishy eye — he lives alone, in corners — he has a great sorrow and the sorrow of his ancient race — he is waiting for the world to go up in flames. There he is at dawn, grumpy, heating tea in a miserable back room, preparing for another day's steamy labour. What does he care about the destiny of man? All *he* knows is that his ancestors like him were patient and lived long lives of silence, and stared.

---

*From the General Prologue to Geoffrey Chaucer's *Canterbury Tales:* "So priketh hem nature in hir corages;/Thanne longen folke to goon pilgrimages." Translated from the Old English it reads: "So Nature pricks them on to ramp and rage/Then do folk long to go on pilgrimage."

I am scared of the Oriental, from what I can gather of him. My Billy Ling in "Road" will be like this Wong Lee of the Lee Laundry, Richmond Hill. — Down the street a still stranger sight. As I strolled in the pre-dawn darkness thinking that Hemingway & Fitzgerald had built their lives around lion-hunts and Yales, and were only really facetious,★ I saw a band of Krug truckdrivers who have wives & kids & homes to worry about forming a picket line in front of the garage. With soft earnestness they decided to block up the entrance and persuade the other drivers to join the strike. Maybe violence will erupt later. Krug is a bread factory. I decided I must be a Fundamentalist at that very moment; but I never stick my nose where I'm not wanted, and walked on ... smugly.

Earlier today I went to N.Y. and dealt out a few chores. Now I am exhausted. I go to sleep. Tomorrow I will be still another man. Every day is different. ("H'm.")

★ *I'll never say anything like that again!* (Mar. 5 '50)

: — ODD NOTES — :

MARCH 1950

The night is atonement for the sins of the day — in America. That is why they want 'the end of the night' — complete purgation from sloppy decadent pursuits of noon. Only the hardworking riveter sleeps at night — the television adman gets drunk. The time has come to pursue the day in honest ways.

*   *

I think the greatness of Dostoevsky lies in his recognition of human love. Shakespeare himself has not penetrated so deep beneath his pride, which is all our prides. Dostoevsky is really an ambassador of

Christ, and for me the modern Gospel. His religious fervor sees through the very facts and details of our everyday life, so that he doesn't have to concentrate his attention on flowers and birds like St. Francis, or on finances like Balzac, but on anything ... the most ordinary things. There alone is proof about the sparrow that falls. It is the crowning glory of such a man as Spengler that he recognizes Dostoevsky to be a saint.

The vision of Dostoevsky is the vision of Christ translated in modern terms. The fact that he is barred in Soviet Russia implies the weakness of the state. Dostoevsky's vision is that which we all dream at night, and sense in the day, and it is the Truth ... merely that we love one another whether we like it or not, i.e., we recognize the other's existence - - - - and the Christ in us is the primum mobile of that recognition. Christ *is* at our shoulders, and *is* "our conscious in God's university" as Cleo says ... he *is* the recognizer in us. His 'idea' is.

The reason "television admen" get drunk at night, as above, is only because the nature of their pursuits shuts them off from meek love of man, which is what we all want. D. H. Lawrence is mere masturbation of self.

Mar. 1st '50

Consider: tonight I went to Lou's house, looking suave and well-contained in my suit, and spoke to him "confidently" about my new plans. Nevertheless I was nervous, and could not help noticing his pale melancholy, even as his mother laughed and chatted with us. Everything I told him — everything that happened — is for me overshadowed by the fact that I *writhed* before this man (famous-young-author-soon-to-be wealthy notwithstanding, also prophet-of-American-strength notwithstanding) and that this was because I recognized his existence with love and fear, and could not bear the mortification of my own senses receiving the grace of his being. Lou is only an intensification of this feeling which I have for everyone; he is a dramatic example of mankind. Nevertheless I could not bear seeing him every day, for fear of boredom, or the fear of boredom — perhaps fear of losing the fear

& trembling which is a dramatization of my being alive. When I left I sighed ... "It's always the same ... My position with one like that will never change ... A relationship is established for eternity ... This world we walk in is only the scene, the temporal scene, of eternal realities; this sidewalk only exists for souls to walk on."

Further than a "dramatization of my being alive" is that such a recognition of fear and love — or the fear and love itself — simply the love — is our existence, and mine too, and yours, and we try to avoid it more than anything else in the world. Thus, tonight, reading my new books, I find that Kafka avoids it in a dream of himself; Lawrence avoids it by masturbating (same thing); and Scott Fitzgerald, though closer to recognition of love, only wrote his story to make money and omitted certain things (in "Crazy Sunday.") Then I read Dusty and it was all there. There is no truth like the truth of the earthly prophet.

I want to become, and pray to be, an earthly prophet.

WED. MAR. 1 — In the evening I met Frank Morley at the Hotel Chatham bar. He was blotto. I got blotto with him. We ended up having a big conversation with Artie Shaw and his girl Anne ... at Artie's house. What a night! At midnight Lucien read me Charles Poore's fine review of my book over the phone, then Tony Manocchio repeated it for Shaw.

Morley is a very great man in many ways. More anon — I'm to see him again in a few days. (I wonder if I should continue this journal; there's too much to tell, and perhaps most of it is insignificant. Who am I telling it for?) The appearance of my book on the market completely shakes me ... it appears among thousands of other books good and bad. A grain of sand in one big American hubbub. A word, however, about Maxwell Perkins' "Letters from Editor to Author." (Well, and I say something with a serious mind but they turn it into small talk. Bah! — "small talk" is the curse of too-advanced civilizations. What's happening in America?) — Anyway, Perkins achieves a tone of pure sincerity, and a consciousness of his own responsible intelligence, in his letters to his authors. This too is but a grain of sand. There are no standards, but that's because the cultural scene is shifting from one focus to another. These foci are but fads, ever so. Why should I bother about them?

That I spent 4 years abandoning the joys of normal youthful life, to make a serious contribution to American literature, and the result is treated like a cheap first novel — which it certainly is not — (in spite of my apparent 'success') — that my Town & City, poor as it is in spots, but over-all *serious*, not frivolous — should be bandied about by frivolous reviewers who do the same thing day after day on countless novels of all kinds ... I'm so confused I don't care to finish the sentence. Apparently nothing is "significant" except a portrait of themselves insofar as commuter-middle-class reviewers are concerned. My Levinsky is received as a useless nut; so Alexander Panos; my Job-like father a "death-of-a-salesman-tearful-lamentation" mediocrity. Even Jack Fitzgerald considers my father insignificant because he is not in a position of worldly greatness ... Something's corrupt in America that such should happen. John Brooks, in some ways, gave the best-understanding review — and I had mistakenly written otherwise (to Justin in Denver) about his Mar. 5 Times review. He sees the characters as *representations,* at least, of the present times ... (and understands how so.)

How is a miserable hitch-hiking boy going to mean anything (in "On the Road") to Howard Mumford Jones who wants everybody to be like him (middleclass, intellectual, "responsible") before he will accept them? Could Dostoevsky make his *lumpenproletariat* Raskolniks figure for such a guy today? — for such a literary class? — as anything but a bum.

The terrible clash, not only of classes, but of groups, and *types,* in America, is better than the uniformity imposed by police states; nevertheless there is needless violence in the clash. No! — let them clash! I can clash as good as anybody. T & C is full of clashing divisions anyhow. It's all true. I'll stop being a child and accept the competitive world, the crazy world.

And what is a book?

I have to write a better one. Universal Love is a lot of hogwash anyway ... in the "daytime world," that is.

Celebrated, in any case. An informal shot of bourbon in a bookstore
(with Goldman) served as my 1st cocktail party. I saw the Lyndons,
Stringham and George at Holmeses; drinking beer, playing bop in the
dark gloomy afternoon of a room hidden from the sun; we don't go
skating like the Scott Fitzgeralds of "decadent" Twenties.

But mainly I was with the beautiful Sara, and practically fell in love
for the first time in weary years. A woman ... a Woman ... of beauty un-
surpassable.

What an enigma a Woman is!

How I love the kind that is!

Who doesn't?

Why do I keep this journal?

Now I read Stendhal "On Love" ... and Perkins too.

MON. MAR. 6 — But to return to details instead of mooning around,
or yelping false exuberances. The day the book came out I went to
lunch with Ed Hodge, Tom Humason & Bob Hill at noon; thirteen
hours later Tom just made the closing gate of what he calls the "drunkard's train." During the afternoon we had drunk and visited a few
bookstores. The evening at Alexandra's, a cynical booktrade bar; where
Treviston (very funny guy, Scribner's salesman) gave me the Perkins
book. I was saddened by my unimpressing publication date, but deeply
consoled by the presence of these good friends. The next day, Friday
[March 3], I signed at school and then had dinner with Sara Yokley of
the United Press, a gorgeous love of a gal. She is upset over her es-
trangement with Lou, who went back to B. Hale. — Next day, I walked
on waterfront, saw an old man with his dog sitting on "back-steps" of
his river-scow house. From there I walked to center of city and the
fashionable bookstores, lurking around my book which no one notices, and why should they notice it any more than a thousand other
novels? In the evening returned to Sara with some cognac. Sunday

morning I came home and puttered around. Monday Morning I got up at 6:30 and planned a tremendous day which I carried out almost perfectly: including the banking of my $750 advance. In the afternoon ate a Chinese dinner with the Holmes; at night got beered-up with beautiful Grace, but I think I am faithful to Sara because I did not — anyway we were both sad. Came home at seven in the morn and spent all day Tuesday answering countless letters.

All this swirl has interrupted the work I was doing on Road. But I'm learning so much from reception of my book that I'm still revising some main ideas for it. One learns so much being published — about the cultural scene and the people of the world who are concerned with it. I believe that my vision needs broadening, like Tom Wolfe's "deathbed window," perhaps to a final bird's-eye view of the world and Time which is like Mark Twain's in the Mysterious Stranger and like something else which is slowly formulating in my mind.

WED. MAR. 8 — Wrote a little in the morning. My mother stayed home with a bad cold. Worried all day about money-problems ... not for me, but for her: she can't work forever. Went to the "Y" gym in the afternoon and played basketball. Came home. Can't write. Will try reading. Maybe physical exercise, the heavy kind like this afternoon, is inimical to mental exercise?

Rave review in Newsweek — ostensibly by Robt. Cantwell? Feel better.*

I decided to use Tony Smith in Road — which completes its conception.

"The diamond upon which existence rests" is a wild and fibrous diamond — and instead of pointing it out, I can now say what its component parts are, completely. One aspect, the major, is that the way a

---

*In its review of The Town and the City, Newsweek called Kerouac "the best and most promising of the young novelists whose first works have recently appeared."

person talks about someone else depends on *who* the talking is to, and it is different in all, all and infinite cases — so "fibrous" is the accurate word to describe this world, with its hint of organic unity.

I want the truth, but not in women ... (a saying of mine.) I want S., not E. But more later. In fact Woman is based on untruth, otherwise nothing could be Mothered; the race would die out.

That 'fibrous diamond': — ask X what he thinks of Z. He will say one thing to you, another to Y, and still another to himself, and still another to a crowd, and still another to A, another to B, to C, D, E, F and Infinitely. *This is the secret of Dostoevsky* and of human existence too in its major, basic form-relations, what Dusty sometimes calls "position."

Am writing a 3,000-wd. story for Jay Landesman, "Hipster, Blow Your Top," for $30. I'll make it wild.

I want the truth, but not in women.

FRI. MAR. 10 — Closing diary a few days — perhaps because so happy with Sara? As for everything else, one-eyed reception of book, *pfui*!! Mon. Mar. 13 I go to Boston & Lowell. More anon ... in this one-eyed world. On Mar. 11 & 12 wrote my "Flower That Blows in the Night," which is that.

MAR. 11–20 — Went to Boston & Lowell; saw the ever-great John MacDonald; autographed books in Lowell; saw Jim O'Day, Louis Eno, Salvey, the Georges. Roger Shattuck and I became fast friends.

APR. 3 — BOOK NOT SELLING MUCH.
Wasn't born to be rich.
Am squaring off a triangle now.

Rain and Rivers

·R·A·I·N· A·N·D· R·I·V·E·R·S·

The marvelous notebook presented
to me by Neal Cassady
in San Francisco

:— Which I have Crowded in Words —:

Standard
B & P
Blank Books
and
Loose Leaf Devices
TRADE MARK
REGISTERED

Standard
Blank
Book

No. 37⅜

Journals Double $ and Cts. no Units

S. E. Ledgers   "   "   "

D. E. Ledgers Full Page Form   "

Records with Margin Line

In 150 and 300 Pages

Made in U. S. A.

TO REORDER THIS BOOK, SPECIFY
NUMBER, RULING AND THICKNESS
AS INDICATED ON BACKBONE OF BOOK

A BOORUM & PEASE PRODUCT

John Kerouac
Jan. 31, 1949
(Begun) 'Frisco—

This journal depicts trips through every region of the country as early as 1949 and one as late as 1954, from New York, through the South and Mexico, into California and the Northwest, and back to New York and Massachusetts through the Midwest. Kerouac has added a heading to each of his pages, to indicate the region he is writing in or about.

Most of the trips and observations in this journal are fictionalized in the published *On the Road*. Toward the end, Kerouac begins referring to his "1951 'On the Road' of Dean Moriarty and Sal Paradise" or "Sal Paradise Novel 'Beat Generation' (Originally titled 'On the Road')," which suggests that he wrote it during the course of this journal.

The journal itself is labeled "JOURNALS 1949–50" on its cover. Its first page reads as follows:

RAIN AND RIVERS
The marvelous notebook presented
to me by Neal Cassady
in San Francisco
: — Which I have Crowded in Words — :

In the lower-right-hand corner is written:

John Kerouac
Jan. 31, 1949
(Begun) 'Frisco —

The last pages of "Rain and Rivers" were filled with an alphabetical catalog of names, not included here. Inserted at the conclusion of this section are the best passages from Kerouac's *On the Road* workbooks.

"RAIN AND RIVERS"

The Saga of the Mist —

Trip from New York to San Francisco, 1949. N.Y. across the tunnel to New Jersey — the "Jersey night" of Allen Ginsberg. We in the car jubilant, beating on the dashboard of the '49 Hudson coupe ... headed West. And I haunted by something I have yet to remember. And a rainy, road-glistening, misty night again. Big white sign saying "West" → "South" ←——————— our gleeful choices. Neal and I and Louanne talking of the value of life as we speed along, in such thoughts as "Whither goest thou America in thy shiny car at night?" and in the mere fact that we're together under such rainy circumstances talking heart to heart. Seldom had I been so glad of life. We stopped for gas at the very spot where Neal and I had stopped on the No. Carolina trip 3 weeks before, near Otto's lunch diner. And remembered the funny strange events there. Then we drove on playing bebop music on the radio. But what was I haunted by? It was sweet to sit near Louanne. In the backseat Al [Hinkle] and Rhoda made love. And Neal drove with the music, huzzaing.

We talked like this through Philadelphia and beyond. And occasionally some of us dozed. Neal got lost outside of Baltimore and wound up in

MARYLAND — WASHINGTON

ridiculously narrow little tar road in the woods (he was trying to find a shortcut.) "Doesn't look like Route One," he said ruefully, and as it was so obvious to everyone it seemed a very funny remark (I forget why now, in its totality.) We arrived in Washington at dawn and passed a great display of war machines that were set out for Truman's inauguration day — jet planes, tanks, catapults, submarines, and finally a rowboat which touched Neal's rueful attention. He is sometimes fascinatingly "great" in this manner. Then, in search of coffee in Arlington Va. We got routed onto a traffic circle rotary-drive that took us whether we like it or not to a coffee shop that was not open. (The greatness of Neal is that he will always remember everything that happened, including this, with significant personal connotation.) We wound out, and back on the highway found a diner; where we had breakfast as the sun came out. (I remember the young proprietor's face when Big Al stole a coffee cake. Rhoda went back to Washington in a local bus; and Al drove, Neal sleeping, till he was stopped for speeding outside of Richmond. We almost all wound up in jail on vag charges with undertones of the Mann act — but paid a $15 fine and went free. A hitchhiker was with us. Neal raged about the arresting officer whom he would have loved to kill. Near Emporia Va. we picked up a mad hitchhiker who said he was Jewish (Herb-

ert Diamond) and made his living knocking at the doors of Jewish homes all over the country demanding money. "I am a Jew! — give the money." "What kicks!" cried Neal (why does the world have to otherwise deprive Neal of his kicks — and I too?) The Jewish pilgrim sat in back with Al and the other hitchhiker reading a muddy paperbacked book he had found in some culvert of the wilderness — a detective story, which he read as if the Torah. In Rocky Mount N.C. we dispatched him to a Jewish home I know of, the Temkos, jewellers. (uncle of Alan Temko), but he never returned. Meanwhile we jubilantly bought bread & cheese, and ate on Main Street in the car. Had I ever been so in Rocky Mt.? — and was it not the place from which I had written a strange melancholy letter to Neal, and where Ann had hath her way, and where the sad fair was? and where my sister almost died? and where I had seen the Forest of Arden in a tobacco warehouse?

Therefore, it is these mysteries in the homely commonplace earth that convince me of the real existence of God (no words.) For what is Rocky Mount after all? *Why* Rock Mt ... ?

In Fayetteville our hitch-hiker failed to produce desired money (in Dunn actually) so we moved on without him, I sleeping. Then I drove in So. Carolina, which again was flat and dark in the night (with star-shiny roads, and southern dullness somewhere around.) I drove to beyond Macon Georgia where one could begin to smell the earth

SONG OF THIS NIGHT-TIME: ECKSTINE'S "BEWILDERED."
GEORGIA — ALA. — MISS. — NEW ORLEANS

and see greeneries in the dark. Woke up just outside Mobile Ala., and soft airs of summer (in January.) We played jubilantly as we had done and did do clear across the continent (Neal & Louanne piggybacking, etc.) In Gulfport Miss. We ate royally with our last monies prior to New Orleans, in a seaside restaurant. (It was Neal's theft of a tankful of gas that saved us; a divine theft as far as I'm concerned, Promethean at least.) We began to hear rumors of New Orleans and "chicken, jazz n' gumbo" bebop shows on the radio, with much wild backalley jazz of the "drive" variety; so we yelled happily in the car. I lay in the back looking at the gray Gulf sky as we rolled — how happy we were! as we'd been through trials and hunger. (Travel is travail.)

"Smell the people!" said Neal of New Orleans; and the smell of the big river (which Lucien has recently characterized as 'female,' because its mud comes from the male Missouri.) The smell of people, of the river, and summer — "the summer's south America," as I had predicted — and the smell of loam, petals, and molasses, in Algiers, where we waited at a filling station before going to Bill's. I'll never forget the wild expectancy of that moment — the rickety street, the palms, the great late-afternoon clouds over the Mississippi, the girls going by, the children, the soft bandanas of air coming like odor instead of air, the smell of people and rivers.

And then Burroughs' tragic old house in the field, and Joan Adams in the back kitchen door "looking for a fire." God is what I love.

Also, the ferry, of course —

NEW ORLEANS

Crossing the Algiers Ferry —

What is the Mississippi River? Near Idaho, near West Yellowstone, near the furthest, darkest corner of Wyoming, the headwaters of the Missouri, modest as a dell of brooks, begin — A log is cracked by elemental lightnings there in the wild corners of wild states ... and meanders restlessly floating downstream. Timbers and hairy abutments (shaggier than those on the Avon-like Hudson) stand in the northern light as the log proceeds. Lost moose from dignified heights stare (pouting) with dignified eyes. ("If I had an eye the trees would have eyes" — Allen Ginsberg.)

Bozeman ... Three Forks ... Helena ... Cascade ... (I've never been there; and now they have power plants and chemical factories along these shores where Jim Bridger was wild, poetic, and rugged with freedom, saintly with hardships) ... Wolf Point ... Williston North Dakota, and Mandon.... The winter snows ... Pierre ... Sioux City ... Council Bluffs (there I've been in a gray dawn, and saw no council of the wagon chiefs, no bluffs but suburban cottages) ... Kansas City.

The Missouri rushes hugely into the floods of the Mississippi at St. Louis, bearing the Odyssiac log from lonely Montana down to the

ALGIERS, LOUISIANA

wide night shores by Hannibal, Cairo, Greenville, and Natchez ... and by old Algiers of Louisiana (where Bill Burroughs sits now.) "Unions! That's what it is! — unions!"

My ferry plows the brown water to New Orleans; I look over the rail; and there is that Montana log passing by.... Like me a wanderer in burrowed water-beds moving slowly with satisfaction and eternity. In the night, in the rainy night ...

But the Mississippi — and my log — journeys by Baton Rouge, where, miles to the west, some underground, supernatural phenomena of the flood has created bayoux (who knows?) — west of Opelousas, southeast of Ogallala, southwest of Ashtabula — and there in the bayoux, too, (and therefore), across my patient soul's-eye floats the wraith of mist, the ghost, the swamp-gyre, the light in the night, the fog-shroud of the Mississippi and Montana and of all the haunted earth: to bring me the message of the log. Ghost by ghost these bayoux-shapes swim by in the hanging night, from mossy palaces, from the mansion of the snake; and I have read the big elaborate manuscript of the night.

And what is the Mississippi River? It is the movement of the night; and the secret of sleep; and the emptier of American streams which bear, (as the log is borne,) the story of our truer fury: —

THE GULF OF MEXICO

the fury of the deadly and damaging soul which never sleeps.... And says in the night, "It's what I always feel, you know?" I know? You know? Who know? But this is vague ... untrue. (Rock-in-the-belly.)

The Mississippi River ends in the Gulf — called Mexico — likelier Night: and my riven, wandering log, all water-heavy and sunken and turning over, floats out to the sea ... around the keys ... where the ocean-going ship (like an eternal ferry) passes again its strange destiny like a wraith. And Old Bill sits under the lamp (reading [Franz] Kafka's diaries), while I, a careless poet, I, an eye, a man, a wraith, a watcher of rivers, night; panorama and continents (and of men and women); in San Francisco scribble.

For the rain is the sea coming back, and the river — no lake — is the rain become night, and the night is water and earth, and there are no stars that show to the shrouded earth their infolded loopings in other worlds no longer we need: I know (and do scribble.)

And the rainy night, a river, is God, as the sea the rivers and rains conceals. All is safe. Secure.

— —

Will I ever see my sea around the riverbend? or merely roll to it at night in silence: some eternity is the Gulf of Mexico.

RICHMOND, CALIF. — 'FRISCO

TEA — DISCOVERIES (riding back to Frisco from Richmond Calif. on rainy night, in Hudson; sulking in back seat.)

Don't get hung up on difficult, miserable discoveries of your "true self" — rather, enjoy and goof off (and thereby avoid these self-knowledges.) Neal's lack. But Oh the pangs of travel! the spirituality of hashish!

And what a revelation to know that I was born sad — that it was no trauma that made me so sad — but God: — who made me that way.

I saw also that Neal — well, I saw Neal at the wheel of the car Allen Anson-ish and more, a wild machinery of kicks and sniffs and gulps and maniacal laughter, a kind of human dog; and then I saw Allen Ginsberg — 17th century poet in dark vestments standing in a sky of Rembrandt darkness, one thin leg before the other in meditation; then I myself, like Slim Gailland, stuck my head out of the window with Billy Holliday eyes and offered my soul to the whole world, big sad eyes ... (like the whores in the Richmond mud-shack saloon.) Saw how much genius I had, too (inasmuch as I could knock myself *out* so?) Knowing the genius, therefore, preferred *solitude* & *decencies*. Saw how sullen, blank Louanne hated me (without fearing me as she fears & wants to subdue Neal.) Saw how unimportant I was to them; and the stupidity of my designs on her, and my betrayal of male friends concerning their women (Neal, Hal, G. J. [Apostolos], even Ed's Beverly, & of course Cru, and unknown unnumbered others in other lives.)

OLD 'FRISCO

The Strange Dickensian Vision on Market Street
I was just walking home from Larkin & Geary where Louanne had betrayed me so dumbly (details elsewhere), in the springlike night of Market St. — filled again, strangely, as always in San Francisco, with moral pangs and dark moral worries & decisions; and walking a mile and a half to Guerrero and thence to Liberty St. (Carolyn's apartment) — when I passed a strange little hash-house near, or beyond, Van Ness, on right side of Market — arrested by the sign "Fish & Chips." I looked in hungrily (though I had just eaten steamed clams and hot broth in Geary St. bar while waiting for Louanne) — Place filled with hungry eaters who haven't too much money to spend. The proprietor was a hairy-armed, grave, strong little Greek of sorts; and his wife a pink-faced, anxious English-woman (as Englishwomany as any in a film.) I had just come from the dawdling company of whores & pimps & some thieves, perhaps even footpads, and was roaming the street hungry, penniless, watchful. This poor woman glanced at me standing there in the outside shadows, with a kind of terrified anxiety. Something went through me, a definite feeling that in another life this poor, dear woman had been my mother, and that I, like a Dickens footpad, was returning after many years in the shadow of the gallows, in English 19th century gaols, her wandering 'blackguardly' son ...

MARKET ST., 'FRISCO

hungry to cheat her once more (though not at once.) "No," she seemed to say as she shot that terrified glance at me (was I then leering in?), "don't come back and plague your honest hardworking mother. You are no longer like a son to me — and like your father, my first husband 'ere this kindly Greek took pity on me, you are no good, inclined to drunkenness and routs and final disgraceful robbery of the fruits of my 'umble labours in the hashery. Oh son! did you not ever go on your knees and pray for deliverance for all your sins and scoundrel's acts! Lost boy! — depart! do not haunt my soul, I have done well forgetting you. Re-open no auld wounds: Be as if you had never returned and looked in to me — to see my labouring humilities, my few scrubb'd pennies — hungry to grab, quick to deprive, sullen, unloving, mean-minded son of my flesh — Please go! Please do not return! And see my sweet Greek, he is just, he is humble ... Son! son!" —

I walked by filled with a whole night-world of memories, all of them so distinctly & miraculously *English* somehow, as if I had actually lived all this — (I was struck dumb, stopped in ecstasy on Market St., trying to re-construct the events that must have transpired between my former sonhood to this poor woman in England up until this one

LOWELL-LIKE FRISCO

haunted moment in San Francisco California in 1949.) I don't jest. But there is no more to it than this. Now refer to the incident of "Big Pop" with Burroughs in Louisiana (in the bookie joint) and to his belief in other lives. On page 79 (ref.)*

Incidentally I walked on from the fish 'n chips place to Carolyn Robinson Cassady's apartment on Liberty St. and noticed as I climbed the steep steps in the yard that only in San Francisco and Lowell Mass. can there be such steep, star-pack't nights — so dark and [Hendrik] Goudt-rich** as in "Farewell Song, Sweet From my Trees"† — tree-swishing, cool nights — so spiritual, so reminiscent for me, of me; and suggestive of "the future."

San Francisco is so homelike to me; and I would live there someday.

*This refers to the page headed "REFERENCE MADE TO TRIPS WRITTEN."
**Hendrik Goudt (1583–1648), Dutch Baroque Era painter.
†"Farewell Song, Sweet from My Trees," a short story Kerouac wrote around 1940. It was un-published until 1999's *Atop an Underwood: Early Stories and Other Writings*.

NEW ORLEANS — THE GIRL'S SUICIDE

That night we crossed the ferry, high, little did we know, & sympathize with soul-thoughts, of a girl who perhaps just then was planning to jump in the water. Perhaps when Neal & I commented eagerly about the old Vulcan's forge of the ship, the boiler furnace — which glowed so dull red in the brown fog of the river night; — or perhaps when Louanne & I leaned on the rail watching the somber, swelling brown flood; or when, gleefully, we laughed; and watched the freighters docked in New Orleans across the water, the ghostly Cereno ships with Spanish balconies & moss, wreath'd in fog; the mysterious mist on the water itself; the intimation and revelation of the whole Mississippi River winding north into the mid-American night (with hints of Arkansas, Missouri, Iowa); and orange New Orleans itself in the night. What was the girl thinking? where was she from? Did her brothers in Ohio scowl fiercely when she was spoken of by men at the taxi stand? Did she walk home nights in the icy streets of winter, huddled in the little coat she had bought from her work savings? Did she sweetly fall in love with some tall, brown, never-available construction-worker who came for her occasionally in his well-pressed topcoat, in his Ford coupe? Did she dance with him at the sad, roseate ballrooms? And make jokes about the moon? And sigh & groan & cry in her pillow? What horror was there in mossy New Orleans, what real final sadness did she see? (In the Latin Quarter streets at night.)

Next day in the paper we read about her suicide, and remembered it; and thought of it.

NEW ORLEANS THINGS

NEW ORLEANS — Algiers Ferry, Canal St., Mickey in the grocery store ("Do you cats blow bop?"); Newton St., Wagner St., the levee down the road; the nightfalls; Basin St., Rampart St., the Bourbon;

Dauphine St.; Latin Quarter; hopping the freights with Neal & Al; high on the grass; Andrew Jackson park; — Joan, Julie, Willie; Helen; playing ball, making shelves; "Big Pop" in the Gretna bookie joint; groceries and Joan's benny; throwing knives; air pistol practice in the living room; crepes; weed; — the radio's Chicken Jazz n' Gumbo show; the "man" with the ice cream wagon — the front room with cot and pad; Louanne the Miss Lou on the trellised porch ... the great Mississippi Valley clouds in the afternoon; the sultry nights; Sunday in the breezy yard, Bill sits all day under his lamp (with shades drawn); and morphine-heavy he drowses or speaks, all's the same. Helen's "plantation" room & bed; the jam and coffee on the front-room floor; shattered benzedrine tubes; the rickety backyard, and the unkempt grass; the smell of piss and rivers; the Gulf rain; Canal street like Market street like any street, Immortal Street leading to the ambiguity of Universal Water whether Mississippi or Pacific.

NEW HAMPSHIRE SOURCES

ROUTE OF MY MERRIMACK RIVER (in New England)
The Pemigewasset is its main branch and begins at Newfound Lake northwest of Laconia, at Hebron N.H., only 85 miles from Lowell Mass. But below Hookset N.H. this Merrimac River begins to assume the depth, rush, personality & loneliness of a great American river, till, by the time it roars humpbacked over the Pawtucket rocks it has accumulated a water-power that is truly awful to hear. (This has been confirmed by Hal, a Coloradoan, who was amazed.)

Here is the route, and some of the feeding sources apparent on the map:

Newfound Lake fed by streams from Mt. Crosby and possibly by the Baker River of the White Mountains. Winnipesaukee is to the east. Pemigewasset flows down through Bristol; Hill; (WEST OF LACONIA) down to Franklin. Meanwhile there are the Franklin Falls and the Eastman Falls Dams — flowing thereby through Webster Place, near the birthplace of Daniel Webster* — to Gerrish, and Boscawen: here there are feedings from Blackwater Reservoir and from Rocky Pond, Sanborn Pond, and many nameless creeks. Now from some Pittsfield Creek, the river is further fed, and named Merrimack. To Penacook, Concord (and Lake Penacook) — to Bow (Turkey Pond), Pembroke; Hookset (SHINGLE PONDS, AND BEAR BROCK) — Manchester and the Massabesic Lake, and a stream from Weare thence Goffs Falls, and by a rock cavern, to Reeds Ferry; Merrimack; Thorntons Ferry — to Nashua and Hudson (fed from Hollis, and Canobie Lake.) and by the Nashua River. To Tyngsboro (Tyngsboro LAKEVIEW pond and creek from Pepperell.) Then *Lowell* — fed by Long Pond (Pine Brook) and Thoreau's Concord River† — on to the Atlantic at Newburyport & Plum Island.

109 Liberty St. 'Frisco   *SECRET, UNCOMMUNICATIVE*
The secret of time is the moment, when ripples of high expectation run — or the actual moment of "highness" itself when all is solved. We know time. Slim Gaillard's knowledge of time.

Danny Kaye's "Dinah" is of course reminiscent of Sebastian ... "Played that record over and over again in the North Pole in 1942." (I said.)

The ripples engendered by many subsidiary events connected with my memory of Sebastian (and his world of "gar-geous womans") finally broke into a rushing stream when I heard and thought of it. This explains my lifelong search for moments of vision when all is cleared ... the big trees in the white desert appearing, and the soft footfall of my approach to them. "We know time." And we anticipate the future when we pigeonhole our ripples as we go along, knowing the joyous solution to come at its given moment. Is this not too unclear though?

---

*Webster was born in Salisbury, New Hampshire.
†Thoreau's first book was *A Week on the Concord and Merrimack Rivers* (1849). It depicts an 1839 boat trip he took with his brother from Concord, Massachusetts, to Concord, New Hampshire, and back.

"NEAL'S CALIFORNIA"

It is a whole new concept, & world, in itself. He explained all about the various divisions of the S.P. railroad the moment we arrived in the state: at the edges of the Mojave outside of L.A., at Tehatchepi, and Bakersfield later. He also showed me (all the way up the San Joaquin Valley) the rooming houses where he stayed, the diners where he ate; even the water stops where he jumped off the train to pick grapes for himself & the other brakemen. In Bakersfield, just across the tracks where I had drunk wine with Bea in 1947 at night, he showed me where a woman lived whom he had entertained — places where he had done nothing more spectacular than sit and wait. He remembers *all*. His California was a long sunny place of railroads, grapes, pinochle games in cabooses, women in towns like Tracy or Watsonville, Chinese & Mexican restaurants behind the tracks, great stretches of land — hot, sweaty, important — And moreover, he is a true Californian, in the sense that everybody in California is like a broken-down movie actor, i.e., handsome, decadent, Casanova-ish, where all the women really love to try various beds. In Frisco, particularly, Neal fits in with the special California type ... where perfect strangers talk to you most intimately on the street. California is as if a land of lonely & exiled & eccentric *lovers* come to foregather, like birds. Everyone is debauched, completely (somehow.) And there is that old-fashioned look of the land, & the towns, (*not* in L.A., but on up) still reminiscent of the Golden American West we think of. The nights are "unbearably romantic" ... & sadder than the East's. [MORE ANON]

OREGON BOUND
WRITTEN IN CHILI RESTAURANT IN PORTLAND

San Francisco to Portland (698 miles) *Feb 4 & 5th '49*
Dumb sullen goodbye with Neal and Louanne after night in Richmond Calif. at wild jazz & whore joint with Ed Saucier & Jan Carter (drum-

mer.) — (the tea; the Pip pulling out her chair; the Billy Holliday gals; and "Shut up!"). Goodbye at the 3rd St. bus station — Greyhound. Oakland. Sleep through Sacramento Valley up through Red Bluff, etc. (Same as San Joaquin?) Woke up at 7 A.M. in Redding. Cold — white bunch-grass hills all around, empty streets ... Up through Shasta Lake by Buckhorn & Hatchet Mts. — spectacular Northwest timber & snow scenery ... (Hal once said it was like Colorado.) Ghostly Mt. Shasta in distance ... Mountain lakes; high blue sky of mountain airs. Lamoine ... railroad shacks; flats. Across spectacular mountains and timbered ridges to Dunsmuir — little railroad & lumber town in the mountains (Mt. Shasta and the walking snows.) Cloud-flirt'd Shasta — Narrow ridge-town, & snow. Vision of little boy: basketball yard at school, father railroader below in hollow; Xmas night; the Shasta snow-wraiths walking; the ghost of the Great Shaman Fool leading him on to white-woman-shrouded sloper. (How the ghost-wraiths disport shame-lessly in the blue high day up there, not waiting for night even — but N I G H T *does* come too ...) On to Mt. Shasta (silly ski-girl.) And then grim weed ... "What'd he do up in Weed?"* The big Inn facing empty spaces north and the coal shuttles; snow & cold — Men in the hotel. Mountain pines. Grim, desolate town.

NORTHERN CALIFORNIA

After weed (big lonely Black-Butte in snow) the great clouds far off over the Cascade Ranges and Siskyous of Oregon (clouds of Oregon Trail.) Then Dorris, Calif., and the intimation of ice caves far to the east down spatial corridors of snow ... Then Klamath Falls in the flats of the Kla-math River: snowy, joyous American town in the morning; "affairs in the sunny town; winter; Geo. Martin; redbrick alleys like Lowell of Du-luoz." A walk in the winey air. Little kids lean over bridge-rail, steam-ing Klamath River, distant Sierra Nevadas of California (No.). Three towns: *Dunsmuir,* Lowell-like, medieval, Alpine, Dr. Saxish — and

*A reference to John Steinbeck's *Of Mice and Men* (1937).

Weed: — grim, western, Oxbow-like (Nevada), rough marshalls and ranchmen — and *Klamath Falls:* joyous, bell-ringing, snowy, sunny, homelike.

Up by great Klamath Lake, on west ridge of timber hills leading to East Oregon craters, wastes, rangelands and that mysteriously unknown junction of Oregon, Idaho and Nevada (east of McDermitt.) Land of Shastas past — land of Modocs now, of lake Indians. Modoc Point. Agency Lake. Long leisurely Sun Pass. Lake in volcanic crater; and prick-point summit that God wouldn't dare sit on (Diamond Lake summit?) Great snowy rocks in the Northwest air, and timber, timber....

(Mt. Shasta haunts poor Dunsmuir, poor Weed, and even me now: a ghostly, shrouded, sneering mount.)

Great Pengra Pass ... four feet of snow. Big glorious redwoods cloth'd in snow, drooping, nodding, standing, serried, gaunt, trimm'd, orchestral in snow, whole arpeggios of snowy redwood, & vaults of blue sky in between.

PENGRA & WILLAMETTE IN OREGON

(Trees grow straight on crooked cliffsides.) The hairy forecliffs leaning over us.) Down Pengra Pass (asleep mostly) to Oakridge ...

The little Willamette Valley, a thin strip of poor farms haunted by distant volcanic craters in the dusk. Pleasant Hill? founded 1848? — how Bourgeois the pioneers were! (The cemetery there full of Oregon pioneers.) Underdeveloped region. Oregon is a wilderness where people have to live in poor little valleys like the Willamette and still be haunted (as they milk sweet cows) by the Encantadas of the blasted West ... Then the snows melt in Pengra and little Willamette floods Eugene, Albany, Junction City, Oregon City, Salem (shows them who's little, and shows up the sterile impotent volcanoes paralyzed in rage out there.)

Ah! — and there's the Columbia for floods, joined by the Willamette (and the big Snake), for the flooding of other cities. Eugene a dull Durham-like college town ... so Corvallis? And Albany & Salem Oregon. But Oregon City, town of Big Watery Willamette now, Holyoke-town of paper mills & gastanks, and ridges with houses above, and whore in the redbrick alley: a definite town.

Portland, like filling stations and hipsters and Portland-sized cities, is the same as any other same-sized city in U.S.A. or like any other gas stations & hipsters all over. Rainy snow here.

THE PORTLAND THOUGHTS

We crossed great dark Columbia over bridge. River once adventurous & commercial pulse of Portland, now barred off from "public" by tug-works, naval bases, etc., etc., as Mississippi River is barred off in Algiers La., with wire fences. Many chop suey joints in Portland, like in Salt Lake City (!!). I anticipated rainy snow in "drenched with suffering" story of 1945, about rooming house in Portland. The mysteries of naturalism & supernaturalism meet.

Many thoughts tonight ... eating chili in Broadway (Portland) restaurant ... O'Flannery's. Saturday night in Portland, Oregon ... girl-and-boy dates.

Pathos of distance softens my anger at Neal & Louanne now. We all are as we are — (and I saw what I was a few times in 'Frisco with horror.) Ah well ... Neal's new morality still stands, but not as an end in itself. More on this in proper pages.

Tonight I sleep across Columbia Valley. Next writing-stop is Butte, Montana. God bless us all. For the wages of sin *is* death ... and eternal life is still ours somehow. This is Neal & Louanne. As for me, I shall be myself as made (no psychology remains, and no philosophy.) There is no beyond behind my beyond, and no behind beyond my behind ... all us say that don't we?

Portland to Butte (Written in Spokane Feb. 6)

Now I will get to the source of the rainy night: The Snow — North, the West that makes Mississippis — that makes the rainy night we cross on tidal highways ... Now I'll come close and touch the source of it all — and thereby, perhaps, what Wolfe meant by "undiscovered Montanas."

Two hobo-panhandlers in back of bus on way out at midnight (2 "scufflers"); said they were bound for The Dalles to beat a dollar or two. Drunk — "Goddamit don't get us thrown off at Hood River!" "Beat the busdriver for a couple!" We rolled in the big darkness of the Columbia River valley, in a blizzard. I could see little but big trees, bluffs, terrifying darknesses — and the lights across the big river (big enough to have its Cape Horn to Mississippi's Cape Girardeau.) Vancouver Wash. across the snowy darkness, on the shore ...

Thought of Hood River and how dismal it would be to get thrown off there: — in the hooded night, on wild watery shores, among logs, crags ... I woke up after a nap and a chat with the hobo ("My originator is Kansas City, Jackson County" and "my place of origination is Texas" — or Bakersfield, or Modesto, or Delano — couldn't make up his mind which lie was most suitable. Said he would be an oldtime outlaw if J. Edgar Hoover had not made it against the law to steal. Said he was going to the Dalles to steal — a small farming & lumber town, he said —

THE GREAT COLUMBIA VALLEY

WASHINGTON

Up ahead there in the frightful night's valley of the Columbia. I lied and said I had driven a stolen car from N.Y. to Frisco. He said he believed me implicitly.) — so after this chat, I slept and woke up at Tonompah (?) Falls —

A hooded white phantom dropped water from his huge icy forehead (which I could not altogether see in the eerie light.) So Dr. Sax had been here too ... in this hooded night of the Columbia. Hundreds of feet high, from the rock-bluff worn shelfwise by the patient frightful Columbia, from icy brows, this water dropped (from its mouthlike hole) and evaporated midways to mist. We were apparently on the floor of the valley now, looking up at ancient shores of rock. I was scared because I could not see what was in the darkness up-&-beyond the hood of ice, the Falls — what hairy horrors? what craggy night (no stars.)

The busdriver plunged along then over mad ridges ... I slept through Hood River, the Dalles.

Woke up briefly, glanced at Wallula, site of the old 1818 Fort (Walla Wall Fort — IN A MESA CUT) — in a Mesa-like country of sagebrush and plains where the Columbia swung around to meet the Snake (in the brown plains of Pasco) and the Yakima a little beyond. On the horizon, the misty long hills called Horse Heaven; and southward (O Oregon!) the Whitman Nat'l Park.

Then northeast through Connell, Lind, Sprague, Cheney (wheat and cattlelands like East Wyoming)

EASTERN WASHINGTON — IDAHO

In a gale of blizzards to Spokane — snowy big town on Sunday afternoon. (Walked in snow to recover my hoary old black jacket.) Sprague a redbrick, wheat-silo, Nebraska-like town.

From Spokane (perhaps really a meditative place after all for my nun-aunt Caroline) to Idaho — Coeur d'Alene —

(But Oh that dark Columbia land!) (I see, tho, how close the Snake River came to be an eastern slope river for the maws of the Mississippi — how it originates a mile from the Continental Divide in Jackson Hole Wyoming; but the Columbia won it, at Pasco; and the Oregon Territory was saved much more — tho the Columbia can handle it, winding all the way from Canada to Astoria's mouth.) (Therefore the Northwest has its rainy night, as Lowell has the Merrimac, and

Asheville its Broad, and Harrisburg its Susquehanna.) Is there any connection between the "ghost of the Susquehanna" and the "Hood River hoboes"? Of course. But to Idaho ...

FEB. 7 — Slept through Coeur d'Alene (Ah well-) — but no mind, I saw the lakes and mountains no less, and could not help it: they came eastward, and Coeur d'Alene like Spokane was in the flatland. But immediately we climbed a great ridge along the frozen snowy lake and mounted to great heights. Fourth of July pass; and the great piney snows, over Coeur d'Alene Lake. The drops were sheer. I thought of the Coeur d'Alene Indians and all this they had.

We came along and down to the waterbed of the

THE BITTERROOT NIGHT

Coeur d'Alene river, to Cataldo. There I saw the clusters of houses homesteading in the wild mountain holes. A car was stuck; a big jovial young man was running out to help; dogs barking, chimneys smoking, children, women. — all the joyous northern life I think of occasionally, like in Maine, with frozen red sunsets, snow, smoke, kitchens of Idaho, home. Then to Wallace ... some big mines ... Then Mullan, in the heart of great sheer slopes rising near. Here I thought of Jim Bridger, and how, when waking in the morning in the valley-hole where Mullan now is, he looked ahead where the riverbed indisputably led him — on across the vast craglands he himself owned, then. I did not see him scrambling slopes, as many of us literally do in civilization, but following the eternity of waterbeds: under those piney heights, under the snow stars. The man who had written a poem:

"I saw a petrified bird in a petrified tree,
Singing his petrified song."   (In Petrified Forest.)

Unknown Jim Bridger, one of the true poets of America; grinding his coffee and slicing his bacon and frying the deer meat in the winter's shadow of the unknown Bitterroot Mountains. What must he have thought? and the men of him, a squawman and solitary?

It got dark and we went over Lookout Pass in the Bitterroots at night. We rose to the great heights in the snowy gray; and way below in the gulch burned one single shack-light — almost a mile below. Two boys in a car

MONTANA ENTRY

almost went off the ridge avoiding our bus. In the silence while we waited for the busdriver to help them shovelling the drifts, I saw and heard the secret of the Bitterroots ... (I've known these things before.) From down the pass to Deborgia, Montana, and on to Frenchtown and Missoula. We followed the Bitterroot River bed (it starts near Butte and winds along these loneliest of mountains to Flathead Lake, north). In Deborgia I began to see what Montana was like: and I shall never forget it. It is something that would please the soul of any man (who is serious, somehow.) Ranchers, lumberjacks & miners in a small bar, talking, playing cards & slot machines, while all around outside is the Montana night of bear & moose & wolf, of pines, & snow, and secret rivers, and the Bitterroots, the Bitterroots ... One small light where they are, & the immensest dark, starpack't. The knowledge of what young men have thought of their Montana (and in 1870?) — and of what old men feel in it. The lovely women hidden. But that was only the beginning.

Missoula I did not like — a college town of skiiers, (at least what I saw around the bus station.)

I slept enroute to great Butte.

And why is Butte — over the Divide, near Anaconda, and Pipestone Pass — greater? Well, look at the names that surround it. Before I arrived in Montana I thought of stopping at Missoula, to rest, & to see; because I had heard it mentioned so much by hoboes (in 1947 in Wyoming, for instance.) But it is only a great rail-junction ... In any case, just to look at the map, and to see Butte in the rough geographies of the divide, is to think of Twain's Nevada, (for me.) And it is so — In Butte I stored my bag in a locker. A drunken Indian wanted me to go drinking with him, but I cautiously declined. Yet a short walk around the sloping streets (in below zero weather at night) showed that everybody in Butte was drunk. This was a Sunday night — I hoped the saloons would stay open till I had at least seen my fill. *They closed at dawn,* if at all. I walked into one great oldtime saloon and had a giant beer. On the wall in back they had a big electric signboard flashing gambling-numbers. The bartender told me about it, and since I was a beginner allowed me to select his numbers in the hope that I would have beginner's luck. No soap ... but he told me of Butte. Arrived there 22 years ago, and stayed. "Montanans drink too much, fight too much, and love too much." I watched the wonderful characters in there ... old prospectors, gamblers, whores, miners, Indians, cowboys; & tourists who seemed different. Another gambling-saloon was indescribable with riches: groups of sullen Indians (Blackfeet) drinking red whisky in the john; hundreds of men of all kinds playing cards; and one old professional house-gambler who tore my heart out he reminded me so much of my father (big; green eyeshade; handkerchief protruding from back pocket; great rugged, pockmarked, angelic face (unlike Pop's) and the

FROM BUTTE TO THREE FORKS, MONT.

big asthmatic, laborious sadness of such men. I could not take my eyes off him. My whole concept of "On the Road" changed & matured as I watched him.) (Explained properly elsewhere.) The whole meaning was there for me, and specifically, it was as tho I were descending from metaphysical "rainy" preoccupations to dear man again ... in all ways, writing & otherwise ... (having now escaped Neal's compulsive *mystique de haschisch.*) Another old man, in his eighties, or nineties, called

"John" by respectful men, coolly played cards till dawn, with slitted eyes; and it amazed me no end that he has been playing cards in the Montana saloon-night of spittoons, smoke & whisky since 1880, (days of the winter cattle drive to Texas, and of Sitting Bull.) Another old man with an old, loving sheepdog (all the dogs, as in Colorado, are shaggy sheepdogs) packed off in the cold mountain night after satisfying his soul at cards. It was like my father's old world of gambling again, but in the Montana night, & *moreso* somehow. Ah, dear father. And the young cowhands; and miners; and wild women. Even the Greeks, who are like Lowell Greeks ... only *moreso* in Montana. How explain? Why bother. Even *Chinamen!*

At dawn I caught the bus. Soon we were going down the slope; and looking back, I saw Butte, still lit like jewelry, sparkling on the mountainside ... 'Gold Hill' — and the blue northern dawn. Again the wild rocks & snows & valleys & rangelands & timber, & sagebrush. In a short while we were at Three Forks ... where the Madison & the Missouri, in strange confluence, act; where the Missouri in

YELLOWSTONE VALLEY

Midwinter lay flooded & frozen, covered with snow, over vast acres of ranch land: — hint of floods in the Natchez cobblestones a thousand miles away, hint of loamy plantations crumbling far around, over, & down the trail of the Missouri (north-wing'd) and the Mississippi (river of southern urge) in distant Louisiana. In Three Forks, in a nippy dawn, I saw the old street, the boardwalks, the old stores, the horses, the old cars — and the distant Bitterroots & Rocky Mountains snow-covered: and the young men who all looked like football players or cowhands; the secret, delicious, unknown women. — At Bozeman I saw the ends of the world again: the Wyoming Tetons, & Granite Peak; & the Rockies & Bitterroots; & something like a distant *glacier* to the Canadian north somehow, all around, all over. This is like looking down the end of the world in Wyoming, in Arizona, in Texas (before El Paso), in Oregon at Mevrill, and many other places in the West. We mounted the Rockies — among mountain ranches & sheep — and descended to Livingston in the Yellowstone valley. The Yellowstone, like the Nebraska Platte, like the Nile, is one of the great valleys of the world: in the snowy waste the trees of the valley endlessly wind away, protecting ranches & farms. Always, in Montana, the great sense of northern distances, in Canada, or southerly to Wyoming — and east to ... *Dakota*. It is one of the most isolated places in the world. Bigtimber, Mont., which I loved, is fine, but it is a world of wildlands from either Denver or ... Bismarck? Boise? Where? Montana is concealed in just this way, and this explains why it is the only state in the union which has its own personality, & the only truly Western state in the West.

BIGTIMBER, MONT.

Butte to Minneapolis
Montana is "protected" by Dakota, Wyoming, Idaho, and strange Saskatchewan from this silly world! — all power to it! — (and at the same time, recall, it is the *actual* source of the rainy night.) Big Muddy's muddy cradle.

Bigtimber. There I saw such a scene, such a thing: all these old-timers sitting around in an old ramshackle inn, at noon, (in the middle of the snowy prairie) — playing cards by old stoves: *even at noon.* Montana is the land of manly life, manly absorptions, and manly laziness! And a boy of twenty, with one arm missing, lost either at war or at work, gazing sadly at me, wondering who I was and what I did in the world. He sat in the middle of the old men, his tribal elders, gazing on the stranger, the alien, the secret Poe or Lafcadio Hearn that I felt like then. How sad! — and how beautiful he was because he was unable to work forever, and must sit forever with the oldtimers, and worry about how his buddies are punching cows and roistering outside. How protected he is by the old men, by Montana. *Nowhere else in the world would I say it were at all beautiful for a young man to have but one arm.* See? I shall never forget also the huge cup of coffee I drank in this inn, for a nickel; nor that poor, beautiful boy, who, though sad, seemed to realize that he was *home*, more than I can say with all my arms. — The bus then rolled on, by buttes, ranchlands, by the Yellowstone trees, by distant canyons & cuts, by Montana ...

In Billings, at about 2 in the afternoon, it was at least 10 degrees below zero. I saw three of the most beautiful young girls I've ever seen in all my life, all within minutes, eating in a sort of high school lunchroom with

"YELLOWSTONE RED"

their grave boyfriends. Ame Montana ... We drove on. And got to the other great Montana town that I'll never forget, & will re-visit ... *Miles City*. Here, at dusk, it was about 20 below. I walked around. There had been many splendid ranches in the Yellowstone bed all the way, and now here were the ranchers themselves, with their families, in town for provisions. The women were shopping, the men were in the magnificent gambling saloons. In a drugstore window I saw a book on sale — so beautiful! — "Yellowstone Red," a story of a man in the early days of the valley, & his tribulations & triumphs. Is this not better reading in Miles City than the Iliad? — their *own* epic? There were many excellent saddle stores; there being an old saddle firm in town, and a leather factory at the east end. The gambling saloons were of course reminiscent of Butte and Bigtimber, though the people looked more prosperous, and it was afternoon, almost suppertime. A man in an old vest, tired of cards, rises from a table (underneath a wall covered with old photos of ranchers, and elk antlers), sits down nearer the bar, and eats a thick, juicy steak. Meanwhile his wife and pretty daughter come back for him, and eat with him. The sons, all decked in new boots, come in from the cold in those Montana sheepskin coats, and they eat. Then, after a few more hours in town, they pack things in the car and drive back to the ranch on the Yellowstone, where the cattle stand in winter pasture, safe from the West's worst winter. It is exceedingly cold in Montana but no —

where else do people dress so well against it — so that the bitterness of the climate is nullified by good horse sense. Most men wear earmuffs — that is, caps with visors & earmuffs, like hunting caps. I saw many a cowboy in the high Texas plateau near Sonora, on horseback, wearing these caps, last month. The final thing I loved so much about Miles City is the perfect unity and meaning of its existence. It is a town (in the original sense of that word's meaning) intended for the preservation, enhancement, & continuation of human life. There is no "decadence," not even so innocent a decadence as hoboes represent. People are lucky in Miles City, they live well, they respect each other, they stick together, & their lives there are a rich chronicle of absorptions, interesting considerations, & solemn joy — no hysteria, nothing "forced" — a mild foregathering of mild birds. They winter and they summer with equal mild strength. Life is joyous ... and yet life is also dangerous there: wherever men are, there's danger; but I consider the danger from mild men the only human danger I should not want to welcome. In Miles City I believe I would mind my own business. And I believe others would do so, too. You can have your Utopian orgies: at least, if it comes down to an orgy, I should prefer an orgy with the Montanans, for just such reasons.

Now an even more *moving* part of the trip was yet to come ... a discovery of the astonishing spirit of the modern West, in "darkest" North Dakota. Yes, in North Dakota there are people I would value more than all the people, taken generally, in New York and all Europe to boot — and I would take these North Dakotans specifically. If I wanted to depend on the blood of men & women, I would go to this No. Dakota and nowhere else.

"HOME IN OLD MEDORA ..."

NORTH DAKOTA — THE NIGHT IN THE BADLANDS

In the bitter winter night of snow-plains we rolled to Terry and then

Glendive, Mont. I had been dozing. Certain passengers got on at this last Montana way-station, and soon we were in Beach, No. Dakota. What a dismal, bitter night — with a cold moon. To my surprise, at Medora, the Incalculable Missouri had worn a rock canyon and this was the Heart of the Badlands. What is it the Missouri does not do? — what lands? — rock? alluvial? will you have frozen rangelands, or black canyons, or Iowa vales, or *deltas*? By January moonlight, in this northernmost part of America, the ghostly snow-rocks and buttes stood in bulging, haunted shapes ... ambiguous heaths for bearded badmen in flight from the law of raw towns. Such a town was Medora; and Belfield ... the great American West that stretches so far from Pasco Washington to places north of Oshkosh, Nebraska. No more "badmen" — not on horseback — but the same rugged, undeniable world for rugged necessary soulfulness. Thus stood my thoughts (which were also haunted by the moony rocks & snows of the Badlands Canyon) when, outside of Dickinson, the mad busdriver almost went off the road on a sudden low snowdrift. It didn't phase him the least, till, a mile out of Dickinson, we came upon impassable drifts, and a traffic jam in the black Dakota midnight blasted by heathwinds from the Saskatchewan Plain. — There were lights, and many sheep-skinned men toiling with shovels, and confusion — and the bitterest cold out there, some 25 below, I judge conservatively. Another bus

DICKINSON, NORTH DAKOTA

Eastbound was stuck; a truck; and many cars. Major cause of the conges-tion was a small panel truck carrying slot-machines to Montana — so that these great commerces were held up by slot-machines so needless in the Dakota steppes. From the little Western town of Dickinson nearby came crews of eager young men with shovels, most of them wearing red baseball caps (or airforce caps, like the caps worn by 2 So. Dakota boys I met on the road in 1947.) And heavy jackets, boots, ear-muffs — led by the sheriff, a strong joyous boy of 25 or so himself. They pitched in — it was an attritive, swirling, arctic-like night: I thought of their mothers and wives waiting at home with hot coffee, as though the traffic jam in the snow was an emergency touching Dickinson itself. Is this the "isolationist" middlewest? Where in the effete-thinking East would men work for others, for nothing, at midnight in howling freezing gales? The scene out beyond the men and the lights was as the plain of Desolation itself ... the Greenland ice cap in darkness. We in the bus watched. Once in a while the boys came in to warm up ... some said it was 40 below, I don't know. Some of the boys were fourteen, even twelve years old. Finally the busdriver, a maniacal and good man, decided to pile on through. He gunned the Diesel motor and the big bus that said "Chicago" on it went sloughing through drifts. We swerved into the panel truck: I believe we might have hit the jackpot. Then we swerved into a

THE DAKOTANS

brand new 1949 Ford. Wham! wham! Finally we were back on dry ground after an hour of travails. For me it was just a good show, I had no boots to go out in. In Dickinson the café was crowded and full of late Friday night excitement — about the snow-jam mainly. All around, on the walls, were photos of old ranchers and even some of fabled outlaws and characters. The Dickinson boys of a less robust breed shot a homey pool in the back. The pretty girls sat with husbands and families. Hot coffee was the big order. Men came in and out from the howling badlands midnight with news of further travails. We heard that the rotary plow had swerved into the new Ford and the mighty rotaries had disposed of the back end in a manner reminiscent of shrapnel bursts — that parts of the new car were so sent to graze in various parts of the snowy range. Or the rotary plow just went sowing? In any case, I hated to leave this marvelous atmosphere, this *real* town, where Nature & Custom found a grand way of meeting and joining forces. Men work against each other only when it is safe to abandon men — only when and where. The Dakotans paid little attention to us now that we were safe; we needed them, they came; but they had no need of us, "Chicago" slickers that we really were. I took one last look at the place, and the pictures on the wall, and the people, and wished that I had been born & raised & died in Dickinson, North Dakota.

NO MORE DAKOTA

We got stuck again outside town but the boys were there again with the rotary plow. A big truck-trailer was stuck deep; the driver was lost in the wastes without them. They hauled chains and chipped ice and shouted, all as if they enjoyed saving the situation. In the East we would despair. We got out and zoomed on across Dakota. I slept in the back, after one interruption when the motor caught on fire. While I slept the bus stalled in Bismarck, in a solid-frozen dawn; all the passengers got out because the heater failed and the inside of the bus was below zero temperature. They huddled in a diner. The bus was driven to a garage and repaired. Through all this I slept calm and wonderful, and had pleasant dreams, of Dakota in June, or of enchanted summers somewhere. I woke up refreshed in Fargo (isn't it a cold-sounding name?) It was –30 below.

And then the trip across the flat, snowy, sunny Minnesota of farms and church steeples was of course uneventful, except for a road outside Moorhead that was obviously designed by a really malignant architect to jiggle one's stomach out in regular, mathematically computed intervals. No mind.

And how dull it was to be in the East again ... no more raw hopes: all was decided and satisfied here. I talked to a fine old man going into St. Cloud, however, who remembered 19th century Minnesota "when the Indians were out at Alexandria" (few miles

MINNEAPOLIS — ST. PAUL

west of Osakis Lake.) Nothing wrong with Minnesota except the middleclass ... which is ruining the entire nation anyway. At St. Cloud great Father Mississippi flowed in a deep rocky bed beneath Lowell-like bridges; and great clouds, as at the destination in New Orleans, hovered over this northern valley. I have only one objection to make to Minnesota, namely, it is not Montana. This is the objection of a man in love — with the western America. We drove to Anoka and then St. Paul.

This famous river port still has the old 1870 brick along the waterfront ... now the scene of great fruit and wholesale markets, just as in Kansas City near the downhill Missouri shore. St. Paul is smaller and older and more rickety than Minneapolis, but there is a depressing Pittsburgh-like sootiness about it ... even in joyous snowy winter. Minneapolis is a sprawling dark city shooting off *white communities* across the montonous flats. The only soulful beauty here is rendered by the Mississippi and also by a hopeless hint of Mille Lacs and the Rainy River country to the North. The people are eastern (of course it's called 'middlewestern') city people; and their corresponding *look, talk, & absorptions*. Blame it on me; I hate almost everything. I would have liked to see Duluth merely because of Sinclair Lewis and Lake Superior.

These are my melancholy opinions.

Then, after a meal in a Minneapolis lunch-house and a freezing walk in the black streets, and

WISCONSIN — CHICAGO — MICHIGAN

a short talk with a young man in the bus station who had a Fire of Phenomenality in his eyes and ended up giving me religious tracts (one more involved & free-thinking than the other, designed for blokes), the bus rolled into Wisconsin and to the charming river-darknesses of Eau Claire.

Eau Claire belongs to a type of American town I always like: it is on a river and it is dark and the stars shine stark-bright, and there is something *steep* about the night. Such towns are Lowell, Oregon City, Holyoke Mass., Asheville N.C., Gardiner Maine, St. Cloud, Stuebenville O., Lexington Mo., Klamath Falls Ore., and so on — even Frisco of course.

After Eau Claire and a glimpse of the flat Wisconsin night of pines & marshes, I slept and was borne down to Chicago at dawn.

The same scraggly streets in dirty dawns ... the eastern metropolis again ... Negro workingmen waiting for work-buses and coughing; the early traffic in cars; the great Rubble of City stretching in all directions like a puzzle and a damnation and an enigma. It was the same Chicago as in '47 ... but this time I did not stop to examine the "riotous, tinkling night" of Bop at the Loop; and beans in hungry diners.

I hated Gary, I even hated South Bend (land of car-dealers and gravelly desolation): what are we going to do?

Then the lovely Indiana and Ohio farmlands I had seen many times before; finally Toledo (Holy Toledo!) — where I got off to hitch-hike to Detroit and walked 3 miles to get out on the highway.

BEAT IN DETROIT
(Sitting on my bag on the floor of the men's room.)

DETROIT Feb. 9, 1949
I got off the bus at Toledo on a wild desire to see ex-wife, ex-love, ex-joy Edie ... I hitched to Detroit in the sunny afternoon. I made it in three rides from three fine men (a young law student from Monroe Mich.; a machinist from Flat Rock Mich.; and another guy who told little of himself.) But I called Edie's mother and Edie wasn't there. I wandered the streets (with my last 85 cents) more beat than ever — (except 1947 in Harrisburg and 2 weeks ago on Ellis & O'Farrell Streets with Louanne.) And I had rages, awful rages. I still have them tonight (but a little less since I learned I can go back to Toledo and on to N.Y. on my ticket.) But I only have 25 cents now, and the Parker family spoke to me over the phone as tho I were a bum and Parker's wife flatly declined to lend me 3 bucks to eat on. Goddamn the whole crummy world. I rested up in the library reading up on Jim Bridger, Montana, and the Oregon Trail ... for my own purposes. Tired and hungry as I am, I worry less about food and sleep than these people who won't lend me $3 — and

who were once my relatives. I wish Edie was here. I talked wistfully to her mother for an hour on the phone. And coincident with this feeling is a growing chagrin about my lost anger at Neal in Frisco five days ago. Life is so short! — we part, we wander, we *never* return. I die here.

NEW ENGLAND RIVER

Further Information Concerning my Merrimack
It is an Indian name, said to mean Swift Water. The spelling with the "K" is "used at places along the river above Haverhill." The Merrimack, with its largest branch, is 183 miles long. It is properly formed at Franklin, by the junction of the Pemigewasset & the Winnipesaukee Rivers. (The Amoskeag falls are 55 feet high in Manchester; the Pawtucket, 30 ft.) Navigable from Haverhill down. The mouth of the river at Newburyport is a tidal estuary, with a shifting sand bar. Drainage area: 5,000 miles. The valley was formed before the glacier arrived and receded: "high flood plain is trenched" & terraced; where new channel did not conform to the pre-glacial channel (Valley was filled with drift after ice retreated) the river has come upon buried ledges, more resistant than the drift below, "and waterfalls have thus resulted."

Thoreau, on the other hand, writes that the Indian meaning of Merrimack is STURGEON (which I think is more likely.) The English encyclopedists are likely to conclude that the "savages" of America called every river Swift Water; with a kind of British wryness —

NEW YORK NIGHTS

NEW YORK SCENE
The night of March 14, when Little Jack's boy Willie suddenly burst into the pad on York Ave. (Allen's) and informed him that the finger had been put on him, & the F.B.I. was looking for him. Little Jack dispatching Hunkey to "dig the heat" around town; and the long melo-

dramatic night of mysterious speculation; & anxiety for Vicki's where-abouts; and story-telling (meanwhile that old man was beating that old Katherine upstairs, and she came to us for refuge.) The "sinister" at-mosphere Hunkey always emphasizes, closing in.

Finally, at dawn, Hunkey returned, ostensibly full of pertinent in-formation, but first going thru an elaborate, almost Shakespearean de-lay ... looking for one, probably, as he came in (thinking Little Jack would not want Allen & I in on it), for when Jack said "What's in the news?" Hunkey opened up his copy of the Daily News and read off headlines & sublines in a mocking tone ... sometimes with a coy twist, sometimes bored a little, sometimes pseudo-dramatically (etc.), always *intelligently* though. Something about a "dead merchant seaman" had its double connotation (all life is double, triple) — for Hunkey once was a seaman, & considers himself "dead." The whole thing was deeply pregnant (I learned a law of drama: drama is mostly ambiguous dan-ger interrupted by funny things, & things like Hunkey's act.) (This has been strangely indescribable.)

BROOKLYN ELS   *NOTES*

Not long after, night of Mar. 16, a Negro woman in the Lefferts El quoted St. John to us "Behold, he cometh with clouds; and every eye shall see him!"* — and then, gesturing towards my feet, cried: "The burning lake is there!"† — A man with a big briefcase, I don't [know] whether he was a lawyer or a madman, said he believed in heaven but hoped there'd be trees and flowers up there. She said we'd all be an-gels, no need for trees & flowers; she said we'd have wings. But he said, "I don't know, I hope there are trees & flowers, because I like trees & flowers a lot."

To me, when I left, she said "Goodnight darling."

*Revelation 1:7.
†Revelation 20:14.

315

She had given me a tract, saying: "Wherewithal shall a young man cleanse his way? by taking heed thereto according to Thy word."

But I am not young, and my way is clean in the burning lake. I have seen the Firmament, & Gold, and did hear them singing: but used these ropes to pull myself back.

The woman's a dusky rose glowing in the golden rain.

— —

One word all night uttering meseems I hear somewhere outside where rain's a muttering so lucid, so near, so tearful on my windowpane: Ah, it's God telling me how dear we are, how mistaken. God hovers over blowing rain.

DARK ZORRO OF THE CALIFORNIA NIGHT

FURTHER NOTES ON CALIFORNA (NEAL'S)

My vision of California, when I first saw it & embraced it in 1947, was inextricably connected to the vision of Zorro riding down a dirt road by moonlight under dense, inky, old trees ... a kind of *Mexican* vision as ancient as the missions — the Camino del Real & the road of flowers — for, as a matter of fact, all "Western" movies practically are filmed in California, and any movies with outdoor scenery, and one grows up seeing the California road & the trees, time and time again. When I got there (especially the nights when I walked across a flowery valley to work, by moonlight) I *recognized* it all — (in '47.) — inky trees and all.

Neal's California fits in with mine, but augments it so beautifully — to include the "brokendown lovers," and the old, sunny, American railroading, and the bars where waiters, bartenders, the owner and customers ALL look like characters in a movie, like seconds, or stuntmen, or stand-ins ... never like the hero. In the East you keep seeing the bloody hero himself. That is why California is poignant. Its nights are pathetic with "end-of-the-continent" sadness ... also *funny*.

I think, also, that California is invested with a kind of "classiness" by the presence of the Mexicans, who are descendants of haughty Spaniards, & know it. The vision of Zorro (with Mexican cape), flying by moonlight on his horse, under old California trees — by groves of lemon, grape & walnut — by old mines — along the silvery dust road — the vision of little kids thinking this — the sea at Monterrey — and Neal.

VISIONS OF CALIFORNIA

One particularly intense night I sat in a swivel chair with my blue uniform, club, & gun (job as a guard, 1947, Sausalito) reading a story about Oregon ... which led me to a "vision" of Northern California. Weed-Klamath-The Modoc country-Oregon-Portland: — This is another matter indeed. It is a kind of "Northwest" vision, (not Mexican, soft, night-like) — but morning, canyon — clear, crisp; timbered; with raw nights, grim men, Weed, Redding, lumberjacks, Shasta, ranches; wolves.

There are *three* Californias in these personal esoteric visions of mine: the "Northwest country" California; the Lowell-like and bejewelled, romantic, night-like, bay-encircled 'Frisco (with its rich old Boston streets); and the soft Southern California of Hollywood ...

Curious that the Valley stretches across these three Californias.

The dividing points are at Redding & Bakersfield. But Sacramento, so Spanish, & hot & sunny, were South of Bakersfield if justice had art. Yet these are *distinct* divisions, as I will continue to show. The value of so innocent a preoccupation is involved with that kind of intelligence which informs European variableness ... One of our most valuable gimmicks for knowledge of man arises out of the wonderful European variety, which dramatizes so much: the French, the Germans, the English, the Dutch, the Swiss, the Italians, et cetera. I will show similar distinctions *within* one state in the USA, for the sake of the poetry of life. The sheriff from Weed, the 'Frisco gambler, & the Bakersfield Mexican ... etc. These things clear themselves.

LONG ISLAND

THE RAINY NIGHT

Let us know then by the rainy night, gift of God, that all our woes are dirt and all complaints chipp'd of marble ... But let us really see. No longer must we fight, or haggle over the price of favors and nosegays, in domesticities wrongly embroiled: — carping, canting, camping, yakking, yipping, contending: —

The rainy night, soft gift, of God given, where all our woes are water — under the bridge is water — and water-falls.

As for me, O God, let me be prosaic and true.

Let me say, plainly, with art, weeping, truly, in the heat of real intelligence and real care:

O brothers, sisters, mothers, fathers — cease! The rainy night surrounds us softly falling, as nothing, exists for us — like the sea says "Shhh-" — O inquietude and restless coughing in the night, end.

Because the rain, in April the rain, is a message from the night, telling of dirt and stone, the end of fretful breathing in wormy congeries: please please please desist and cease, no longer consist of mad, all worried gnawing; consist instead of flowers, of momentary, perceptive, all-darkened, all-enkindled fire and flame of joy, gladness ... Pater Nostrum! — eyes, eyes! Mater Nostrum:! — Kisses! Only a step away, you, expectant, watch me.

What Might	How long dark?
Have Been a	How much wait?
Sign — but Which	Why so dumb?
Is Only a Dumb	What so dumb?
Doodle, no Macro-	What so big?
cosm — a Mackerel	When we hear?
	What was done?

— The above is the result of emotions aroused by the sum of feelings sprung from this long preoccupation with rain & rivers, and all the rain & rivers across the continent of America: the desultoriness due to an avoidance of actual detail, in one general cry without real, built-up foundation. This is a lesson in art, that art, like life, is an organic of details, no sigh ... Moreover, the above Sign of the Mackerel, while an exemplary attempt at unconscious, automatic writing — in imagistic form, is still only a "doodle," a dawdle as long as it does not spring from an actual trance (no sigh.)

It is better to go on with the facts, whose poetry speaks for themselves, and *often* enough, finally, to pile-up a kind of epos in sum. And wait for a sign, a trance, a vision of gold — and for work.

LONG ISLAND

THE TRANCE IN MY QUEER HOUSE

The night of the eclipse of the moon, 11 P.M. April 12, 1949, I had a dream and a trance, in my queer house in Ozone Park ... that is to say, it was suddenly the same ambiguous house of my dreams, with many meanings and existences, like a great well-placed word in a line of poetry or prose. It was that very house that sometimes rattles ... and is set on the edge of the world instead of Crossbay Blvd.

Earlier in the day he who is known by name, Allen Ginsberg, and I, discussed the "shrouded stranger." This stemmed from a dream I had of Jerusalem and Arabia long ago. Traveling by dusty road in the white desert, from Arabia to the Protective City, I saw that I was inexorably pursued by a Hooded Wayfarer with a staff, who slowly occupied and traversed the plain behind me, sending up a shroud of dust slowly. I know not how I knew he followed me, but if I could make the Protective City before he caught up with me, I knew I would be safe. But this was out of the question. I waited to waylay him in a house on the side of the road, with a rifle: yet I knew no gun would save me. Allen wanted to know who this was, and what was meant by this. I proposed that it was

"FAR ACROSS A LOST LANDSCAPE"

one's own self merely wearing a shroud. What does this mean. It will be explained.

In the dream dreamed during the eclipse of the moorish red moon tonight, while the earth significantly turned, I was on the West Coast of America: in the true, real America, the mysterious Chinese-Egyptian America that we dream of. I guess it was St. Augustine transposed to Los Angeles ... in a land I've never actually visited, for all my 45 states. Here, on a kind of Denver University campus, were many young people engaged in some sort of Universal Production (an Eternal Hollywood.) It was to be a musical. There were songwriters, lyricists, singers, boys, girls — all wandering in the soft moony night on the campus and in Immortal Sodafountains. A girl sang the same song over and over again. The writers kept smiling at me, asking, "Good?" They all wanted my opinion. But I was very unhappy. I wanted to go back home to Lowell (an Immortal Lowell I've never seen) where, in my mother's house, I lived on my back half-sitting up on two elbows. (the realization of the elbows was the deepest, most difficult thing to remember about the dream.) This Lowell, far across a lost landscape (which was yet within walking distance) haunted me for the fact of so much unfinished business there ... concerning G. J., Scotty, Paige's Sodafountain, the

AN ETERNAL HOLLYWOOD

strange saloons, my mother, my *mad* father, and queer hilly streets like Mt. Vernon or Lupine Rd. etc. — I was unhappy in this spectral California, especially since I would have to travail to get back ... hitch-hiking and so on; and among the singers and songwriters it was not that I was so concerned whether they liked me or not, but merely that I might be happy or unhappy over the arrangement, the very scaffolded *arrangement* of the world. What right had I thus to presume on God's wisdom, eh? As a matter of fact, the young people seemed to like me. I say *seemed* only because I was not sure whether I like anyone there or not, or anyone in the world; and further, it seemed to me ... in the trance that followed, also ... that it was impossible to like anybody in this other world that haunts our sleep like the shrouded stranger — a mean and hellish and helpless atmosphere where it is clear that insanity is in the nature of things, is true, inexorable, where falseness is the only possibility ... to such a degree that one's ordinary machine-thinking about falseness and insanity begins to change. The world's upside-down but is the bottom of the world really gold? In any case, my falseness with the young people was something else with a different name suddenly, and my insanity ... quite, quite universal.

I walked along with one young man who confided his plans in me concerning the song

IN THE PIT OF THE NIGHT

he had written. But just before the conference of songwriters began I learned from a clever girl that this song was practically stolen, in part, from a famous semi-classical melody. I forget the name of the composer; I think of the names Buxtehude and particularly Beelzebub. So I entered the conference room armed with a long Knight's Lance, to use in this information about the song, though I quickly dropped the lance as "going too far" and tried to think up some other object without success. I stared triumphantly into all their faces; they sensed I had arrived with something to contribute, and smiled at me. He who smiled the broadest was that same poor young man whom I was about to obviously discredit ... although (here's the point of the dream) it wasn't so much that I was "betraying" him but simply that I was too insane to understand that he, being the same young man, would be "betrayed" by my disclosures, my contributions ... which were after all only the type of contribution the world gets from critics and such people ... he, being the same young man, seemed to make no impression on me, because I wished to address the entire company as a *body* — and for this purpose could blind myself to him individually. I stared blankly *into his equally blank face.*

What did this mean? All along, he too was insane and false — I have no doubt of

WHAT MEANS THE BABE?

now — and had the dream continued ... ?

But I began to fall into my waking trance for the purpose of re-membering and catching these things. I am a workman in an old moth-eaten sweater, complaining, sweating, hustling to catch the fresh dream — a writer, a fisherman of the deep — but someday I'll wear white robes flowing and write with a Golden Pen of Fire.

In my trance, sitting there half-awake in this queer house, I saw that there is definitely another world ... the world which appears to us, and in which we have our other existence, while dreaming. This is our Shrouded Existence. What means this?

Whatever ambiguous intentions we each have for being alive — for why should we live? — are rooted in our Shrouded Existence. Each newborn babe is a new ambiguity for this queer world. What secrets has the babe? — what means he? — what does he want? — what does he know? — what will he admit? Only a Celestial Tongue can tell. I know however that each of us is born in darkness, but dies in light. I have some doubts about an extension of this: is the darkness from whence we come, hell? — and is the earth in which we have our exis-tence, heaven? — or purgatory? I believe it is heaven we live in, and that when we die we are buried here in heaven forever. — It is hell we come from. What is the Shrouded Dream? It is the vision of hell from which we come, and from which we tend, towards heaven, here, now.

This needs further explanation, and is the most serious matter I can think of.

Love, for instance, particularly true, loving love in the bower, is the meeting of two Shrouded Existences in a tangle of shrouds. It is the moment when a man and his mate see the hell in each other's eyes, the hell from whence they came, and from which they tend in the LIGHT of heavenly life. We cannot admit that the other world is anything but helpless (no will), mean (unloving), and hellish; an abyss, over which "dove-like" we brood with spread wings; a lost landscape and flat on our back on two elbows. If we are to *admit* this world, this otherworld, as our ambiguous intention itself, we — we do not exist alive, but dead. But bear with my foolish hopefulness ...

I say that, being born in the darkness a Shrouded Infant, we come, ambiguous & secret, to the actual world, with a mission, a personal holy mission of light, which outs one way or the other. The dream is our reminder of darkness, the Shrouded Stranger pursuing us *on* to heaven which is great life on earth; and if we lag, he may catch us and cast us down in the darkness again —

But wait. First ... I believe in God on one level, I definitely do; I see God in the concerned heart and in the rainy night; but on another level, the Plane of Falseness and Insanity as in that dream, in that mean and helpless atmos-

YES, AN OZONE PARK DREAM

phere, I think nothing of the sort is allowed to exist. It may be true therefore that God does not, cannot possibly exist. He did not exist in that dream ... there was nothing. But when I woke up I realized all we were doing here was trying to do our best in whatever worlds we found ourselves. In a dream? — dumbly arranging and re-arranging the memories of other dreams, other existences, like file-cards, and so on — How stupid now!... all the secrets are rushing out of me, I have spilt no gold, & it's too late. But wait ... In the real world? Well, the little duties and involvements, something a baby cries about at first, (or Hunkey complains), even though that baby knows perfectly well he has a Shrouded Existence.

Supposing, dear reader, the Mystic Seven should approach you, surround you, and, in chorus ask — "What do you mean by your existence?"

And what means God by giving us this situation wherein we can't be sure of anything, even His existence? What is He trying to Say? Eh? "Care" is only a concern for this fact, that the world is mean and loveless maybe (but I did mention the change of thinking) — yet what is care? just an old-garb'd complaint of mine, & my family totem pole should represent just this dull, rheumy-eyed routine under a joyful sun ... a trifle silly and really, meanly unpleasant, no Lucien-goldenness. My old man and I, muttering complaints.

ALL ABOUT THE SHROUDED EXISTENCE

Yet what does my father know now that he is dead? Is there infinite light incarnate in his corpse, his cropping, mouldering, cracking corpse crumbled underground? Did he come from hell and is now buried in heaven? — or is there an actual celestial heaven incarnate in the sky?

Ah, this is all a puzzle, just like my dream, an arrangement of puzzle-cards, and cries: "What does *that* mean?!!" "And *this*?"

The Shrouded Stranger is oneself from hell.

Jethro Robinson got mad at Allen Ginsberg because the Shrouded Existence (whatever it means) really scares him and he does not want to giggle.

What is this ambiguity of existence, of intention, of meaning; communicating *what* from hellish depths? What is this evil genius of that dream, mine own.

O Immemorial Pearl!

The more men are born, the more die, the more light is dispersed from their graves. Therefore we must know more now than ever before, and so onwards. Yet why do the Egyptians seem silent? *Are* they?

Music hints the Shrouded Existence, but not only music, — musical language of course: the Celestial Tongue ... which holy Dostoevsky had.

What means God by giving us this kind of hand? for he is playing the game with us undoubtedly, the game concerning light and darkness.

A Chorus of Mystic Seven:

Allen, Bill, Hunkey, Neal, Lucien, Hal, and I.

Going about saying "What do you mean?" — which

DREAM, DREAM

would be the most important poll in the world. Or Eliot, Van Doren, Empson, Merton, Auden, Spender, and Dylan Thomas.

Or better — Dostoevsky, and others like him.

Our life on earth is heaven compared to this other hellish existence that haunts.

O dull journeyman putting down all your notes! (But necessary now, until I flow gold.)

The "unhip hip" who think more of awareness than of the beauty of it. This is why Allen is great. Today he said, "I liked him a lot on the Queen Mary" — and then bit his lip because it was such a strange, beautiful thing for anybody to say. This is the recognition of at least the beauty of *what we mean*. During my trance I got messages (personal?) of Allen's great mind. Perhaps he sent them himself? — "Bit his lip" is also the recognition of the awful-and-beautiful, hell-and-heaven. Therefore we must be awfully immortal, to recognize, whatever happens, that something's being *done* to us. O awful hell! — O beautiful heaven!

In "Town & City" George Martin arrives in the "riotous tinkling night of Times Square a dusty, shabby traveler from the desert of the night." And then goes to see an ambiguous, gray-worlded movie about queer people under a crooked roof. Ah.

And my mother doesn't want to be hid away like a "grandmother," she wants to mell in the ambiguous Easter Parade, where is the Queen of the May.

THE MOON

Having this dream, & the trance, tonight during an eclipse of the moon, has a definite connection not only with astronomical matters but with others far stranger.* The world swirled.

To be holy is to be in touch with the other world, in a naive trusting way?

Finally, the rainy night is itself a shroud; and rain and rivers explain, in an epic of water, how rainy nights come about; once come about, and with all signification, a rainy night can tell all ... and shall tell all 'ere this book is crammed.

—   —

*NOTE** Not long after the moon caused an earthquake in Washington State.

:   =   :   =   :   =   :   =   :   =   :   =

"The moon feeds upon organic life on earth." — Gurdhieff*

Therefore, when eclipsed, visions of eternal life may be most propitious.

I did not receive a vision comparable to this until Oct. 29–30 of this year, around midnight (recorded in looseleaf notebook) when a heavy

*G. I. Gurdjieff (1872?–1949), Greco-Armenian mystic, founder of the Institute for the Harmonious Development of Man.

fog, rare for N.Y., obscured the vicinity of Richmond Hill and perhaps deflected the moon partially. This vision, by the way, exceeded and superseded the one just described, and was on exactly the same (moonless?) level of apprehension.

MASSACHUSETTS

A BEGINNING FOR DOCTOR SAX

"I once hitch-hiked along the Merrimack River through New Hampshire and Massachusetts; and came at night to a dark place along the river where it started to rain, and I had to take cover under some heavy trees on the shore, where piles of leaves were still dry. There I sat, warm in my old sweater, in the glooming overfolded April darkness, by glistening waters. There were no lights except on the deserted highway where the town limits ended — rusty halos from dull poles hanging, with vain spearing from the Infinite Dark all around and overhead — I was abandoned in the woods, by the rainy river, in the loops & shadows of night.

Came a flash of lightning and lo! across the river, among trees, stood a castle with turrets that I had never seen before. It was on a hill right above the water, a queer manse with crooked roofs, and many dolorous windows, and weeds.

I never came back that way. But I have since learned the entire story of that castle. It is called the Myth of the Rainy Night."

—   —

The Merrimack could as easily be the *Susquehanna* at Harrisburg; or the *Willamette* at Oregon City; or the *Chippewa* at Eau Claire, Wisconsin; or the *French Broad* at Asheville; or the *Kennebeck* at Gardiner, Maine or the *Tennessee;* or the Mississippi at St. Cloud; or the *Missouri* at Jefferson City; or the *Red,* the *Arkansas;* or the *Sabine* at Logansport,

Louisiana; or the *Columbia*, the *Colorado*, the *Bitterroot*; the *Humboldt*, the *St. Mary*, the *Merrimac* in Missouri even; or the *San Joaquin* ...

THE OLD MAN OF RIVERS

NEW ORLEANS TO TUCSON — JAN. 1949

We left at dusk — waving goodbye to Bill and Joan and children Julie and Willie; and to tall, sad Al Hinkle and his wife Helen. Just Neal, Louanne and I in the big Hudson; bound for California 2,000 miles away. Wheeled through Algiers in the sultry old light — once more crossed on the dolorous ferry to New Orleans, by crabb'd ships at muddy-splashed river piers, by the bulging flood of the Brown Old Man of Rivers, and into the ancient slip at the foot of Canal Street.

Neal and I were still dreamily uncertain of whether it was Market St. in Frisco or not — at dreamy moments. This is when the mind surpasses life itself. More will be said and must be said about the sweet, small lake of the mind which ignores Time & Space in a Preternatural Metaphysical Dream of Life ... On we went into the violet darkness up to Baton Rouge on a double highway. Neal drove grimly as the little blonde dozed, I dreamed.

At Baton Rouge we looked for the river bridge.

And lo! my friends, finally we crossed the River of the Myth of the Rainy Night at a place magically known as Port Allen, Louisiana. O Port Allen! Port Allen! — my heart on your tidal highway doth spread and fall like rain, with love and an intelligence like unto softest raindrops. O lights! — lights at the river cape and at the port; warm, sweet, mys-

POEM OF RAIN & RIVERS

terious tapers burning here at the place of places where is the fruition of the fleshly rain. For rain is alive and rivers cry too, cry too — Port Allen like Allen poor Allen, ah me.

No, no — to cross the Mississippi River at night, at night in violet

Louisiana, Oh Inviolate Louisiana, is to bridge the Bridge of Bridges — to assume for once the dark, dear knowledge of a heritage which has yet no name and of which, poor heritage, we have never spoken aloud, and need not speak.

For what is the Mississippi River?

It begins in Montana snows and flows to the Mouths of the South ... to the Gulf that is Night ... and outward to return in Rain, Rain, Rain that sleeps.

O what is the Mississippi River?

It is the Water of Life, the Water of Night, the Water of Sleep — and the Water, the soft brown Water of Earth. It is that which has and does receive all — our Rain, our Rivers, our Sleep, our Earth, and the White Night of our Souls ... the Lamb that White Tears weeps.

And what is the Mississippi River?

It is the River we all know and see. It is where Rain tends, and Rain softly connects us all together, as we together tend as Rain to the All-River of Togetherness to the Sea.

For this is mortal earth we live on, and the River of Rains is what our lives are like — a washed clod in the rainy night, a soft plopping from drooping Missouri banks, a dissolving (Ah! — a learning), a spreading, a riding of

"LITTLE RAINDROP THAT IN DAKOTA FELL"

the tide down the eternal waterbed, a contributing to brown, dark, watery foams; a voyaging past endless lands & trees & Immortal Levees (for the Cities refuse the Flood, the Cities build Walls against Muddy Reality, the Cities where men play golf on cultivated swards which once were watery-weedy beneath our Flood) — down we go between shores Real and Artificial — down a long by Memphis, Greenville, Eudora, Vicksburg, Natchez, Port Allen, and Port Orleans, and Port of the Deltas (by Potash, Venice, and the Night's Gulf of Gulfs) — down along, down along, as the earth turns and day follows night again and again, in Venice of the Deltas and in Powder River of the Big Horn

Mountains (name your humble source) — down along, down along — and out lost to the Gulf of Mortality in Blue Eternities.

So the stars shine warm in the Gulf of Mexico at night.

Then from soft and thunderous Carib comes tidings, rumblings, electricities, furies and wraths of Life-Giving Rainy God — and from the Continental Divide come Swirls of Atmosphere and Snow-Fire and winds of the Eagle Rainbow and Shrieking Midwife wraiths — then there are Labourings over the Toiling Waves — and Little Raindrop that in Dakota fell and in Missouri gathered Earth and Mortal Mud, selfsame Little Raindrop Indestructible — rise! be Resurrected in the Gulfs of Night, and Fly! Fly! Fly on back over the Down-Alongs whence previous you came — and live again! live again! — go

MISSISSIPPI RIVER NIGHT

gather muddy roses again, and bloom in the Waving Mells of the Waterbed, and sleep, sleep, sleep ...

God bless Life, oh God bless Life.

Then, with the radio on to a mysterious mystery program (and as I looked out the window and saw a sign saying "USE COOPER'S PAINT" and answered: "Allright, I will.") — then we rolled across the Hoodwink Night of the Louisiana Plains to Opelousas — and towards the Bayous at DeQuincy and Starks; where we were to read the Chinese Manuscript of the American Night.

But first we stopped for gas in Opelousas.

In the rickety streets of the soft & flowery night of January's Louisiana, I wandered into a grocery store and came out with a bread and a jar of cheese. Every *cent* counted if we were to reach Frisco. There was no one in the haunted store. We rolled on across the dark pasture-plains of the delta south; playing more mystery programs on the radio.

We passed through Lawtell, Eunice, Kinder, Ragley and DeQuincy ... western rickety Louisiana towns becoming more and more a Sabine-like bayou country; till finally between Starks and Deweyville we passed over a dirt road through the bayou wilds. An elevated road, with mossy trees on each side, and hints of darkest swamp-water, and no road-lamps ... sheer snaky dark. The mansion of the copperhead, the moccasin, & the mottled adder; drooping vines, silence; star sheen on dark ferns, and the reeds of the mires. Neal stopped the car and turned out the lights.

We were in the silence of this mireful, drooping dark.

LOUISIANA BAYOUX

The red "ampere" Lutlon glowed on the dashboard ... the one red eye in the swamp of the dark. Louanne shuddered and squealed. Neal turned the headlamps on again; they but illuminated a wall of living vines.

Then we crossed the Sabine River on a new bridge and zoomed on over the Neches (these secret swamprivers of the Deep South night) into oily-fragrant, dark, pinpoint-sparkling, misty, vast, mysterious Beaumont Texas. (NOTE: North of Eunice is *Ruston,* Big Slim's rickety hometown, his home in Louisiana; I thought of it at Eunice. "Maw, I wanta be a hobo someday," Wm. Holmes Big Slim Hubbard said to his mother as a child in Ruston.)

But now Texas, the East Texas oilfields; and Neal saying: "We'll *drive* and *drive* and we'll still be in Texas at this time tomorrow night." Across the beginning of the Big Texas Night, across the Trinity River at Liberty, and on into Houston and more hints of Bayou Dark.

Evocations of Bill's old house here in 1947 ... of Hunkey, Joan, Julie, Allen & Neal; and the Armadillos. And Neal driving the car through haunted night-streets of Houston at 3 A.M. reminiscing of former beat adventures with Hunkey, on this corner, in that amusement center, in that bar, down that street. The rickety niggertown. The downtown commercial streets. A Houston wrangler suddenly roaring by on a motorcycle with his girl ... a poet of the Texas night, singing: "Houston, Austin, Dallas, Fort Worth ... and sometimes Kansas City, sometimes old San Antone." Neal singing: "Oh look at that gone cunt with him! Wow!"

We get gas and proceed, now, towards the range-West I so dearly want to see again ... to Austin ... through Giddings and Bastrop. I sleep thru Johnson City and wake up at Fredericksburg. Louanne is

TEXAS RAINY NIGHT

driving, Neal is sleeping. Louanne and I talk. It is cold; there is snow in the bunchgrass hills. It is the worst winter in western history. I take over the wheel at Fredericksburg and drive carefully over snowy roads through Harper, Segovia, Sonora, about 200 miles, while they sleep.

IMPORTANT NOTE: I just said I slept from Houston to Austin. I had forgotten that I drove that night in a lashing rain while they slept. At Hempstead, near the Brazos River, in a haunted rain-lashed rickety cow-town, a raincoated cowboy-hatted sheriff on horseback (the only human abroad in the abysmal muddy night) directed me to Austin. Outside of this little town, in the rain-mad night, a car came in my direction, headlights flaring. Rain was so heavy the road was but a blur. The headlights were coming right at me, either on my side of the road or I was on their side. At the last impossible moment of this blurry head-on collision, I swung the car off the road into the flat shoulder of deep mud. The car backed up. It had forced me off my own side. In the car were four sinister men, drunk, but grave.

"Which way is it to Houston?" I was too stunned and dismayed to demand that they help me out of the mud. Also I didn't want to get mixed up with them in this rainy wilderness. The rainy night in Texas, and in the American wilderness past, is not at all protective, but the greatest of menaces.

They went off towards Houston at my mute direction.

Then I woke up Neal and for half an hour, while Louanne was at the wheel, we kneeled in the mud in torrents of rain, and pushed ... pushed the very night.

We finally got the tormented Hudson out, and got all wet and muddy, and cold and miserable; and it was then I slept, to wake up to the snows of Fredericksburg. Neal lets Louanne and I drive because he knows that each one at the wheel knows precisely what to do, though we might deny it, and "everything takes care of itself, everything is all right." (NOTE WITHIN A NOTE: When I went to Frisco again in August of some year, Neal's shoes in the closet had not been cleaned yet of their cake of Texas mud from that night.)

In Sonora, to return to the next day, we repasted on bread and spread-cheese, and Neal drove then clear across the rest of Texas. I slept some and woke up in the orange-rocked, sage-brushed Pecos Canyon country, in golden afternoon light. We delightedly talked of many things, blasted, and finally all three of us took our clothes off and enjoyed the sun in our bellies as we drove westward into it at 70 miles per hour.

Ozone ... Sheffield ... Fort Stockton. I told them of my idea for a western movie using all of us in an epical cow-town and our likely transformations in such an atmosphere: Neal a wildbuck outlaw; Louanne a dancer in the saloon; I the son of the newspaper publisher and occasional wild rider on the plains; Allen Ginsberg the scissor-sharpener prophet from the mountains; Burroughs the town recluse, retired Confederate colonel, family tyrant, opium-eater and friend of the Chinese; Hunkey the town bum living in Chinese Alley; Al Hinkle the haunter of gambling tables ... and so on. (Good idea for movie story someday.) We visited an old stoneheap monument Spanish church-ruins in the sagebrush, naked under coats.

Then on towards El Paso and Tucson.

NEW ORLEANS TO FRISCO VIA TUCSON — JAN. 1949

I slept through Ft. Stockton and Van Horn and woke up at Ft. Hancock
near the Rio Grande River. Another river! It was late afternoon. We descended, as I say on P. 44, from the plateau of Texas into the great
world-valley that separates Texas from Mexico. Rolled under valley
trees through Fabens, Clint, Ysleta, with the river and the reddish
mounts of Mexico on our left. Neal told me a long story about the unbelievably repetitious radio station at Clint, whose program he used to
listen to in a Colorado reformatory. Just records, Mexican and Cowboy,
with repetitions of advertisement for a "high school correspondence
course" which all the young wranglers in the West at one time or another think of writing in for ... because, uneducated, they feel they
should have a diploma of some kind.

We came into El Paso at dusk. It was to be a year and a half later
the same Neal and I would make the amazing jump from Texas into the
Indian land of Mexico. But now our eyes were bent on Frisco and the
Coast. However we were so broke it was decided something should be
done in El Paso. To be honest, we thought of hustling, in some inno-
center way, with the attractive blonde, but nothing ever came of it. It
was cold as fall in El Paso, and grew dark. We buzzed the Travel Bureau
but no one was going West. We lingered around the bus station to persuade would-be customers of the Greyhound Bus Lines to switch to our
Slow Boat to China. Actually, we were too bashful to approach any one,

THE KID ON HIS WAY TO OREGON

even the college boy who watched Louanne so flusterdly (she was giving him the works for exercise.) Neal finally ran into a 'buddy' — some
dumb kid from reform school who said 'Let's go mash somebody on
the head and get his money.' Neal made him talk, and laughed, and enjoyed, and ran off for five minutes with him, while L. and I had our-

selves a ball of sorts in the car. So it went, in the dark sidestreets of El Paso and all that desert in front of us and no gas-money. Finally Neal returned and we decided to chance it to Tucson, Arizona, anyway, where my friend Harrington could feed us a meal and lend me gas money. 'On the way,' Neal said, 'we will pick up hitch-hikers and get a half-buck from each one; that's 2 gallons and forty miles.' Well, right outside El Paso, after we skirted the Rio Grande in its Juarez night all a-glitter over yonder, and reached a main highway, there stood our first (and last) hitch-hiker. Forget his name, but he had one embryonic, useless hand, was about eighteen, quiet and sweet natured, and said he was going from Alabama to Oregon without a cent ... home was Oregon, poor kid. Neal liked his sweetness so, and him too, that he took him on anyway "for kicks," and that is the goodness of Neal. Off we went towards Las Cruces, which Neal had negotiated earlier on his way to our meet in North Carolina, and now we actually had "another mouth to feed." I slept through Las Cruces, in the back seat, and woke up at dawn to find the car stopped on a mesquite mountainside, everybody sleeping, Neal at the wheel, the Kid beside him, Louanne in the back, and a cold fog at the car-windows. I got out to

REFERENCE MADE TO TRIPS WRITTEN

stretch my legs and look at the West. It was very cold indeed. But what a scene met my eyes when the dawn-fog dispersed and the sun appeared all of a sudden over the mountains. I didn't know where we were, but it was in the vicinity of Benson. Dewy cactus, red gold sunrises, giant mists, a purity so intense it takes a city man a double take to understand what he's seeing & smelling — and hearing from the birds. Trucks far down the mountain growling on the dew road.

(The rest of this trip is carefully and completely recorded in the 1950 "On the Road" of Dean Moriarty and Sal Paradise — the trooper in Benson, the stay in Tucson, the Okie hitchhiker outside El Paso, the drive thru Techatchapi Pass & Bakersfield & Tulare & on into Frisco where I had the Market Street Vision)

----------------------*----------------------

LIFE, LIFE

T-NOTES — Here is how I think we look at each other & get to know each other in this strange existence of ours. (Isn't it strange?) We all know what a certain someone is when he is alone, we have our private portrait of him, sometimes even a set, loving image. (How this "loving image" can be shaken when we see someone who has changed over the years.) The private portrait of someone is so funny, so awful, so very beautiful: especially someone we love, — that is, dote upon? — IN just this way, when I saw Joan's rocky, gaunt, red face after a year — and she was so pretty, so plumpishly German once — my "loving image" of her underwent a kind of defamation. It is that serious.

But the main point here: when someone we dote upon turns to us from his immortal solitary posture and seeks to speak to us, to communicate, to cadge, cavil, enjoin, persuade, anoint, or impress, with appropriate expressions and exertions, we see, instead of the loving image, a kind of horrible new revelation of reality, so suddenly existent, and forever, so ineradicable too, and fear for ourselves and our poor private portraits and notions; we quake; yet at the same time, in a kind of sweet simultaneity that *redeems,* (and life is so full of redemptions we never acknowledge!) we also see the dear 'routine' of this person, his manner of 'coming out' to us, that pitiful admixture of pride, deceit, shyness & underlying real regard, tender hope, and all, which is seen to have existed before anyway, and is compared and noted with regard to other revelations, & related to the loving image again — again — and again.

I have had the pleasure of noting this in the way that Louanne watched Neal over many days & nights of driving. First she sullenly, ruefully observed his set, rigid posture at the wheel while he drove; his little demonstrations of will & vigour in the way he flicked the car around curves; and most of all, his hangjawed wonderment as he suddenly fairly forgot he was not alone and dwelt in his "eternity," with sad silence. She would sit there doting over his sullen air of male self-containment, his absentminded rumination, his very *bulgant* face; then a small smile would come across her face, because she was just so amazed he existed, and that he knew her, and was so amazingly himself all raging & sniffy & crazy-wayed. Ah, that smile of hers, that which all men want from their women, the smile of tender dotage & sinister envy. And she *loved* him so much — so much so that she would want to keep his head in some secret place, there to go and gaze at it every day; or one of his hands; or feet ... the bony manliness of him.

But, lo! there was Neal suddenly turning to her, seeing her (with absorbed afterthought), realizing she was watching him *that way*, & realizing she was there, and smiling the false, flirtatious smile of his. I, in the back seat watching, and Louanne in front, would burst out in simultaneous glee. Moreover, Neal, far from being "found out," or disturbed or anything, would merely grin the way men grin when they know people are laughing at them because they love them and see them: a grin of knowing consistency lightened by a mixture of watery, good-natured buffoonery, & self-acceptance. This is by the way one of the few human gestures without words, a wordless realization that one is after all funny.

ARIZONA THINGS

ARIZONA

Some notions: in Wickenburg, in 1947, tho it was a hot desert day, dry & sunny, I saw a man and his wife and kids in a small buckboard dragging trees from their yard, in the shade of many trees: it was a kind of joyous Arizona suddenly. This was all later confirmed when I travelled up through Prescott, Oak Creek canyon, and timbered Flagstaff, where, in high woodsy airs viewing distant desert-horizons far off, one feels the peculiar joy of canyon country, high country, timber country: a kind of mountain gladness (is it not logical that the yodel originated in the mountains?) When crossing the Colorado river near Indio, you see an Arizona of desolations ... especially near Salome ... a desert, with a shack a mile off the road every 30 miles or so, and crossroad towns — and far off, the Mexican mountains where the gila monster sung himself; and mesquite, gopher holes, cactus, buttes, lonely mesas way away.

In the mountains near Benson it is a kind of heaven at sunrise — cool, purple airs; reddish mountainsides; emerald pastures in valleys; the dew; the transmuting clouds of gold.

Tucson is situated in beautiful flat mesquite and river-bed country overlooked by snowy ranges like the Catalina. The people are transient, wild, ambitious, busy, gay; downtown bustles & promises to bustle much more; it is "Californian."

Fort Lowell Road, following riverbed trees, is a long green garden in the mesquite plain.

EL PASO & TEHATCHAPI, CALIF.

TWO VIEWS — EL PASO & MOJAVE

There are two interesting vantages in the West I can think of where you can see unbelievably vast valleys — valleys so all-inclusive that they floor three or four rail roads, and you can see locomotive smoke miles apart simultaneously puffing.

There is the valley of the Rio Grande as seen from east of El Paso. Here, at reddening sundown, we drove over a long straight road under trees (a riverbed road again.) To our left, across the river, across the green farmlands, were the jagged mountains of Mexico — a reddish wall, a monastery wall too, behind which the sun seemed to be setting, sadly, to the accompaniment of some brooding Mexican guitars we heard on the car radio. I am sure there were no better way for me to see Mexico for the first time. And to think of night settling down behind those mountains, — ! in secret, soft Mexico, a purple shawl over their vineyards and dobe-towns, with stars coming on so red, so dark; and perhaps that Moorish moon.

Straight ahead the valley seemed to drop us off some topmost level of the world, down to territorial slopes where the separate locomotives toiled in various directions ... as tho the valley were the *world*.

Same thing just before the town of Mojave in California, in the kind of valley formed by high Mojave's plateau descending to the west, with the high Sierras of Tehatchapi Pass straight ahead north: again, a bewildering view of the ends of the world, & the rail roads in the various distances, like smoke-signals going from nation to nation. And *after* Tehatchapi?

A view of the whole floor of California!! (Bakersfield.)

COLORADO

THE DIVIDE   May, 1949

The Continental Divide is where rain and rivers are decided ... and in the shadow of this central event in the myth of the rainy night, dwell now I. Westwood Colo. might have, should have been called Foothill Colo. This is where I live. I am watching the wrath of sources here ... and the Lamb is in my bed.

And here too, the melodious airs and rumorous murmurs of summer afternoon, — in Colorado fields — vast afternoon excitements blowing in from the Plains — and to our west the severe yet smiling mountains of day.

I am Rubens ... and this is my Netherlands beneath the church-steps. Here I will learn the Day.

NEW YORK TO DENVER; MAY, 1949

The trip on which I spent 90 cents for food, in order to save money in my search, in Denver, for a house in which I dwelled when I wrote words on opposite page 70. Took a bus all the way. As we rolled out of New York at midnight, and as I fondly remembered A.'s love-bed of an hour before (Spanish girl), and as I contemplated this important move in my life which would consume my first $1000 advance from the publishers but would settle the family once and for all, as we rolled on into the red, red night of America, towards that home-town Denver, I sang the following song:-

> "Been to Butte Montana
> Been to Portland Maine
> And been in all the rain —
> But tell my pretty baby,
> I ain't goin' back to New Orleans;
> Tell my pretty baby
> I'm goin' on home to Denver-town."

I had intense visions of the sheer joy of life ... which occurs for me so often in travel, coupled with a grand appreciation of its mystery, & personal wonder.

After the usual run to Pittsburgh over the uninteresting garden-like drives of the East, in this case the Pennsylvania Turnpike, in a hot noon I got off the bus to wait for the Chicago coach. Walked in downtown Pittsburgh to find a cheap lunchroom.

Was already weary from the night's traveling.

PENNSYLVANIA — OHIO RIVER

I found a lunchroom and had two 5 cent cups of coffee with some of my sandwiches. (Let me repeat that I was practicing an ascetism necessary to my soul & my plan for the folks, even though Paul the night before, after driving me to the bus station in N.Y., had spent almost $5 on a movie & parking lot. Possibly I spent only 90 cents on this trip to Denver *because* of that. I should have *foreseen* enough at that moment.)

The trip to Chicago was more interesting. In the lullal afternoon we rolled into the Pennsylvania hills with their mounds of dug-out sand, and scarred mine-sides, and general doleful industrial ruination — although green else about. At Weirton, West Virginia, it was pretty much a town risen from these things — a mining town, haunted by scarred mountainsides beyond each sooty backstreet. Main Street was a beehive of shopping activity in the Friday afternoon, the excitement of a work-week ended ... men in shirt-sleeves, women, & children.

Yet the moment we crossed the ever-so majestic Ohio River on the other side of town, and rolled across the bridge, to Steubenville, Ohio, it changed — from mining-country bleakness to a Wabash-like shore of soft trees; even though it's a kind of factory town, Steubenville.

In the late afternoon we rolled across a hillier Ohio than that I had known before northwards around Ashtabula & Cleveland. (Joe Martin itinerary.)

At dusk, into the spacious avenues of Columbus.

Then on to Indianapolis, Indiana, across the moonlit night. I watched the moony fields

INDIANA — ST. LOUIS

which in the Fall, as I had seen them Fall of '47, are shrouded in a moon-mist & haunted by the frowsy shapes of harvest stacks ... Indiana corn. But in May-night, Indiana is precisely that which you feel when you sing "Oh the moon is bright tonight along the Wabash" — so I sang it. Later, I conversed with a fellow-passenger, a young actor named Howard Miller, from Muncie, Indiana, who had lain in the night long ago dreaming of Broadway, and was coming home to work in his father's grocery store awhile. He reminded me of Hal Chase.

After Indianapolis I fell asleep, in spite of the beauty of the night and its moon, and woke up just as we rolled into East St. Louis, Illinois, about nine in the morning. I had known all about this wild old town from Burroughs before ... a redbrick river-town. Was not chagrined for sleeping, as I knew the land between Indianapolis & St. Louis from previously.

Across the bridge! — across the Mississippi River! — under morning sun-clouds! — in cool May air! — into St. Louis. *Again I crossed the River.*

I shaved in the men's room of the bus station, using a young fellow-passenger's razor — a psychiatrist, of all things; then took a walk to the riverfront, where I'd been before, and loafed on a corner, like a veritable young Wade Moultrie.

Back to the bus — and across the beautiful afternoon of Missouri, with its balsamic odours of clover, fresh-cut hay, & sun-warmed, rich earth. Whole vistas of this.

MISSOURI AFTERNOON

No land could be more fertile than Missouri land. It is still odorous from the relatively recent presence of the River — rank with greeneries. There must be more beautiful trees in lush Missouri than anywhere in the world. And such fields, such ripeness, such summerlands! No wonder Missourians are vain of their home. No wonder Mark Twain's "Campaign That Failed" was such a pleasant failure.* In this world of fields, knolls, and hazy green distances, I almost regretted we would start climbing the gradual climb to the Higher Plains, to the Kansas prairies, & Colorado rangelands, for say what I will about the West — Missouri, and Illinois with its enchanted rivers, Indiana and Ohio, and New York State & New England, & all the South ... represent the soft, sweet East of this world, as distinguished from the wild and

---

* "A Private History of a Campaign That Failed" is a short story Twain wrote about his brief stint as a Confederate soldier in Missouri in 1861.

arid west — and to make a choice between the two is like tearing out & examining the foundations of one's heart, where all ideas about life are stored. Shall it be the soft, sweet life of the Idyl? ... or the wild & thirsty life? The life of enclosed horizons, the life of the sweet trees — or the life of vast, yearning plains. What does it do to any town, That at the end of its street at night, one either sees the *groves* of night — or the *desert* of night? Citizens take deeper note of this than they know.

MISSOURI

Somewhere in Callaway county I got off the bus and took a walk from the way-station into the heart of these lovely drowsing greeneries. It was dry & hot; there were cows; I sat in the grass. I wished I lived in Missouri — especially in afternoons.

We had passed through St. Charles & Warrenton: we now proceeded to Columbia, and at Boonville cross't the mighty Big Muddy. Pathetic that I should dwell so much on earth & rivers ... for Boonville is one of the most ironic & ugly-souled towns in this world, and I do Love-of God no honor in avoiding issues of men. Boonville (a beautiful town outwardly, with ancient trees, shady streets, old houses) is remarkable for its preponderance of old men, octogenarians who look like Civil War vets and crawl along the sidewalks. Nothing wrong in the freedom of many old men, except that there is a large boy's reformatory in Boonville — those who can walk, may not; those who cannot, may.

I slept some on the way to Marshall. It rained. Somewhere along the line we picked up a poor slatternly woman and two children. I sat one of them on my lap; and he never budged an inch, or said a word, and ended up taking my hand in perfect understanding that I was his good friend & father-like fellow traveller. No "rich kid" would behave like that, but in little Missouri Ozarkie it is natural. Part Indian.

At Lexington, in the gray rain, the magnificent Missouri River showed its big face to me just as rainbows bloomed. A huge island split it into two wide, muddy channels.

This is a great river of rivers. I think the Mississippi is less patriarchal. The Missouri is wild & beautiful. It comes from stranger sources than Minnesota — nameless sources at Three Forks (the Gallatin, the Madison, the Jefferson) which are not *names* for what is up there, and will never do for me. — I opened the window to smell Big Muddy. A man from Kansas City conversed with me.

We entered Independence, or that is, bypassed it, and I saw no signs of what it used to be in the days of [Francis] Parkman not Truman.*

We entered Kansas City. I checked my bag and took a 5-mile walk down to the railroad yards overlooking the confluence of the Missouri and Kansas Rivers, an airport, and amazingly high levees. You can see the flood danger. The Missouri has a mean flow at this fork.

I walked back uphill through the old K.C. riverfront warehouses & meat packing plants; past fruit markets where extremely strange old men sat with extremely strange old dogs — in a long sunset. I noticed old K.C. and the new high-suburban one uphill — just as St. Paul; a city moves away from its original source, with all the brash forgetfulness of an ungrateful child grown fat & silly. But I cannot judge this century; besides I love this century; only, I love the last much more ... or, in a different and personal-interesting way.

I walked up Broadway far as W. 12th St. It was Saturday night, all humming with excitement in the heat. The buffet bars are marvelous places.

*Francis Parkman wrote of the Missouri River in his classic travelogue *The California and Oregon Trail.*

NEW YORK TO DENVER, MAY 1949, (CONTINUED)

I walked in the downtown section; entered a tough poolhall-bar; had a beer in a buffet, & went back to the bus. I kept thinking how hot it was in Kansas City and dearly, eagerly, joyously looked forward to climbing out of the low Missouri Valley, to that place of my hopes —

High on the hill of the Western night
Denver, where the stars are wild ...

I even sang this, tho I forget the exact words. I invented this song for motorcycle wanderers of the midwest night. He is in hot K.C., he wants to zoom down to Tulsa and Fort Worth, or out to Denver, Pueblo, Albuquerque — anyplace but here, in the hot Missouri night. He wants to go *up the hill* — and what a hill! — to where it's cool and clear and starry. At nine o'clock our bus rolled in that direction. Across the river, and zooming to Topeka.

In Topeka, I had a terrific frosted strawberry malt in a wild bus station on Saturday night. A crazy motorcycle kid, without any preamble, all decked in boots & studded cap, told me he had just wrecked his new motorcycle. He was proud as hell, and mad-eyed.

The bus zoomed on along the Kansas River to Manhattan. The prairie grew more desolated — it was dark out there. I kept my window part opened; the ladies in back of me complained. I slept a little. That psychiatrist who had traveled to St. Louis — what in the hell for was he coming out here to

THE PRAIRIE NIGHT

psychoanalyze such wonderful people like that motorcycle kid? Which is best — wreck a motorcycle on a Saturday night, or stay home reading Freud? What is the earth for — what is the night for — what is food & strength for — what is man for? For joy, for joy.

In Manhattan, about one o'clock in the morning, it was wild and crazy. At the end of the streets you could see & mostly sense that great, wide, impenetrable prairie darkness, the likes of which exists nowhere else in the world. Though you cannot *see* the plane, you can *feel* that all this is in flat, black endlessness — that it is all around, and once blew tumbleweed, and still does. I once saw a cheap movie about Kansas with Randolph Scott and Robert Ryan, and though it was probably just filmed in a California backlot, somehow — by some accident and some love of my attention — it seemed just as I saw Manhattan, Kansas, that night ... it was a ghost town ... at each end-of-street nothing but the wall of dark, and hugest humming silence of an entire territory of grass rustling in the wind, and little feelings of blown dust quietly in the darkness, dust from hundreds of wide miles away. The feeling that there are no hills, no roads — just grass, just flat.

Though Manhattan, Kansas, in 1949 was not surrounded so wildly, so desolatedly any more, it was still *true* to its past — almost truer.

From out of this incomprehensible desert of

MANHATTAN, KANSAS

night came wild careening jaloppies driven by drunken boys. They roared into town at the other end, abruptly from the plains, and were suddenly zooming around where I stood in crazy U-turns. Above, the sky was black; as black as the walls at street's-end. They paid no attention to this. They wanted to go in the wild dance-bar which adjoined our bus-stop lunchroom. They piled out of the cars. A fight was developing among the revolving doors; sides were lining up; girls were peeking from the bar windows. Time and again I looked around us all at that incredible plane of darkness; never have I been so aware of the existence of man on his dark plain, in his pit of impenetrable night; his furies within it; his comings & goings, carelessly, on the *plane* of his haunt, his earth, his cruel & sightless, huge universe. I was also awed, on another level, by the great wild joy which existed here, *further in* on the plains from K.C. and Topeka; as though, isolated and doomed off from the life of cosmopolitan cities, they here took on the craziness of the native coyote instead. I never saw such crazy kids ... the way they drove, the way they wanted to fight, the way they ate and drank. No old folks were in sight, just kids in a haunted town in the plains. The smell of the night was sweet ... a prairie May-night — the smell of the Kansas River, of hamburgers, of cigarettes ... and that strangely haunting smell of gasoline in the air.

KANSAS-NIGHT COW

On our way in, just outside Manhattan, near the bend of the Big Blue River, our busdriver had rammed into a cow on the highway. Everybody made jokes about steak. It was a terrific bony concussion. In Manhattan we all signed as witnesses to the event — an event which struck me as being sad. An old white-faced cow, in its world of darkness, its rummaging, foraging, joyous, peaceful existence, doth cross the hot pavement of man from clover to sweetest clover — musing perhaps — and out of the dark comes the monster with the blazing eyes and the sign says 'Denver' — and WHAM! Dead cow; cloven brain-pan; blood on the hot road, on the hot radiator. To this — from the incredibly sweet moment-before. For a cow in the night, with all the sweetgrass in the prairie to loll over, has thoughts of its own in the secret wides out there ... thoughts which are not far from mine when I ride by.

This is my elegy to the *Kansas-Night Cow*

KANSAS-NIGHT COW
Bovine skull, so lately stored
With cuds of grassy thought,
And eyes a moment before
Which kenned dark plains
And airy deeps — stairy-secret,
Ghostly, white-faced, silent cow —
Thou nun of night in prairies —

347

I sympathize with thy bones
All broken on this hot highway.
　　The fool eats hamburger of thy doom
　　Yet learneth nothing of thee so shy.

WEST KANSAS WILDS

— Finally I slept, and as the bus made its slow upward mount to the High Plains, dreamed — but what it ever was who will ever know or understand? Someday we'll all have died and nothing settled ... just the forlorn rags of growing old,* and nearer, to the bleak affinities of grave & history. Woke up, having slept through Abilene, Salina, *Ogallah*, — in Oakley, where we all had breakfast in a ramshackle inn in the cold gray morning.

At Cheyenne Wells in sunny Sunday morning a blue eyed cowboy got on the bus & smiled at everyone as he hustled his bag to the rear, his clothes smelling of the clean Plains — his smile so sincere & open everyone was embarrassed & looked away — and I knew we'd reached the True West. This same cowboy told me where to go in Denver for fieldhand work.

Afternoon thundershowers partially hid the wall of the Divide as we rolled down East Colfax into Denver.

That night I'd finally contacted Brierly and he flashed his spotlight on me on the corner of Colfax & Broadway, our meet.

Inside 3 days I has the cottage out Alameda Avenue & was cooking

---

*Kerouac would put this image to use in the heartwrenching final line of *On the Road:* "the evening star must be drooping and shedding her sparkler dims on the prairie, which is just before the coming of complete night that blesses the earth, darkens all rivers, cups the peaks and folds the final shore in, and nobody, nobody knows what's going to happen to anybody besides the forlorn rags of growing old, I think of Dean Moriarty, I even think of Old Dean Moriarty the father we never found, I think of Dean Moriarty."

up steaks in the backyard & reading cowboy stories in the furniture-less house at night, HAPPY!

DENVER TO SAN FRANCISCO, AUGUST 1949
— Recorded in Sal Paradise Novel 'Beat Generation' (originally titled 'On the Road', 1951)
— The pimps with the Travel Bureau car, the God-clouds at Utah border, the old huts & covered wagons in Nevada, Frisco in the glittering cold night, Neal at the door at 29 Russell Russian Hill house naked-

SAN FRANCISCO to NEW YORK; AUGUST 1949
(Trip carefully & completely recorded in Sal Paradise "On the Road" (1951) — the jazz in Frisco, the trip in the Gag Plymouth, the Talk in the Backseat, Salt Lake City & Neal's broken thumb bandage, Denver, the Carnival night, Ed Uhl's ranch in Sterling, the Cadillac Limousine to Chicago, Detroit, the Chrysler to New York.)

NEW YORK TO DENVER TO MEXICO CITY: 1950
(Trip in Sal Paradise *On the Road* (1951) — the kid in the Ft. Wayne pen, Kansas City, selling his suit on Larimer St., Neal's arrival in a 36 Chevvy in Denver, Frank (Jeffries) "Shephard," Bru, Ed White (Vi, Tim Gray) trip thru New Mexico & Texas to San Antone, Laredo; whorehouse in Victoria; Jungle at Limon; Sierra Madre road; Zumpango Plateaus, & the Valley of Mexico.)

MEXICO CITY TO NEW YORK: AUGUST 1950
Ferrocarril de Mexico Pullman to Laredo Texas — then bus to San Antonio — to Baltimore — to N.Y.
    (with a kilo of cured shit 'round waist in a silk scarf)–   –

—   —

: — SONG — :

I left New York
Nineteen forty nine
To go across the country
Without a dad-blame dime.

———————

T'was in Butte Montana
In the cold, cold Fall
———I found my father
In a gamblin' hall.

———————

"Father, father,
Where have you been;
Unloved is lost
When you're so blame small."

———————

"Dear son," he said,
"Don't a-worry 'bout me;
I'm about to die
Of the pleurisy."

———————

We headed South together
On an old freight train,
The night my father died
In the cold, cold rain.

———————

"Dear son," he said,
"Don't a -worry 'bout me;
"Lay me down to die
of the misery."

———————

Oh father, father,
Where have you been;
Unloved is lost,
When you're so blame small.

———————

NEW YORK TO SAN FRANCISCO; DECEMBER 1951
Recorded in VISIONS OF NEAL
(1952)

Jack Duluoz
(Jog in cold Pittsburgh, beans in Chicago, old maniac in Omaha —
Nebraska blizzards, bench in Big Spring — snowfields of old
Wyoming, — Nevada, gamblers, snows of Truckee, Sacramento bus
station, old Lawyer W. C. Fields on Frisco Graymist).

—   —

SAN FRANCISCO TO MEXICO CITY, APRIL 1952
IN THE 1949 Chevvy station wagon with Neal, Carolyn & kids,
straight to border at Nogalez, Arizona — then on alone in second class
bus to Navojoa, Culiacan, Matzatlan & Guadalajara & the City, with Enrique Villanueva as guide & buddy — the greatest trip. ("Culiacan"
story has part of it.)

("Lonesome Traveller")

WILD NIGHT IN BROWNSVILLE

BROWNSVILLE TEXAS TO ROCKY MOUNT, — JULY 1952

Hitchhiking all the way, with a 5-dollar bill and a big packbag — No time to stop cause I wanta be home for 4th July — Start off walking from Mexican bus across Matamoros, out dusty streets, to border, American guards, & into Brownsville — out to connecting highway, where I'm picked up by Hotrod Johnny Bowen of Brownsville who wants me to have a beer with him — A few beers in roadhouse — Now he wants me to drink with him all night — wants me to get a job in Brownsville — He is a crazy lonely kid — wants me to go see his pregnant wife — we drink and do, she throws him out (they're separated) — Wants me to meet his Drive-In sister, she says "I don't wanta be told who to go out with" — he's crazy

— He plays pinball machine all up & down the highway, we get drunk, drive 100 mph thru intersections, play pool with a buncha Mexicans downtown Brownsville one of whom "borrows" $1 from me & I so drunk I give it, out of my 5 —

At dawn I'm broke — we sleep in his house, Texas cottage — Next day I'm sick & also dysentery fever

— Have soda, he gives me back my $5 — I go out on road & am sick in gas station toilet — sit a long while resting — Then I hitch — Got 3000 miles to go — Immediate ride to Harlingen along endless fence of King Ranch, with old hillbilly who hearing of Mexican whores thinks it wd. be a good idea to bring a truckload to Chicago — Long wait in hot sun at Harlingen, I drink cokes, — Get ride to Rosenberg Texas from young Mexican medical student — Then spot ride into Houston where drunken construction worker invites me into his motel room for shower & when I come out he on his belly naked begging me to screw him — I leave, wont do it — he's crying — I get ride from little faggot who owns Dandy Courts, says "Hitch out here in front of my court (motel), if you don't get a ride come in & sleep" but I do get ride from oil truck driven by wild talking rhythmic Cherokee Indian mentioned on p. 74 of DHARMA BUMS, to Liberty Texas at dawn, where I sleep on railroad loading platform — There ride with flat truck carrying pile of black-eyed peas in bags, we stop to fix load under "tarpolian" he called it, thru Beaumont to Baton Rouge — Hot sunny highway I suck on flavored ice in a cup, get a ride up to Mississippi from some pleasant Mississippian — Many spot rides thru the night, little towns, to Jackson Miss. — One guy picks up another hitchhiker a strange pale blond kid coming back from a Billy Graham revival meeting! — I wind up in mid of night in sleepy village of Newton Miss., no rides whatever, in fact no traffic, I just sit on curb in hot summernight sad, try to sleep a little in tiny bus station, sitting up head on war bag — In the morning a fine breakfast strengthens me (I ate so heartily tourists stared at me, pancakes & eggs & toast!) — Bam, a sudden ride from a fine gentlemen, kinda hip, in a new car, takes me up through Montgomery & Tuscaloosa Alabama & on up thru Georgia where he buys me great meal of Southern cornbread, blackeyed peas et etc (great restaurant on curvy country road) & up through stopping in Tobacco Road crossroads for a beer among the strange Georgia Crackers, funny! — then up to Florence S.C. at dusk, end of ride, long ride, where I call Ma long distance & then hitch, getting final ride from big fat Walter Brown of Baltimore chugging 30 miles an hour up swamps of S.C. & southern N.C. (stopping midnight in diner with 10-year-old girl plays "Rocket 69" on jukebox) & Rocky Mount at dawn — Hungry! Exhausted! Grateful! Broke! Gaunt! Home!

DOWN TO CAROLINA

NEW YORK TO SAN JOSE — FEB. 1954
Wearing silly new tan Dragnet raincoat & carrying 'essential pack' for Baja California hermit life but inside temporary expedient American

suitcase, walked home & Ma's love in cold night to Sutphin (wearing railroad gloves, earflap hat, 2 jackets under coat, 2 shirts) (& two pair jeans!) — E train to Port Authority, & thus began a voyage I shouldn't have taken — Bus to Washington at 10 P.M. — Sitting relaxed in front-up seat, practising rest & meditation, avoiding looking, thinking — bus takes NJ turnpike and rolls uninterrupted to Delaware, the Howard Johnson's only flashing by — At H.J.'s I get out and stand in cold deep-breathing — At Washington it's a little warmer, dawn, sun, I get off bus and hurry to Virginia bridge, stopping first for free breakfast of Farina, toast & eggs in Cafeteria — walk over bridge & realize awfulness — all these details — my hand hurts — thousands of cars raging around in a gasoline stink, haggard faces don't care, I abandoned bleakly in evil blank universe — Why didnt I go back home then? Would have saved $250 — But it was an 'instructive' trip. At the rotary drives with (earlier) Neal & Louanne & Hinkle I'd driven around in snow, now I stood, on cold brown grass, cant get a ride — Walk further. Finally near Pentagon a businessman picks me up — we talk of mushrooming population of Washington & Alexandria (when I get there I realize I know & remember & can talk about everything). — He drives me to outside Fredericksburg where I have quick snack in ice cream stand & cut out, thumb, for ride from Negro truckdriver ambitious, married, smart, quiet, like Willie Mays — Ride to Richmond, bleak, in cold gray I walk stretching truck-tucked legs, to junction, where ulcer-suffering carpenter rides me — I advise him to rest & think nothin, — All this time I've been radiating mental peace in silence to my benefactors & now I speak a little wisdom — He is surprised and interested — Drops me at James River bridge where I buy $60 of Traveller's Cheques foolishly, in bank, thinking I'll hitch all the way to San Jo-say ————

Ride from guy who sells used cars, his brother behind him somewhere on road in their own car — Driving he is to Sanford, N.C.(!) — Good ride — I relax — We go thru Petersburg, South Hill, Novlina, Henderson, (all fated places. In So. Hill a dozen times I've passed, The Universal Ghost in All of US) — thru Raleigh, Sanford. There I tried to get a good night's sleep in a railroad hotel by the seaboard tracks, & did — Fine bed, old hotel, brakemen & conductors in the old lobby playing cards — I drank my brandy a bit — Practiced dhyana at dawn, resting mind from dreams of sex with "Eddie Fisher's Jewish girl" — Great freight trains balling by all night, B W A M ! — Sad mist nightlamps of Carolina-like Obispo but another, sadder railroad) Dogs & cocks at dawn ...

Morning, big sausage & eggs & pancakes breakfast; bought nose inhalors, cough drops, gum; stood on road (Hiway No. I) at 9 A.M. fresh & ready for California.

Sinister bad luck — the foolish look of my raincoat shoulderstraps & hat with earmuffs, like eccentric killer on road — No rider — Walked 3 miles up a hill, out to country, angry — Finally, ride at afternoon, late, from big Armand, Okie, to Southern Pines — beautiful burnt gold warm afternoon with sough of pines & fragrance — Wanted to sit down there, why go 3000 miles to sit down & be Buddha?

Ride from non-committal soldier swiftly to Rockingham — Where, night falling, I buy ticket to Los Angeles at little Greyhound station, giving girl my precious $60 Travellers Checks — Waiting for bus I wander Saturday Afternoon streets among farmers & feed stores & conversations of sidewalks — Buy a bag of peanuts but clerk didn't tell me they were unroasted but eat them anyway in empty car fender lot, for proteins — amen, Negro children — One peanut has worm in it I can tell, as I swallow soft salty rot of something sad soup & crackers in North Carolina beer lunchroom with fat funny jokesters — Crazy conversation in street with Negro bus porter who tells all local histories, I radiate him mental peace — He tells of local Negro family had just slaughtered all its hogs & smoked them for the year & fire burns down house & hogs & feed & furniture, all — (just the other night) — Sun sets on sad little countrytown — Bus comes, crowded, I give my seat to old man to all as far as Charlotte.

Then in the night to Spartanburg, and Atlanta at dawn. I see the Southern Railroad tracks —

To Birmingham Alabama and Bessemer, vast mournful city with Negro shack slums & Sunday morning bicycles —

At Columbus Mississippi at noon I go up little hill to Faulknerian Sunday mainstreet and eat Duncan Hines lunch of soup

SWEET ESCAPEE IN JUAREZ

& exquisite croquettes & Caesar salad & homemade invisible lemon meringue pie that melted away — among Southern aristocrats in suits talking of huntin & fishin.

Across Mississippi all Sunday afternoon with hills suddenly dropping into flat Delta and passenger tells me local news & says lots of snaky at last delta hills — insisted on sitting with me to talk — We cross spectral Faulkner countries & I hear his dialect — till Greenville Mississippi at Sunday Night silence at last Mississippi Gene's hometown) and I take quick walk to levee and see great silent river moveless, in the peace & old Showboats now Nightclubs tied at shore — and haunted trees of Arkansas Huck Finn 'cross the way — crossing the Mississippi once more —

Across the night to El Dorado Arkansas where suddenly I look up & see the stars & feel great joy and say:

Release yourself sweet escapee,
Death owns bones;
But Infinite Emptiness
Of pure perfect Mind
Who how much owns?
All, all of it

———————————

Dallas at dawn and take quick brisk walk around streets, after shave & puttin on jeans, and buy bag of fresh donuts & eat them with coffee in bus station — All day across Texas in the crowded bus — stop at Boomtown Odessa where I walk & get soup in lunchroom — whole town brand new, long on the highway, rich, useless, lonely in the vast plain with its oil towers mistlike on endless horizons — On to El Paso, arriving 8 P.M. — I walk quick to railroad hotel and get stuffy inside windowless room but sleep —

In morning I get out for day of exploration of El Paso & Juarez — Clear blue sky, warm sun, redbrick sorrow & fences this side, dusty gray dobes and sad dry earth of Tarahumare other side of Rio Grande — Get big pancake breakfast in American Mexican restaurant — whole town Indian, rickety, secondhand clothing stores with ancient sheeplined cowboy coats — I go across sad railroad plazas of dust to Juarez Bridge & cross for 2 cents — into the blissful peace of the Fellaheen village at hotsun noon — smells of tortilla, drowse of children & dogs, heat, little long streets — I go

A TARAHUMARE AFTERNOON

clear out of town to river levee and squat on ground & see America across the way and on this side an Indian mother kneeling at the river washing clothes with little baby son clinging lovingly to her back as he stands there — Thought, "If my mother was only simple as to do her wash at the river" — Felt happiness. But no-good drunken kid insisted on talking to me, bumming Bull Durham, offering tea, etc. — But I get him to talk Tarahumare dialect for me — We stroll — He explain- it Mexico — he's a good kid actually but stoned — We met two hipsters in a field who look like gangsters, which they are — they beat my Indian for his money sometimes — I avoid them and they cut, zoot-suited thru the bushes — In the field the ancient farmer and his wooden plow and his peace — Across the river the SP yards, spuff up smoky heights head West for Lordsburg & Yuma — It never occurs to

357

me to continue the journey by SP freight — Ole 373! The Zipper! — (next time)

I give kid 99 cents for tea & he never returns, going up into bare sand humps where Indians forage in junk up to their knees — Family are building new adobes — I meditate in sun on levee, cruiser goes by & vanishes — I put on shoes & roam the junk hills of the Tarahumare of El Paso — I circle way around — find tattered Mexican comic books — pass Indians taking shits in plain sight of women — examine how dobes are made — Watch Tarahumare dobe-makers knead manure and mud with shovels then dump it in frames and smooth and remove frames & leave block to harden in sun — Indian seeing me watch says, smiling "No sabe?" — I go back to downtown Juarez, roam in markets selling desert cactus and herbs & mysterious seeds & roots, wow — dig girls, cant stop looking at brunette lovelies — Have beer & raw oysters in cool bar — Beers & write in guitar-singer bar — Visit railroad station & dig funny yardgoats & boxcars &

BOOMIN TO YUMA

big fiesta crowds milling round station platform in hot sun — I eat coconut delicacies & sit on rail — sit in sun listening to guitar singers near bridge, on sidewalk with back to wall — Next time I get straw hat and practice "siesta" meditation in streets of sweet Mexico — Return to El Paso, buy for $2 an Army field coat with huge pockets, go to dusty hike & dance alley & sit while little Negro girl plays around me — Give her Mexican gumballs — Go to El Paso station & roam around in hot red sun — rest feet in park — Get on bus at sundown, roll across redness —

Lordsburg at night, big freight pulling in from West as we stop rest stop — I rush out and buy bread & butter from almost-closed Chinese grocer and rush back to bus and three hoboes off eastbound freight panhandle me but I got nothin — They say they coming from California — Young Big Slim hobo says, "We been over that San-Luis-Obispo-*Bump!*" — hump! —

Bus rolls in night, I eat bread & butter humbly as two soldiers goof in backseat loud — Tucson in midnight, nice & warm, dark desert invisible but downtown lonely bright like Denver — On to Yuma, at dawn, where I sit on Yuma Yardoffice bench up a flight of wooden stairs from the bus station, watching SP freights coming east & west, & spread butter on my bread & eat like student just in — In empty lot below I see mesquite bushes with still pieces of the yellow alogoraba pod hanging, one of Indian desert mysterious delicacies — (ripe in August) — Bus rolls on in opening dawn into Imperial Valley, to El Centro where cars parked diagonal on broad lonely Main Street — Beyond strip of irrigated agriculture the Imperial Valley is a desert — Orange groves, cotton — new houses — On into San Diego desert of rocks and cactus and lone sand hills — I see the Little Agave out there, with cabbage below and 12 foot stalk reaching up, the

STORMY MASON

great desert delicacy of the Cornhusk Indians — not a sign of em — nothing — a great lone desert for the hermitage, full of hidden food & water (kopash cactus has water inside) — But grim — On into San Diego, warm, sunny, down off the desert mountain pass — (Forget to mention Jacumba, stop between Yuma & El Centro, on the border, thus, birds at misty dawn & a man walking out of the trees of Mexico into the American sleepy border street of shacks & trees & backyard dumps) — (Future place for me) —

San Diego rich, dull, full of old men, traffic, the sea-smell — Up the bus goes thru gorgeous sea-side wealthy homes of all colors of the rainbow on the blue sea — cream clouds — red flowers — dry sweet atmosphere — very rich, new cars, 50 miles of it incredibly, an American Monte Carlo — Up to LA where I dig city again, to Woody Herman's band on marquee — Get off bus & walk down South Main St burdened with all pack and have jumbo beers for hot sun thirst — Go on down to SP railyards, singin, "An oldtime non-lovin hard-livin brakeman," buy wieners and wine in Italian store, go to yards, inquire about

Zipper. At redsun five all clerks go home, yard quiet — I light wood fire behind section shanty and cook dogs and eat oranges & cupcakes, smoke Bull Durham & rest — Chinese New Year plap-plaps nearby

— At 7 I get foolishly on Zipper caboose and talk to rear brakeman as train is made up — BRAM! SLAM! brakeman struggles to fix mantle and lamp and start coal fire — Conductor is Stormy Mason — Doesn't bide by my papers, order me out of the caboose — train is underway to Santa Barbara

— "Then get on out there, you cant ride in here or I pull the air!" — I curse and go out crummy door and light lamp (leaving gear in crummy) and tender brakeman tells me "Be careful" and I climb up ladder at last boxcar's side and run over walkramps keeping lamp un-lit until watching switchman finished thinking I'm a hobo and yelling "There's a flatcar

"HE DONE MADE A BUM OUTA ME"

up ahead!" because if lamp lit they be confused — That's me! — all over! — and as train rolls & clacks I run & jump & come to flatcar, which has big machiners lashed on (SP trucks) and I get under & sit & sing "He done made a bum outa me!" and for first time in months, in cold rushing night air of California Golden Coast, uncork wine & drink up — raw, bad, rotgut — but I warm and sing all the way —

It gets cold in constant nightwind so I wrap up in my coat & huddle & freeze & sing —

At Santa Barbara I've had enuf but I see there's nothin but cold misty swamps beyond the tracks, & the cold seashore, so I wait till Stormy Mason is gone from crummy at his run's end & sneak back 12 cars to empty caboose, remove suitcase & bring it back to the flatcar, where I unpack blanket & wrap up & drink wine — Soon new crew gets Zipper underway for San Luis Obispo.

Now comes colder bleaker grimmer coast of after Gaviota, up by Surf, Tansair, Antonio

— I don't dare even look but over wild clack of wheels huddle & meditate, shivering — under stars — At San Luis Obispo, straightshot run, I get off shakey, no more wine, I get off before train stops, at roadhouse, & walk down to old Colonies Hotel of my brakeman days

— Closed, asleep — So I go downtown among familiar bleak palms & cottages to hotel & pay $1.50 for room & sleep, tearing up SP timetable & throwing it away "No more SP for me!" Blue morning I eat donuts & go out on 100 and hitch — Bah! I see a freight is leaving over overpass & I could have hopped it! But a ride comes just then from a crazy guy ex-infantry in new car, and up the San-Luis-Obispo-Bump we fly, to Santa Margarita, arriving one hour or 40 min. before the freight — So I have soup in ole familiar sweet Margarita where I'd made my first student-run breakfast & seen the

THE GOLDEN AGE IN A BOXCAR

Pome sectionhands at dewy morning — Bar that sells little bags of beef jerky & pinon nuts is closed, so I buy candy & sit in siding grass near my old hillswinger's shanty (to which I no longer have the key), in hot sun on moist ground wait —

Here comes the train, because an Eastbound is a-comin he'll stop — I get on engineer's side of tracks, right where I'd dreamed of the murderous hoboes chasing me (!), and calmly get in a boxcar, not a soul in sight —

Soon we start & on we go to Templeton, Hanery, Paso Robles, Wunpost, and on up the Salinas Valley

— The great riverbottom at Wunpost, another place for a bhikku hermitage!

— Hot sun pours into wide open door, I drowse — Train heads in at Templeton, I get out and lay in green bankside, still & happy, bliss, ignoring calls of hoboes 10 cars down — This where we'd had our break-in-2, conductor MacKinnon, & I'd talked to some bo's in my brakie past — Toot toot, I get back on as slack echoes up and on,

— We fly to Salinas and Watsonville in the hot delight of California in the afternoon — And I think "Death is the Golden Age."

At one point I force myself to throw up all that bad candy —

At Watsonville, familiar sad Watsonville, now only 50 miles from my goal, I get off, walk to west end of yard, sit in grass by the piles, & wait for next train — A little sick

— Meditate — Passing hobo sees me & lets drop one of his free cabbages — Later I pick it up & munch on it — My nausea disappears!

Red sun is like liquid in the rails — Night, purple, Watsonville across the lettuce fields & my old Pajaro river-bottom lights up sad — I ask harder about next train

— Soon I see its number

— I make sure, asking car-knockers, & get on in dark

— At 8:30 we thus

THE MOON OF SARIPUTRA

roll right on out to Aromas and Chittenden, to sleepy Gilroy again, & sweet Madrone, & Morgan Hill, and ole Coyote, & into San Jose — by this time I'm dancing and singing at top of my lungs in the whole big rattling black boxcar, glad, healthy, full of raw cabbage & guts — Arrive S.J. yards where I drop off my boxcar east of the yard-office so none of the familiar brakemen see me — As I wait at crossing for crummy to pass, so I can get out on Neal's avenue bus line, a switchman, seeing me, with pack, thinking I'm trying to get on eastbound rail, says, "Get on the Zipper, she's leaving in a minute for LA!" Ho! — I go to gas station & call Neal — He comes to get me in his jaloppy that makes our voices hum & throb as in a dream — I buy beer & we talk all night. I tell Carolyn "Do you realize that you're God!" I run the parking lot for a few weeks, getting kicks, playing chess in the shanty with Neal getting high in the afternoon of old — Every night after supper I go & sit under a Western Pacific railyard tree in a field, a great unfolding infolding bodhi tree, & meditate under the stars an hour — sometimes in the cactus grove I sit, & hear the fieldmice snore — The moon of Sariputra shines down on me and the long night of life is almost over. — Adoration to the Buddhas!

July 26 1950
Richmond Hill

— — — • — — —

GONE ON THE ROAD

CHAPTER ONE: An Awkward Man

It all began when I came awake and a terrible, certainly most terribly beautiful thing was TAKING PLACE only for a few moments but enough to make the change in my life that led to the events I implore God to help arrange in my mind so I may bring them to light.

It was I had no idea what time of day or night, behind drawn shade that on first waking seemed like something else, in a rickety old hotel room with a crooked ceiling, all in a city impossible to remember that this special awe possessed me *in* the space of five or six seconds in which I completely lost every faintest, poorest, most woful recollection of who I was, and may the Angels of the Eternal Dream bear witness.

So in the moaning void — of — my hollowed mind, the realization came unimpeded like an unkind dream that I was growing old and I would die; just when, in the late afternoon outside, early-waited leaves were flying in their first Autumnal wind and everywhere all forlorn window-panes rattled up the new winter.

Then by some means I don't recall, from the darkness of my pillow, I saw that the smoky railyards, where freights were slamming, which I could see through a chink of shade were — the railyards of Des Moines, Iowa, "of course, naturally," and I remembered who I was be-cause I remembered why I was there (which was) to find a job within a few days, or certain I'd go hungry soon.

July 26 '1950
Richmond Hill

GONE ON THE ROAD

*

An Awkward Man

CHAPTER ONE: ~~A Lonely Man~~

~~Here is what happened.~~ It all began when I
came awake and a ~~most~~ terrible,
certainly most terribly beautiful thing
was ~~happening to me~~, TAKING PLACE ~~that~~ only for
a few moments & yet enough to make
the change in my life ~~that~~ led to the
events I implore God ~~to help me~~
arrange in my mind so I may bring
them to light, BACK ~~for the~~
~~of all concerned, the dead is alone back~~
It was I had no idea ~~how I~~ what time
of day or night, behind drawn shades
that on first waking seemed like
something else, in a rickety old
hotel room with a crooked ceiling, all
in a city impossible to remember
that this spectral awe possessed me in
the space of five or six seconds, x
in which I completely lost every faintest, poorest, most woeful recollection
of who I was; ~~& I~~ # So in the
moaning void ~~of~~ my hallowed mind
the realization came unimpeded like
& may Angels of the Eternal Dream
x or the ~~Blessed Angels~~ bear witness.

In a proud dream of life, like life after death of an angel that has died,

I lay as if revealed, in bed, to a mighty gaze that became, in time, more personal and merciful and assumed a voice, reproachful, even friendly and complaining in tone like the voice of a dead ancestor, tell it because my own ancestral voice as it grew dark.

Stranger in the earth, who are you? How come you to make by thoughts such as these in your living days? The city, the city — how could you tell what city it was, just what poor place you brought yourself to sleep, to rest your numb and broken flesh. Lord, Lord, Chicago, N.Y., San Francisco — what does it matter? You are growing old, you will die, and you lie a bed, on the first Autumn night, alone. They'll husk the corn before the coin could open your eyes, and you will die no less. Where will you go? What will you do? And doing what in this sad old hotel by the tracks? Where is your father, your mother, your wife, your friend? For are you made to groan in these pits, shafts, beneath these crooked roofs, these levels, staircases, and balconies, all, great dusty racks and dear & trustful dark, these mysteries your position so makeshift and foolish among them, just to forget your father, your mother, your friend, your wife in the grave beneath these? Lest you open your heart to the hints of sweet light pouring somewhere near?" It did seem to me there was such delight at that instant.

Won't you hear my plea? My plea in this, too: you loved me when I was yours, if you hate me now I'm old it's too much to bear. I did love you quite a bit as a youth — a real youth-like youth I was — and had secret plans for our future, always thinking, whenever I took a shower on a hot day in Manhattan, at once I was in the Adirondack cabin with you; when I dried with a towel, it was to rush to meet you at the convertible so we could dine at a mountain lodge. This is what I dreamed for you in our future. Even though it's so absurd now, I still dream it. I'm going mad again; I've been full of reason for years, ever since we went our different routes on this gnashing map. All life is barbs now, when once, like for Tony, it was bombardment of grace.

Thou that comest from a perfidy of dirt waking in this dark house of eternity that leans beneath the molten clouds — not knowing if up-stairs, downstairs, in the back or in the cellar — orphan, scrub of the mysteries — not knowing which eye watches you — what your name is — loveless, friendless, love — shade of a rack of days — go home, go marry yr. love, another winter's come and catching you."

And I had grown old.

I felt my arms, my chest, my belly, which had become soft unmuscular flesh it seemed in only the past few months and for no reason for I'd worked & worked. Rising apprehensively, I stared in the mirror to see the damage of the slob, grieving, all-grieving at the sight of it, astonished at the suffering face I saw, fairly horrified by the drawn, hooded eye that looked at me.

Gone on the Road   That's what Dean says, when, after his green-tea visions, someone leans over the couch and asks how he is. "Gone on the road ..." Life is a road-journey, from the womb to the end of the night, ever stretching the silver cord till it snaps somewhere along the way ... maybe near the end, maybe not till the end; maybe early in the journey.

Where are we all? Gone on the road ... What's at the end? Night ... whatever Celine meant by giving death that name, whatever kind of death he meant.

The Saint's Thoughts

This world, which made us, but only imperfectly, that is to say unsuited to its every barb and to most of its inevitable commandments, is I now think but the place of preparation of our souls for the other world, where perpetual ecstasy shall finally prevail, unfleshed and all in the immortal mind, for all of us. Therefore this world, for me, is losing its own importance (what do I care if the wind makes the leaves rustle? (or the sun shines on my flesh, or by the same law that I cannot make love with a woman 24 hours a day) and, year by year, the contributions that it makes to the formation of the other world, by slowly building a universe in an unending series of dreams, night dreams, unconscious dreams, sleep dreams in which I am awake as never before and in whole landscapes my life is one perpetual amazement and love, *ecstasy*, in brief, is taking in the only importance at least left for me.

This world is bad. Sinister nature, that made Jacobs predicate the Lord around a bunch of stinking goats, has given over to sinister art, that entombs men in mines, blows up innocent bystanders (at the war front) and sinks sailor-souls into perfidies of salt with all their useless steel.

My aim is to find good. I shall not find it in such a world, for which I was not made I believe I shall find good in the other world.

The Second Coming is the death of each man when he steps, weary of this, amazed into the next and cries in his dying flesh, "So this is what I was made for! Glory be to God!"

I have nothing but sympathy for all of us.
I definitely feel everything is
   coming to an end; I hear the
     bells ringing.

Nature is just a great big vegetable. Nothing happens in it. To me it's just a desert, a waste, of time. I will not wait within it. The grass rustles, the wheat takes too long to grow. I will not eat any more wheat. The grass is adapted to this world, not me. I need ecstasy at once. Failing its appearance, I rather will die, and go into my own world which is all our own world, and find my love immediately there. This world seems to wait unsympathetically on anything I am about to say or do Very Well Then, this world is not mine and I owe it nothing. I never asked to be made, and so unsuited born. I only ask, now that I am alive and conscious, for the ecstasy which my soul requires. I know where it is in the other world. I shall go there when it is ready for me, and that is soon enough.

Nevertheless, nature has instilled in me the refusal to die, and a dark determination it is, wherefore this world like a gallstone weighs heavily in my patience and makes me cry, and sigh, and seek, in vain, for the ecstasy I know will only come much later after much sweat and useless hankering.

Did I not say it was a waste of time?

Why do you suppose people are always sighing when they sit around a table?

Why has God been so cruel to his living creatures?

Because this is their only means of preparation for ecstasy of the eternal dream to come.

In this work I will deal with this world and its connection with the other world as it appeared in dreams to Roger Boncoeur, the Walking Saint.

I ain't afraid to roll in the bottom of things.

(How can people be so furious in this metaphysical void? — that's what a *living narrative* is.)

Music is a dream.

The flesh has ceased to mean anything to me. What does it matter whether I gain the meager satisfactions of the penis or not? What has that foul, insuitable, lame worm to do with me? — even if it fills at the sight of a thigh? So no? The sun goes up, the sun goes down — so? The sea is golden; does that make me golden? does that make me salt

What's *me*? *Me* is that which want to be amazed without natural cessation, in an eternity of ecstasy.

Rules? Laws? To me, *what*?

I am free to want what I want.

I want uninterrupted rapture. I believe this has been made manifest to me in dreams, and in music, and in the pages of Dostoevsky, in the lines of Shakespeare, in sexual joy, in drunkenness, and in being high on tea. Why should I compromise with anything else or with the "Bourgeois" calm of the backyard lawn, The Edgar Guest* concession to wild, wild happiness.

On tea I have seen the light. In my youth I saw the light. In my childhood I bathed in the hints of light; I hankered, eager.

I want a blaze of light to flame in me forever in a timeless, dear love of everything. And why should I pretend to want anything else? After all, I'm no cabbage, no carrot, no stem! a burning eye! a mind of fire! a broken goldenrod! a man! a woman! a SOUL! Fuck the rest, I say, and PROCEED!

I was fascinated by everything that pertained to this girl and to her life, her man, her thoughts. All too soon I would never see them again "Hoik!" I cried in my mind. The stars above became a manifestation of my rapture at the discovery of these mad new people, (Even then I was old, so old.) She told me all about herself of which to this day I remember nothing, of course; and why should that be of boon or beneficence ? More anon, more anon.

Suffice it to say, all at once her boy woke up, she called him Roger, he walked over to us, I watched amazed and ... it happened. The old man with a white beard marched out of the night into the circle of light.

The first time I met Laura was in a place called Dilley, Texas, at three o'clock in the morning on the road, in summer of 1941, in the months before Pearl Harbor. That time of strange innocence and of strange ro-

*Edgar Guest (1881–1959), English-born popular American poet; known for his simple, happy poems, Guest was often called "the poet of the people."

mantic flavor when jukeboxes played Artie Shaw's forlorn clarinet all over the nightland and kids thought it was magnificence to go follow the howl of a train to the source of rich heroic truth. Obviously nothing of the sort was found. In fact how can I forget a poor friend of mine, a Dakota kid, son of a railroad brakeman, whose ambition it was to be a beachcomber in California; who delayed doing so till the Army drafted him, and made him a medic, ending up on the beach at Peleliu beach — combing among washed-up salt corpses.

MADE BY THE SKY

Is it a sin to my loved ones that, being made by the sky, I cannot sit quietly with them in this vegetable world in which they see greatly valuable things; that having a grave in my mind, and being a poet, and one of many emissaries sent from the sky to go through this world, a spright, watching its shape and form of things (not having to "know how it works") before receiving that thoughtful post in heaven so blue when I shall have seen it all and shall know the duties of the Creator's wishes, I must strive my poor abilities in this rounded skull to greater work and cannot enjoy the benefits & peace of lettuce nature. Besides which I am naturally unable to understand it, not being born of the apple womb, only its son. What is that iron wheel that flies through the vegetable roofs of city night? It is the genius of the hierarchal inventors of Western Civilization, most complete & most knowing of the heavenly combinations to come, to whom, like Burrows, I stem an idiot child because not being of the vegetable world, and not of theirs, where then do I come from and from what universal purpose?

Most lonely of men, no beak, no claws, no squawk, they wonder at this careful, gentle, secretive passage of mine through things — if they wonder at all, and mayhap they do not.

Many are chosen, few came

This world, through the ragged means of civilization, which in the West is Utopia-seeking, may go through a gate of iron now, wrath, into an earthly Utopia that shall have crowned the meaning of Utopia, which is how to die gently; or explode and go at once, bypassing the problem of death, to the eternal world when the Heavenly Wheel shall begin the forming of its spokes and rack. Other planets, other worlds, may contribute long after us, but in Heaven we shall not be impatient. The Eternal Wheel is Infinite joy. My thoughtful post up there ...

To stare into the heart of it and bring back my knowledge to the angels of the rack, the poll of The Universe, but doing so under great fleshy duress, without nicety, in my weakened hands — born thus, of course, for sky is sky — and not loaf my honorable sending, is my life.

I'm really willing to be conscientious

I am not bored and depressed at moments we describe by these words, but near the point of death for all purposes worth mentioning. Death ... death ... and nothing else. I have to be joyful or I die, because my earthly position is untenable in gloom and I betray God in spite of myself therein.

I don't have to go to museums, I know what's there ...

Journal during First Stages of On the Road

All of a sudden, in the mail,
a Texas Univ. (Austin)
brochure listing autograph
manuscripts including my
78-page diary in pencil
of 1748-49... and a
picture of the first page
... a diary I didn't know
I ever lost! —
    So I look over my
remaining diaries & find
that the great "NOTES"
diary of 1947-48 is also
missing! This latter diary
was definitely stolen in
Northport only this last
year. Who? What else
was stolen, like from the
file cabinet? My friends —

Back in the early 1960s, when Jack Kerouac was living with his mother in a modest home in Northport, New York, comfortably situated in Long Island's famed Gold Coast, an essentially homeless Gregory Corso came to visit. Even more than Allen Ginsberg's, Kerouac loved Corso's exquisite poetry, considering "Gasoline" and "Marriage" the literary highwater marks of the so-called Beat Generation. While the two artists enjoyed swapping tales and catching up on old friends there was a tension between them. Corso had become a heroin addict, and junkies, sometimes glamorized in Beat lore, are notoriously untrustworthy: a point Kerouac's mother, Memere, drove home when Corso showed up at their door.

At some juncture during that strange visit, Corso, desperate for money, stole a seventy-eight-page pencil-written "On the Road" journal (1948–49) from Kerouac's vast archive. A criminal poet great at casing rooms, Corso, in fact, purloined one of the most valuable items from the collection: an early meditation on *On the Road* morphed with the development of the *Doctor Sax* concept. After telling Kerouac good-bye, Corso headed into Manhattan where he sold the notebook to the House of Books, LTD in New York — located at 16 East 60th Street — for a few hundred dollars, enough "bread" to purchase plenty of "smack." Meanwhile, the House of Books sold the manuscript to the University of Texas at Austin for $1,000. "Herewith the Kerouac notebook," bookseller Marge Cohn wrote to Warren Roberts at the Harry Ransom Humanities Research Center at the University of Texas. "I think I should charge extra to have myself fumigated after having Gregory Corso here, what he needs is a bath and not a bed."

The four months which this journal spans include some of the most noteworthy events in Kerouac's life to date. In January 1949, he takes his first road trip with Neal Cassady. That journey, fictionalized in part 2 of *On the Road*, is touched on briefly in this notebook and is covered in greater detail in Kerouac's "Rain and Rivers" travel journal. He returns to Ozone Park, New York, in mid-February, and then in March *The Town and the City* is bought by Harcourt, Brace. Editor Robert Giroux accepts the manuscript, in part, because of an enthusiastic recommendation by Columbia University's professor Mark Van Doren, an expert on twentieth-century literature.

Because this stolen notebook has long been available to scholars to study at the Ransom Humanities Research Center, we did not include it in the hardcover edition of *Windblown World*. There I chose only previously unavailable diaries. But since many Kerouac devotees can't make their way to Austin I decided it would make a suitable "postscript" for the paperback edition. With only a few minor edits the stolen journal/diary appears here for the first time.

Douglas Brinkley
New Orleans
December 2005

MONDAY NOV. 29 — That's 32,500-words since I started on Nov. 9, or better than 1500 words per day ... per sitting, very high. Altho this is only the first draft, and I still have no idea where I'm heading with it, I delight in the figures, as always, because they are concrete evidence of a greater freedom in writing than I had in Town + City. However, who knows about the quality? I have been sitting down + writing with perfect equanimity, and I hope I can go on like this from now on and write a great many good books all intertwined. Still — lately — I've had a feeling of emptiness ... *not* boredom, just emptiness + even falseness. These are not the reverent, mad feelings during Town + City, altho I'm convinced it indicates "artistic" growth; as for "spiritual growth," I can't say at all ... yet. My whole feeling + knowledge now is concentrated on people, and not beyond them in the realms of "spirituality" — (I do believe.) So a new notebook (the other one was sloppy to write in due to the bulge of the pages.) This is better. These absurd little interests in notebook-paper are connected with the gravity of early boyhood diaries. We need out *petit* absorptions like campstools in the wilderness. (How neat.) Tonight wrote **1500 words**, good ones too. To bed reading anthropology.

TUESDAY NOV. 30 — No news from Little, Brown yet. Wrote **1000** words in the afternoon. A little bored in the evening ... finally a sort of fit of rage, which I tried to face during a walk and saw that it was a paranoiac attack (daydreams of destruction.) This I can't understand ... and the source I'll never see. I was just mad at everything, in a mean mood, picturing myself shooting at cars who bore down on me in the street and choking people and "making up my mind once and for all." I can see all this with knowledge, but where it stems from *inside* — and even my psychoanalytic investigations (I always pounce reluctantly on the "answer" that seems most absurd) seem stale and nowhere — where it actually comes from I don't know. This hasn't happened to me in some time, now, especially since I started to leave the house regularly to go to school and see the others. Whatever names we give to this — frustration or whatnot — it is still undiscoverable and the most dangerous thing in our lives. I used to call it "moods," but now I want to "exterminate the brutes" by complete self-honesty and no equivocation in calling it a mood that's inevitable. It may not be inevitable at all. John Holmes says he wants "honesty and safety and knowledge." His use of the word "safey" is significant of his sense of danger in delusions, either self-delusion as in a fit of rage, or mythic delusions of others as in fascism.

But where does this moralizing get me unless I get the details, the "life of it"? — and the life of that fit tho short-lived, was all complex and rich with details I didn't grasp. Next time, then ... (and we'll get it.) Wrote **2800 words** at night, and also read a lot of Stendhal, + [Harry] Slochower's crap.* It is perhaps Stendhal, and the vision of Hal, that depressed me partly — but the rest?

DECEMBER —

WEDNESDAY DEC. 1 — wrote **500-goodly words** in the afternoon, completing "Tea Party," a very good chapter. "On the Road" it appears now will slowly grow into a great book and I shall have learned at last how to really write. There is no more of the heaviness of T + C and as much, if not more, of true beauty. I'm proud of the progress in Road — I got a great letter from John Holmes concerning my work and especially my "journals" I let him read. The thing is so comprehensive I can't mention it like this — but will do so in dribbles — and on the whole I find he is great. It is a guy who refuses to let life slip out

---

* Harry Slochower (1900–1991) was a New School professor and a prolific writer whose work spanned philosophy, literary criticism, and psychology.

of his hands — intense he is, and avid with interests. His vocabulary may be heavy with expressions like "come to terms with" but he himself digs in when he least realizes it. My days lately are filled with him and I have yet to judge his tendencies, but as a friend he couldn't be more satisfying, absorbing, and good. I have yet to see his own prose writing, but *believe* in his avidity ... and he is so honest-seeking that I perversely feel dishonest (tho with Ginsbergian style, the "giggle") John's drive is the same as Allen's, on another kick, and yet they look askance at each other: they both want a love-belief. John is nearer to it by nature, and actually *in* it. I'd not known he had migraine headaches in the Navy, or that he went through a period of wild avidity during the early days of his marriage. It may even be true that I refuse to admit something about him; or, more accurately, it hasn't clarified in my mind as yet what his *substance* means to me, as it was with Ed White a long time. *John is watching me closely* (reading my diaries even) and I haven't learned a thing about him yet and this is a complaint. Two observant novelists observing each other and that is a vacuum. But as I write all this I have the feeling that it's all words, that I'm deliberately hedging, that he's "watching" me, and that "I won't tell." *What* won't I tell? I won't tell that I am afraid of forming an opinion of John Holmes because I am too happy knowing him and something unhappy will come of my opinions ... *at this stage* ... and anyway it doesn't matter, as we all know. I simply bask in his company, feel at ease, enjoy, talk, tell stories I'm not self-consciously involved with him as with Burroughs, say, (whom I fear), and I fear Burroughs because he fears me. Not so in this sweet relationship with grand Holmes.

Yet even then I have the feeling that I force these observations out because he has read my diaries and *may even read this one someday*. I'm not disturbed ... this is not a private diary, I have nothing to hide that is worth hiding — Listen here John Holmes, go fuck yourself! Put up your dukes, as Neal says. Come on, man, let's hide nothing and no more, tell all, all. Are you really telling all? Am *I* really telling all? Who's telling all? Put up your dukes, everybody, this is the way we'll live from now on — we'll all put up our dukes and dissolve the hypocrite's agreement and become same and sane. Come on! — Because this is what really makes us want to live and work and love, this myth-breaking and unveiling for each other, and the confession of daydreams. There will be no follies left when this last folly is done, this refusal to admit what daydreams *really* signify ... they signify that we want to be admired by everybody in the world *on our own grounds*. I am already admired by John Holmes, therefore, I grin ... What?!! — he has a few criticisms to make about me? Who does he think he is! I'll show him! So he wants me to admire him, hey? — well, allow me to grin. There's much time. We'll see, I'll think about it ... And if he suddenly left town without a word and I never saw him again, why naturally he'd be hiding somewhere hating me with all his might and even laughing. So this is the material we have to work with in this life, and out of it, though, come the most beautiful things and situations in creation. Come on John Holmes, my fit is over, shake hands. By this fit I see what you see maybe. You see, I don't arrive at conclusions — I'm not a bus-driver, I'm a wrestler — I wrestle to my conclusions. *I don't believe in the mind*, man. That is why I am so sly ... Yes, why am I so sly? Why do I write such shrewd books? He-he! Since we're all children of the earth, *real* flesh + blood children of the ground ... so what does it matter what opinion I have of you, when, especially, I have none of anybody, only a look-see at them and that is enough for me. I see you, peekaboo ... That's all and that's ALL, to me so sly and big-eared. Hawthorne's crown is not Melville's crown, (opinions also), but Hawthorne's flesh is Melville's flesh and *that* is more than crowns. And as Ed White says, "it's all pepsicola," and the world still turns on its axis. The waiter says, "Cognac?" and Ed White says, "Sure, shoot it!" — and *grins*, though. But this would lead us into Ed White endlessly. — Time to eat.

Went to Kazin's class, and then went by appointment to Diamond's house. There a series of things began. First, Diamond informed me that he was shocked at my behavior (drinking, parties, calling up late, etc.) and at my "terrible reputation" in the village. I asked him where he had heard that I was a "dope-addict" — and acted like a "maniac" at "certain parties" and so on, but he named no names. "People at San Remo's." He said I would not become a great artist if I went on this way: moreover he said he was shocked by my attitude and my "opinions" — that I did not work like a true artist, or think properly, etc., and that I was on the road to ruin. He said people like Louis Ferdinand Céline (whom he knew in Paris) are better off dead for the sake of "culture" and "progress." He even castigated Jesus in the course of our argument. (Incidentally, Brom Weber* says exactly the same thing about Céline.) He said he had no use for people like me without a "mature sense of values" and that he never wanted me to see him anymore because I was "childish" and "enervating." Finally he told me soothingly not to feel sorry because I couldn't have him for a friend. I felt sad for myself. I said nothing after awhile, and left — wondering what on earth to think about all this. I almost decided to clout him one but I'm glad I didn't. Lucien later said D. would have loved that, and anyway, of course, one doesn't go around clouting composers of beautiful music, especially when they are small men, of course. I now consider him, first, a jerk, and second, insane. I cannot be responsible for his insults which were repeatedly thrust at me without provocation and for my possible future reaction after tonight's moment of sadness before his madness. He said he could not risk his reputation with people like me (an insult to my family), and at one stage demanded that I go to bed with him (an insult to my manhood after all), and finally said it made no difference I had written "Town + City" because immature kids before me have "memorized symphonies and conducted them prodigiously" (an insult to my artistic will). All these things are uncalled for, rude, deeply untrue, insulting, snide, and finally ... obvious to all. My indifference to his attack fed fuel to it. However I am not indifferent to the insult, only to him. I cannot give him the pleasure of responding. I feel no opposition to any counter-thrust I might make, therefore I understand his intent to be an attempt to provoke my person. I gain no

* Brom Weber was a literary critic, Hart Crane biographer, and professor to Kerouac at the New School in fall 1948. Their often contentious relationship continued into the spring of 1949.

satisfaction from the thought that I have acquired an impolite enemy whose low opinion of me only stems from a general low-mindedness only to be found among respectable homosexuals in the arts. I do however gain much satisfaction from stating my position in this formal manner, since it is irreversible.

Next, in a black mood that always comes over me whenever anyone criticizes me, I went to Lucien's. Barbara and Bob Lisles were there. Lucien told a story about a murderer of 40 people in Tacoma with such glee that I finally understood that crime has its own punishment *only part of the time.* Lucien with this terrible knowledge which only L. could have imparted to me, I went to Bickford's on Times Square and wrote a "confession of three murders." I imagined so strongly that I had murdered three people that when my mind drifted momentarily from the subject I could feel a horrible (the worst yet) guilt creeping up out of my *unknown.* I saw that it was possible to be a murderer and be glad of it. This is so much nearer to the facts than my stupid naïve Lou last year — "Do you ever feel sorry you killed D.?" In those days ... well, who can say? ... in those days I didn't know this. I went to visit Hunkey at the Roxy Hotel on 42nd and 9th avenue, but only stared happily at the hotel from the street, and retraced my steps. All these actions are inexplicable to me. Looking at the hotel, the confession, even my deliberate refusal to "answer" Diamond when he was most insulting (I was however thinking of not ruining a contact for my book; this tactic was later justified in a Burroughs letter the next day advising me to "use all my contacts" to get published; since Diamond said also he was still my friend.) — I went and slept in Tony Manocchio's room and when I woke up in the morning I was guilty of murder. (It appears I murdered Diamond in my reveries, and two others to boot.) What strikes me is the way I felt in the morning, such is the power of the imagination. But Tony's sweet good presence began to revive me. I went to school and spent a long afternoon listening to Brom Weber criticize my novel. He finally concluded I might "save parts of it" for future use. In other words, to judge from the events herein described, I was not only a "childish adolescent" not worth knowing, but someone who had unsuccessfully tried to write a novel and failed in the end. This is what David Diamond and Brom Weber have told me in the past 24 hours. I am struck by the neatness and dispatch of their performance; and conclude with these two remarks of my own addressed to young writers of the future:—

1) Do not believe in what criticizers say of you.

2) Because all men who do not criticize are silently watching the criticizer, not you, and can only judge you from the silence of your works but not from the noise of the criticizers and are perfectly aware of what is going on.

However, if the pathos of the situation does not victoriously comfort you, you may bask in the glee of "Every-knock-is-a-boost." But do not at any time be seriously swayed by words of criticism. The criticizer in the moment of his noise is not what you are in the silence of creation, i.e., a maker instead of a destroyer. If however destruction appeals to you, embark on true destruction, become an outlaw and a plunderer, and accept the responsibility of your risks, but do not at any time hide behind the skirts of Mother Respectability while a destroyer. Among other things this will earn you the deepest contempt of silent men. If you do not accept the value of silent men (creative men also) you must, as I say, state your position unequivocally and become a destroyer of silent men — which is of course impossible and earns its consequent risks, moreover; although it is not a "dangerous" risk. The loss of the respect of silent men is risk enough since it is the loss of undeviating support in the flood-flux of devious existence. I myself am horrified by the loss of Hal Chase's friendship, and though I cannot determine whose fault it is we parted, I feel that much less alive and "safe" in living. It may be that I criticized him by laying his woman, and it may be that it was no criticism at all, only an urge directed to her — but I feel this loss and always will. Therefore, it is well to ignore all criticism and to know it for what it is (frustration), and work on in silence, and depend on the support and finally the love of men who similarly engage themselves in your midst. Anything else will lead to a universal disbelief in you, which is as though God had given you up to float in the ocean (forever alone) ← forever alone

If these moral postulations sound stiff and are frightening, it is well to ignore even that, but keep silent and work on. I only know, myself, that I don't believe what these two men said of my life and my work, and that if I were to believe them there would be nothing left to do but die. They want me to die. All criticizers will want you to die. ("Céline would be better off dead"). If you don't want to die, don't believe in what they say. If you want to kill them, do so — accepting risks, — but this will kill you too in the end. So ignore those who want you to die and you might even forgive them — but this is where I get off. It is well to know that all these things I've said about these two men were better not said, it's only that I feel responsible for the situation which they began but cannot finish. I do it out of a sense of duty to the honesty of this diary, too. But beyond that, silence is best — and work. It is true, finally, that everybody is the same — although this is God's truth which at the moment, in my mortal heat, I find hard to accept. It is the hardest of all truths (but I believe it.) I'll have to be an old and meditative man before I'll accept it. Right now I feel my blood, my pride, my fists knotting. The world will have to "breakthrough" someday because this paralysis of madness cannot organically last — there'll be a new Spring season, these brown leaves of our time will fall — there'll be a Winter too in the between — but I have pride in my flesh which silently, swaggeringly jibes at men like that and especially men like "females," for which I'm sorry, and glad too, and it is hard for me to admit that God's truth is over my head in my hotter days. Enough. This is tightrope-walking, I want ground. I want a lot of things, not *this* certainly. God can hate me for abandoning his truth — that everybody is the same and everything is really ecstasy, it's only *we* who are fools — he can hate me for reveling in human follies. I have no right perhaps to inhuman godly perfection of moral insight ... only the kind of feverish outsight I have at this moment, and if not born with, certainly bound to. — I had dinner, on Thursday evening at Geo. Bouwman's home in Brooklyn, a writer and yachtsman. He has a lovely wife. He has just begun to write, and has natural ability. He plans to date me with a millionaire's daughter from Chicago, after Xmas, which sounds charming inasmuch as he describes her as being very beautiful and sexy. At night, I got Tony into Lenrow's course. A Gil Kraft, just back from Paris, told me Temko had asked him to look me up concerning a possible publisher. I took his address. In the same moment Adéle Morales popped over. She and I and Tony had a snack in the Italian restaurant, Joe's, on Sheridan Square. It was a warm, sweet night, comforting me greatly after all the horror of Diamond + Weber. (Retraction: Brom Weber isn't so bad as I make him sound, it's only that he criticized my work at a wrong time, and it isn't his fault; also he has his own literary standards and I'm not the one to deny him his calling as a critic.) I gave Adéle parts of my novel to read. However, the next night, she didn't turn out to be the warm sexy Spanish girl I figured her as — a kind of educated Bea Franco — It seems she is "confused" and is being psychoanalyzed and so on, and we argued too much, partly my fault for not respecting her dependence on psychoanalysis. Oh there's something wrong with me too, no doubt of it ... it seems that I have a habit of wanting to lay women, or at least start affairs, without preliminaries and such ... a throwback to my ancestors the cavemen. I keep forgetting that this is a civilization and that I am dealing with sensitive people, over cultured and refined people. It is true, though, that I ought to practice a little finesse in these matters. I took her home deep in Brooklyn, kissed her in the hall, (a throwback to High School days), and went back to Holmes'. Slept there. In the morning Rae Everitt was there, and Barbara Bowles, and of course sweet little Marian whom I love more and more (Alan Wood-Thomas says she is a panda bear.) (He also says I am a tiger.) We spent a nice afternoon, doing little talking, cleaning the house. I knocked off a letter to Alan Harrington in Tucson. John and I had a long talk ... I even told him about my entry in this diary concerning his peeking-over-my-shoulder. We agreed that complete honesty is the only answer in that situation as in all situations. At night we went to the Wood-Thomases and spent another delightful evening among their children and neighbors. The great and beautiful Pauline,* perhaps the finest woman I'll ever know, was there again. I think I'll ask her to marry me someday; I wonder if she'd do it, and if so, how happy I'd be, and she'd be, and all. We danced and sang and talked and told jokes and had a wonderful time. Alan just sat there coloring prints, an owl ... "The Boss," as Pauline calls him. Rae Everitt finally sexed up to me and I tried to take her to Ginsy's apartment nearby but she ran off home. If sex is what makes the world turn I'm damned if I'm turning with the world. I always end up with such stupid neurotic women — as Ed Stringham pointed out. I give up, I've been writing in this diary for hours. But I love Pauline.

SUNDAY DEC. 5 — Bolted down a large meal and slept ... feeling physically lost and don't care much. At night I had a fever. I also read "Bartelby the Scrivener,"† which almost revived me to something until I realized why "we modern intellectuals" are so fascinated by Bartelby and his "I prefer-not-to" routine: — it is our dead-end souls in the cities. The hero of that story is really Bartelby's old employer, a man of sympathies and sense. Bartelby is after all a catatonic case, a depressive ... I am one, too. Even at 16 "I preferred not to" work, I remember that. Well, I don't blame Bartelby, or Russell Durgin (who is very similar), but I myself "prefer" some other line of willfulness that is closer to human communication. Still, you can't say that Bartelby was *not* communicating; he is beautiful; it's only that all of us feeling like that would perish, though I don't deny this might be acceptable, too. I don't prefer to die. As Ginsberg said in a letter today, "because I have no angle to offer keen-eyed employers I curse myself ... my being, not my existence." Bartelby exists. Existential Melville (!)

---

* Pauline was a married woman from New York City with whom Kerouac had a brief affair in the winter of 1948–1949. He fictionalized her as Lucille in *On the Road*.
† Melville's "Bartelby the Scrivener: A Story of Wall Street" (1853) is the tale of a young scrivener hired to a Wall Street lawyer's office who withdraws from work, and eventually life, by stating "I prefer not to" anytime he is asked to do anything.

MONDAY DEC. 6 — Went to [Elias] Tartak's class at school. On the way home I stopped off in Brooklyn to find out about a longshore job from a longshoreman on State Street. His story of indecisive employment depressed me. I came home, bolted another large meal, + slept again. Then I spent an entire night of nausea — and tried to read "Benito Cereno" but was too nauseous.* It seems as though it doesn't make any difference — even a nauseous night doesn't bother me, I've drawn a blank in my soul. Carolyn + Paul are pretty definitely coming to live with us in Ozone here, around January. All the better. It is Little, Brown with their seven-week silence that depresses me. They ought to let me know if they want T + C or not, and if not cease wasting my miserable time. One surprising thing, however — I resumed work on "Doctor Sax" temporarily. This way I'll write two novels simultaneously. But *why?* — when I make no living from it and go on being a "loafer" in the house. Going to school, for the sake of $75-per-month, has resulted in my receiving the following sum of money with which to pay the rent: — $SHIT. No word, no money, nothing from the Putnam short story, nothing, + nausea. — However, Burroughs writes that he is making $ with his crops. I must visit him in January and see how he does it.

TUESDAY DEC. 7 — Besides my nausea yesterday the house was frozen ... no heat. This is better than Pearl Harbor, though. Today I finally heard from Little, Brown. "Town + City" is too long and too "risky" to edit, etc., etc. What gets me is that when I read these diaries later I won't feel disappointed because the novel is not being accepted. I will however feel a weary sadness, and say "poor struggling bastard." "Poor fool." "Poor asshole." Running headlong into all available stonewalls, I am. Just now I was whistling a merry little tune. So this afternoon I resumed a few pages on "Doctor Sax." I'm tired because Town + City will be hailed as a great book, I'm bored by the prospect of such retarded ignorance all over. What can you do about the stupidity?

---

* Melville's "Benito Cereno" (1856) is a gruesome novella which tells the story of a slave revolt on a Spanish ship. It has often been published in single-volume form with "Bartleby the Scrivener."

Nothing. Stupidity works around the clock. When they finally "discover" it they'll all blast like sheep and I'll fall asleep watching them jump over my by-then-broken-down fence. It won't matter then. *And I'll tell them.* At night I wrote a letter to Neal and proposed that we go to sea together, save our money, and try to start a farm in California later with our savings. I also wrote a letter to Burroughs.

WEDNESDAY DEC. 8 — Not writing lately, although this afternoon I typed the Tea Party chapter from "Road" to show around (for Weber in the class, and to send to Burroughs.) Went to Kazin's at night. He was very cool to me — I think maybe Diamond has warned him against me, but I'm not sure. If so, more's the pity for Diamond ... or for me if it isn't "so." Ginsberg and Holmes were with me. We argued practically all night. John was depressed and there was a curious tone of hurt in his voice. He is sweet and I am only derisive: Barbara Hale says I am derisive and it's quite true. More's the pity for me. We saw Marian later, and I slept there on the couch. Ginsberg said that Tony Manocchio "started into a nightmare." Everything is sad now — but more than that, it's "in the air" that we're all rejecting each other. For instance two guys, Ed Stringham and Jerry Rauch, wrote to Allen G. and told him they preferred not to see him any more. And I have recently been called "immature" by four people. ... Diamond, Weber, John Holmes (indirectly) + Putnam. What does all this mean? I wish Neal was in N.Y. to join Allen and I in this awful debacle.

THURSDAY DEC. 9 — Went to Weber's class after a chat with the Holmeses. Allen came with me. He started the dull Weber class "vibrating" and it was a weird four hours of arguments with this dry critic about God and prayers and modern-day sainthood. I also told Weber I did not believe in criticism of any kind and wrote because it was a prayer to God. He told me criticism should be accepted on an intellectual level, not emotional. "But everything is emotional," I said. Allen said many similar things in his own lush language. Weber concluded we were "mystics" of some sort. Some in the class laughed but mostly it was all vibrating. Dear Allen did it. He wondered how I could stand this school — "you really work for your money!" What money? Saw a lot of people during the long day — Geo Bouwman, Barbara, the Neumanns, Bill Welborne, Adéle finally. Got mad at Allen + Barbara for their conspiracy against my romance with Adéle (even though poor Barbara had just given me a sweater.) Went off with Adéle after leaving the "Times Square" chapter with Lenrow, a fascinating (to me) instructor in the American novel course. ... Shabby, dogged, rocky, earnest, Dreiserian; almost Wolfean in loneliness too. Said he wanted to see what the new young writers were doing. I like this man. Adéle and I kissed in Shine's bar + grille and both of us were dizzy from it ... The most tremendous love-sensations for me since Mary Carney, whom she resembles (dark). Again, later, we went mad in her hall in Brooklyn. This is a real down-to-earth relation based on sexual vibrations (we look into each other's eyes raptly) that can only end (and begin) in bed. For once I can wait. I hope everything works out. I really love her in the eyes of God and not according to talk and worry.

It's the Forest of Arden's real attraction between a man and a woman — bodily, spiritually; (tho not "intellectually," we argue about "ideas") — and what more is needed? That's what I mean by the eyes of God. This is the way swains love lasses; it's not "modern" and not a Goethean "passion," it just happens as among deers and doves in God's creation. It is not "bad" and it is not the Devil's works, or difficult or even complex. — Putnam for the second time ran into me accidentally in a bar, and said I had better start growing up and go to work (job). As an artist I am more and more becoming vermin. And it is not "American commercialism" that says this, *remember this important fact*, it is all these Diamonds + Webers + Putnams of the American intelligentsia — and please remember that. American Commercialism isn't bothering me, it's these people who are supposed to be the bearers of the torch against commercialism. I'll remember that if you won't. And if I wake up some morning a vermin, like Kafka's Gregor, I'll not languish in the room, I'll crawl out and devour them all.* I have rages growing in me now and I will not *submit*. Came home at 5 A.M.

FRIDAY DEC. 10 — Wrote to Hal Chase finally in the afternoon. The manuscript is back from Boston, with a rather personally snotty letter from a certain man named Blanchard. Don't know who he is — but he lies, mostly.

At night lugged the ms. to Kazin's house in New York, where I left it with a porter. Came right back home. I am more discouraged than I've ever been, and what's worse I can see now that my three years of work on Town + City were the years of a madman. I keep telling myself now that it's all my fault for being so childish as to compose a large, sincere, all-encompassing, heart-serious work of life in the midst of this kind of world, this day and age. I tell you, the gadding forum of this world which judges the poor simplicities of such a heart as mine (*when it is at work*) is the ugliest spectacle I have been born to see. It's none of their business! What are they all mad about? I only wrote a big novel ... No one asked me to write? Would I say "no one asked you to do this" if some poor guy gave me a gift, no matter how stupid he is, or how paltry the gift. Shame on the world! I can see now what it's done to others and what it will yet do. A Liberal Utopia of Enlightened Individuals? — tonight in front of the "Leftist" New School, in the cold winds, I saw a limousine waiting. It will always be the same, a *malice* in the world continually gadding and working itself — nothing will ever stop it. I can only droop when I think of it, even what it will do to me. Sad, sad I am. In my mind I have the memory of a good man like my father, and the dream of a race of man gleeful, affectionate, and fair. It is so strong in my mind that even now I refuse to believe people can be so ugly. I cannot picture them when I'm in bed at night. In bed at night I think of children, of strong, kind fathers, and strong, sweet mothers, and loyal brothers and sisters. Can they accuse me of sentimentality for refusing to face the malignity of man? Can I not *chase* it, like Melville?

* Gregor Samsa, the young protagonist of Kafka's *Metamorphosis*, transforms into a monstrous insect overnight. His family locks him in his room, but he escapes in a frenzy.

After all, "sweetness and light" is a bore, we want that inscrutable malice, don't we? I sometimes think that people who love malice do not realize what it is. And I sometimes think they have somehow been shattered from the rawness of it. And I think of Mark Twain who laughed because he was afraid to die crying.

SATURDAY DEC. 11 — Today I received a check for $160.00 from the Vets Administration — Good! I'm grateful. Now I have a little money for once and can go to California to ship out if Neal is willing to go in January. Also, it's money for the rent for Christmas, for the house, for a few shirts, and maybe I'll buy a few good records. I'm happy again today. We'll start saving our money now, all of us, for a farm someday. And I'll go on writing. Worked on Doctor Sax in the afternoon ... about six words all told. (?)

SUNDAY DEC. 12 — The only thing that has ever disappointed me is men. How much wiser I was, as a boy, depending on the sky for sustenance gazing at it from galley, jail, and sickbed with perfect trust and love. It is still the same world that used to smile on my joys, therefore why should I begin being so unhappy now? It's the same, same world ... Now they have properly shown me what a fool and madman-child I am, put me in my place moreover, I think I will die, give up, go mad, and begin to be happy again. I will walk down the road again singing "Without a Song" to the sky, and when I can afford a marriage I'll sing to my wife and children perpetually — I'll say, "Dear ones, mad little ones, birds, how sweetly I adore you! Do not believe in the world. Believe in yourselves. Because in the world, in the name of justice of all kinds, they will judge and judge till you, believing, walk sincerely condemned to all gallows ... No, no, lives, you lives, believe not in the world, it does not exist. All is ecstasy. Give up the world, jump gladly down the street, sing, seek each other out." — Last night I saw Pauline again. It was very sad. We can't reach each other through the prison-bars of the world. On all sides there are warders, judges, attorneys, witnesses, and executioners. I don't even know if I can reach her through the mail, but I'll try. Talked with John and Marian in the afternoon, and then came home, depressed — for real reasons, for Pauline, and for me mad. But I'll reconcile myself to my "madness." I will not "grow up" and reject the innocence of birds for the company of men. I am a bird. It no longer concerns me that birds are mad, that they twit and quiver and sing to God all day: and that finally, as the bird in Scranton at 5 o'clock in the morning in August of 1947, it gets run over by a car in the midst of a song and has it all squeezed out of it by the heavy wheel — "SQUIT!" Besides I'm tired. And I will do something decisive about Pauline, a dear bird. Who knows? She is perhaps the great woman I sought, and I am perhaps the loving man she seeks. Thought all night.

MONDAY DEC. 13 — First thing in the morning Pauline called me, and I've been feeling happy all day. Amazing how we seem to understand each other. I cashed the check and deposited $60 in the bank. Took out two books to study for school. Went to school and signed, and talked with Bill Welborne — who is going to Mexico in May to lay the foundations for a Mexican movie career, if he can make it. Came home, ate, chatted with Ma, and settled down to what I have to do: term papers, letters, Doctor Sax, studying, and writing to Pauline. Last five days of depression were horrible — simplicity, perhaps, is sublimity.

TUESDAY DEC. 14 — Not so simple as that with me. What have I done these days? — a big nothing ... all those big projects to begin ... and last night I slept eleven hours. When will I start living? All I did today was write letters and sit around. I read my "On the Road" and see that it is a powerful and singularly GLOOMY book ... but good. Ray Smith comes amazingly to life, also Warren Beauchamp. I wrote a large prophetic letter to Temko in Paris, and a silly tho honest letter to Ginsberg. Wasting my time, Doctor Sax is supernatural, On the Road is naturalistic ... This I decided ... but I have no normal discipline with which to view them. And the term papers have to start ... I started Tartak's Tolstoy paper. But this kind of angry uprooted work drives me silly. Enough, enough, enough for God's sake.

A little silence is a good thing too.

Since in any case half of life is death.

Jack O Lanterns....

1949

JAN. 3 — Much happened in past 2 weeks. Reason why I don't want to continue the diary is because it disturbs me by its falseness ... and actually impedes my living. —

Ma and I went to North Carolina, in a train, laden with Xmas gifts. Neal Cassady arrived there a day later from 'Frisco, in his new car ('49 Hudson — our big 1949 car) and Lou Ann and Al Hinkle with him. We dashed up to N.Y. in a trip memorable for the cold and dry misery. Settled at Ozone, did a million things. Dashed back, Neal and I, to No. Carolina. Came back with my mother and some of Nin's furniture. Big New Year's Eve party at Herb Benjamin's ... great times these. Nin + Paul moving in.

In 2 weeks we're off to New Orleans, and the sea of 'Frisco. Diaries are for lonely men. I'm sorry I can't keep on — but I won't forget a thing, watch.

Kazin reading the novel. My "last chance" as far as I feel. I'm off. New things, new things ... The great things are yet to come, watch. And great books for me, watch.

Neal — "Everything's always alright."
And that's *it*.

LINES IN THE FINAL ANALYSIS

In my wild, sweet circle
This winter, we'll visit the summer's
South America for gourds;

With umbilical intelligence
Departing, to bongo jungles we'll go,
Like the last sweet little drops
By milady's finger jingled out.
And we're hip: —
God is what I love, you know.

Children come out of nowhere, and they pick up. Someone, one
night, says "Where's your father?" and they say "Not here!" — just like
that so quick. Where? where? where are they from? So quick and wise
the little voices? Under the rainy roofs ...

Under the rainy roofs I go, a-thinking and a-thinking of rain and
roofs and little kids; that's me, Jack, crazy, rueful, guilty, happy golden
Jack O Lanterns.

ME CAREER

This world is the city of God;
And though I'm supposed to stay
    on the same block,
In the house winding spools of thread,
where I was appointed to be,
I have thrown up the threads
And his the streets of God —
And though he is mad at me
I *am seeing what I will never see again.*

*   *   *   *   *

The streets of God, the streets of God.
(But in my room, at sad dusk,
the red light quivers on the drape,
and I have died a rueful die.)
Yet now, behold, I still live.

MONDAY JAN. 10 — Ball in the erotic night with Luanne ... although like Al, I really don't care. Wrote to Pauline and stated that I only failed to keep our appointment because I overslept. Who but a woman will accept the rawest truth? At York Avenue we goofed all day ... as we've been doing for 2 weeks now, laugh, ... laugh ... laugh; imitated "B" movies; blasting hay; talking. Allen is there in his silk bathrobe wondering when he'll ever get a moment of solitude again. But it's a "great season," as we all know. With strange Ray Smith-like Al I talk of visions, angels, feelings on the road, girls, experiences, the sea ... with Neal of Everything, with Allen too; with Louanne of love and love-affairs and sometimes of that slow-boat to China. And then ... through it all, completing my term at school and waiting for word on my book. (Kazin handed it to Harcourt, Brace.) Through it all, too, Nin + Paul and Paul, Jr., and a '49 Ford convertible (canary yellow with green top) moved in with us ... and I helped last Saturday to move the house here around like a mountain. Naturally, there was no need for a diary. But looking over this one (previous pages) tonight, I saw how beautiful it was for me to keep a diary if only to set down that I told Neal + Allen in the West End: "This life is our last chance to be honest ... really the Last Chance saloon,"; or that I'm going to subtitle "Doctor Sax" — "The Myth of the Rainy Night." — ; or just to set down that Neal said this or that, or Allen said: "How did we get here, angels?" — or that Louanne is telling me her life-story, and ding-dong the knell of winter's springtime, and I said to Pauline in the letter: "Nothing is true but everything is real." (I have finally resolved Nietzsche's aphorism again.) Literally speaking, Neal's arrival did not strengthen my naturalistic intentions for "On the Road" (and that part of my soul concerned with such things) but, surprisingly, even "miraculously" my supernatural Godly intentions for Doctor Sax. And listen ... I foresaw Al in Ray Smith I foresaw even the Scandinavian sweater in the story. And I even foresaw that America's young "furtives" (like Ray and Al) are concerned with visions + God. Why? Why? you see how great? The future of man is secure in my mind now. And then ... by abandoning the frowning honesty of the first sixteen days of this diary, and losing it, I however valuably gain a kind of creative insouciance which will lead (you will see) to great things. My "great things" are inevitable but still as yet wanted. As Neal says, "If you but see." Well, you, then ... if you but see, see that I love God and will write it.

At home they worry about me because I'm away so much (especially, they having just arrived, feeling that I'm avoiding them) — no, no. I am placating all around happily, and this is life ... But I'm a bastard to Pauline (and Adéle) now. Also owe a thousand letters. Life like a sea envelops my thirsty island's mouth ... I placate and swagger, long-haired, boppish, high-cat, crazy; enjoying secrets of existence; and loves, and love of knowledges; and of rains, swirls, the Alls of the All; mystic making no mud. Floating down the steps; gazing back at the caravan on the wall; looking for Hunkey; engendering new intentions. And we're all making and destroying new plans every day: — today it's New Orleans, no 'Frisco ... to work in N.Y., keep the car, develop Allen's place into a real pad with photographs, heater, wire-recorder, midnight teas (there is a face of Baudelaire on the wall, and a cracked kitchen.) Later to go to sea ... or New Orleans and 'Frisco. Carolyn, meanwhile, wants to buy a couch for the house; which would have been money for shirts + little things. So it goes, as an example of it all. And through it all a sweet little infant sleeping in my room in the very corner where my father's deathbed lay ... Well, well, well ... so this is — ; but what is it?

It is I and ... they ... and Him.

TUESDAY JAN. 11 — Went to Brooklyn with Paul to see about his telephone job. Lately, since I've felt that there are "no more problems" in life, I've had instead a kind of knot in my stomach (like Louanne has) and I wonder, I wonder. The domestic life in my house now satisfies my soul to the utmost ... a baby, a sister, a mother, a brother — and my thoughts. But there is that conflict in my stomach arising from the fact that I don't know my next step. Today I got a letter admitting me to the

Sorbonne (!) And Paul told me that we might all be able to move into the caretaker's 8 room house on Frank Sarubbi's farm in Morristown N.J. next September. For that goal (and keeping the car in the family — and getting my mother on her farm at last) I would work and not goof off in Paris ... although I regret the lack of experiencing Paris with one such as Ed White, and all the fine French girls there. Perhaps I'll simply go to sea — with Neal and Al. But they may change their minds tomorrow ... I'll end up going alone. I *do* want to travel, at the same time earn for our life. Still, I'd like to go West again — maybe ship out of 'Frisco. And write "Doctor Sax" and "On the Road" — and go to Paris ... and have women ... and eat ... and save money ... etc. etc. — thus, I think, the knot in my stomach. But I'll decide.

Went to see "Red River" at night with Paul, a great picture.* Paul and I are good friends but we never talk ... except about plans. — Still haven't written the last of my term papers, on myth. Last week I knocked off papers on "Satanism," "Whitman," "Dreiser and Lewis," and "Tolstoy." Tonight I'll draft the paper. And where are my sweet lunacies tonight? — my sweet mad children of the pads? I'm sometimes amazed by my own *range of solicitudes* ... because all today I've been so solicitous about such different things than yesterday. But God is leading me by the hand to my destiny, which is to make up for my crime by learning all and laboring great books. God is leading Neal by the hand to the answer to his question: "Why must I deceive?" and leading Allen to the circle-swirls of life from which he was once curiously banished; and leading my mother to the heaven of the exploited saints (on earth?) — and leading us all by the hand to *what we really want.* Therefore there *are* no problems, see? How I believe in God now! He's with me all day. Where did he lead Edie by the hand? —*where* is she now? She who loved the rainy fool ... I got a haircut today, though.

WEDNESDAY JAN. 12 — I might have died today ... I'm not superstitious, I know *God.* Went to N.Y. to school; signed; drove off with

* *Red River* (1948), a classic John Wayne/Montogomery Clift western about a cattle-driving family in turmoil. The film fed Kerouac's fascination with the American West.

Neal — we sent $18.00 to his wife in Frisco, my money (just for the hell of it). He told me of the mad party I had missed Tuesday. Then Neal beat up Louanne ... Lucien and I were a little shocked. However we all went to the Clique bebop nightclub, where Neal took $2 from Lou's wallet. I am disappointed, but interested in this savagery of Neal's. Lucien was in his glory for once ... if you see how I mean. It gave him great joy. Can it be that Lucien is oldfashioned? At dawn Lou and I drove around in the Hudson and picked up Tony and gave him a ride. I drove back to the pad alone, and went to bed. — Next day Neal felt a little better ... and at night we went to the nightclub once more, with Al and Rhoda. Next day we felt even better, and ate porkchops, and all went to the movies. (I can't describe life any more.)

SATURDAY JAN. 15 — Home in Ozone. Now it is definite that we're all moving to Sarubbi's farm in the Spring, and share an alfalfa crop with him ... but my joy is indefinitely darkened because the mother feels that it will all come to naught and her hunches are always right; Goddammit. I'll go to sea in 2 weeks + we'll see what happens in the Spring. Meanwhile, tonight, I read parts of T + C to find out if it is anything. It is not anything but "inevitable." Then *what* are they waiting for? If my soul depended on the way in which my book is being received I would not be alive to write these silly lines, tonight. But "men of destiny" like me are always martyrizing their own joys. I say this objectively. Who am I? — I burn. That's all, period. There is no satisfaction in this heart. Even heaven is frightful (I'd be alone there.) What do I want? — I want to burn, that's all. I got a silly letter from that whore Pauline who says someday I'll go to hell where the Devil will prod me with his pitchfork when I wish to recline — as I "always do you lousy bastard." She wiped her ass good on me ... now she's happy, the whore. Let her be happy. I won't give her the benefit of what I think of her. Said her husband wanted to kill me ... let him come, the whore. We're all whores. What's one whore or more less. I'll disarm him with my feet, an old trick, and break his arm. What's the matter with me tonight? Imagine Pauline writing this to me: "My husband isn't a bastard like the likes of you. You couldn't even polish his shoes. The pity of it all is this, that I can't get you to go out and work. I'd make you work so damn hard the sweat would fall from your brow like the rain you keep talking about. That's the only thing that will save you. Work, Manual Labor." (Her capitals.) "I suggest that you try writing about *real people* like us and not jerks like Doctor Sax and his rainy nights. Don't ever call yourself a religious writer again, you don't know your ass from a hole in the ground about religion. You brought me down to your level, but that won't be for long." She'll have her Easter morning, she will. Once — (I wonder if she's right?) — Lucien does say he is worried about my loutishness (which I glorify, you know, *literarily*) — Once I would have considered becoming an imbecile and going out to shine her husband's bloody shoes — but it's too much for me now, it's too late.

Gad, what a life I'm leading.

SUNDAY JAN. 16 — You think I care? Don't crowd me, world! (He-he!)

FEBRUARY 12 1949

And then the 8,000-mile trip to New Orleans, Arizona, Frisco, Portland, Spokane, Butte, No. Dakota, Minneapolis, Chicago, Detroit, etc. (inc. Florida).

I have just returned — came home and ate in the middle of the night all the eggs + bacon in the house. Trip described elsewhere.* Registered next day.

I was just in time to see off Ed White + Bob Burford + Frank Jeffries on the Queen Mary. Hal Chase + Lucien Carr were on the ship somewhere, as well as Ginger, Barbara, Tom Livornese, Julie — Ed Stringham, Johnny, Marian, and of course Allen. Didn't find Hal or Lou ... it was the ship of the world, just too big.

So much has happened in past weeks, since Dec. 24th actually — 11,000 miles of traveling — and all the developments — that I am

* Most of the trip is described in detail in the "Rain and Rivers" travel journal.

exhausted, and refuse to describe it now. Later. Now I'm back at school, and forming Doctor Sax swiftly, and writing it.

Map of trip elsewhere.

Resting. Very happy. New soul.

Composing Doctor Sax, which is become a description of darkness.

Feb. 20 – 21 ... Spent total of 16 hours writing essay "The Minimization of Thomas Wolfe in His Own Time." Not too good ... Though my best essay yet. Wrote with extreme care, with an eye on critical demands (form, tradition.) Imitating Eliot maybe.

The distinction between the intellectual and the metaphysical mind is involved in this ... that a situation, a thing, needs to be accounted for — and in this analogous instance, let us say it is the choice of words used to deal with the spectacle of a man "musing on eternity." For my purposes here, and not without validity, I would suggest that the intellectual, in his haste to dispense with the matter conveniently, would describe the thing as "wonderingly thinking." This is the description. The label: the intellectual moves on from there to the re-arrangement of other labels and other systems of labelings. But our metaphysical, or Shakespeare-type, will use these words — "Dumbly mulling."

"Wonderingly thinking ... "

Dumbly mulling ...

Not only has the metaphysical function found a more beautiful set of language here, and attacked an esthetic deep, but the meaning is more accurate and more useful. Why? And what, further, is to be learned from this distinction between prose-sense of the intellectual and the poetry-sense of the metaphysician?

There are beauties in "dumbly mulling," the rhythm of the "U" vowels as well as the rhythm of the words together; plus the easy loll on the tongue (two "Ls"); plus, finally, that indecipherable mystique of the *seen word*. We know that — great ships are whistling in the harbor at night, — but it requires the metaphysical prowess (at its height) to show us, further, that, really — great boats are blowing in the gulfs of night.

This estimate of the beats is one that, if applied to its author Thomas Wolfe (usually not metaphysically sharp) may be analyzed on useful grounds: it is this: he has evidently affixed some kind of living quality to his concept of a ship, as being more than plates + bolts, hull + superstructure — as being, really, something almost alive. Likewise, the "night" has been more than darkness to him — something space-less, timeless, spherical, misty. "Boats blowing" in "the gulfs of night" is reminiscent (to me) of Aeoleus with puffed cheeks; or of the foghorn that blows fog from its mouth: what it was to Wolf is left in obscurity, we cannot know his "emotional complex" which went to work producing the "objective corollary" we have in print; we only sense the transcen-dental lull which has come into perfect being in these lines. No scien-tific measurements can tell us much more. We only know that these lines, in that they are simpler, more elegant, yet pursue the abstract idea to the least abstract point of concentration, reach further, tell clearer.

And there is more fact in "dumbly mulling." No doubt "wonder-ingly thinking" (perhaps an unfair example for the intellectual choice) indicates some other meaning, touching on some kind of meditation of action: "How will I do it?" "Why did he do that?" "How does this happen?" "Dumbly mulling" gives its picture of hangjawed wonder-ment of infinity, on the other hand, is more accurate. There is accuracy in language — (and tone). The metaphysical intelligence is concerned with the furthest possible reach of an idea, or image, and the most ba-sic, simple, possible way of evoking this feeling on the edge of relative meaning (no meaning is absolute, only God perhaps is absolute); but the intellectual perception, in the limits of the present definition, stops at the description of a thing and makes its label, files away the mean-ing of absolute, and moves on — dumbly mulling all the way, rear-ranging, pasting, pigeonholing, balking, sulking up. There is the sulkiness of such a form of mind.

Many metaphysical intelligences are however ambiguous. An example: — "Ah the mildness of this year!" This is a line which tells that a year has been mild, not harsh: perhaps the climate itself, or the mild events, the mild doings of people in a given season. There is a double meaning. In context within a dramatic structure it could tell all that were required of it.

But if the metaphysical impulse in its author is taken lightly, — if poetry becomes verbal, general song, — if there is a loss of control from the rigors of structural meaning (as in a context), the line might deteriorate, as far as clarity and far-reachingness are concerned, to — "Ah the mildness of the year."[1] This is a general song: any year, any mildness perhaps, any edge of any meaning; any metaphysical swirl in any space. It does not *refer.*[*] The sin, however, is far milder than the sin on the intellectual prosody: —

"It has been a year of warm weather, and the people have behaved themselves nicely, as though the weather had something to do with it."

There are other distinctions, to be made later.

The most total distinction, perhaps, is implicit in this feeling — that metaphysical men are not more important than intellectual men, only more interesting. Shakespeare's rue is to me an interesting, varied rue; because he evidently has a knowledge of his shift + position on the edges of the very limits of knowledge (where he is only brilliantly performing, while the others are bootless). No more can be done. Other men mull dumbly on the unattainable secrets, but he pursues them with the great charm of concern. When we hear that Shakespeare himself did not understand the artistic failures in "Hamlet" we are saddened and see the great clown stopped on the edge of the world. We love him because he has understood so much else for us, + danced to all plaints for us. (I believe he began "Hamlet" bravely and then decided it would be too much to have Hamlet carry the action out to its intended end, namely, marrying Gertrude someday; + Shakespeare spooled it out; and *knew* the failure.)

[1] Which means something else, and is perhaps a superior line.
[*] That is, not as unmistakably for the reader.

No, the secrets were perhaps in the possession of Dante:-
[JK drawn atomic figure] A metaphysician supreme.

Notes from 1945 Notebook:

"Scattered matter straying too far from essence." "You are not bound for heaven, you just came from there: and the idea is to re-discover your loss in the well."

Sum-up, 1949: — Even though all is fore-ordained, we are still free, for we know not. (Supreme Reality of 1943.)

—   —   —   —   —   —   —   —

It is not only fruitless yipping, but ignorance, to complain in this eternity: yet men do so, and do so, and do so — and some complaints are songs, and some are rage. Boethius himself complained when he hoped to make it understood that pre-ordainment did not imply hu-man helplessness, in Pavia.*

I am not helpless because my big, dull "Town + City" cannot sell; it doesn't matter so much. My own stupidity is involved. Now I want to go into a little conspiracy of understanding of eternity with a lovely girl — and write "Dr. Sax" — and come to direct feelings with God. (If my love of God is a death-instinct, then by the same terrestrial cogni-tum all neurosis-theory is a manifestation of anxiety.)

Where will I eat? (Why must I eat?) Where shall my mother rest her tired feet? Let us all be clever and steal fruit from the wired gardens.

Does my dog Pete continue in eternity, for he has a dogsoul — a sight of the world, a "silling" softness, and he returns to me when I call him ... he returns across the plain to me and to no one else. This is a soul.

Oh God, by degrees I can as easily drop from you as rise to you. It is not that I "need faith" but need nothing. Can this be? Now I'm ready to

---

* Boethius (480–524?) was a Roman philosopher and Christian martyr who was falsely ac-cused of treason and sacrilege, imprisoned on Pavia, and executed for his crimes. While in prison he wrote his meditation on the human condition, Consolation of Philosophy, to which Kerouac is referring.

cross the mountains ... maybe the Asian plateau ... to the Guarded mount, where like a Japanese maid, I must obviously assume that the jump to spacelessness is next. It is not despair but loneliness. For the dark spaces I see whirling are not an Easter Resurrection in Palms, not Paradiso: — wrathful lights. These are the wrathful lights ...

Beyond the bay of the night is the sea, the Pacific unknown to me which I have not traversed ... Soaring up (and therefore below) this sea, my (soul?) in great whirl, whirls. ... There are spaces, and all is known. I am not freed by the whirlwind, nor consoled, nor softened, rendered, nor calm'd, nor seen ...

The One Eye alone sees.

To this Eye I proceed with drawn whiten'd face up-staring, mad eyes (as of the heed in the snake's mouth) outpopping — sheer small terror of no consequence — swirled in the consequential hurricanes of the spheres.

The One Eye makes a light over the ledges of the planetaries — to which I, drawn without quarter, speed — God be praised that the whole universe knows.

We the myriad angels meet in heaven.
We the angels meet in earth.
We the angels cry in hell.
We the angels never die.

Rueful dancer to these plaints, Oh Lord, firgive, forgive ... forefend, foresee, forelength, forechange, foreshorten, foretake. But life lives.

*   *   *

And in combinations, too. This past weekend (March 5–6), I saw, after a lot of things, that experience may be characterized as a series of combinations that appear at first overwhelming and simple, and later — after inundations in life — less overwhelming, more complex: more to be termed "interesting," less to be termed "tremendous." Once one is wise to the rudimentary combinations, one overlooks them, in search of the hidden combination. Like art, life is best when varied. And these "later" combinations, new with nuance, alter the relative "position" of phenomenae (in one's mind), only, and do not "change truth" in any way. There is no truth, only degrees of light. My light is growing smaller ... The big flashes were tainted, as by the dome: but these small lights are pure and white and are like tapers burning in my wilderness.

Here is one of my latest combinations:

First ... the vision of the Silly Subway. A young man one night grinning irrepressibly, in the subway, tho I know not what for, yet for my purposes ostensibly at the silliness of the subway ride; which is, after all, absurd: rocking mildly thru tunnels of darkness towards further dimensions of the brick-heap. This given, I myself looked around and saw that everybody in the subway was silly. Our young man: most, and most charmingly, silly — and conscious of himself as such, like our Don Quixote. The people — particularly one man with his hat perched squarely upon what seemed to be two layers of hair (two wigs) and a red nose and small, close eyes, and wisps of hair sticking out at unfortunate angles — were silly, and did not know it, + tragically clownish. A woman leaned forward eagerly in her "grief" (her camp): a man moped; all were hung up in their personal traditional poses, like actors (and this stage so grim). Given, then, our mad positions on earth, our mad insistence to strike a pose, and hold it, and grieve by it, and die by it like patriots (patriots of the self). In this serious air ... Even one who notices this dull absurdity, a Lucien, is silly; and I; because on the subway, on the hard shelves, you can't escape looking silly ... Why, after all, should you have given yourself over to it? Why aren't you standing under the boughs? — in the morning?

Now Lucien, seeing this, proposes that all life is hopelessly silly, + defunct even, but maintains ruefully that at least some of us may stand on "solid ground." This is done by my Lowell friends Geo. Murray + Connie Murphy (last night at a party) while the others, the mad

Maryjohn, the desperate, helpless Rhoda, Les, George, Ed Stringham, even poor John drunk, agitate furiously in the nothingness — wondering vaguely, sadly, "what is wrong?" Those with their feet on the ground contemptuous of these demonstrative, agonized others — and these others bored by the former. And, midway, Adéle murmuring her incoherent complaints to the surly air: — "But these people are so lost — so-so-so — they're all looking for-for-for —" She concludes that "our society is sick." Meanwhile, on the street, I see a crowd gathered around some old man who has just been knocked down by a car — in the merciless floodlight you see his bloody face, his hand over his heart, his mute, prayerful fear, and his glassy sense of sudden, absurd drama (one thinks of the idiot who knocked him down "accidentally"). What is the meaning of this combination?

Not only is it obvious, because it *is*, but, to go beyond it, stop the machinery: i.e., *stop thinking*. (This too is part of this particular combination.)

It is interesting because it proposes an end to unnecessary anguish, with its co-existent silliness + waste. (Anxiety.) The old man in the street has something actual to worry about — and he was belabored by a car, by a driver whose mind was wandering in anguish: the old man himself must have been wandering. Not in visions of fire, like St. Francis, but like our "grieved" lady in the subway. There is nothing to worry about save the possibility we may not all die and melt into the universe — in short, nothing to worry about in this melting all the poses are cast out, like husks, and actually calmly affirms itself. Actuality is this: — existence. ("You call that living? —it's just existing.") it's the point ...

To worry and harry and fret at silly parties, to deal in the interchange of vague hysteria, to wonder and not admit anything, not even admitting one's silliness essential, to mope and accuse, and swoon because of it all (like drunks), this is being on the outer peripheries of life's swirl. In the calm center, in the area of the Eye, (where I, silly, believe myself now to be, and probably stupidly am, or shrewdly) there is a recognition of the end of life and the beginning of life, and the glory of the universe. Man is a fool. It is in him to be sweet, true, and fresh, as at morning, caring not where he is, or how, or why, or when — but always. Do not be afraid of any thing. Stop thinking.

Someday — at 35 perhaps — I am going to stop thinking, at least for awhile (that is, stop writing). It is unfortunately essential that I be right, the others wrong: — as in these writings in solitary (with silly headphones). That is why I will someday stop thinking even that.

And "silliness" is a futile preoccupation: in the end, the air is grave.

"You may be very sure she thinks of nothing. She goes from day to day, hour to hour, as they did in the Golden Age. I can imagine nothing more vulgar."

— "Mrs. Costello" in "Daisy Miller"
by Henry James

(But delightful Swiss music over my shortwave radio saves my soul — O the myth of the world night!)

"As Adam early in the morning walking forth from the bower is refresh'd with sleep"[*] — so all of us.

A WRITING-RULE —

No need to create effects, as in "recreating atmosphere," when these mere effects come naturally (as in life) as a result of desired events. Thus, write as you might live

---

[*] From Whitman, "As Adam Early in the Morning" in *Leaves of Grass*.

I saw the Shrouded Angel standing in the Hooded Tree
And below, **The Urn of God** covered
With a cloak, and all such awful
Silence as I had never known:
Meseems a **Cape of Darkness** followed,
Widely lowered over the sea;
And on the **Sheering Mount** the walking
snows,
All swirl, disported on before mine **Eyes**.
Here the **Olive** dies, and the aged **Grape**,
the **Tangerine**, the **Banana** + the **Gold**
go **pale**, + **Freeze** in the **Hand**.
So the whiten'd **Sun** the **Moon** becomes,
And all but the **Arm of the Angel** dies.

      (when writing poetry, more than this
      go bold)

The Vision of the Hooded White Angel
Follows
The Myth of the Rainy Night ...

The eyes of Sax go golden,
 the firmament of morning
  follows the wizard night.

Of fire be serious,
in pearls is frozen
the golden flame of roses.

The aerial ice, the eagle's eye,
and the condor's Chinese claw
are made of rain.

The violets and lilacs
are sleeping in the rain
at night: and rain sleeps.

And the mountain's upside down
looking at the bottom of the world:
and the bottom of the world is gold.

Do not cry out,
the falcon of darkness
is in love with your eyes.

And the rose is glowing
in the golden dark
where vermillion eyes are blue.

And bones become water
and fly in the air
to feed the brown night-shore.

Marble melts, flowers shine,
and dirt turns green + dark,
in the land of rain's love.

MAR. 25 '49

Thought up further definitive ideas for "On the Road," No more Ray Smith, except in the person of a narrator — the hero's Panza, the hero's Boswell, the hero's Pip — who tells the story with ravenous absorption, + with great beauty (naturellement.) The hero is a man in his late 20s who has lived a lot, and who ends up in a jail, thinking, finally, that he needs to "seek an inheritance incorruptible, undefined, and that fadeth not away," in the words of Bunyan. This is a "mature," experienced, variegated even learned man of many talents + personalities, whose background, like Melville's Confidence Man, or like that of any man of spiritual merit (if we can measure these things) is inexplicable in terms of logical thumbnail data — in other words, an artist of life. (like Burroughs.) He has an old father somewhere out West, and after lingering in N.Y. awhile (after his release from jail) with Junkey + all the others connected with the "T + C" New York, he sets out, on the road, with his Pip, his crony (an almost idiotic boy with a nature too soft, too sweet, too saintly for this world) to seek out his father.

In the past, with his father, mother, uncles + cousins, he was a boy living in a valley in California (where he fancied himself Zorro, in keeping with the concept described in the "Record" notebook). It had been a life, grand and rich, which somehow had not come into his inheritance. Now he seeks to recover it. His other great friend is Vern Pomeroy, whose own father, an old western-Texas hobo, had once worked on the Moultrie lands; and Ray Moultrie (the hero) had grown up with young Vern. He joins Vern out west. The three young men find old Bruce Moultrie in Butte; and old Pomeroy in Denver. They go on to California. This is a rough idea of the beginning of the quest. The Pip — Smitty — goes with them.

Ray Moultrie had been a minor league outfielder, a jazz drummer, a student at London University, a seaman, a truck-driver, and, among many other things, a jailbird in his strange, spotted career. (Just think how many actual men like that, and just as brilliant, exist in America. I met them on ships, in jail, in psycho wards. Slim Hubbard is only one of them.)

Also — will they wonder why a man who has gone to jail for being an accomplice in a big robbery, also reads the Bible and prays? On his knees? If they wonder, they fail to know man.

PROGRESS ON DOCTOR SAX

SAT. MAR. 25 — For the first time in months I walked by my old house + old church on the old road back here by the tracks, and perhaps I was not wrong supposing "Sax" is only the poem capping T + C. I need some such idea — the theme is too frivolous for me sometimes, too influenced by mystic, mad Allen G. The thing is so beautiful I can't abandon it; and the idea so *loony* I can't *get on* with it. If it is really loony, which it may not after all be, still it is a poem, a description of darkness, a midnight lark instead of my usual dark-toed midnight *labour*; and I like to consider it sandwiched between "Town + City" and "On the Road." So I'll do it. Also, in order to do so, I must put my nose to the grindstone again, if only half so strenuously ... with a discipline, a schedule: with an approximate date: May 31st. I have some 10,000 words written, if not more, and plan the novellina at 60,000. That's 50,000 constructive words till May 31st — (with only one provision: — that I might be interrupted by the successful acceptance of T + C, and would have to bend to a revision of that + put off Sax for this summer or ... fall). So tonight I *officially* begin the schedule. Pace: at least 5,000 careful words per week. Sax requires a slower pace; it is more poetry than prose, and the organization must be watertight, no detail wasteful, no word slack. So here goes. Uneventful, stupid days; and in the end, a manuscript writhing with its own strange life, — si? Wrote a few hundred unsatisfactory words.

SUN. MAR. 26 — Tonight I wrote a remarkable little piece called —; well, not decided on title, "Ling's Woe" at least. I wrote it in about 2 hours, and it seems complete. Then I decided what to do about Knotty Sax — to make it simple, + closer to my heart, in the same spirit with which I'd decided to make T + C understandable to both intellectuals and regular readers. This only means earnest simplicity (maybe). We'll see. Revised the plot. (By the way, "Ling's Woe," like a dream, is not *completely* analyzable in terms of symbolic personal representation, is, rather, a mystery of identifications; not quite an allegory, either. It is a dream, and also a feeling I have about what the Chinese must really be. It is also satisfactory to me because it proves to me that *care, warmth,* are real, forever, and possible even in a world of catastrophe like eternal fog, in a Second Coming; it is my own solacement; + was sorely needed.) — (I am very happy over it.)

MON. MAR. 28 — Saw Mark Van Doren today, who called Harcourt, Brace for me; got books for my library; + saw Seymour, Allen, Vicki, etc.

TUES. MAR. 29* — I thank you, God, with all my heart, for this undeserved good fortune ... coming years after I prayed for it to you. Now I see that all good luck and all bad luck are unintended by you; that it is *something else* you wish to reveal — and that is, humility and care wherever + whenever, whatever + whichevers and what-all, on *earth*.

And I promise you, God — and I think you know it — I will continue to be conscious of my debt to life itself and be *grateful* whatever happens.

Teach me to remain yours, and not of the world's; and heap your Grace upon my writings, as you have done.

Teach me to *see*.

Teach me to *pray*.

Preserve me in care and humility, make me honest, make me helpful, and true.

This I want of you foremost — this I *have* wanted — this I want to go on wanting. God preserve my *want* of your mysterious wishes. Don't frighten me with your gratuitous heapings of good fortune, as I have been needlessly frightened by the bad. Teach me no Fear of you, but Understanding of your Mysterious Wishes, so I may Comply.

(And God is the only critic who cares little for style.) Eh?

NOTES — "ON THE ROAD" — ETC.

It is one of those pathos of life, perhaps the "strangest" pathos, that we need *contrast* to create. In N.Y. I can write with magnificent unction

---

* Kerouac composed the following upon learning that Harcourt, Brace had accepted *The Town and the City* for publication.

about Lowell; in Paris, I'm sure, about America; in the West about New York; so on — in the same way that it was undoubtedly necessary to think of God in contrast to the Devil, or heaven to hell, or, most mysterious, good to evil. The *unction* of this childish contrasting is the source of our most precious creation, springing from instinct, childlike at heart, and it is a creation we might identify with the various states known as sympathy, loyalty, care ... But isn't this all too dry! Therefore, is it not unintelligent?

What do I mean by unction? That it is not entirely *proper*, not "rational" to depend on the pathos of contrast to make hay; perhaps we should make hay anyway without dividing things. But isn't it true that you can't make hay when it rains?

The child is unctuous when, by pointing out a bad dog, he displays the goodness of his own dog: but isn't it sweet + true?

On the Road — a note. In 1848 certain wagon trains were bound for the West: men with their families + belongings + tools, going out to find their great though arduous inheritance in the magnificent territories. What could have been better for man! But the moment they heard about the gold at Sutter's mill, some men unhitched the horses from the loader, ramshackle, homey wagons, left their families behind, and took off on horseback, sweating for gold. All the gravity and glee and wonder of their lives and their loves was forgotten, for mere gold ...

This is what is still going on in America. They've unhitched the horses from the wagons — from their souls — and gone off like whores for a little gold. Sometimes, in this age, the cupboard of home is bare for the sake of some golden automobile, which is used to go around in traffic circles. *De profundis Domine!* It has always been so, and we refuse the joys of life, which is essentially as simple as a tree, with birds in it!

Same way with our "liberal" intellectuals: they too have unhitched the horse from the simple truth, and gone off sweating after the golden, glittering, false solution. It's all a big *gold strike* in the 20th Century — but those old wagons are still rolling!

"However I should like to enjoy what the competences of life procure, I am in no wise dashed at a different prospect. I have spent too many thoughtful days and moralized through too many nights for that." — John Keats, from a letter, 1819.

That's an old wagon, right there.

And do you think these old wagons of simple belief in like and death, these faithful souls, plod like oxen? Keats again — writing to Fanny Brawne —

"I will imagine Venus tonight and pray, pray, pray to your star like a Hethen."

The maternal instinct of a woman is always somehow so much more sublime, + expertly so, than her other instincts. (Old Bruce's wife.) The woman kneeling on the sidewalk in front of the Culture Conference, with that silly sign about "half-baked intellectuals." It would be laughable if it were not true that she has in her God's greatest gift to the earth, the mothering instinct ... emerging even at such a ridiculous moment (that is, in her face).

Red Moultrie — 3 years in jail. His past life: — marriage to a Mexican Bea? And all the other things. Admired from afar a certain great beauty in his youth-world (as young men admire Ava Gardner + Lana Turner) who has become a famous singer in jazz (a la Fran Warren, or Frances Wayne, etc.) She is another matter in his "return" to the valley. (So. Platte? — near Denver? — wheat?) Red lost his mother at birth, got stepmother at age four. (I'm aware of what this means, + even in a vindictive way.)

Mexican Bea waited for him until he loused himself up with bad behavior + got full 3 years. She drifted away ... tho sadly. He meets her later.

Road-runs from NY to Chicago to Butte to Frisco (or any old way; get *seasons* straight.) Red looks like a bigger, rougher Red Rodney. (?) Participated in robbery of a safe (intact) in 1946 (Feb.) (or Xmas 1945.) Let out Spring '49. Knows Liz Martin, thru having known Joe Martin when Joe was on the road in 1941; and meeting Joe later in N.Y. in Fall of '45. (time of Joe's return on troopship with Hathaway.) And therefore knows whole Junkey-Fredericks-Dennison-Levinsky group; tho never saw Peter but once. In On the Road Liz goes all out, a la V. In Denver Red knew Jeff Hames + others, + of course Vern Pomeray; and the gang (Ed, Burf, et al inclusive.) One of Red's great buddies is Big Slim Holmes (Hubbard). His women include Jeanie, etc. Vern has his Marylou. This is *it!* — + growing all the time.

What of Doctor Sax?

I think I'll put off Sax till On the Road is finished. And make Sax *all phantasy.*

The girl in On the Road. She returns from Paris, after a vacation, to the valley (where she meets Red). (I'll go to Paris in the Fall?) The American-in-Paris theme through the eyes of a girl like that.

But it's not so much the *valley!* — it's *humility!* Remember that — the valley is only an association. Humility + that spirit of revelation which goes on endlessly in someone like Allen + Bill too.

Red Moultrie's first memory of life: the brown mountainside in the blue morning air long ago in Colorado. (My old cliff-dream?)

I told George ← candy store tonight that the feeling I've had since selling my novel to Harcourt, Brace is like what you feel just as you're walking into a whore-house for the first time, at the age of seventeen, with your little two bucks, and you just *know* you're going to "get it," and there's a nauseous, silly excitement in your stomach.

It is the fear of getting what you've wanted for so long; and *getting it* but good — the abyss of your own nature staring back at you from its mysterious other side, way over there and all your own "fault" and doing ... though it all seems, also, the work of the Almighty.

This "butterfly" excitement will fade in a week or so — + then I'll earn perspectives.

Regard the slow ruin of the rose,
Think about it in the streets;
For Jinny, the little princess
Weighted down by the horror of her kingdom,
Jinny is my Italy, my work woman.
(CULLED FROM NOTEBOOKS)

One thing certain: — my notebooks were better when I was seriously at work. And when I'd say, as in 1946: —
"Money is only a step in the drama of Faustian becoming."

As Red travels West right after jail he is in that state of mind like one who has almost died — *every moment counts*. Thus, in his depressions and joys, he seizes on everything around with that great saintly intensity ... anything along the road. This trance will last for several weeks. *Pilgrimage.*

"Forgive everything!" — smile up to God and you will see what I mean," — and then, a hot-coat deal! (as in coy, Mar. 11, 1947.) This is like his prayer in jail, so strange.

STATES OF RED'S SOUL

1) *Purity* of jail + early road (Susquehanna.)

2) Miserable indifference + haschisch of Vern + later road

3) Incomprehensible, unhinged winning of $40,000 in Butte

4) Effort to regain purity: — rational: —

5) Repentance + old joy

(SEQUENCE MAY BE DIFFERENT.)

All the horror in the world lies before Red's eyes when he can't *move on* (in hitchhiking or anything). Inhospitable earth, malign struggle. But then gravity returns, + the sorrow in it. ... the humility of traveling-life ... (travailing-life.)

Look here, all, goodbye now.

My interest in the "beat": — it must be because they're not only poor, but *homeless* — without the consolations of the poor family man. Their lives have an *exterior* air of pilgrimage (wandering + impoverished) and as in the case of someone like Neal or Al, a kind of mystic signification (which some wino-hoboes seem to lack, of course.) (Notes on road-age Calif. 1947, etc.)

In Arizona, after the beautiful sunrise, + then after the cops in Benson, Red just gapes into space thinking he has his right to be glad about the sunrise and no right to be mad about the cops. This brings in the "mixing-of-men-with-stars" theme.

ALSO: —

Remember: On the Road is also a study of the great places like San Joaquin Valley, Butte, the Mississippi River, the Susquehanna, the So. Platte, 'Frisco, Arizona, Nevada, the Dalles, minor league night game in Rocky Mount, New Orleans, Texas, Chicago, Iowa, Grants N.M., carnies, and so much else. This is the rockbound spine of it, as town of Galloway + N.Y. City is spine of T + C events. Opelousas ... Truckee ... Salome ... Battle Mountain ... Laramie ... Longmont ... Algiers ... Lookout Pass ... Bigtimber etc.

CRAZY JAZZ: — April 5, '49
*Willie Jackson,** blowing tenor, with Cootie Williams' group, on "Gaitor Tail," is an example of crazy jazz. I don't care what anybody says (and in any case it isn't *jazz* properly) but I'm pulled out of my shoes by wild

stuff like that — *pure whiskey!* Let's hear no more about jazz critics and those who wonder about bop: — I like my whiskey wild, I like Saturday night in the shack to be crazy, I like the tenor to be woman-mad, I like things to GO and rock and be flipped, I want to be stoned if I'm going to be stoned at all, I like to be *gassed* by a back-alley music ... I want it to be reminiscent of red whiskey, muddy alleys, creaking beds, women and all-night balls (and maybe a hint of the Memphis train smashing by across the shacks, by dark starlight.) I like everybody yelling, everybody drunk, everybody *going!*

If it's going to be anything, let it go all-out like *Willie Jackson* does! (And the "deplorers" can stay home deploring.)

Since in any case my Sundays are so quiet.

UNITIES IN "ON THE ROAD"

1) The seasons in America

2) The places in America

3) The search for inheritance ?

SPRING*— New York City; The South; The Mississippi, New Orleans
Rain — rainy nights; soft moon-nights; chill, windy nights; Spring mornings

---

* Willie Jackson, jazz saxophone player. In a 1958 *Esquire* essay on the Beat Generation, Kerouac identified Jackson — along with Wardell Gray, Lester Young, Dexter Gordon, and Lennie Tristano — as the quintessentially beat jazz musicians.

SUMMER — Iowa, Nebraska; Denver; Nevada

Hot sun — sleep in fields; walk in road; baseball; nights so soft; swimming. Plus Frisco summer.

FALL — Chicago — San Joaquin Valley; St. Louis; Indiana

Dry Husk-Winds — winds whipping street-lamps; leaves; sunsets

WINTER – Butte; No. Dakota – Portland; Idaho

Snow – freezing cold; icy star-nights; blizzards

Other "Road" Notes in black notebook "Night"

PETIT

I found another world — it made me so happy — where the night-birds warble in living trees: — and a queer house that yawked at me as I passed. All this in Ozone Park the night of the eclipse of the moon, and of my trance of the shrouded existence. Oh.

APR. 17 — Waiting for word from Robert Giroux to begin revising T + C. I feel like working. Also I like the idea that we're going to "work in his office in the evenings" — with its quarts of coffee in cartons; in shirt-sleeves (good Arrow shirts); maybe a pint of whiskey; chats; the big city nights of April and May outside the windows of Harcourt Brace, and the thought of ships and women, and old Broadway glowing — this is also suggestive of "working" in Hollywood, or the way successful songwriters must work.

Then finally the book will come out in actual print, in a big *black* vol-

---

* Four seasons filled into itinerary of *"travails"*

ume, indicative of the darkness and solitary joy (+ affright) that went into its writing.

Soon, I think, I will actually be happy at the prospect of my worldly success.

Meanwhile, I have great ideas for my future. Hollywood career. Imagine making the following movies — "Benito Cereno," "Look Homeward, Angel" and, of course "Doctor Sax" (as now again revised.) And "Heart of Darkness" — and "Passage to India." There's no end. [Conrad's] "Nigger of the Narcissus." [Dostoyevsky's] "The Brothers Karamazov." [Kafka's] "The Castle." [Goethe's] "The Sorrows of Werther." [Celine's] "Journey to the End of the Night." [Wolfe's] "Of Time and the River." A really great "Huckleberry Finn." Alan-Fournier's "The Wan-derer."[*] Etc., etc., etc.

"Roughing It," even. *Real* things.

Lives of great men like Thoreau, et. al. in a series. To present these things unpretensiously, yet accurately — for great men were neither pretentious nor dull, and the "people" appreciate these es-timables.

There ought also be a "new kind" of Western historically accurate, without silly heroics (which no one believes any more anyway), and therefore more interesting.

Wouldn't it be interesting to everybody to see Bat Masterson and old 1880 Denver exactly as they were and the things that happened? I don't mean a mere Realism, but something like a *deepening* of the facts that appear on the face a reality — that is, actuality.

APRIL 23 —

In the space of this past week, Bill down in New Orleans, and Allen, Hunkey, Vicki and Little Jack were all arrested and put in jail — Bill for narcotics, the others for robbery + etc. in N.Y.[†] God knows what's hap-

---

[*] Alain-Fournier (1886–1914), French novelist killed in World War I. The lyrical coming-of-age story *The Wanderer* (1913, translation 1928) is his only full-length book.
[†] Burroughs had been arrested in New Orleans for possession of drugs and weapons; the

pened to Vern + Louanne. It is like a season, ending in jails, begun in furtive, imaginary hideouts.

What are they hiding out from?

Who pursues them?

Because of that damned radio I might be questioned myself.

It's about time for me to start working again, on "On the Road" in earnest. Yea.

I see there's too much actual paranoia in all this — as if, to tempt a hated society, one has to defy it and actually get enmeshed by its laws, and then rage righteously about it.

It's never "society" — only the soul, that is "wrong." This doesn't mean Allen, who is too kind hearted to be of this world.

The more society is "goaded," as here, the more it will *exist*. Ignore, ignore — all is in the soul. Everything comes from inside. Forget it. Have joy.

I'm mainly worried about Allen — and then, smugly, about this matter of compulsive lawbreaking, which is like a criminal revolution sweeping the country, + so *dumb*.

Now, for the first time in ages, I want to start a new life.

We are going to move out to Colorado — the whole family — within a year. And within 2 years I'm going to marry a young lady. My aim is to write, make money, buy a big wheat-farm, + actualize further consideration in the flesh ... with sons + daughters. An actual new life.

What kind of novel will I be writing at 57? (year of Dusty's "Karamazov"?)

This is the turning-point, the end of my "youth" and the beginning of manhood and its proper absorptions.

How sad.

How necessary.

How true.

---

others were jailed when police raided Ginsberg's Manhattan apartment and found the drugs and stolen items he was housing there for Herbert Huncke and Vicki Russell.

The closest thing to Fascism in America, after the Ku Klux Klan and racial discrimination of all kinds, is the liberal intellectual *demand* that everyone comply with the rules set down as to how to think and what to do.

In this sense, therefore, I am a reactionary, but I do not demand that anyone believe and act as I do, nor that they believe and act in any other particular way.

I do believe in what they mean by "progress" but also believe that it may only be effected by work (no talk) + by each of us generally minding his own business, etc.

So ends this Notebook — The 'Road' notebook. All Notebooks have a lifetime . . . from beginning to end. I thought it would exclusively report my wordage-progress on 'On the Road.' Instead, it was another kind of progress. We follow the turn of the road, and it leads us on.
Where? To actuality, ourselves, others, + God. ?

And they spake unto him the word of the Lord, and to all that were in his house.

ACTS 16.32

INDEX

Page numbers in *italics* refer to illustrations.

Adams, Walter, xxxi, 112, 116, 121
Adventures of Huckleberry Finn, The
   (Twain), 103, 104
African Americans, 8n, 56, 117, 136,
   145, 166, 214–17, 251–52, 259, 267,
   354, 355
   in the Brooklyn El, 315–16
   Cleo, 269–70, 274
   of the corn-rows, 109, 111, 118
Alabama, 353
Algiers, La., 287, 288–89, 328
Algren, Nelson, xxviii
Allen, Steve, xxviii
American Indians, 13, 59, 353
Amram, David, xxviii
Anderson, Sherwood, 25
"And the Hippos Were Boiled in Their
   Tanks" (Kerouac unpublished
   novel), 55n
Anglophiles, American, 146–47
Ann (Kerouac's girlfriend), xxxi, 96, 97,
   99, 107, 113, 286
Anna Karenina (Tolstoy), 128
Ansen, Alan, xxviii
anti-communism, xxiii–xxiv
Apostolos, George (G.J.), xxxi, 291
Arizona, 72, 172, 335, 337–38, 359
Arkansas, 356
Arnold, Edward, 57n
art, 198, 267
   excluding age in, 4, 7
   healing effect of, 81, 87
   as holiday of dreams and themes,
     80
   intellectual concentration in, 170
   as retirement from life, 139–40
Asheville, N.C., xviii
As You Like It (Shakespeare), 35n
Atlantic Ocean, 91–92
atomic disease, 53, 142
atomic energy, 170, 193
Atop an Underwood (Kerouac), 39n, 61n,
   292n
Ayer, A. J., xxxi, 171

Baker, Chet, xxvi
Baker, Jinny, xxxii, 106–18, 108, 163
Balzac, Honoré de, 95, 109, 120, 137,
   150, 172, 210, 252, 264, 266,
   274
Barnes, Djuna, 166, 168
Barrymore, Lionel, 66n, 172n
baseball, xvi, xl, 76, 77, 80, 84, 89, 96,
   119, 188, 225
   in Denver, 214, 216–17
   JK's novel about, 61
Beard, Charles, 59
Beard, Mary, 59
beats, Beat Generation, xxii, xxiii, xxix,
   xxxviii, 100
   JK as "avatar" of, xxviii
   meaning for term, xxiv–xxv
   novels of, xxxiii; *see also specific works*
   parties of, xxxi, xxxix
   poetry of, xxxvi
bebop, 36, 52, 117, 142, 254, 256, 262,
   266, 268, 277
Beethoven, Ludwig van, 267

Benjamin, Herb, xxxii, 168, 171, 172, 175
Berlin crisis, 60n
Bernard, Carol, 169, 171
Berry, Chuck, xvi
Bigtimber, Mont., 306–7
Billy Budd (Melville), 263
Birdland, 263, 267
Black Spring (Miller), 163
Blake, Caroline Kerouac (Nin), xxxii, 59, 115, 126, 128, 173
  in Colorado, xxxii, 183, 202, 217
  health problems of, 90, 286
  JK's correspondence with, 60n, 124
  JK's visits to, xxxii, 16n, 90
  in North Carolina, xxxi, xxxii, 16n, 60n, 90, 102, 175, 199, 286
  in Queens, 186, 187, 190, 245
Blake, Paul, Jr., xxxii, 90, 123, 175, 185, 189, 202, 245, 341
Blake, Paul, Sr., xxxi, xxxii, 16n, 59, 72, 90, 102, 105, 128, 183, 186, 189, 190, 202, 217
  JK's correspondence with, 60n, 96, 97, 175
Blake, William, 107, 108, 189, 239, 242, 246, 249
Blanchar, Pierre, 42
Blue Angel, 221–22
Bogart, Humphrey, 60n
Book of Dreams (Kerouac), xxx
Bop Apocalypse, The (Lardas), xv
Bop City, 254, 267
Boston, Mass., xli, 120, 279
Bouwman, George, 241, 269
Bowen, Johnny, 352
boxing, 97
Brabham, Ann, 174
Brady, "Diamond Jim," 57n
Brandel, Marc, 161
Brando, Marlon, xxviii
Brandt, Alan, 168
Bridger, Jim, xvi, 59, 288, 302–3, 313
Brierly, Justin, xxxii, 200, 269
Brooklyn, 34, 85, 96, 150, 241, 245, 251, 270
  Els in, 315–16

Brooks, John, 276
Brothers Karamazov (Dostoevsky), xx, 9, 16, 47, 112, 120, 194
Brown, Walter, 353
Buddhism, xv, xxiv
Burford, Beverly, xxxii, 64, 88, 199, 291
Burford, Bob, xxxii
Burger, Sando, 169, 171
Burmeister, Dan, 193, 194, 195
Burroughs, Joan Vollmer Adams, xxxii, 32, 37, 68, 288, 328, 331, 336
  School for Comedians and, 226, 227, 228
Burroughs, Julie, xxxii, 328, 331
Burroughs, William S. (Bill), xv, xxiv, xxxiii, xxxvii, 31, 37, 68, 89, 117, 169, 174, 176, 193, 229, 325
  background of, xxxiii
  JK's collaboration with, 55n
  JK's correspondence with, 96, 97, 98
  JK's discussions with, 30
  JK's travels and, 288, 289, 292, 328, 331, 333, 342
  in *On the Road*, xxiii, xxxiii
  School for Comedians and, 226, 227, 228
  wife killed by, xxxii
Burroughs, Willie, xxxii, 328
Butte, Mont., 303–5, 307

California, xxiii, xxxvii
  of Cassady, 296, 316–17
  JK in, xxxvi, xli, 11n, 21n, 203, 225, 283, 290–92, 295–97, 299, 316–18, 333, 359–63
  JK's interest in, 90, 98, 103n, 105, 271
  in *On the Road*, 123
  view of the Pacific in, 145–46
  visions of, 317–18
Cannastra, Bill, xxxiii, 85, 95, 175, 237
  death of, xxxiii, xxxvii
Canterbury Tales (Chaucer), 272n
Cantwell, Robert, 278
Capp, Al, 167, 187
Captains Courageous (movie), 172–73
Carlyle, Thomas, 24, 94, 166
Carney, Mary, xxxiii, 77

Carr, Lucien (Lou), xxxiii, 121, 127, 176, 229, 258, 261
  girlfriends of, xxxvi, 88, 277
  JK's correspondence with, 220
  JK's friendship with, xxiii, 67, 68, 77, 79, 85, 106, 116, 117, 122, 129, 161–62, 166, 173, 219, 224, 235, 274–75
  JK's work read by, 117, 118
  Kammerer stabbed by, xxxiii, xxxviii, xl, 55n, 80n
  at parties, 101, 171, 233
  School for Comedians and, 226, 227, 228
  at UPI, xxxiii, xxxix, xlii, 44n
Carter, Ed, 296–97
Cassady, Carolyn Robinson, xxxiii, xxxvi, 103n, 168, 291, 292, 351, 362
Cassady, LuAnne Henderson, xxxiv, 215, 216, 313
  travels of, 285, 287, 290–91, 293, 296, 328, 331–35, 337, 354
Cassady, Neal, xxiii–xxvii, xxxii, 82n, 105, 204, 215, 216, 219, 222, 235, 239, 245, 258, 261, 263, 304, 325
  background of, xxxiv, xli
  in California, 296, 299, 316–17, 349, 351, 362
  JK's correspondence with, xxvii, xxix, 41, 96, 97, 98, 102, 103, 114, 118, 168, 286
  JK's notebook as gift from, 282, 283
  JK's success and, 240, 254
  JK's talks with, 95n, 254–55, 267
  "new psychology" demanded by, 107, 108
  in On the Road, xxiii, xxiv, xxvi, 119n
  at parties, 233, 241, 263
  romances and marriages of, xxxiv, xxxvi, 290–91, 299
  School for Comedians and, 226, 227, 228
  travels of, xxv, xxxiv, xl, xli, 183, 203, 285–87, 290–91, 293, 294, 296, 316–17, 328, 331–35, 337, 354
  as Wild West protagonist, xvi, xxvi, 333
Cass Timberlane (Lewis), 50

Cass Timberlane (movie), 50
Catholicism, 268, 272
  mystical, xv–xvi, xx, 207, 233, 234
Celine, Louis-Ferdinand, 67, 95, 98, 101, 109, 170, 205, 235, 242, 260, 266, 267, 366
censorship, xxiii–xxiv
Cezanne, Paul, 229
Chagall, Marc, xxviii
Charters, Ann, xiv
Chase, Ginger, xxxiv, 37, 41, 58, 60, 62, 64, 85
Chase, Hal, xxxii, xli, 59, 60, 72, 73, 85, 93, 117, 174, 192, 193, 291, 325
  background of, xxxiv
  driving of, 60, 62, 63, 64
  JK's correspondence with, 186
  JK's talks with, 53, 55, 58, 62, 64
  JK's travels and, 24, 62, 63, 294, 297, 341
  JK's work read by, 50, 64
Chaucer, Geoffrey, xxiv, 272n
Chicago, Ill., 238, 271, 313, 349
children:
  JK's desire for, 7, 72, 75, 77, 109
  JK's views on, 16, 21, 143–44, 163–64, 189, 207
Christianity, 97, 199
"Christmas in New York" (Kerouac), 26
cities, towns compared with, 13, 147, 308
classless society, 77–78
Cole, Nat King, 168
Colorado, 305
  JK in, xxxii, xxxvi, xli, 190–203, 191, 225, 258, 262, 267, 339, 340
  JK's interest in, 58n, 62, 72, 75, 76, 80, 88, 103n, 190
Columbia University, xv, xxxi, xxxiii–xxxviii, xli, xlii, 176, 253
Columbia Valley, 299–301
communism, xxiii–xxiv, 31
"Composing Diary," 155, 159–76
Confidence Man (Melville), 246, 247
Conrad, Joseph, 123, 138n, 149–51
consciousness, xxx, 16, 75, 80, 89, 129, 145, 168, 211, 275–76
Continental Divide, xxvi

Cooper, James Fenimore, 121
cowboys, xvi, xxiv, 308, 348
Cowley, Malcolm, xxvii–xxviii
Crabtree, Mary Pippin, 85
creative writing courses, 143
Crime and Punishment (Dostoevsky), 120, 145
Crime and Punishment (movie), 42
Crime and Punishment (play), 42
critics, xviii, 34, 42, 87, 121–22, 149n, 150, 256
Crockett, Davy, xxiii
Cru, Henri, xxxiv, 11n, 291

Danellian, Leon, 221
Daniels, Josephus, 143
Danilova, Alexandra, 221
Dante Alighieri, 233, *234*
Darin, Bobby, xli
Dark Eyes, 26, 29, 30, 97
Dave Garroway at Large (TV show), 271
Davis, Miles, 267
Daytona Beach, Fla., 92
death, 15
    JK's views on, 14, 16, 19, 21–22, 64, 91, 126, 170, 173, 174, 198, 204, 205, 209–14, 224, 237, 257, 267, 367
    obituaries and, 20–21
de Berri, Corinna, 118
decadence, 54, 58, 111, 308
Denver, Colo., xxxiv, xxxviii, xlii, 190, 202–3
    JK in, xxxii, xxxvi, xli, 202, 214–17, 225, 258, 262, 267, 340, 348–49
Denver University, 194, 195
De Quincey, Thomas, xxvi, 189
Desolation Angels (Kerouac), xxviii
destiny, 64, 224
Detroit, Mich., 100, 201, 203, 313–14, 349
Dewey, Thomas E., xxxvi, 96n, 160n
Dharma Bums, The (Kerouac), xxiv, 223n, 353
Diamond, David, xxxv, 94, 95, 113, 115, 161, 162–63, 165, 173
Diamond, Herbert, 286
Diamond Jim (movie), 57
Dickens, Charles, 95

Dickinson, Emily, 148, 249
Dickinson, N.Dak., 309–11
Dietrich, Marlene, 57n
Doctor Sax (Kerouac), xxviii, xxx, 155, 159–60, 165, 167, 169, 183, 185, 205, 206, 225, 236, 238, 263
Donne, John, xxvi, 237
Dos Passos, John, 252
Dostoevsky, Fyodor, xix–xx, 18, 30, 34, 56, 73, 81, 95, 97, 109, 124, 148, 160–61, 170, 176, 214, 229, 272–76, 279, 325, 369
    greatness of, 273–75
    "H'm" in, 266
    JK compared with, xxv, 266
    wisdom of, xx, 9
    see also Brothers Karamazov; Crime and Punishment; Idiot, The; Raw Youth, A
Doxey Tavern (later Glen Patrick's Bar), 55n
drugs, drug dealers, xxxii, xl, 142
Duel in the Sun (movie), 66
Durante, Jimmy, 140
Durgin, Allen, 100
Durgin, Russell, xxxv, 100, 101
Durham Medical Center, 90

Eager, Allen, 112
Eau Claire, Wis., xvi, 312–13
Eckstine, Billy, 145
Edison, Thomas, 142–43
editors, 30, 121–22, 215, 242
    see also Giroux, Robert
Einstein, Albert, 193
election of 1948, 160
Eliot, T. S., xxvi, 213, 266, 325
Elizabeth, Princess, 29
El Paso, Tex., 334–35, 338, 357, 358
Elwitt, Elliott, 245
"Encantadas, or the Enchanted Islands, The" (Melville), 109, 247
ennui, 203, 208–14
Eno, Louis, xxxv, 279
Enright, Ray, 57n
epigonism, 141–42
Epitome of Ancient, Mediaeval, and Modern History (Ploetz), 260n

"Essentials for Spontaneous Prose"
(Kerouac), 125n
eternity, 107, 208, 210–11, 232–33, 245,
268, 337
Everitt, Rae, xxxv, 171
evil, 86, 129, 135, 137, 139, 151, 235
Eyre and Spottiswoode, xxi, xl

fame, 52, 86–87, 115, 116, 135, 215, 264,
265
"Farewell Song, Sweet from My Trees"
(Kerouac), 292
fathers, 119, 143–44, 168
"Fenimore Cooper's Literary Offenses"
(Twain), 121n
Fields, W. C., 236
Fiorini (editor), 30
"first thought, best thought" philoso-
phy, 125n
Fischoff, Ephraim, 226
Fitzgerald, F. Scott, 4, 7, 79, 273, 275,
277
JK compared with, xxi, xxiii
Fitzgerald, Jack (Fitz), xxxv, 37, 72, 85,
163, 164, 190, 202, 245, 260, 268,
270
JK's correspondence with, 168, 176
at parties, 40, 269
Fitzgerald, Jeanne, xxxv, 37, 85, 163, 164
Fitzgerald, Mike, xxxv, 85, 163, 164
Fitzpatrick, Jim, 85, 101
Fleming, Victor, 172n
Florida, xiv, 91–92
football, xv, xvi, xxxii, 64, 175, 263
Ford, Henry, 142–43
"Forest of Arden," 35, 137, 286
"Forest of Arden" journal, 131–51
forgiveness, xxx, 127, 129, 168
Fournier, Mike, xxxv, 49, 72, 90, 167
Fourth of July, 99–102, 201–2
France, Frenchmen, 83n, 93, 142, 259,
267
Americans compared with, 34
Francis, Saint, xxiv, 274
Franco, Bea, xxxv
Frank, Robert, xxviii–xxix
freedom, 9n, 73n, 242, 368
of JK, xv, 25, 66, 81, 168

Freudianism, 127, 140
friendship, 49, 58–59, 97

Gabin, Jean, 93
Gable, Clark, 168, 172n
Gaillard, Slim, xxvi
Gambetta, Leon, 83
Garroway, Dave, 271
Garver, Bill, 37
Gaynor, Don, 221
Geismar, Maxwell, 149n, 150
"Gentle Maiden, The" (Dostoevsky),
124
Georgia, 353, 356
German Americans, 55n
Gide, André, 151
Gielgud, John, 42
"Gift of the Magi, The" (O. Henry), 26n
Gillespie, Dizzy, 267
Ginsberg, Allen, xv, xxxiii, xxxiv, xli, 31,
37, 85, 87, 117, 173, 193, 219, 235,
237, 245, 270, 288, 315, 324
background of, xxxv, 88–89
at Columbia, xxxv, 253
"dead eyes see" and, 208, 232
drugs and, xl
expressions of, 261
as Jewish, 35, 258
JK compared with, 35, 94, 110
JK photographed by, xiii
JK's correspondence with, xxviii, 79n,
82n, 102, 165, 173, 215
JK's discussions with, 30, 35, 43, 96,
238, 240
JK's dreams and, 319–20
in JK's fiction, xxiii, xxxvi, 200n
JK's views on, 35, 43–44, 67–68,
88–89, 101, 106, 125, 185–86, 193,
204, 325, 333
JK's work and, xvii–xviii, 84–85, 88,
94, 169, 198
mental instability of, xxxv, 43, 67,
88–89, 193
at parties, 101, 106, 112, 171, 233
School for Comedians and, 226, 227,
228
travels of, 285, 286, 290, 294, 296
vision of life of, 35

Giroux, Robert (Bob), xxv, xxxvi, 183, 199, 203, 219–21, 224, 235, 239, 242, 244, 254, 265, 272
  Denver visit of, xxxvi, 200, 201, 214–15
  JK's socializing with, 221, 255, 263
Go (Holmes), xxxvii, 166*n*
God, 9, 11, 13, 17–20, 139, 187, 193, 206, 211, 224, 232, 233, 245, 274, 287
  existence of, 323, 324
  happiness and, 34
  JK's letters to, xxiv
  JK's praying to, xix, xxx, 53, 157–58
  in one's self, xxii, 78, 223
  as the should-be, 143–44
  thanking of, 57, 76, 154, 155, 176–77, 200, 240, 318
Goethe, Johann Wolfgang von, 31, 38, 64, 112, 114
Gone on the Road (Kerouac unpublished novel), xxix
Gordon, Beverly Anne, xxxvi, 75–80, 82
Goudt, Hendrik, 292
Gould, Joe, 86, 166
Grace (Kerouac's romantic interest), 171, 269
Grasse, Peggy, 76
Great Britain, xxi–xxii, xl
  Wolfe-Lewis experiences in, 45
Grey, Zane, xvi, xxvi, 128, 150, 151
Grimald, Nicholas, 190
Guest, Edgar, 369
guilt, 97, 106, 129, 143–44
  of JK, 85, 88, 111, 162, 169
Gurdjieff, G. I., 233, 234, 326

Hale, Barbara, xxxvi, 85, 106, 116–19, 122, 129, 161, 162, 166, 173, 277
  JK's work read by, 117, 118
  Macmillan and, 88, 113, 119
  at parties, 101, 171
Hamanaka, Conrad, 171, 172
Hamlet (Shakespeare), 235, 237
Hampton, Lionel, 254
Hansen, Allen, 85, 87
Hansen, Diana, xxxvi, 239, 245
happiness, 34, 45, 77, 78, 208, 211, 369
  knowledge and, 100, 142

possibility of, 28, 145
  in statement of sanity, 132, 149
  truth and, 12
  work and, 72, 73, 115, 117, 118
Harcourt, Brace, xvii, xviii, xxi, xxv, xxxvi, 183, 186, 187, 255
  JK's work at, 219–21, 244
Harrington, Alan, xxxvi, 85, 87, 97, 101, 112, 127, 129, 160, 172, 173
Harrington, Mrs. Alan, 97
Harrington, Steve, 97
Haverty, Joan, xxxvii
Heart of Darkness (Conrad), 123, 138*n*
Heinrich, Tommy, 225*n*
Hemingway, Ernest, xxvii, 120, 273
Henry, O., 26*n*
heroes, xvi, xxiv, 9, 60, 61, 105*n*, 216, 316–17
Herrick, Robert, 190
Hill, Bob, 277
Hinkle, Al, xxxvii, xl, 328, 333, 354
Hinkle, Helen, xxxvii, 328
"Hipster, Blow Your Top" (Kerouac), 279
hipster generation, 266–67
history, 13, 17, 57, 142, 233, 270
Hodge, Ed, 277
Hoffman, Diana, 112
Hollywood, Calif., 145, 317, 320–21
Holmes, John Clellon, xxxv, 165, 186, 188, 198, 219, 224, 235, 237, 239, 277, 278
  background of, xxxvii
  JK's correspondence with, xxvii
  JK's talks with, 168, 169, 175, 240, 255
  at parties, 101, 171, 263, 269
Holmes, Marian, xxxvii, 162, 174, 175, 224, 239, 277
  at parties, 171, 263, 269
homosexuality, xxxviii, 56, 142, 352
Horace Mann Record, xlii
Horace Mann School, xv, xxxiv, xxxv, xli, xlii, 168
Hornsby, John, 85
Huescher, Harold, 69, 85, 147, 192
Hulme, T. E., 246, 247
Humason, Tom, 277

humility, 10, 17, 21, 23, 51, 53, 65, 74, 75, 77, 86, 126, 143, 270
Huncke, Herbert (Hunkey), xxxiii, xl, 37, 100–101, 106, 171, 199–200, 314–15, 324, 325, 331, 333
  background of, xxxvii
  as beat, 100, 102
  School for Comedians and, 226, 227, 228
Huston, John, 60n
Huston, Walter, 60n

Idaho, 301–2
Idiot, The (Dostoevsky), 88n, 120, 129n
Idiot, The (movie), 129
Illinois, 73–74, 342
I Married a Savage (movie), 245n
immortality, 106, 135–36
Indiana, 313, 341–42
Indianapolis, Ind., 341, 342
intellectuals, xli, xlii, 47, 54, 103, 140, 142, 245, 253, 270
  despair of, 133, 142, 147–49
  female, 77, 79
  New School, 166–67
  revolutionary, 166

Jacobs, Muriel, 235
Jamaica, Queens, 8n, 186, 221
James, Jesse, xvi, 83
Japan, U.S. occupation of, 136, 137
jazz, 36, 52, 112n, 113, 119, 142, 296–97
Jeffries, Frank, xxxvii, 194, 349
Jesus Christ, xx, 9, 56, 187, 199, 238, 267, 269
  death of, xxiv
  JK's prayers to, xxiv
  love and, 135
  as philosopher-prince, xv–xvi
  teachings of, xv–xvi, 11–12, 15–19, 75, 78, 271
Jews, 35, 258, 259, 286
Joe Gould's Secret (Mitchell), 86n
Johnny (Jerry's mother), 195–97
Johnson, Harriet, 162, 165, 166, 171, 173
Johnson, Samuel, 64

Jones, Howard Mumford, 276
Journey to the End of the Night (Celine), 98
Joyce, James, 13, 48, 120, 237, 242, 246, 260

Kafka, Franz, 126, 194, 275, 289
Kammerer, David, xxxviii, 68
  Carr's stabbing of, xxxiii, xxxviii, xl, 55n, 80n
Kansas, 345–48
Kansas City, Mo., 344–45
Kansas-Night Cow (Kerouac), 347–48
Kazan, Elia, 38
Kazin, Alfred, xxxviii, 97, 258, 268–69
  JK as student of, 161, 163, 165–66, 169, 172, 173
  JK introduced to, 87, 95
Kelly, John, 221, 222, 263
Kennedy, Jackie, xxix
Kerouac, Caroline, see Blake, Caroline Kerouac
Kerouac, Gabrielle Levesque (Mémère), xxxviii, 52, 57, 59, 98, 103, 125, 126, 326, 353, 354
  expenses of, 122–23
  gold teeth of, 237
  health problems of, 278
  husband's death and, 19
  as "it," 174
  JK's conversations with, 31–32, 40, 55, 175
  JK's correspondence with, 96, 97
  in JK's fiction, xvii, xxxviii
  on JK's friends, 49, 238
  JK's living with, xxxviii, 5, 7n, 15, 29, 55n, 102, 113, 119, 183, 238, 257
  JK's work and, 70, 71, 105, 128, 146
  movie going of, 50, 54, 174, 245
  in Richmond Hill, 183, 220
  shoe factory job of, xxxviii, 31, 122, 201, 278
  travels of, 16n, 62, 63, 90, 102, 183, 202
  on women, 31–32
Kerouac, Gerard, 237, 258–59

Kerouac, Jack:
ambitions and dreams of, xiv,
xvii–xviii, xxi, 7–8, 52, 57, 62, 63,
65, 72, 77–80, 86, 90–91, 172, 185,
225
Americanism of, xvi, xviii, xxii–xxiii,
xxiv, xxvi, 20, 83, 112, 146–47, 172,
262
anger of, 121, 129–30, 162, 168, 198,
299, 313
anxiety of, 51, 110, 111, 112, 114, 187,
194, 198
appearance of, xiii, xxix, 84
bail of, xl, 80n
at beaches and swimming, 104, 106,
124
book reading of, xviii, xx, 9, 11, 29–31,
36, 42, 45, 56–60, 63, 66, 72, 97,
98, 99, 101, 103, 114, 123, 124, 128,
187, 189, 218, 220, 236–37, 238,
241, 247, 248, 260–61, 264, 313
as character, 17, 31
clothes of, 59–60, 186, 265, 274,
353–54
club going of, xlii, 36, 42, 52, 117, 119,
254, 263
confidence of, 129–30, 274
cooking and eating of, 114, 271, 287,
291, 353, 354
dancing of, 29, 58, 84, 104
death of, xiv
dreams and visions of, 32, 40, 51, 87,
103, 241, 249, 254, 258–59,
291–92, 317–18, 326–27
drinking of, 24, 28, 30, 32, 40, 44,
46, 55, 58, 61, 62, 72, 86, 87, 95,
100, 106, 118, 119, 129, 161–63,
168, 171, 173, 174, 202, 275, 277,
304
education of, xv, xvii, xxxi, xxxiv, xxxv,
xxxvii, xxxviii, xxxix, xli, xlii, 39–40,
78, 80, 122, 159, 161, 162, 165–69,
172, 183, 185, 224, 226, 240, 253,
265
eye problems of, 64, 104–5, 113, 117,
118, 119, 124
family background of, xiv, xvii, xxxii,
xxxviii–xxxix

farm or ranch as goal of, 7, 62, 72,
76, 79, 80, 82, 90–91, 102, 103n,
105, 109, 123, 148, 188
fears of, xxix, 11, 29, 34, 52, 68, 72,
86, 91, 110, 113, 119, 168, 169,
274–75
in fiction, xxxvii, 81, 207
film treatment prepared by, xxxv
financial concerns of, 7, 26, 30, 39,
59–60, 62, 65, 72, 73, 75, 86, 88,
90–91, 93–94, 97, 115, 116, 138,
162, 185, 188, 192, 199, 200, 203,
224, 257, 264, 265, 278, 313,
340–41
first novel begun by, 172–73, 259
freedom of, xv, 25, 66, 81, 168
future of, 7, 52, 57, 69, 72, 80, 90–91,
107, 225–26, 258, 271
guilt of, 85, 88, 111, 162, 169
health problems of, 39, 40, 58, 74,
89, 103, 104, 220, 249, 352
horseback riding of, 196–97
identity of, 51, 258, 259
impatience of, 98, 199, 205
loneliness of, xv, 15, 17, 18, 25, 33, 54,
71, 72, 74, 76, 77, 80–81, 87, 90,
91, 93, 97, 104, 112, 113
madness and, 27, 32–33, 49, 52, 66,
72, 90, 94–95, 98, 110, 111, 167,
189, 206
marriages of, see Haverty, Joan;
Parker, Edie
melancholy and depression of, xxx, 4,
7, 24, 40, 61, 62, 71, 72, 80–81,
83–84, 90, 169, 192, 202, 210–17,
239, 249, 250, 257, 286, 290
in merchant marine and navy, xv,
xxxiv, 11n, 38, 39n
movie going of, 37–38, 42, 50, 54, 57,
60, 66, 112, 124, 129, 172–73, 174,
236, 245, 346
as myth-maker, xiv, xvi, xxiii, xxix,
169, 176
myths about, xxv–xxvi
newspaper reading of, 25, 37, 46, 54,
60, 64, 103
nonwriting jobs of, 21n, 88, 105, 122,
124, 126, 253

own works read by, 26, 38, 43, 61, 65
photographs of, xiii, 187, 189, 245
piano playing of, 40, 55
popularity and success of, xxviii–xxix,
  52, 90, 209, 264, 265, 276
radio listening of, 46, 96, 97, 199,
  225
religiosity and spirituality of, xv–xvi,
  xix–xx, xxiv–xxv, xxx, 9, 11–12,
  15–19, 62, 135, 139, 142–43, 157–58,
  160, 176–77, 186–88, 193–94, 205,
  211, 223, 224, 232–33, 234
romantic relationships and interests
  of, xxxi, xxxii, xxxiii, xxxvi, xlii, 26,
  29, 30, 75–80, 82, 96, 97, 99,
  106–18, 108, 162, 163, 175–76, 257,
  269, 277–79
School for Comedians and, 226, 227,
  228
screen play of, xxviii, 30, 37
self-doubt of, 8, 10–11, 20, 48, 72,
  76–77, 100, 104
sexual experience of, 41, 162, 163
sleeping habits of, 39, 51, 54, 65, 66,
  120
start of journal keeping of, xv
theater going of, 42, 221
travels of, xv, xxv, xxxii, xxxiv, xxxviii,
  xl, xli, 21n, 22, 23, 163–64, 165, 183,
  190, 199, 201, 203, 257–60, 266,
  269–71, 279, 283–363
TV appearances of, xxviii
twenty-sixth birthday of, 50n, 57,
  59–60
typing paper of, xxxiii, 44n
walking of, 8, 9, 24, 36, 37, 51, 54, 55,
  65, 74, 80, 81, 100, 105, 190, 204,
  238, 265, 343
Wood-Thomas's sketch of, 176
work methods and habits of, xxv–xxvii,
  28, 54, 65, 95, 97, 120, 220
Kerouac, Jack, writing of, 20
  mastery in, 25, 26, 29, 30
  middle vs. end of, 74
  myths about, xxv
  problems with, 8, 10–11, 24, 27,
    29–30, 38, 46, 51, 53, 74–75, 204,
    218, 223, 241, 244

purpose of, 12, 17, 24
as secondary struggle, 72–73
spontaneous prose in, xx, xxvii, xxviii,
  xxix, xlii, 125n
Wolfe's influence on, xviii, xxi, xxii,
  xxvi
see also specific works
Kerouac, Leo, xiv, xx, xl, 12, 60–61, 126,
  127, 168, 230–31
  background of, xxxviii
  death of, xvii, xxxviii, 5, 19, 21, 204,
    205, 207, 243, 324
  in JK's fiction, xvii, xxxviii
Kesey, Ken, xxvi, xxxiv
Kingsblood Royal (Lewis), 56
Kingston, N.C., 19
Kipling, Rudyard, 172n

Lakeside amusement park, 195–96
Landesman, Jay, 245, 279
Lardas, John, xv
La Touche, John, 221
Lawrence, D. H., 274, 275
Lawrence, Seymour, 112–13, 121
Lenrow, Elbert, xxxviii
Letters from Editor to Author (Perkins),
  275–76, 277
Lewis, Sinclair, 45, 50, 56, 312
liberalism, 253, 270
"Life and Millions" (Kerouac), 38
Life on the Mississippi (Twain), 66n
Lincoln, Abraham, 73, 143
literary agents, 85, 87
  see also Everitt, Rae
Little, Brown, 172, 176
Livornese, Benedict, 268
Livornese, Maria, xxxix, 84n, 119
Livornese, Tom, 8n, 37, 65, 84, 104, 113,
  117, 124, 165, 174, 186
  background of, xxxix
  "death" of, 268
  JK's collaboration with, 118–19
  parties of, 40, 269
Lockridge, Ross, Jr., 101n, 209n
London, Jack, 49
Long Island, 318–20
  see also Lynbrook, N.Y.
Look Homeward Angel (Wolfe), xviii

Lord, Sterling, xxi
Los Angeles, Calif., 359–60
Lost Weekend, The (movie), 173*n*
Louis, Joe, 97
Louisiana, 287–90, 292, 328–31
love:
  Christian, 135, 274
  Dostoevsky's views on, 273–75
  JK's views on, 19, 33, 35, 36, 69, 73,
    74, 76–77, 80–81, 93, 100, 101,
    106–17, 108, 125, 135, 139, 145, 168,
    170, 174–75, 205–8, 211, 232, 235,
    237, 257, 268, 273–75, 277, 336
  self-, 135, 139, 174
Lowell, Mass., 54, 259, 263, 265, 292,
  294, 301, 320
  in JK's fiction, xviii, 10*n*
  JK's visits to, 63, 279
  JK's youth in, xiv–xv, xxiv–xxv, xxxi,
    xxxiii, xxxv, xxxix, xl, xli
  The Young Prometheans in, xl, xli
Lowell Sun, xx–xxi
Lutcher, Nellie, 136
Lynbrook, N.Y., 8*n*, 40, 118–19, 268,
  269
Lyons, Martin Spencer, 144

MacArthur, Douglas, 136, 137
Macauley, Sam, 37
McCarthy, Joseph, xxiii
McDonald, Ian, xl
McDonald, John, xl, 279
McGhee, Howard, 52
McGraw-Hill Company, 53*n*
Macmillan, 88, 113, 115, 119, 128,
  129–30
madness, 53, 67, 230
  JK's views on, 17–18, 27, 32–33, 36, 49,
    52, 66, 72, 78, 88–89, 90, 94–95,
    98, 110, 111, 142, 167, 189, 206
Maggie Cassidy (Kerouac), xxxiii
Mailer, Norman, xvi, xxviii, xxxix
Manhattan, 54, 85
  Bowery, 85, 86, 106, 171
  East Village, xiii
  454 Twentieth Street, xxii, xxv
  Greenwich Village, xxxviii, xlii, 85,
    161, 166

  Harlem, xxxv, xlii, 100, 101, 147
  Times Square, 38, 166, 167, 172, 245,
    265, 325–26
  Yorkville, 55
manliness, 7–8, 24, 49, 67, 74, 100
Mann, Thomas, xxiv
Marcus Aurelius, *132*, 149
Massachusetts, 283, 327
Melville, Herman, xvi, 39, 43, 56, 59,
  95, 109, 173, 207, 214, 242, 246,
  247, 249, 263, 266
  see also Confidence Man; Moby-Dick
Mendocino Forest, 90
Meredith, Burgess, 221
Merrimack River, 294–95, 301, 314,
  327–28
Merton, Thomas, 237, 238, 325
Mexican Americans, 215, 216, 317
Mexico, xxxvii, xxxviii, 201, 283, 334,
  338–39, 349, 352, 357–58
Mexico, Gulf of, 289–90, 329, 330
Mexico City, xxxii, 257–60, 349, 351
Miles City, Mont., xxiii, 307–8
Miller, Henry, 163
Miller, Howard, 341
Millstein, Gilbert, xxviii
Minetta Tavern, 166
Minnesota, 311–12, 344
Mississippi, 353, 356
Mississippi River, 287–90, 293, 299,
  305, 311–12, 328–31, 342, 344
Missouri, 83*n*, 342–45
Missouri River, 287, 288, 305, 309,
  343–44
Mitchell, Joseph, 86*n*
Moby-Dick (Melville), 16, 237, 246
modernism, 86, 111
Mohammed, 8
Monacchio, Tony, xxxix, 44, 79, 91, 92,
  122, 124, 129, 168, 275
  baseball and, 76, 77, 80, 84, 96
  JK's loan from, 76
money, xv, 88, 93–94, 115, 116, 122–23,
  135, 138, 172
Montana, 112, 289, 299, 300, 303–10,
  313, 329
Morales, Adele, xxxix, 189, 263,
  265

morality, 16, 17, 18, 25, 56, 65, 126, 149, 193
  organic, 67
  of Tolstoy, xix–xx, 9
Morley, Frank, xxi–xxii, xxxix, 275
Mort a Credit (Celine), 247
movies, 93n
  JK's views on, 37–38, 42, 50, 60, 66, 129, 172–73, 200, 236, 239, 245, 333, 346
murder, 14, 66–67, 230
Murel, John, 66
Mureray, Wally, 195
Muriel, 237, 241, 245
Murphy, Connie, xxxix, 84
music, xlii, 118–19, 145, 147
  New York scene for, xxxix, 36, 42, 52, 117, 119, 254, 263, 266, 267
  see also bebop; jazz
"My kingdom is not of this world," xv, 15–17
Mysterious Stranger, The (Twain), 263, 278
myth making:
  about JK, xxv–xxvi
  of JK, xiv, xvi, xxiii, xxix, 169, 176
  reality vs., 176
  of Wolfe, xviii
"Myth of the Rainy Night" (Kerouac's proposed third novel), 204

naturalism, 268–69
Nature, 126, 127, 137, 161, 186, 367, 368
Neumann, Dick, 169
Neumann, Marion, 169
Neurotica, 245
Newcombe, Don, 225
New Hampshire, 62, 294–95, 327
New Mexico, 349
New Orleans, La., xl, 287–89, 293–94, 328
New School for Social Research, xxxvii, xxxviii, xxxix, xli, 159, 161, 162, 165–69, 172, 183, 224, 226, 240, 265
  intellectuals of, 166–67
Newsweek, xx, 278
New Testament, xx, 11, 199, 230

New Year's Eve, 40, 263
New York, N.Y., xv, xxii, xxxi, xxxiii, 38, 349
  bars and restaurants in, xlii, 55n, 76, 161, 166, 221–22, 238, 277
  intellectual circles in, xli, xlii, 140, 166–67, 245
  JK's goodbye to, 186
  music scene in, xxxix, 36, 42, 52, 117, 119, 254, 263, 266, 267
  nights in, 314–15
  parties in, xxxi, xxxiii, xxxix, 32, 77, 85, 86, 95, 100, 101, 106, 112, 161, 171–72, 175, 233, 241, 245, 263
  subway in, xxxiii, 52, 57, 102, 109, 166
  theater in, 42
  see also Brooklyn; Manhattan; Ozone Park, Queens; Richmond Hill, Queens; *specific schools*
New York Daily News, xl
New Yorker, xx, 86n
New York Public Library, xxv, xxxiii
New York Times, xx, xxviii
Nicosia, Gerald, 35n
Nietzsche, Friedrich, 151
Nightbeat (TV show), xxviii
Niles, Bob, 173
"1949 Journals," xiv, xxix, 181–371
  road-log in, 182n, 185–87
North Carolina, xviii, xxxi, xxxii, 99, 102, 190, 199
  JK in, 5, 16n, 19, 39, 90, 285, 286–87, 355–57
North Dakota, 308–11
Notes from the Underground (Dosto-evsky), 123
novels, 94, 95, 145, 242, 243
numbers, magic, 233, 324, 325

O'Dea, Jim, xxxix, 279
Of Time and the River (Wolfe), xviii
Ohio, 313, 341, 342
Olson, Charles, xxviii
On the Road (Kerouac), xiv, xv, xxi–xxix, 125, 155, 165–67, 172, 173, 179–371
  autobiographical elements in, xxii–xxiii, xxxii–xxxix, xli, xlii, 21n

On the Road (Kerouac)(*cont.*)
    characters in, xxxii–xxxix, xli, xlii,
        119*n*, 169, 172, 173, 186, 201,
        202–3, 223, 231–32, 239, 244, 264,
        265, 268–69, 278, 283
    final line of, 348*n*
    myths about, xxv
    new title for, 218
    notes of 1950 February for, 262
    original voice in, xxii
    plot of, 219, 264
    popularity of, 192
    rain-and-rivers study in, 198
    rejection of, xxi
    "Remember? Okay" chapter of, 169
    reviews of, xxviii
    revisions and editing of, xxvii–xxviii
    search for father in, 119*n*, 348*n*
    start of writing of, 165, 225
    Town and the City compared with,
        236, 241, 244
    trips as basis of, xxxiv, xxxviii, 21*n*,
        183, 283–363
    two different manuscripts of, xxvii
    workbooks for, 283, 363–71, *364*
    working notes for, xxv–xxvi
    writing style of, 167, 169–70, 241–42,
        243
Oral History of Our Time, The (Gould),
    96*n*, 166
Oregon, 297–300, 335
orgone theory, 62, 141–42
Orlovsky, Peter, xxviii
Overland With Kit Carson (serial), 59
Ozone Park, Queens, xvii–xviii, xxii,
    xxxviii–xxxix, 5, 18, 55*n*, 57, 62, 167,
    183, 186, 319

Paris, 93, 112, 115, 122, 137, 165, 200,
    204, 222
Parker, Edie, xxxii, xxxiv, 67, 100, 102,
    203, 204, 268, 313–14
    background of, xxxix–xl
    JK's marriage to, xxxix–xl, 80*n*, 98,
        101, 111, 122, 225, 243, 313
Parkman, Francis, 344
"Partners, The" (Kerouac), 128–29
Patis, Jackie, 117

Pauline (Wood-Thomas's model),
    175–76
PEN, xxviii
Pennsylvania, 340–41
Perkins, Maxwell, 275–76, 277
Pettiford, Oscar, 117
"Philip Tourian Story, The," *see* "And
    the Hippos Were Boiled in Their
    Tanks"
photography, xiii, xxviii–xxix, 187, 189,
    245
Piazza Tales (Melville), 109*n*
Picasso, Pablo, 111
place names, xvi–xvii
Ploetz, Carl, 260*n*
Poe, Edgar Allan, 38
poets, novelists compared with, 94
Polo, Marco, 189
Poore, Charles, xx, 275
Possessed, The (Dostoevsky), 120
Poughkeepsie, N.Y., 163–64, 190,
    269–71
poverty, xv, 15, 19, 82, 187, 343
"Private History of a Campaign That
    Failed, A" (Twain), 342
"Private Philologies" journal, xxix, 183,
    190*n*, 191
Proust, Marcel, 170, 252
"Psalms" journal, 153–77, *154*, 183
psychoanalysis, 30, 193, 271, 345
psychology, 62, 118, 129, 149, 159
    "new," 107, *108*
Puccini, Giacomo, 267
Puerto Ricans, 147
Purcell, Duncan, xl, 167
Purcell, Edeltrude, 167
Putnam, James, 119, 161–62, 165, 166

"Rain and Rivers" journal, xxix, 183,
    186, 203, 263, 281–363, *282*
Raintree County (Lockridge, Jr.), 101*n*
ranches, xli
    JK's interest in, 62, 72, 76, 79, 80,
        82, 90–91, 102, 103*n*, 105, 109, 148
Raw Rookie Nerves (Kerouac), 61
Raw Youth, A (Dostoevsky), 29, 31, 34,
    41*n*, 44, 47, 87, 139–40
reality, 46–47, 176, 232

Reich, Wilhelm, 62n
Reichians, 141–42
Republican Party, 96, 160n
revolution, 36, 74, 198
    sexual, 163, 165, 167
Reynolds, Allie, 225
Rhoda (hitchhiker), xl, 285, 286
Richmond, Calif., 290, 296–97
Richmond Hill, Queens, xxii, 183, 203,
    218, 220, 238, 241, 257, 263, 264,
    327
Rimbaud, Arthur, 151, 267
Rise of American Civilization, The (Beard
    and Beard), 59
"road" genre, xxii–xxiii
"Road Workbook 'Libreta America'"
    (Kerouac), xxix
Robinson, Jethro, 324
Rocky Mount, N.C., 60n, 286–87
rodeo, 196–97
Roosevelt, Franklin D., 143
"Rose of the Rainy Night, The" (Ker-
    ouac), 201
Rouge et le Noir, Le (Stendhal), 29
Russell, Bertrand, xxiii
Russell, Lillian, 57n
Russell, Vicki, xl, 37, 106, 113, 171, 200,
    315
Russia, 35, 47, 60n, 270, 274
    U.S. compared with, 122–23, 142–43
    women of, 31–32
Ruth, Babe, xvi, 119

St. Louis, Mo., 342, 345
Salvas, Roland (Salvey), xli, 279
Sampas, Charles, xxi
Sampas, Sebastian, xviii, xxi, 231, 243,
    295
    background of, xl
    in JK's fiction, 10n
San Antonio, Tex., xxiii–xxiv
Sandburg, Carl, 270
San Francisco, Calif., 90, 91, 98, 103,
    105, 271, 317
    JK in, xli, 109, 146, 203, 282, 283,
    291–92, 296, 299, 333, 349, 351
San Francisco (movie), 172
San Luis Obispo, Calif., 361

San Remo, xlii, 166, 238
Saroyan, William, xxvi
Sarubbi, Frank, 99
Saturday Review, xx
Saucier, Ed, 296–97
School for Comedians, 226–27, 228
Scribner's Magazine, 71, 81, 83, 85
"Sea Is My Brother, The" (Kerouac's
    unpublished novel), 39n
seasons and months, notes on, ix,
    27–28, 158, 189
selfhood, self, 110, 135, 146
sexual revolution, 163, 165, 167
Shakespeare, William, 9, 35n, 109, 120,
    168, 170, 235, 237, 249, 267, 273,
    369
Shapiro, Meyer, xl, 235, 240, 258
Shattuck, Roger, 279
Shaw, Artie, 275, 370
Shearing, George, xxvi, 117, 254
shrouds, 242, 243, 246, 248, 249, 251,
    319–25
Simpson, Louis, xl, 112
sin, 17, 34, 186, 188, 192, 273, 370
Sloane, Ruth, 241
Snyder, Gary, xxiv
solitude, 139, 148–49, 150
Some of the Dharma (Kerouac), xv
Specimen Days (Whitman), 170n
Spengler, Oswald, 274
spirituality, 270, 315–16
    of Americans, 142–43
    see also God; Jesus Christ; Kerouac,
    Jack, religiosity and spirituality of
Spoilers, The (movie), 57
Spontaneous Poetics of Jack Kerouac, The
    (Weinreich), xviii
Steinbeck, John, xxiii, 297n
Stendhal, 29, 36
Sterling, Colo., xli, 349
Stewart, Stephanie, 171
Stringham, Ed, xli, 87, 94, 97, 129,
    162–63, 171, 186, 277
success, xv, xxviii–xxix, 52, 90, 93, 172,
    209, 215, 264, 265, 276
suffering, 16, 18–19, 65, 80, 101
suicide, 14, 84, 161, 209, 210, 293
Sunday Mercury, xxi

Taine, Hippolyte-Adolphe, 238
Taleyke, John, 169
Tchelitchev, Pavel, 222
Tejeira, Victor, 111, 115
television, xxviii, 271, 274
Temko, Allan, xli, 98–99, 104, 165,
    269, 286
Texas, 83n, 331–35, 349, 352–53, 357
    censorship in, xxiii–xxiv
Theado, Matt, xx
Thelma (Kerouac's date), 117, 119–20
thinking, thought, 14–15, 16, 18, 25, 53,
    80, 103, 133
    "true," 102, 123, 125
"This Is the Beat Generation" (Holmes),
    xxxvii
Thomas Aquinas, Saint, 210
Thoreau, Henry David, 143, 148, 295
Times Literary Supplement, xxi
Tolstoy, Leo, xix–xx, 9, 128, 188, 267
Town and the City, The (Kerouac), xiv,
    xvii–xxii, xxviii, xxxviii–xli, 145, 160,
    165, 167, 187, 206
    Apres-tous in, 115, 118, 128, 129
    autobiographical elements in, xvii,
    xviii, xxxii, xxxiii, xxxv, xxxvi,
    xxxviii–xl, 49, 200n
    characters of, xix, xxxii, xxxiii, xxxv,
    xxxvi, xxxviii–xl, 10, 25, 31, 36, 49,
    50, 80, 145, 172, 200, 325–26
    City Episode of, 41, 45, 47, 50, 52, 53,
    56, 60–63
    dedication of, xxxvi
    English edition of, xxi, xxii, xl
    finishing of, 81, 82, 105, 114, 115, 118,
    120, 130, 159
    funeral in, 65, 66, 71, 74–75, 82,
    113
    "Greenland narrative" in, 38–39
    "Hah?" in, 266
    length of, xix, 4, 7, 30, 54, 105, 112
    "mood log" of, xix, 5, 7–11
    moral theme of, 56
    one-year anniversary of, 45
    On the Road vs., 236, 241, 244
    plot of, xix, 41, 45, 52, 54, 59, 61, 66
    publication of, xvii, xli, 65, 70, 71, 72,
    77, 81, 83, 84, 105, 113, 115, 119, 130,

    155, 183, 185, 187, 203, 219–21, 225,
    240, 244, 246, 257, 264, 277–78
    "rain" chapter of, 107, 109
    rejection of, 72, 83, 121–22, 129–30
    reviews of, xviii, xx–xxi, 275, 276,
    278
    sales of, 279
    Scribner's and, 71, 81, 83, 85
    sea-chapters in, 55, 114, 115, 119–22
    as "tremendous story," 50–51
    Wake fragment of, 113, 116, 117, 118,
    121, 125
    "Wartimes" section of, 44
    Wolfe's influence on, xviii, xxi
    worklogs for, xvii, 3–130, 133
Tracy, Spencer, 50n, 172n
Treasure of the Sierra Madre, The
    (movie), 60n
Tree Grows in Brooklyn, A (movie),
    37–38
Treviston (Scribner's salesman), 277
Trilling, Lionel, 25, 87, 253
Tristano, Lennie, 36, 52, 102, 223, 224,
    237, 267
Tristan und Isolde (Wagner), 98n
Tristessa (Kerouac), xxviii
Trollope, Anthony, 49
Truman, Harry S., 160, 286
truth, 11, 12–13, 24, 48–49, 82, 106,
    107, 108, 124–27, 208, 252
    of Dostoevsky, 274, 275
    turning away from, 67
Truxell, Ann, 175
Tunney, Gene, 263
Turner, Lana, 50n
Twain, Mark, xxvi, 60, 66n, 99, 109,
    121, 123, 128, 143, 263, 266, 267,
    268, 270, 342
    life of, 65, 150–51
    pathos in, 160
    see also Adventures of Huckleberry Finn,
    The; Mysterious Stranger, The

Uhl, Ed, xli, 349
Ulysses (Joyce), 13n, 237, 238, 246n,
    248
Understanding Jack Kerouac (Theado), xx
Union Theological Seminary, xxxi, xxxiii

436

United Press International (UPI), xxxiii, xxxix, xlii, 44*n*, 76
JK's proposed job at, 122, 124
Unruh, Howard, 230

Van Doren, Mark, xviii, xxxvi, xli, 65, 84, 115, 169, 183, 239, 325
Vanity of Duluoz (Kerouac), xiv
Vidal, Gore, xli, 221, 222
Viking Press, xxvii
Villanueva, Enrique, 351
Virginia, 354
Visions of Cody (Kerouac), xx, xxvii, xxviii, xxx, 57*n*, 95*n*

Wagner, Richard, 98
Wake, 113, 116, 117, 118, 121, 125
Walcott, "Jersey Joe," 97
wars, JK's views on, 36, 47, 60, 61, 103
Washington, 300–302, 326
Washington, D.C., 285–86, 354
Washington, George, 143
Weber, Brom, 162
Week on the Concord and Merrimack Rivers, A (Thoreau), 295*n*
Weinreich, Regina, xviii
Weirton, W.Va., 341
Wellbourne, Bill, 169, 171
Wells, H. G., xxiii
West, the, xvi, xxiii, 83, 190, 257, 265, 271, 285, 342–43, 348
history of, 57, 59
see also cowboys; *specific places*
Westwood, Colo., 183, 190–203, *191*, 339
White, Ed, xli, 25, 37, 55, 84, 85, 176, 192, 193, 194, 223, 291, 349
JK's correspondence with, 102, 165, 186
JK's work read by, 50, 55
White, Frank, xlii, 194–95
White, William Allen, 143
Whitman, Walt, xvi, 16, 60, 116, 170–71, 271
"Whitman" (Kerouac), xxxviii, 172
Whittelsey House, 53
"why," philosophic, 144–45, 206, 232
Wilder, Billy, 173*n*

Williams, Ted, 89, 91
Williams, William Carlos, xvi
Wingate, John, xxviii
wire-recorders, 95, 267*n*
Wisconsin, xvi, 312–13
Wolf, Don, xli, 168
Wolfe, Thomas, 20, 60, 73, 95, 109, 117, 118, 126, 143, 147–51, 300
critics' views on, 42, 87, 121
inclusive art of, *4, 7*
JK influenced by, xviii, xxi, xxii, xxvi, 105*n*, 278
Lewis's experiences with, 45
loneliness of, 151, 249
see also You Can't Go Home Again
women, 72, 101, 116
JK's views on, 19, 41, 55, 57, 75, 77, 79, 93–94, 98, 106–20, 129, 168, 196–97, 206–7, 269, 277, 279, 290–91
Russian, 31–32
Wood-Thomas, Alan, xlii, 168, 175, 176
Wood-Thomas, Annabella, 168, 175
Wood-Thomas, LeeAnne, 175, 176
World War II, xli, 75–76
writing:
artistic-ethical struggles and, 133, 149–51
JK's views on, 10, 11, 24, 47–48, 52–53, 72–73, 74, 82, 92, 121–22, 140–41, 169–70, 185, 190, 192
Wyse, Seymour (Nutso), xlii, 219, 224, 235, 237, 245
in JK's fiction, xxi–xxii

Yellowstone Red (book), xxiii
Yellowstone Valley, 305–8
Yokley, Sarah (Sara), xlii, 220, 224, 233, 235, 257, 277–79
You Can't Go Home Again (Wolfe), 16, 42, 45*n*
Young, Bob, 104
"Young Jack Kerouac, The" (Lenrow), xxxix
Young Prometheans, The, xl, xli

Zorita, 245